Ritzy

British Hotels
1837 - 1987

by

Derek Taylor

*For Bill & Gordon,
our oldest friends —
almost in both senses.
As ay.*

April 2003

The Milman Press.

First published in 2003
by The Milman Press.,
3, Avenue Close,
Avenue Road, London. NW8 6BX.
Phone: 0207-449-9385.
FAX: 0207-449-9386.

Printed in Great Britain by
The Book Factory,
1a, Mildmay Avenue,
London. N1. 4RS.

ISBN No: 0-9542684-0-7 (Hardback).
0-9542684-1-5 (Softback).

This book is published in association with
The Hotel, Catering & International Management Association.

By the same author:

The Golden Age of British Hotels (with David Bush) 1974.
Fortune, Fame & Folly (*The Caterer* 1878 - 1978) 1978.

British Library Cataloguing in Publication Data
Taylor, Derek, 1932, August 5th.

Ritzy

(**Ritzy** *adj. colloq.* 1. High class, luxurious. 2. Ostentatiously smart.) O.E.D

For Diane
and with gratitude to the Caterer & Hotelkeeper
and the Hilton Group for their help.

Contents

Illustrations.

Front Cover: From left to right:

The Langham Hotel, London, The Midland Grand Hotel, London, The Midland Grand Hotel, Manchester, (now the Crowne Plaza, Manchester), Durrants Hotel, London, Longs Hotel, London, The Savoy Hotel, London, The Athol Palace Hydro, Pitlochry, (now the Pitlochry Hydro), The Grand Hotel, Brighton, (now the De Vere Grand), Chewton Glen, New Milton, Hants, Gleneagles Hotel, Auchterarder, The Hilton Hotel, Glasgow and the North British Hotel, Edinburgh, (now the Balmoral).

Back Cover. From left to right:

The Zetland Hotel, Saltburn, The Great Northern Hotel, London, The Piccadilly Hotel, London, (Now Le Meridien Hotel), The Victoria Hotel, Sheffield, The Cecil Hotel, London, The George Hotel, Stamford, The de Keyser Royal Hotel, London, The Grand Hotel, Scarborough, The Palace Hotel, Buxton, The Westminster Palace Hotel, London, The Royal Station Hotel, York, (now Le Meridien Hotel), The Grosvenor Hotel, London (now the Thistle Hotel, Victoria), The Metropole Hotel, Brighton, (now the Hilton Brighton Metropole), The Caledonian Hotel, Edinburgh, (now the Caledonian Hilton), The Mermaid Hotel, Rye, The Midland Hotel, Derby and The Connaught Hotel, London.

Thanks are due to the following organisations for permission to reprint the photographs on the front and back covers: Durrants Hotel, De Vere Grand Hotel, Brighton, Rocco Forte Hotels, Savoy Hotel, Crowne Plaza Hotel, Manchester, Connaught Hotel, Gleneagles Hotel, Chewton Glen Hotel, Hilton Group, Caterer, Thistle Hotel Victoria, The Connaught Hotel, Unilever plc., The Thistle Hotel, Victoria, The Mermaid Hotel, Rye and Sheffield City Council.

Preface

As this is the most detailed history of the British hotel industry yet attempted, you might well ask yourself what are my qualifications for writing it. I suppose I could claim to have some first hand knowledge on the subject matter from around 1941. When war started in September 1939, the family headed for the South Coast. We had some furniture shops in London and my father commuted every day. In 1941, however, my parents decided that they'd had enough of that and moved back to London to live in the Cumberland Hotel at Marble Arch. So did my great grandfather and my grandparents. For the next four years, when I was on holiday from school, I would come to the Cumberland and there would be an extra bed for me in my parents' room.

With less than brilliant timing, my parents returned to London at the height of the blitz. There were raids every night while outside, in Hyde Park, 300 anti-aircraft guns would blaze away, with barrage balloons hanging in the air to bring down low flying aircraft. Whether the shells ever hit anything or the balloons got entangled with any bombers, we never learned. The noise was comforting anyway. The hotel was always packed and the residents were augmented by guests in every kind of uniform. When the war ended, London hotels were again needed for normal business; tourists, particularly. The Cumberland had a strong Commonwealth clientele and the country was in desperate need of foreign currency. So it was decided that the residents would have to leave and the family departed. Later we lived at the Mostyn Hotel near the Cumberland for a year in 1953/4.

After reading History at Cambridge, I went into the industry in 1954 as a salesman for three little London hotels, largely because I wanted to get back to London, from which I'd been evacuated and also because I found that hotel workers got four weeks holiday, rather than the national average of two. The hotels eventually grew to be Grand Metropolitan, which itself became the 10th largest company in the UK. I stayed for 27 years, moving up as if I had come in first at low tide. As a salesman for all the hotels, I was a member of Head Office. So I started in a small room opposite the managing director and from the beginning it was life at the top. I was very lucky that the managing director, Fred Kobler, was more like an uncle to me than a boss and was a hotel genius to boot.

Ritzy

When I got married in 1961, I couldn't live on my salary. As the Company didn't propose to raise it to pay for my new status as a husband, I had to consider other sources of income. One was writing for the trade press. I had the marketing knowledge to impart - very unusual at the time - and, as an arts graduate, I had been taught how to write essays. Reading again my early efforts as a journalist, the novelty of the content must have made up for the atrociousness of the style.

I was delighted to find that trade journalists were not thick on the ground. My articles then went on non-stop for the next 28 years, including nine years writing for the Hotel Review 10 years between 1973 and 1983, writing a weekly column in Catering Times under the name of Michael Archer and six years as a weekly columnist for Caterer.

By 1973 I was a director of Grand Metropolitan, so I could write what I liked. I used a pseudonym because I couldn't be seen to be writing the views of the Company. My views were often extremely contentious and you couldn't maintain your anonymity for very long. Many were the occasions when my chairman, Sir Maxwell Joseph, was confronted by angry members of the industry's top management, demanding that I be stopped from attacking their views or practices. Joseph adopted the policy of Horatio Nelson, put his chairman's telescope to his information blind eye and refused to acknowledge that I was writing anything.

If you agree to write a weekly column you are constantly in need of new material. To make matters worse, I had agreed to cover two or three topics every week for Catering Times. So I just had to study everything that was going on in the industry to fill the space. It was an excellent discipline and it does mean that the vast majority of the material in this book covering the last 40 years, has a good deal of first hand reporting in it.

30 years ago I wrote a book called The Golden Age of British Hotels with the late David Bush. The early part of this book is based on that volume and its preface is still relevant. So, enough about me; let's have a look at what's in the book.

Introduction

The Preface to the Golden Age of British Hotels.

Books about hotels are very often really books about the people who stay in hotels. "Imperial Palace", "Grand Hotel" and "Hotel" are the best fictional examples but a great deal of non-fiction has really covered the same type of ground. The stock hotel characters regularly appear; the temperamental chef, the aristocratic manager, the head porter with a heart of gold, the kindly old waiter and the housekeeper with a "past". The background is equally familiar, from the magnificent display of flowers in the Prince's suite to the delicate bouquet of a Château Beauregard '87. The immaculate dinner jacket of the tall, dark haired restaurant manager never creases as the guest ponders deeply before deciding between the Filet de Sole Emmanuel X and the Oreilles à la Rouennaise. The world has stopped in a fairyland where no-one grows older, accounts are settled discreetly, and the lowliest chambermaid knows exactly how much hot water Lord C. likes in his bottle.

This, however, is a book about the hotel business, not as it might have been but as it was. The heroes and villains are the hotels themselves, and the people who succeeded or failed to make them profitable. For money was the name of the game; the opportunity to make a fortune, to climb out of the gutter, to keep the family from starving or just to keep a roof over your own head. The players are still famous, like Cesar Ritz and Auguste Escoffier, or they are nearly forgotten like Frederick Gordon, Sir Polydore de Keyser, Sir William Towle and John Smedley. We think they deserve more than obscurity, for they were seldom dull in their own lifetimes. They were pioneers, building and creating something quite new - a modern hotel. Very little has changed since the Golden Age; a soupçon of air conditioning, a few more floors in height, and some different building materials, but otherwise it is still the way the Victorians and Edwardians left it.

Who built all those hotels whose origins seem nearly as obscure as the statues on Aku Aku? Where did all the mystique come from, and the snobbery and the servility? Why did the business attract so many continentals and where did all the money come from?

A hotel is a factory producing goods as surely as tinned pears

Ritzy

come off a conveyor belt, but it's a special sort of product, vanishing like the fairies when dawn breaks and the room was not let, the restaurant table empty, the bar stool unoccupied. As an industry, the world of hotels is fascinating in its own right, and needs no carefully concocted literary plot to keep the reader's interest. If we fail to do so, the fault is in ourselves and not in the tale we have to tell.

That preface was written 30 years ago. Alas, David Bush - and so many others - have died in the meantime but the material we all helped to gather, was almost entirely accurate. Readers kindly pointed out one or two very minor errors at the time but, overall, the facts were not challenged.

In bringing *The Golden Age* up to almost the present day, however, a pattern emerges which is almost as strange as those prehistoric markings across vast distances in South America, which you can only see from hundreds of feet up in the air. It appears that the hotel industry, in its growth, has broken most of the classic rules you find in case studies in business schools: have a look.

Are we agreed that a hotel is no different from a manufacturing company in that, to survive, it must provide a product or service that the public wants? Right? Now, sometimes the public knows it wants a product; clothing, housing, alcohol. Sometimes it finds itself attracted to new inventions; electric light, the motor car, television. For whatever reason, the products are normally geared to the world the public lives in. Shops today sell the fashions of today. Washing machines can deal effectively with cleaning today's fabrics. Motor cars are of a size suitable to today's roads.

So it was in the beginning of the hotel industry in Victorian times. Hotels were just another service designed for the Victorians. The staff were dressed like Victorian servants. The food was served in a manner which the Victorian guests would have recognized, because it mirrored their own way of life in their own homes. Hotels were marketed much as were other products, using the same language and the same technology.

Within the hotels, the staff were treated as were any other kind of workers. The French revolution had brought some excellent - and unexpectedly unemployed - French chefs to noble homes, while the early hotel industry had some standards which would please guests who had often been on the Grand Tour of Europe. The industry, primarily, used the technology of the home, although hotels were among the first to introduce many new inventions to the public: lifts, private bathrooms, electricity.

We are now over 150 years away from those early days of the hotel industry. The hotel world has developed out of all recognition. It is a major employer in the UK economy and it has provided a large number of the jobs that were needed to replace those lost, as manufacturing industry declined and the surviving companies became more mechanised. It plays a full part in the highly successful British tourist industry, helping the UK to maintain its position of sixth in the world league table for incoming tourists, both in terms of numbers and the value of their spending in the year 2000.

And yet....and yet....the service hasn't changed. It is still almost exactly as the Victorians would have expected to find it; the uniforms of many types of staff, waiters serving from the left, reception desks and brochures "to peruse". It is an industry which, in many ways, has been caught in a time warp. So many of the developments which have characterised other parts of the British economy in the last 150 years, have been, almost totally, absent in the hotel industry.

For example, other parts of the economy have recruited university graduates for their management, changing the old Victorian precept that a gentleman should not be involved in trade. Most of the commercial industry management have come from the higher socio-economic groups. By contrast, in the hotel industry, the management is off the factory floor. There is practically no recruitment from the major universities; graduates normally only come from hotel schools, which consist of a few new universities, those polytechnics which have, even more recently, been granted university status and Colleges of Further Education. The graduates have been taught severely relevant subjects, rather than the academics having, as their prime consideration, the broadening of the students' minds.

Even in the few early chains of hotels, the stigma of having a job in the industry could keep its members from senior company positions. As we shall see, in the board room of Gordon Hotels, the largest chain of British hotels in the 1920s, there were four directors who were barristers, but only the managing director had a hotel background - and he'd been to Marlborough and Cambridge, because his father was head of Midland Railway Hotels !

Ritzy

There have, effectively, been no unions. There have been practically no strikes during the whole period. From a bird's-eye view of the 150 years, that's astonishing. Another factor in hotel staffing, which for many years would have been unthinkable in much of British industry, is the, overall, perfectly cordial relations between different nationalities. In 1948 the British government agreed to accept 100,000 immigrants from Displaced Persons Camps in Europe; some of the desperately sad cases of people whose lives and homes had been wrecked by the Second World War. The government was only able to allow the immigration of these refugees when agreement had been reached with the TUC on the many industries in which they would be forbidden to work. The same thing happened with Hungarian miners fleeing in 1956 from the Russians. The hotel industry, to its credit, welcomed them without demur.

Successive waves of immigrants have come into the British hotel industry over the years with no problems to speak of. From the Italians late in the 19th century, to the Polish Army demobilised in Britain in 1945, the Displaced Persons, the Hungarian refugees, the Caribbean immigrants of the 1960s - all were absorbed with a minimum of hassle. The last were the Phillipine workers in the late 1960s.

The retirement age in the UK is normally 60 for women and 65 for men. In the hotel industry it has always been the case that, if you can do the job, the age doesn't really matter. So many remain in harness beyond retirement age. It has also been normal practice until recently for workers in industry to stay for many years within an organization. A CV which showed continuous movement from one employer to another, would have been considered a sign of unreliability for most of the period under discussion. Not in the hotel industry. Most employees would move from job to job without any adverse effect on their future prospects. Equally, there was little job security.

Most staff work for wages. Until 1943 all hotel restaurant waiters worked almost solely for tips. It was an industry where tips loomed very large in the benefits package. Some staff would actually pay management to get the available jobs; London West End commissionaires for example and many cloakroom attendants.

Consider, most governments try to help their native industries flourish. Public money is poured into enterprises as varied as British films and British motor cycles. Ambassadors seek to help British

14

exporters and governments will subsidise foreign companies who may be prepared to build factories in the UK. Yet the funding for the British Tourist Authority is puny by comparison with other state investment. What is more, the British hotel industry was almost totally ignored over the 150 years by successive governments - but has grown to its present size and importance nevertheless.

The lack of influence on government by the industry had many original causes. The absence of unions made the Labour Party indifferent to it. The Liberal Party, with its strong 19th century temperance wing, didn't like hotels either. Tory landowners often created hotels, but normally to help turn their agricultural land into industrial building land. They wanted no interference from a hotel lobby.

Then again, most industries expect to be built up with the support of the City of London. Raising capital for investment, they expect the help of banks who recognize the potential, and the interest of institutional and public investors. Yet throughout most of its history, the hotel industry has been something of a pariah in the City. Agreed, it showed little sign of being a sound investment in times of recession, but it wasn't the only sector to suffer in those days. Yet, apart from a few decades from the 1960s - 1980s, the hotel sector has found great difficulty in raising sufficient funds from the City. It has stifled its growth.

Almost all other major British industries gave birth to large companies who controlled substantial parts of their outputs and total markets. Yet, for well over 100 years the hotel industry didn't. It remained a vast array of individual small companies. The percentage of the industry represented by major companies was minute. There are still a very large number of small companies.

Where other industries work closely with suppliers to design new products which will enable them to run their businesses more effectively, this is seldom the case in the hotel industry. Large expanses of carpet are still cleaned with domestic vacuum cleaners, baths are cleaned with cloths and cleaning liquid, much of the kitchen equipment is little different from that found in the home.

Again, if you compare hotel advertising today with Victorian times, you will find very little has changed. The holiday page in the Daily Mail is practically identical with Edwardian times. The hotel brochures use almost exactly the same language. Hotels are still "ideally located" with "superb cuisine". There is still no colour photography in the menus or wine lists of luxury hotels, even though the technology to reproduce colour photography in print was available for most of the 20th century. Within the chains of hotels, there is little use made of test marketing, few TV commercials and little use of focus groups. The sales people in the hotel industry seldom know much about techniques like Buying Signals, Body Language, and Closing Techniques - skills in which sales people in other industries are automatically trained.

All very odd but, as a result, we can look at an industry where there was little discrimination against outsiders, little interest by the "Establishment", an international dimension, scope for small entrepreneurs and the ability to make an enterprise successful because of personal involvement.

It was ideal on all these grounds for ethnic entrepreneurs and they took the opportunity. The influence of men like Cesar Ritz and Polydore de Keyser in the 19th century, followed by a wide range of key first or second generation migrants, helped tremendously in the development of the industry. Newcomers from Asia in recent years carry on the same tradition.

The question, therefore, arises of whether the accepted principles of running a business are valid! The hotel industry has flourished so often without using them and manufacturers and retailers who have, have often found them unsuccessful.

Of course, the changing life style of the population and the increasing affluence over the period have had an effect on the growth of the hotel industry. Nevertheless, a study of the history of the industry and the way in which its methods developed, throws an interesting light on aspects of company operation which are, largely, taken for granted in the present economic climate. Also we see an industry which, initially, reflected the life style of the public, change to one which almost reflects a bygone age.

There have been adverse results as well. The hotel industry has lost a large percentage of the eating out market which it dominated up to 1945. Here, the public were not prepared to put up with an old fashioned product, except on special occasions. The primitive advertising has made it more difficult to get a larger share of the public's disposable income. The absence of unions has resulted in depressed wages and this, in its turn, has led to serious staff shortages, particularly as tipping has become far less the normal behaviour by customers. The industry has also suffered from a lack of the contribution which would have come from its fair share of the best young university brains in the country.

It is an unresolved question whether the glamour of the hotel world has been beneficial or detrimental. There is considerable prestige in owning great hotels. In deciding whether to buy the Dorchester in Mayfair, it's less likely to have been a purely commercial decision for the Sultan of Brunei than buying a factory making shoe polish. Hotels have been lavishly decorated to gain their owners admittance into society (The Royal Bath in Bournemouth in the 1880s, for example), hotels were built to put passengers on train lines (Turnberry in the 1900s and Gleneagles in the 1920s), and hotels could accommodate Victorian buyers (Furness Abbey in Barrow in Furness). These all distort normal business practices because they lead to a level of value for money which is normally unsustainable.

Although the hotel industry has developed in a different way from most other industries, it has been subject to its own internal differences; notably between those who saw hotels as a business selling beds, and those who concentrated on the sale of food and drink. The latter cultures were strong in the days of stage coaches and were strengthened by the increasing influence of continental hotel managers in London. On the continent, the culture of Switzerland, France and Italy, in particular, included a greater emphasis on haute cuisine and wine connoisseurship than was normal in Britain.

Out of all these practices - there were seldom any academic theories - there developed a very successful 21st century British hotel industry. It is one of the great success stories of the British economy over the last 175 years - not always a smooth and continuous advance, but a development which eventually came to strengthen the British economy to a marked extent. With the opportunity, thanks to HCIMA, *Caterer* and the Hilton Group, of bringing *The Golden Age* up to date, this book is about how that happened.

I'd like to thank all the friends and colleagues in the industry who were kind enough to give me invaluable help and information: Douglas Barrington, David Battersby, Professor John Beavis, Neil Benson, the late Eric Bernard, Michael Boella, the late David Bush, Clive Carr, Victor Ceserani, Bob Collier, Bob Cotton and the British Hospitality Association, Jacques Courivaud, Harold Delvin, Henry Edwards, Peter Eyles, Sir Rocco Forte, Norman Fowler, George

Ritzy

Franks, Elizabeth Gadsby, Stanley Green, Dennis Hearn, George Hill, Roy Tudor Hughes, Lisa Jenkins, Kit Jones, Rex Joseph, Peter Leather, Len Lickorish, Don Marshall and Oxford Brookes University, Michael Matthews, Professor S. (Rik) Medlik, Peter Mereweather, David Michels, John Guthrie and the Hilton Group, Lord Mishcon, Forbes Mutch and Caterer, Ramon Pajares, Giuseppe Pecorelli, Sir Michael Pickard, Miles Quest, Nick Redman, Professor Paul Richardson, Susan Scott, Diana Self, Ernest Sharp, Giles Shepard, Joanna Shepherd and the *Fuller Library*, the late John Tanfield, Alistair Telfer, David Wood, Ann Corrigan and the Hotel, Catering and International Management Association, Philip Webb, Oliver Westall, Richard Walduck, David Wood and Brian Worthington.

I am particularly indebted to Professor John O'Connor, a stern critic of poor literary style, with an eagle eye for a non-sequitur or a doubtful judgment and an expert in his own right on the subject. Valerie Taylor did a great deal of very valuable research and proof read with meticulous care. Suzy Taylor produced a stunning cover and Jack Da-Costa and The Book Factory were the soul of patience. My wife, Diane, continues to put up with my obsession with the subject with unfailing good humour; sine qua non.

Every effort has been made to acknowledge those who have the copyright of the photographs in the book and I am grateful for permissions which have been readily given.

Derek Taylor.
London, 2003.

1
The story so far.

"Forty years ago" said the *Daily News* in 1887 "it was almost a sign of eccentricity to put up at a hotel. Where the hotel was not ultra-fashionable, it was suggestive of Leicester Square. Families came up every season for the sights, and took their lodgings in Norfolk Street. Many of the old-fashioned houses still stand. The front room is a sitting room; the room behind it is a bedroom; the small enclosure behind that will hold trunks and with them, at a pinch, a son or daughter, or a maiden sister in the spare bed. The bill of fare was limited, and the cooking never professed to go beyond 'good plain'. It was roast and boiled and they were served at four. An odd man, not innocent of the odour of spirits, pervaded the street and was the herald of the modern commissionaire." In retrospect it certainly wasn't very attractive and the decor received few plaudits, being labelled by another contemporary writer as dingy and fusty which the visitors "endured with a flickering belief that they were enjoying themselves, the appalling discomforts of early Victorian furniture, grim in its ugliness, glistening malignly in its sticky beeswax and pricking maliciously through its horsehair seatings."

Of course, there had been hotels for centuries. They may have been called inns but they provided a roof over the traveller's head and a certain amount of refreshment. Mind you, it could come in useful to bring your own furniture. When Richard III was killed at Bosworth in 1485, his war chest of £300 remained hidden in the base of his bed at the Blue Boar at Leicester for very many years. The man who eventually found it was promptly murdered for the loot, and the money hasn't been seen since.

The most famous inn was the Tabard at Southwark which was immortalised in Chaucer's *Canterbury Tales*, and, indeed, throughout the Middle Ages, English inns had a good reputation. Because those which remain today are often public houses, we tend to think that they were always regarded in that light when, in fact, the best were among the most important commercial buildings of their time. In one inn on the Great West Road, the Spanish Ambassador was invested with the Order of the Garter by Henry VI in 1445, and the King of Denmark was put up at the Ship Inn at Gravesend when he reviewed the Royal Navy as the guest of James I. Lengthy discussions with

Ritzy

William III on the terms of James II's abdication were held at the Bear at Hungerford.

It was as well to plan your journey so that you *were* near a decent inn. When Queen Henrietta visited Tunbridge Wells in 1630 they had to have timber cottages brought in on sleds and most of her entourage slept in tents. Charles II's wife, Catherine, found houses at Tunbridge in 1663 but still nothing like a decent hostelry, and when Bath was at its peak in the 18th century, the Saracen's Head which was built in 1713, couldn't cope with the 8,000 visitors to the city a couple of years later. Instead, the travellers took lodgings with families or rented houses for themselves. Scotland's oldest hotel is the 17th century Salutation Hotel in Perth, which accommodated Bonnie Prince Charlie.

In the 18th century there was a great increase in the number of stage coaches and their speed depended to a large extent on the inns that lined their routes. Within these substantial houses were stabled the fresh horses which could be harnessed up in under a minute - a necessity if you were trying to keep to a schedule of London to Holyhead in 26 hours, or London to Exeter in 17. It was nothing unusual for the coaches to need 20 changes of horses for a long journey and the major coaching inns had far more room for the animals than they did for the people. A busy posting house could stable 600 horses and would expect to gets its main additional revenue from selling food and drink rather than bedrooms. The coaching inns were a combination of hotel, stable and travel agent. It is still possible to see good examples, like the Angel at Guildford, with its double entrance, one for guests through the front door and the other through the tall wooden gates for the coaches. The gates led to a courtyard, on one side of which was the stabling and, on the other, the bedrooms and public rooms. Inside the hotel it would be possible to buy tickets for the other coach routes which stopped there and, at Cheltenham, for example, 23 passenger services ran regularly from the Royal. At the George Inn in Stamford there was an 18th century dining room where the doors which faced North and South were labelled Edinburgh and London respectively. To reach the coaches for those destinations, you went through those doors.

In most of the inns the majority of the travellers had only a communal kitchen in which to eat, and dormitory accommodation if they stayed overnight. Only the wealthy were able to get private rooms where they could be served in any degree of comfort. Even if you could afford it, the rooms were often in short supply, particularly in the more remote parts of the country. In Hawick, in the only inn suitable for the stage, you had to arrive early "lest other travellers should be there before you; there is but one sitting room at Hawick and only one tolerable bed-chamber with two beds." If the coach was carrying you further on your journey, there was very little time to eat in either room or kitchen, and landlords were accused of being in league with the driver, who was bribed to call the passengers from their set meal before they had time to finish and get their money's worth. As a consequence, the same cold joint could be offered to many different parties.

As the English road system improved in the latter half of the 18th century, so the number of stage routes proliferated and, by 1825, as many as 10,000 people a day were using the regular coach services. The development of roads was slower in Scotland, which accounts both for the smaller number of staging inns and for the greater speed with which its hotel industry developed when the country became a popular destination for tourists. At that time the few existing inns were almost immediately unable to look after the rush of visitors brought by the railways.

Although it has been estimated that over two million passengers a year were carried at the peak of the coaching days after the Napoleonic Wars, conditions were extremely rough. There were occasions when people actually froze to death in the coaches during the winter, and there was the very real danger of highwaymen holding up the stage and robbing the travellers. It was easy to catch cold at a time when influenza and pneumonia were deadly killers and you were crowded together in a confined space with strangers, who might have any one of a variety of contagious diseases. All of which only emphasises the primitive conditions of that era. Oh, for a train to take the strain.

The origin of the word "hotel" is French and it roughly equates to the English word "mansion". French innkeepers were permitted to use the diminutive "hotellerie" to describe their business but could not use "hotel" before the Revolution. During the Napoleonic era the aristocracy were hardly in a position to object, and in addition many of their best servants found themselves out of a job and became innkeepers. The former staff then used the word "hotel" frequently, as they felt themselves a cut above the rougher image of an inn. In Britain there is an early record of William Pitt writing to his mother in 1780 on the headed paper of Nerot's Hotel in London, so that we know the word had been copied by that time and was in fairly general use. In the early part of the 19th century it had genteel connotations but this restriction did not last. The situation in London was somewhat different from the rest of the country, in that the capital offered a wider choice of hotel, and if a visitor had his own coach, he would not stay at an inn which catered for the stage passengers. Of course, many wealthy people had their town houses as well as their country homes and did not need hotels at all. Many others received hospitality from their friends or stayed in lodgings. Nevertheless, there were a number of fashionable hotels, many of them in the Mayfair area.

London at the beginning of the 19th century was a loosely connected series of towns and villages and it might well be necessary, for instance, to take a bodyguard on a journey from Hyde Park Corner to Knightsbridge. The City was the business heart of London but the entertainment centre was around the Strand, with Mayfair the finest address in which to live. It was in Mayfair that the great houses of the aristocracy were to be found, together with hotels like Pulteneys, the Clarendon and Longs. Pulteneys was at 105, Piccadilly and was built on the site of a house which had cost the Marquis of Queensberry (Old Q) 4,350 guineas (£4,567) in 1792, but unfortunately it burnt down soon after he bought it. The new hotel was good enough to be patronised by the Emperor of Russia and his sister in 1814 and would have been conveniently close to St. James Palace. The Clarendon was at 169, New Bond Street and could count among its guests the Elder Pitt, who lived there in 1741. It also housed a literary society founded by Sir Joshua Reynolds and Samuel Johnson. Even when the country was at war with Napoleon, the Clarendon had the reputation of being the only hotel in London where you could get a genuine French dinner, even if it did cost you £3 or £4 (around £300 today) with a guinea (£1.05p) for a bottle of champagne. Longs, also in New Bond Street, was an early 19th century centre for dandies and country bachelors.

In Marylebone there was Durrants Hotel, which still survives, a perfect example of a Georgian hotel, elegant in design, charming and gracious. Then, for the racing crowd, there was Limmers, who had a waiter called John Collins and he created the famous long sum-

mer drink. There was a rhyme which went:
"My name is John Collins, head waiter at Limmers,
At the corner of Conduit Street, Hanover Square.
My chief occupation is filling up brimmers,
To solace young gentlemen laden with care."
Another solace for the patrons was a secret passage through the back of the hotel into Bond Street if the bailiffs were after them, a fate to be expected by unsuccessful gambling men. Officers on leave or business used Stephens Hotel in Bow Street, while Louis XVIII stayed at Grillons Hotel in Albemarle Street and, as was natural for a guest of his distinction, had his own apartments in the hotel and used it as he would his own palace; he would expect the servants to be provided with liveries and, indeed, it was very unlikely that they would have been able to afford suitable outfits otherwise. This is where we find the origins of hotel uniforms, because, in the stage coach inns, the staff would have been dressed in their normal clothes.

The owners of the hotels were often men with experience of service in aristocratic houses and would acquire their first clients on the basis of this reputation. Like William Claridge, who took over Mivarts at 49, Brook Street, Mayfair, with his wife, Marianna, in 1853, changed its name to his own and died highly esteemed in 1882. George IV had wanted a hotel which he and his friends could use discreetly and he set up James Mivart in No: 49 in 1813. It was from such questionable beginnings that the hotel became almost an annex to the palace. In 1827 the *Morning Post* described Mivarts as: "the fashionable rendezvous for the high corps diplomatique." It grew to five houses by 1838. Claridge too was very much a courtier: "Mr. Claridge's bows were celebrated; they were of a different depth according to the rank of the person to whom he bowed, and there was even the delicate difference in the salute that he gave to a Serene Highness to that with which he welcomed a Royal Highness."

As was to be expected, the coaching inns of London included some of the largest in the country. Like La Belle Sauvage in Ludgate Hill, the White Bear Inn which stood on the site of the present Criterion in Piccadilly and the famous Golden Cross opposite today's Charing Cross Station. For many years the Golden Cross was known as Morleys Hotel. Put all the London hotels together though, and they were still a relatively unimportant section of the available accommodation, for most people still sought lodgings.

Ritzy

Even in the 18th century, however, there were a few exceptions to the plebeian coaching inns outside the capital. In Buxton, for example, the 5th Duke of Devonshire, copying the Royal Crescent in Bath, spent no less than £120,000 on building his own magnificent Crescent :"a stately pillared stone building in the form of a segment of a circle with an arcade running the whole length of the segment." Over 100 yards (94m) long, the Crescent was used first for the Grand, the Centre and the St. Ann's Hotels, the ground floor fronts were occupied by shops, and nearby were the great stables which now house the Devonshire Hospital. Such munificence in 1784 was only possible for someone like a Duke who had resources like his own copper mines. The Crescent is Doric and the guests in the hotels could well believe that their temporary home was superior to many a manor house.

After Waterloo, in the era of Nash, many new hotels were built in country towns and can often be seen to this day. They were usually three-story buildings, like the Bold Hotel at Southport, whose: "wooden portico with coupled Doric pillars underlies the Greek lineage of Regency architecture." One of the best known in its time was the first Adelphi Hotel in Liverpool. This was built as part of a terrace in 1823 and by 1828 a London hotelier called James Radley had acquired the lease. As he was new to the city he decided to circularise his potential clientele and under a woodcut of the Adelphi with its address, he wrote: "James Radley begs respectfully to inform the nobility, gentry and public in general that he has taken a lease of these premises and fitted them up at considerable expense to form a complete hotel. The situation is central and good and the house combines the peculiar advantages of a private entrance for families, and an excellent coffee room contiguous to the general door in Ranelagh Place. The extent of accommodation is great, including good sitting room, bedrooms, baths, etc. etc. on each floor. Immediately behind the hotel are good lock-up coachhouses etc. J.R. has had much experience in this business in London and he begs to assure those families and gentlemen who may honour him with their patronage, that the most strict attention shall be paid to their comfort and convenience in every respect." Customer benefits in profusion.

James Radley was an excellent hotelier and his advice was later sought by others in the profession. When royalty needed accommodation in Liverpool they would choose the Adelphi and Charles

Dickens was very fond of its cuisine. He stayed at the hotel in 1842 on his way to America and commented: "I have not enquired among my medical acquaintances whether Turtle and Cold Punch, with Hock, Champagne and Claret and everything usually included in an unlimited order for a good dinner - especially when it is left to the liberal construction of my faultless friend, Mr. Radley, of the Adelphi Hotel - are peculiarly calculated to suffer a sea change; or whether a plain mutton chop and a glass or two of sherry would be less likely of conversion into foreign and disconcerting material - I know that the dinner of that day was undeniably perfect."

The quality of hotel food might be good or bad, but it was better anyway to eat, drink and be merry because tomorrow was very uncertain. The expectation of life was well under 40 at birth, and was one reason why there were only 14 million people in the whole of England, Scotland and Wales in 1821. Smallpox, cholera, typhoid, tuberculosis, diphtheria and bronchitis all made it unlikely that you would grow old enough to die of a coronary or cancer. Life was still: "nasty, brutish and short" and the search for better health was conducted with vigour and almost unquestioning faith. There were two main streams of thought which affected hotels. They both sprang from the continuing and growing belief in the good magic of water as against the bad magic of alcohol, and resulted in the Temperance Movement and the Hydropathic Institutes.

The beginnings of the Temperance Movement coincided with the passing of the 1830 Beer Act, which was a measure of Lord Melbourne's Whig government and intended to reduce the amount of spirit drinking by making it easier and cheaper to drink beer. The Act permitted anybody to open a beer shop on payment of a fee of two guineas (£2.10p) and resulted in 20,000 new beer shops opening in the following decade. Far from reducing drunkenness, the Act ensured one of the greatest British binges of all time, and although the original temperance pioneers could not place the blame for this solely on a few hotels, they were, in principle, against anything which helped people to drink. There might be a tendency to regard the present day temperance movement as a little out of date, fighting battles which modern common sense has already won and a bit reactionary even in a politically correct society. Irrespective of the truth or otherwise of such an assessment - and there are estimated to be nearly 1 million alcoholics in the country today - the Victorian temperance movement was a powerful influence in a different world, just as a 19th century Tory, like Disraeli, might consider the present day Conservative party very left wing. To visit the past is really to be a stranger in a foreign land.

In the beginning the temperance advocates wanted to reduce the amount of drinking, not to abolish it. It was only when the hard-liners took over the infant movement that the taking of the pledge of total prohibition became the sign of the true follower. Not to drink alcohol was initially regarded by the vast majority of the population as anti-social, foolhardy and unhealthy. It was anti-social because to offer a drink was the equivalent of a cup of coffee today. It was a sign of bonhomie, a touch of friendship and it was used to seal bargains, to mark the initiation of apprentices and in countless other aspects of business and social life. It was foolhardy not to drink because the water supply was too often polluted. Patients in hospital were always given mildly alcoholic drinks rather than plain water, and in private homes water would have to be brought up from the well if you had one, or carried from a public well: "Even in upper class households in the 1850's mains (water) supplies were intermittent" and in 1859 there was still a real need for the formation of the Metropolitan Free Drinking Fountain Association. It was during Victoria's reign that it was discovered that both cholera and typhoid could be traced to infected water and there was a good deal of common sense in using alcohol to kill some of the bacteria in it.

The general public also considered it unhealthy not to drink because it believed that drinking gave you strength and did you good. Those old advertisements of musclebound giants drinking their: "beer for men" are first cousins to the popular Victorian image. Many people when they want to say "thank you" still say "cheers". As a consequence of these arguments and conditions, the early temperance preachers often had a difficult time and even had to flee the wrath of enraged mobs. The hard core of the pioneer temperance leaders were, however, made of stern stuff mentally, even though a surprising number of them did suffer physical ill health through no fault of their own.

The health improving properties of certain wells had been known for centuries and flourished in a series of spas from Bath, Sadlers Wells and Tunbridge Wells in the South to Buxton and Harrogate in the North. The waters often had iron in them and these are known scientifically today as Chalybeate springs. Some of the wells were credited to saints, like St. Ann's at Buxton but, from whatever foundation, they attracted visitors with the freshness and purity of their surroundings, contrasting so vividly and favourably with the stench and dirt of the cities. The water was drunk and it was used for bathing.

In most circles of early Victorian society bathing was considered something of a fad, appropriate to the spas where drastic methods might be needed to restore one's health, but not all that necessary and sensible otherwise. It was only about 50 years before that Frederick the Great of Prussia, having failed to wash for 30 years, cut his leg and not unnaturally died of gangrene. Wealthy young men on the Grand Tour of Europe might visit Versailles and reflect that the palace of the Sun King, Louis XIV, had been built with one bathroom and two toilets. It wasn't surprising that hydropathists could believe that bathing in special water might have wonderful recuperative effects. Indeed there were and are ailments which respond to this treatment and tens of thousands of sufferers who have had their pain alleviated by visiting the spas.

The spas had, however, also been an excuse for people to go on holiday, and for them the social round in a city like Bath could well be the highlight of the year. The spas were the 'seaside' before many people thought of going to the seaside. There was a more informal atmosphere about life at the spas and there were balls and concerts, lectures and recreational activities of all kinds. It was often a method of finding a suitable husband for a daughter or a wealthy wife. Although the spas had never been part of a moral crusade, as the temperance movement was now launching, they did have common ground in advocating the greater use of water.

Far away in Austria there lived a farmer's son called Vincent Preissnitz (1801 - 1851) who was busy claiming that the water on his land was exceptionally pure and capable of curing many diseases. By about 1830 he managed to receive very favourable publicity and became extremely fashionable. From Preissnitz came the hydropathists and the hydropathic institutions, which began in Britain soon after, and of which hotels like the Atholl Palace at Pitlochry, the Norbreck Hydro, Blackpool and the Peebles Hydro are surviving architectural examples. Vast sums of money would be spent on creating such establishments and they eventually became part of the hotel industry.

Ritzy

For such a craze to catch on, there had to be powerful support. It came from eminent thinkers, like Charles Darwin, who wrote "I feel certain that the water cure is no quackery" and from public figures like Gladstone and Tennyson. It came from Sir Charles Scudamore, who went to Graffenberg in 1843 to report on Preissnitz and came back convinced by his methods. As a doctor, Scudamore immediately fell foul of the College of Physicians who considered the idea nonsense and, indeed: "Homeopathists, Hydropathists and Morrisonians were the dissenters in the Medical World, threatening its established church - the College of Physicians." If you were very ill with, say, tuberculosis, however, and Dr. John Balbirnie said that you could use water from the Highlands to treat the illness, then the gullible and desperate had little to lose. In defence of the water cure, it would certainly have done little harm in the treatment of any illness, particularly by comparison with some of the hocus-pocus practiced.

It was also natural for the British to turn to the country spas because they had their roots deeply in the land and the village. The growth of the grim industrial towns and the movement of labour from the fields to the factories throughout the century, only made the people more anxious to get away from the smoke and the dirt when they could. Admittedly, in the early days of the century, the country was never all that far away; in 1840 the pigs for London hotel kitchens were raised in Notting Dale just up the road from Mayfair. Cows were kept in pastures off the Strand and there were sheep to be sheared on Hampstead Heath as late as the 1930s. The wealthy might flock to London for the season but they went home to the country after that.

There were also a large number of coastal resorts which had become fashionable and attracted a large number of visitors. Brighton was the most famous, but the pattern of accommodation was the familiar one of lodging houses and private homes, with a small number of inns which could provide a bed. The attraction was not so much the sea bathing - indeed a number of the early lodging houses were built with their backs to the sea - as the many social events, and, of course, the town was a favourite of the Prince Regent who had first visited it in 1784. As late as 1853 Thackeray called it a city of lodging houses for, like all the smaller seaside towns, almost any inhabitant would take in visitors.

While a number of resorts had been favoured by visits from royalty - George III went to Weymouth, for instance, and the Princess of Wales to Worthing - the overall development was still slow. In Worthing in 1800 there was only sufficient room to feed 42 guests in the two inns the town could boast, and if you were looking for good cooking, you were better advised to get invited to the home of an epicurean aristocrat. Even in those days it was accepted that the best chefs were to be found in France and many were hired to lend lustre to a noble's hospitality. It was in this way that Marie-Antoine Carême came to Brighton after Waterloo, to act as joint head chef to George IV, but he did not settle down, largely because he could not find any trained assistants. For the greatest chef in France, a man who had been Chef de Cuisine to Czar Alexander I, to have to rely on young kitchen maids if he did not want to do the work himself ! It was not only intolerable as far as he was concerned, but the clearest example of the paucity of experienced staff at the time. And if royalty couldn't get them, what chance did a humble hotel have?

Although there might not have been sufficient demand for resort hotels in the early part of the century, the seaside soon became very much a growth industry for trippers. In 1815 there were 21,000 visitors to Margate, who came by sail from London, but this figure rose to 40,000 in 1820 and 100,000 in 1830.

The reason for the lack of hotels, both at the seaside and in other cities where the habit might have been created earlier, had much to do with the simple question of money. To build a large hotel was feasible for a Duke of Devonshire, but out of the question for lesser mortals. It was the kind of project which would require capital from the public and many difficulties were deliberately put in the way of raising it by such means. Of these the most awkward was the absence of limited liability. If you invested in a business as a shareholder and the business foundered with debts owing, above and beyond the capital you had put in, then you were personally responsible for a proportion of those debts; you would not only lose all the money you had paid for the shares, but in addition you could be called upon for more money by the creditors. This legal condition had been devised as a consequence of the famous South Sea Bubble debacle in 1720, when thousands of investors in trade to the South Seas, had been defrauded of their capital and the scandal had proved most embarrassing for the government of the day.

So legislation was brought in to protect the public against directors of companies who might try to leave the shareholders and creditors holding the baby. Exceptions were only made when it was impossible to count on individual businessmen building an industry brick by brick. Normally an entrepreneur would be expected to start, say, with one spinning wheel and finish up, after investing his profits steadily over the years, with his own mill. This system was too slow, however, if you wanted as a government to create, for example, a national canal network; so canals were excluded by Special Parliamentary Acts. So were a number of public utilities, but nobody would have been permitted to raise money for a private limited company to build as speculative a venture as a hotel. This was the situation right through the early years of Victoria's reign, and it accounts in part for the small size of the vast majority of the hotels in 1840.

It was architecturally feasible to build a large hotel. The first was the Tremont Hotel in Boston, Massachusetts, which covered an entire city block and had nearly 200 bedrooms, although it was only three stories high. It was opened in October 1829 and could boast a main dining-room with seats for 200 guests, carved walnut furniture and wall-to-wall carpeting in many of the apartments. Among the innovations, which were not to be copied in Europe for a long time, were free soap beside the bowl of water in the bedroom, an electromagnetic buzzer which enabled the staff to see that you wanted service, and a special reading room. The Tremont, of course, did not have a lift and this restricted the hotel's tariff. If a guest paid a reasonable price he was not prepared to climb long flights of stairs every time he wanted to reach his bedroom and, indeed, if he was elderly, might not physically be able to do so. In British hotels as well, therefore, the top floor bedrooms had to be let more cheaply and were often used for the guests' personal servants. A Victorian hotel which was anxious to cater to the wealthy patron would have as many as half its total number of bedrooms set aside for the servants, and this explains the difference in height between the upper and lower floors, the difference in size and all the small windows the higher up you went.

The United States was not only to be responsible for pioneering the large hotel, but would also produce the first lifts, electric light, telephones and some of the most advanced building contractors for the international hotel industry.

The catalyst which was eventually to transform the cinderella of the accommodation market was the railway, and the British Hotel industry owes George Stephenson a debt of gratitude for his enterprise. The railway had a shattering effect on the pattern of transportation, ruining the elaborate system of stage coach routes and leaving almost derelict the coaching inns which had provided the horses and the refreshment for travellers. By the 1830s it was questionable whether you would get a worse reception in a coaching village as a railwayman or as a temperance preacher, but neither was at all popular. What the railways destroyed, however, was nothing to what they created, and we can look first at the point the railways had reached by 1837.

Although the first Parliamentary Act was passed in 1811 to permit the building of a railway line in South London, the railways didn't really get under way until the 1830s. They had from the beginning aroused great passions and great enthusiasms; passions from people who would suffer from their success, and enthusiasm from those who could see the fortunes to be made. As the growth of the railway hotels was a part of the development of the railways themselves, it is worth describing briefly how you had to go about getting permission to build a railway. It was first necessary to survey the route and to lodge the subsequent plans at the House of Commons. As the railway would cross the fields and property of many landowners, a Book of Reference to all the owners affected had to be compiled as well. This, with 10% of the estimated cost of building the railway had then to be given to the Clerk of the Commons and only then could a Bill be introduced for permission to purchase the land compulsorily. If the Bill was approved, the price had to be agreed between the two parties and, if this was impossible, the local Justice of the Peace would arbitrate. As they were often part of the anti-railway lobby, there were many difficulties.

Railways brought noise, dirt and rough navvies and they spoiled a lot of the scenery. They also brought industry, capital, work for the unemployed and the possibility of substantial profits. Consequently, two diametrically opposed schools of thought existed about the desirability of railways; opposition to the routes themselves came both from people who didn't want the line on their property, and from people who objected to the fact that it wasn't on theirs. The railway companies bought the land as cheaply as they could, and in the cities would endeavour to locate their main stations in a part of the town which was either completely undeveloped or run down. On such property most of the railway hotels in the provincial towns would be built.

The railway companies needed to build hotels for three main reasons. In the earliest stage of railway development small hotels were put up at the country stations, for the benefit of passengers who had to travel a long way to reach the line. These hotels were invariably leased to other people and the railways didn't put up the money for them. Many of the larger pubs in the country, still called the "Station Hotel" today, would have had their origins in this way. Because of the capital needed to build railways, the government classed them with the canals and public utilities as an area where money could be raised from the public, but in order to offer the maximum protection, the money thus produced had to be used exclusively for the railway itself. When this was not done and senior railway executives used their finances for purposes like building steamers, or even buying collieries to ensure the coal travelled on the right railway, any shareholder could object in court. The Chairman of the West Hartlepool Harbour and Railway, who had almost literally built the town by his own efforts, was totally ruined in a long drawn out court battle in the 1850s over misuse of the funds of this nature.

A separate bill had to be passed through Parliament to build a hotel, or the money had to be raised through a separate company. There were a number of breaches of the law where hotels in the early years did benefit from the original share-holders' money, but fortunately for the directors concerned, any complaints failed to reach the courts. Many shareholders did object on moral grounds, insisting that they had been asked to invest in railways and not in establishments selling drink, but it was never suggested that the board was lining its own pockets in some way.

The second reason for the railways' interest in hotels was that punctuality could not be guaranteed on the early trains and many would arrive late in the evening, stranding the passengers without anywhere suitable to sleep. Many trains also left on long journeys early in the morning and these created more hotel custom as travellers stayed the night before their journey. Some hoteliers were not above making the check-out time an hour or two before the departure of popular trains, so that the guests either had to vacate their rooms at an inconvenient point or pay extra for the privilege of staying until the train was ready to set off.

The third reason was that the railways soon started to compete for traffic among themselves and some of them, like the Midland and the South Eastern believed that putting up hotels would give them a competitive advantage. There were to be many railway lines to the different South Coast ports and resorts and many provincial cities were also served by more than one company. We can examine later the economics of this kind of travellers' perk, but the principle highlights the haphazard development of hotels, as of so much else, in Victorian Britain.

The Victorians were devoted to *laisser-faire*, to economic freedom to get rich or go bankrupt, with the minimum amount of interference from the government. It was inconceivable in that climate, as indeed it is today, to gear the demand for hotels to the supply. Once it appeared that a hotel developer was on to a good thing, once a company thrived or an individual prospered, there was no lack of imitators. A decision to build the Zetland Hotel at Saltburn for the rich burghers of Middlesbrough who wanted to get away from the town's grime to the seaside, made admirable sense in isolation. What could not be foreseen was how long the people would be content to travel just a few miles to go on holiday, whether they would prefer another fashionable resort in time and where the money was to come from to improve the buildings, as new inventions were introduced. The small station hotels existed from the earliest railway age, but the larger ones, like York, Derby and Paddington, did not appear until after the railways could turn to the minutiae of their projects in the period from 1837 onwards.

Life in an early 19th century hotel depended on your purse. At the top end of the market, the hotel had many amenities; there would be a lounge and often a billiards room. Billiards had been a popular British game for centuries; Mary, Queen of Scots, complained to Queen Elizabeth that her captors had taken her table away from her. It was popular with the aristocracy throughout the 18th century. White's standard book on billiards in 1807 describes the same game we play today and, apart from the improvements in equipment, such as the slate bed to ensure that the balls roll truly, there has been very little change. At a time when people had to make their own amusements in the evening, the billiards room was very popular and often very lavish.

If the hotel could boast its own dining-room, all the guests who did not wish to take their meals in a private sitting-room, would be seated round one large table, with the landlord or host presiding at the top. There would be a set menu, which is the origin of the term table d'hôte, and a choice of cold dishes.

At the other end of the scale, the common lodging-house for the poorest travellers and the near destitute could hardly have been worse. The bedding was filthy, there were lice and rats, it was wise to sleep with your boots on for fear they would be stolen during the night, even if sleep was impossible with the noise of the other members of the dormitory, who could be drunk, half-mad, or using the place as a brothel. Lodging house guests would bring their own food, or buy it raw from the lodging house keeper and then cook it themselves in the large kitchen. It was very rough indeed, but there were thousands of itinerant workers who could afford nothing better.

It was a long way from a city common lodging house to an inn, deep in the country, but these might offer accommodation as well. Thomas de Quincey, the author and essayist, writing about his travels in Wales in 1802, speaks highly of the numerous inns which had been put up about 15 miles from each other for the accommodation of tourists. A small English spa like Matlock could muster 3 hotels, even if they did look exactly like large farmhouses.

Britain in 1837 - for hotels a developing seaside, new hope for the spas, a wide network of doomed coaching inns and a small group of city centre hotels. Ready to change it all came the steady march of the railway navvies, building lines like the strings of a net which would finally gather up the diffuse communities throughout the country and make them accessible to each other.

2
The pioneering years. 1837-1862.

Hotel development during the 25 years between 1837 and 1862 was geared to the progress of the railways. Each new line opened up the area it covered, altering the existing communications industry, increasing or reducing traffic. Villages which had been staging posts on the main coach routes declined dramatically and large and prosperous coaching inns, which had throbbed with the bustle of arrivals and departures, soon took on the aspects of a deserted stage set; the weeds spread through the derelict yards, the stables which had housed hundreds of horses echoed the foot-steps of the few employees left; landlords were reduced to trying to sell the local butter and cheese as if they were running a roadside stall, or making ends meet by mending shoes or competing with the local blacksmith. The rare visitors remarked on the deserted corridors and the general air of decay and despondency.

It was a very bad time for the districts affected, and with unemployment came a drop in land values, reduced turnover in the village shops and emigration from the area to the new industrial towns. There was nothing the villages could do. any more than a petrol station on a main road can replace the business when a new motorway diverts the traffic. All that was left was to sell drinks to the local inhabitants, which was not sufficient to keep a lot of the inns solvent. All over the country they soldiered on as best they could and finally a lot of them closed.

Where the coaching inn was in a sizable town, much depended on its position *vis-à-vis* the new station. Some inns in the early days were taken over by the railways to provide carriers' quarters or booking offices till more permanent arrangements could be made. If they were fortunate enough to be near a busy railway station, the change from coach passengers to railway passengers would be comparatively painless, but not many were so lucky. Some relics of the Elizabethan Castle & Falcon Inn remained at Aldersgate Station in the city, as did parts of the 16th century Swan with Two Necks and the Catherine Wheel near other London stations. In the provinces the Adelphi in Liverpool was one which found itself very close to the new terminal. Partly through this, and partly through James Radley's expertise, it was able to expand by absorbing other buildings in the terrace. For the most part, though, the inns were in the wrong places.

It is, of course, one of the major risks in building a hotel that the existing economic and transportation patterns can change radically. If an area is fashionable when the hotel is built, the hotelier must still be able to attract visitors when the area has gone to seed, even though the new conditions locally are no fault of his. There's an old saying in the business that the three most important factors in a hotel's success are "Location, location and location" but the best location today can still be a back-water or a slum in a few years' time if the environment changes.

In 1833 the national total of coach and mail travellers had reached a peak at just over 2,500,000, with about another 25% arriving on post-horses, canal boats or in private carriages. That traffic withered away for the most part, but by 1863 the total number of railway journeys was over 204 million. So this was a time of massive growth in travel rather than overall decline.

The railways produced hotels in two different ways; by creating the traffic for others to risk putting up new buildings, or by building hotels themselves. But where there was competition in a town between two railway companies for permission to build a terminus, one of the common arguments used was the location of the existing hotels in relation to the proposed site for the station. In Manchester, the Liverpool and Manchester Railway wanted to put up a terminus at Store Street while the Manchester & Leeds wanted it sited at Hunts Bank and argued "The superior convenience of Hunts Bank as a central station is attested by the fact that of the 28 inns and hotels in *Pigot's Directory* for 1841, 19 are nearer Hunts Bank, 2 are equidistant, 7 are nearer Store Street". New Street Station, Birmingham, situated 100 yards (90 metres), from the Royal Hotel, which was the best in the city, and the Oldham Road Station in Manchester in 1836, also near to the local hotel, are further examples which obtained approval partly for that reason.

If the railways were competing with each other for permission to build a terminus, they might use the location of existing hotels to bolster the case for a central site, but ideally the railways wanted to buy inexpensive suburban land for terminii. When successful, there would not be sufficient suitable bedroom accommodation and then the railway would either hope that hotels would spring up without their assistance or, alternatively, they might invest themselves. Hotels weren't the status symbols they would become, though.

The first railway hotel was, in fact, two hotels at Euston which were opened in 1839 by the London & Birmingham Railway. The prospectus for the raising of the capital was headed "London and Birmingham Railway Hotel and Dormitories" and the money for the hotel was raised by the creation of a separate company, in keeping with the laws on the use of railway funds. The idea was to build a hotel on the east side of the station and dormitories on the west. The railway directors would be trustees of the land on which the buildings were to be erected and the money would be raised in £25 shares. Throughout the Victorian period, the nominal value of shares was much higher than we normally find today; £5, £10 and £20 shares were the usual units and this, of course, restricted the share purchasing section of the population to a very small percentage.

Fifty years after the building of the Euston Hotels, the manager of the Metropole Hotel in London, one of the finest and newest, would earn only £10 a week. To most people, £20 was a small fortune. The new hotels at Euston were not licensed and were completely separate buildings. Although a number of the rooms in the dormitory building might have had several beds, the word 'dormitory' did not automatically imply this, but rather a place in which to sleep. A proportion of the dormitories had small sitting or dressing-rooms attached to them. The hotel was to have a splendid coffee-room and there would be another in the dormitory building. The coffee-room was open to the general public where the expression 'dining-room' would indicate for some years that only hotel guests and their friends were admitted. Charges for sleeping depended on the floor occupied and: "the scale of accommodation". Public bathrooms were placed in each building.

It was not until 1881 that the two hotels were joined together by a connecting block and altogether the original scheme was a limited effort. Even so it provided good accommodation for the time, and an improved setting for the railway directors, themselves. These men were engaged in enterprises involving vast sums of money and they sometimes needed a prestigious building. The first attempt to raise over £1 million to create the Great Western Railway was at a meeting which had to be held in a Bristol inn. Such a location was not considered a good enough stage setting for the sale pitch.

Ritzy

Euston Station had been opened in 1838 with the hotels as an afterthought, but at Derby the design for the station incorporated a hotel. It was opened in 1840 and was called the Midland. Three railway companies used the station; the North Midland, the Midland Counties and the Birmingham & Derby. To modern eyes the brochure illustrations look modest enough, but to an eye- witness at the time: " This is the most complete and magnificent Station yet erected. It has a frontage of 1050 ft (320 metres) and the whole interior, comprising sheds, workshops, engine houses and offices, is on the same stupendous scale." It also looked so large because everything around it was so small. The buildings were detached with a wide street between station and hotel, along which carriages and pedestrians alike would move without any danger of obstructing each other. Most people had no reason to take large buildings or big crowds for granted and each new large hotel would have the impact of a Canary Wharf for years to come.

York and Hull soon had hotels as an integral part of their station designs. Another early railway hotel was the Furness Abbey. This is a good example of a hotel built in an area made industrially attractive only by the invention of railways, and specifically needed to serve the buyers visiting the town. The 6th Duke of Devonshire was chairman of the Furness Railway Company and also the owner of the slate quarries and much of the other industry which was opening up the district around Barrow-in-Furness. A hotel was needed to accommodate the businessmen who came to negotiate for slate and the Duke is said to have paid for it. He certainly took a great deal of interest in the design for, like the 5th Duke at Buxton, he was an amateur architect. The hotel was built in a narrow, well wooded valley and looked like an old-fashioned country house; indeed, part of it had formed the home of the abbots of the Abbey.

To a people who only knew travel in terms of walking, riding horses, or enduring a stage-coach, the railways were an unparalleled marvel, but the early trains were hardly luxurious. For the poorer travellers the coaches were open to the elements and the speed must have seemed to many to be extremely dangerous, even though the *Rocket* averaged less than 30 mph when winning the competition for the most effective engine. Whatever the drawbacks, there was enormous excitement in taking a railway journey and, by the early 1840s, the growth of excursion trains had started.

The pioneering years

The first excursion train was run to see a public hanging in Bodmin in Cornwall. One of the earliest was Thomas Cook's famous arrangements for the supporters of his local Temperance Association; a rally in Loughborough in 1841. No less than 570 people paid a shilling (5p) each to travel from Leicester to the meeting in nine open coaches. Cook organised it as a keen temperance advocate but soon realised the opportunity which now existed to make a good profit. He continued with it as a side-line, arranging similar outings. Very soon these began to cover longer distances, the railways themselves became interested, and many visits were organised to destinations as far afield as Scotland.

There the growth of the tourist trade could be attributed to the popularity of the works of Sir Walter Scott and Robbie Burns and to a visit which Queen Victoria and Prince Albert paid to the country in 1842. With the trains making it possible to cover the miles in a reasonable time, Scotland found itself host to many more tourists and, if they were led by a temperance man like Thomas Cook, the hoteliers could expect to take both money and advice. Reminiscing in 1886, Cook recalled: "We had always a difficulty in Scotland in making hotel arrangements of a satisfactory character, and this was in great measure owing to the inveterate love of whisky which has been the drink and the curse of that country.....Nevertheless.....the example I set before my travellers who accompanied me through these districts and the example others had upon Hotel Proprietors, produced effects of a very beneficial character."

Individual travellers were very welcome, but to the railways in England seeking traffic for their wildly expanding system, the excursion traffic was an additional boon, and its increasing popularity was one reason for the 'railway mania' which swept the country in the late 1840s. Hundreds of bills were passed by Parliament for new lines, and eventually and inevitably - as with the modern 'dot.com' mania - the stock market crashed, temporarily calling a halt amid the cries of the ruined investors.

Cook also found that there was a lot of drinking in Ireland and when he addressed a meeting of Irish hoteliers on the principles of the temperance movement he was not amused that the owner of the hotel at which they gathered was very drunk indeed. Ireland was a very poor part of the United Kingdom, but before the potato famine in 1846, with its resultant starvation and emigration, over one third of the population lived there. Dublin itself had declined after the Act of Union, which transferred the parliamentary business of the country, together with a large number of the Irish aristocrats, to London. The economy which had, among other products, supplied England with much of its corn during the Napoleonic Wars, was hit by inflation and the relaxation of import duties. In that climate it was surprising that one Irishman, Martin Burke, had sufficient confidence in Dublin's future to invest heavily in the creation of the Shelbourne Hotel. In 1824 he opened it in the heart of fashionable St. Stephen's Square and even then could see the possibilities of the city as a tourist centre.

The hotel offered private drawing-rooms for between three and four shillings (15p - 20p), and Thackeray wrote later that a guest: "is comfortably accommodated at the very moderate daily charge of six shillings and eight pence (33p). For this charge a copious breakfast is provided for him in the coffee-room, a perpetual luncheon is likewise there spread, a plentiful dinner is ready at 6 o'clock; after which, there is a drawing room and a rubber of whist, with tay (tea) and coffee and cakes in plenty to satisfy the largest appetite." Thackeray also wrote about the Shelbournes' cocktails, a useful source of hotel industry profits in much later years. The luxury of the Shelbourne must have contrasted very strongly with the want and deprivation in the meaner streets of the Irish capital.

The future German Chancellor, Otto von Bismarck, also remarked on the food in British provincial hotels when writing to his father during a visit in 1842, but in slightly less glowing terms. "It is the country for heavy eaters. The variety in the cuisine is small: roast beef, mutton, ham (boiled), bacon, roast lamb, veal, eggs and potatoes are on the table at every breakfast, to which fruit and a vile fruit tart are added at dinner. The soups are so strongly spiced with black and red pepper that few foreigners can eat them. The system of allotted portions is unknown; even at breakfast the most enormous pieces of each of these kinds of meat, such as we never see, stand before you, and you cut and eat as much or as little of them as you like, without any difference as regards payment. In the hotels when I have taken supper and breakfast....and spent the night there, I have always paid 8 or 9 shillings (40p - 45p) - that is with a tip." One would imagine that the average Victorian guest was hard put to it to eat lunch after such a breakfast.

The railways retrenched, amalgamated and prepared for the

The pioneering years

Great Exhibition of 1851, when the total attendance of 6,009,948 visitors finally showed beyond doubt not only the new trend to mass travel, but also the need to cater for it. Of course, the attendance included vast number of Londoners, but Thomas Cook brought up 165,000 people from the provinces himself, and such hotels as existed had their best year ever.

The 1851 *Exhibition Guide* provided what advice it could, but there was little to choose from: West End hotels like the Clarendon, Fentons, Wrights, the Brook Street and Mivarts were booked completely. In the Covent Garden area, the Bedford, Tavistock, Old Hummums and New Hummums were equally packed. In the city a room would cost 6-7 shillings (30p-35p) a day, full *pension*, but in the West End a sitting room and bed-room was anywhere between 10 shillings and 6 pence and a guinea. (52½p and £1.05). The *Guide* recommended that you asked the price at the earliest opportunity as there was said to be a tendency for hotelkeepers to name a figure the guests looked as if they could and would afford. In addition, it was customary for the waiter and chambermaid to receive 1 shilling (5p) a day between them and the 'boots' 6 pence (2½p) as well.

A minute proportion of the visitors to the Great Exhibition would have stayed in hotels but many an investor around the country saw the way the wind was blowing. One railway hotel was approved in the year of the Great Exhibition when in February 1851 a meeting of the GWR directors authorised: "An hotel with Refreshment Rooms, Dormitories, Stables, and other conveniences for not more than £50,000" to be built at Paddington. The hotel was to be leased to a company directed by shareholders and officers of the GWR and the resulting Great Western Hotel was, at its opening: "the largest and most sumptuous hotel in England." The Philip Hardwicks, père et fils, were the architects and persuaded the directors to accept a design which was in the style of the French renaissance which was just beginning to be fashionable again. This is one of the earliest examples of the close connection between hotels and the flights of Victorian architectural fancy.

Victorian architects had passed the period where stucco was used instead of brick to imitate the rustic stone, and retreated from the simplicity of Georgian and Regency design which they now condemned as monotonous. Professor Pevsner, in his monumental *Buildings of England* explains the background very clearly: "Monotony had become the worst offence. It was detested as much by the advocates of the Italian as of the Gothic style. This high Victorian desire for richness, for rich relief, for ornate decoration also explains the next of the 19th century revivals, that of the French renaissance."

For the directors of hotel companies in the luxury category, there was to be a continuous conflict of interest in the years to come, as the architectural fashions grew steadily more lavish. On the one hand they wanted to have a new hotel which could be seen to be as stylish as possible, but they also wanted to keep the excessive expenditure, which Victorian architecture could easily involve, within reasonable bounds. At the Great Western Royal, John Thomas produced a splendid pediment on which carved figures illustrated the great Victorian virtues of peace, plenty, industry and science. It was stylish and artistic, but did it attract more customers to the hotel? It added nothing to their comfort, but it would be a talking point, and where did you draw the line anyway, for no hotel has an entirely utilitarian decor?

Time and again there were to be arguments along these lines, and many decisions were taken for reasons which had little to do with economics or marketing. The directors were often concerned with their own prestige and that of their company, which the hotel was designed to enhance, and it must have been a great satisfaction to the board of the GWR that the hotel's success was immediate and: "unheard of dividends were the result." Prince Albert, himself, made a tour of inspection before the hotel was opened for business on June 9th 1854. Large hotels were very novel and it was natural that royalty should visit them, in the same way that they might look over a new city skyscraper today.

As the GWR had no professional hoteliers anywhere near board level, the chairman of the hotel company was the great engineer, Isambard Kingdom Brunel, who: "found the supervising of the management a very agreeable relaxation from his other duties."

Although the: "sad spectacle offers itself of England throwing away her heritage of originality and returning to a style of period imitation as barren in its neo-Wren as in its neo-Georgian form"- and presumably neo-Gothic, neo-Italian Renaissance and neo-everything else - it is also true that hotels provided the Victorian architect with the opportunity to create a new type of building, or at least to push the frontiers for that type of building further forward. But the Hardwicks'

The pioneering years

Great Western was not typical of its day, and the Great Northern Hotel, which was opened at Kings Cross in 1854, was a far more modest and standard construction.

There was another aspect of Victorian architecture which was strongly advocated by the influential theorist, A.W.N. Pugin. In his pamphlets and buildings he endeavoured to make the neo-Gothic revival into an act of faith. It might seem a little far-fetched today, but he wanted a Christian country to reject any form of architecture which was derived from pagan civilizations, like the Greek or Roman. This attitude was in keeping with his times. The Victorians could produce the weirdest extremes and extremists and when you remember that the legs of a piano would be covered in many households as a seemly precaution against erotic thoughts, nothing is beyond belief.

It was also an act of faith for the temperance movement to go into the hotel business, for many of their leaders realised that the best way for temperance travellers to avoid the pitfalls of a licensed hotel, was for an alternative to be provided. So: "in 1836 the first temperance boarding house....was opened in London, and the first temperance hotel appeared in Aldersgate Street in the City, financed by William Jansen, who was also knows as Barley-Water Billy". Unfortunately for guests who habitually used temperance hotels, a firm faith in prohibition did not automatically guarantee that the proprietor was also capable of running a hotel. Temperance hotels: "were often opened by those who had failed at normal inn-keeping and by reformed drunkards who, with no aptitude for the job, were set-up in business by local sympathizers." The hotels were often very small indeed; like the one near Penzance which consisted of one room over a general store.

A temperance historian wrote in 1865, when there were nearly 200 temperance hotels in England that: "temperance hotels had in many cases, brought a reproach upon the movement because of their mean appearance and unsuitable management". It would be unfair, however, to tar all the temperance hotels with the same brush. Among many other dedicated proprietors, Mrs. Thomas Cook opened her own hotel in Market Harborough in Leicestershire and the Cooks built a new temperance hotel in Leicester itself in 1853 for £3,500. The hotel was popular and well run, as one would expect from a man who always looked after the comfort of his tourists with such care.

While one temperance leader could complain of the management of temperance hotels and call them: "Penal settlements of Teetotalism", the hotels did at least enable the temperance guest to carry out his pledge without enduring from servants or other guests the small slights which indicated that they thought his conduct mean, odd, or unfriendly. Temperance hotels: "were really attempts to enable teetotallers to survive in a drink-ridden society" though they were also used on occasions as fronts for less legal activities, as a funeral parlour in Chicago in the 1920s might conceal the entrance to a speakeasy. Gambling and disorderly conduct in certain so-called temperance hotels got them banned even by teetotal societies, and some brothels called themselves temperance hotels in order to allay suspicion. It was true that many of the hotels were drab and it would have been helpful if there had been some recognized standards of practice, because the hotel keepers would probably have followed their society's instructions with care. Unfortunately they didn't develop in such an organised way.

There was one temperance enthusiast, however, who did make a fortune out of accommodating guests and that was John Smedley who started with the unlikely asset of a stocking mill in Matlock in Derbyshire. Smedley in his early years was a strong churchman who felt so deeply on the subject that he discouraged his work people from going to chapel; but he became converted in time into a dissenting preacher, and a very powerful one at that. John Smedley was the epitome of the self-assured, enthusiastic, dynamic, God-fearing, Victorian entrepreneur and he had the useful skill of being able to persuade others to his way of thinking. At one stage, for example, he went overboard for a particular kind of quack pill and managed to dose his entire factory staff with it. Throughout his later years he waged guerrilla warfare against the more conservative parsons and doctors.

The railway reached Matlock in 1849 and not long afterwards Smedley fell seriously ill with typhoid and was taken to Ben Rhydding, at Ilkley, to convalesce and to try the hydropathic water cure. This was a great success. He fully recovered his strength and, as a result, the cause of hydropathy gained for its ranks a formidable advocate. Smedley immediately started testing hydropathic techniques on his own long-suffering work force. To his delight the practices seemed to work and in 1853 he bought a small existing hydro and started to run it himself.

The pioneering years

When Smedley began to operate the hydro, the spa of Matlock had almost ceased to exist because it was no longer fashionable. Throughout the length and breadth of the country the spas had had a long run, but they badly needed a new gimmick to correct their image as an old-fashioned holiday. The social side had overtaken the medical to a great extent and the wealthy were seeking new and more modern methods of healing themselves. They were no longer satisfied with the cures of their parents and grandparents. In 1818 the Old Bath Hotel at Matlock had accommodation for 100 visitors and there were smaller hotels like Saxtons and The Museum, as well as a number of lodging-houses. By Smedley's time, though, it was a quiet village, slumbering in its beautiful countryside.

The hydro proved popular and Smedley put up a larger building on the site very quickly. The rumour was that he built it like a factory, so that if it proved a failure as a hydro, the money would not be wasted. Smedley had no need to worry, however, for his fame spread through the non-conformist world. He wrote a book with 512 pages called *Practical Hydropathy including plans of baths and remarks on diet, clothing and habits of life* which, by 1872, had reached its 14th edition, and his supporters you couldn't come into contact with him without imbibing at least some of his zeal and enthusiasm.

Matlock possesses tepid springs and the hydro did offer a formidable range of special baths and massages. In addition, much was achieved for the visitor by the regime he was expected to adopt. This consisted of plenty of exercise in the fresh air, going to bed early and taking the pledge, at least temporarily. The diet leaned towards vegetarianism and tobacco was frowned upon. It was an unusual kind of hotel where elderly gentlemen sometimes took offence at being fined for arriving late at the dining table. After the meal they had to lie down with a cushion on their stomachs to help their digestions. It would be wrong, however, to think of the hydros simply in terms of hospitals. Indeed, for nearly 20 years, Smedley had no qualified doctor attached to the hydro. Treatment, at first, was just the application of water to the affected places, the use of wet sheets, douches and baths. Even so there were many cures and the hydro was soon very popular.

After Smedley's death the hydro became a public company in 1875 and eventually paid 20% dividends with great regularity. It would have been surprising if this enviable combination of miraculous cures and a seemingly unlimited clientele had gone unnoticed or uncopied: "Smedley's success soon induced others to build similar establishments for the treatment of rheumatic and other complaints." The hydros were far more than this though, as they looked after ladies who had more money than sense and a great deal of time to fill in, finding imaginary ailments to suit the cures. On the positive side, the hydros helped reduce obesity in women after pregnancy and dried out many a country gentleman who had imposed too great a strain on an elderly constitution. The fate of the hydros and how most of them eventually came to be purely hotels, is part of the industry's story in later years.

There was another haven for invalids and that was the seaside. Blackpool, for instance, was noted for the therapeutic effect of drinking the sea water as early as 1784, and the custom continued until around 1850 in a number of other resorts as well. The seaside between 1837 and 1862 also grew because of the development of the railways, and the best example of this is probably Bournemouth, just because the railway did not reach there until 1870. The town had had a very early start thanks to the enterprise of the local landowner, Sir George Tapps Jervis, who realised the potential for the seaside earlier than most. He built the first hotel in Bournemouth, which was called the Bath, and opened it on Coronation Day 1838. The hotel was described as a: "very elegant, spacious and convenient structure under the careful management of the occupier, Miss Toomer."

The railway was quickly built to nearby Poole, but the growth of seaside towns was initially due to day trippers and, for them, the journey by road from Poole to Bournemouth was too long. The credit for the first railway excursion train belongs to Sir Rowland Hill, who is, of course, better known for creating the Penny Post, but only three years after the first penny black, his Brighton Railway Company was running them. In the North a Lancashire Manufacturer took his 650 workers to Fleetwood one year later in 1844 and in the South, by 1859, as many as 73,000 Londoners travelled to Brighton in a week, a figure which included almost no commuters and represented 5% of the total London population.

Traffic in such volume justified the resident population of Brighton growing from 40,000 in 1831 to 90,000 only 40 years later, but the influential citizens of Bournemouth did not want the excursion type of business. They believed that it was impossible to mix

The pioneering years

wealthy invalids and lusty trippers together and the best way to avoid the problem was to stop the railway. Consequently the town stagnated and hotel development was slow. As, however, there was still a shortage of accommodation in hotels at certain times of the year, the existing hotels did quite well. The Belle Vue boarding house in 1840 flourished to such an extent that it became the Belle Vue Hotel in 1855 with the Union Jack flying from its new flag staff and a gazebo in the grounds. The ability to stop a railway was only one indication of the power wielded by a comparatively small number of people in deciding the way a seaside town should develop.

In the early resort days there was much of the atmosphere of the original spas. Apart from the sea bathing, the visitors would fill the time, taking long walks, visiting the Assembly Rooms and searching for interesting fossils. The first dinosaur bones were turned up at Lyme Regis. There was gaming with a faro bank at Scarborough in the 18th century and many guide books pointed out later the antiquarian appeal of the neighbourhood. At the libraries there were organized sweepstakes and raffles and auctions were conducted; greens were made available for archery and others for bowls. Into this calm and sedate society the masses of trippers arrived like a sudden tsunami wave, and the middle classes who had formed the backbone of many of those resorts, took flight for new pastures. This is the reason for the development of those additional towns which are so often found, cheek by jowl, with the original watering places; St. Annes near Blackpool, Saltburn near Redcar, Cliftonville near Margate, and Westcliff near Southend.

The mere existence of such new resorts was a warning to far-sighted investors that the potential seaside clientele was fickle, but few entrepreneurs seeing the immediate prospects, could be blamed for letting the long-term future take care of itself. As the great economist, John Maynard Keynes, himself, remarked many years later: "In the long run, we are all dead". The problems would come home to roost for future generations.

The older resorts had, themselves, grown from different foundations; Ramsgate, Torquay and Great Yarmouth were examples of original fishing ports. Scarborough had been a spa. Some of the ports were to grow even more important because of the additional speed of railway connections, and here again there was severe competition between competing lines. The South Eastern Railway had built the line to Dover and, to stop travellers embarking from other South coast ports, were prepared to offer them every comfort and inducement. As many passengers wishing to take boats for France, wanted to stay overnight at Dover, the railway decided to build the Lord Warden Hotel, which was sumptuously opened with a grand public dinner on September 7th 1853. It was a Doric building, named after the greatest - and about the oldest - living hero, the Duke of Wellington, who was Lord Warden of the Cinque Ports and who took a keen interest in the original design of the 111 bedroom hotel.

Although the Lord Warden was built and furnished by the SER, the directors, unlike those of the GWR at Paddington, sought a tenant from the beginning, rather than go into the hotel business themselves. The hotel might have: "a spacious *salle à manger* and a noble coffee-room" but they decided it was a far cry from operating engines and carriages. Certainly, a contemporary illustration of the dining room at the Lord Warden would have been enough to over-awe all but the very sophisticated. It was a large room dominated by the one enormous horseshoe table, and amid the acres of snowy white tablecloth sat large fruit bowls on pedestals, each topped with an uncut pineapple. The table was so wide that it would have been quite impossible for a guest to speak comfortably to his neighbour on the other side, even if etiquette had allowed. For those with a taste for display and formality it was a splendid sight, but for the shy and retiring it was a sufficient explanation for the number of guests who chose to take all their meals in their own rooms. Authoress, Lucas Malet, wrote: "Persons who in the security of their island homes are well bred and really quite delightful, become as awkward as chased hens in an hotel". For the railway companies, however, there was am-ple precedent for both tenancy and self-management to be the wrong decision.

In Swindon the GWR had opened both refreshment rooms and a hotel on the station platform in 1842. Originally, all they had wanted was 300 workmen's cottages for the staff at their new engine factory, but in order not to pay for the houses, they had of-fered the builders two incentives; the rent from the workers and a peppercorn rent of one penny (1/2p) a year for 99 years for the re-freshment rooms. To ensure that the refreshment rooms were well patronised, an agreement was also reached that every train would stop for 10 minutes at Swindon Station. The builders then sold the lease of the refreshment rooms to the Queens Hotel, Cheltenham, for a premium of £6,000 and a rent of £1,100 a year, and later sold the whole lease for £20,000. After that every succeeding owner tried to make the maximum profit, but it all hinged on the trains stopping and that meant that the GWR couldn't run any through expresses. One owner lost £10,000 in five years and another sold out with a profit of £35,000 after only 12 months. The GWR, in desperation, went to court in 1875 to get at least two mail trains through Swindon with only a five minutes halt. That was the limit of their success, however, and in the end they had to buy the unexpired portion of the lease for £100,000 in 1895 to get out of the whole mess.

These were the pioneering years for the railways and the hotel industry often benefited almost by accident. There was no justification, for instance, for three different railway lines to be constructed to Harrogate: "The spa was not large enough to attract early railway promoters: the country was difficult for construction and seasonal passenger traffic alone would not justify the building of a line." There were only 3,500 inhabitants in 1851 and yet, in the rush to build tracks during the 'mania', three came to Harrogate. The York and North Midland Line trains halted opposite the Brunswick Hotel (Later the Prince of Wales) in 1848 and the existing hotels could smell the beautiful aroma of massively increased business in their smoky wake. The White Hart Hotel was rebuilt in 1846, the Crown in 1847, the George in 1850 and the Brunswick in 1860. The Leeds, Sheffield and Manchester merchants had already found the delights of Harrogate, and the hotels soon attracted specific clienteles. The Crown: "was the choice of the aristocratic invalid who wished to be close to the waters. In contrast, the Dragon and the Granby were sacred places. The Lords only graced the latter, while the wealthy commoner pleased himself in the former."

The first really large London hotels were built after the Great Exhibition of 1851. The Great Western led the way, and in 1858 the Grosvenor and West End Railway Terminus Hotel Company was formed. Known as the Grosvenor, which came off the tongue rather more easily than the G&WERTHC, the resulting hotel adjoining Victoria Station, was not easy to build. The foundations had to be sunk through a series of quick sands, mudbanks and old peat bogs. The architect, James Knowles, had not chosen a simple structure. The Grosvenor today is the best example of the French Renaissance revival, with its pavilion roofs and broken skyline. It has a massive appearance, with a great many architectural frills and furbelows, which do not detract from the overall impression of great solidity. There are touches of Italian Renaissance as well, and on the first and top floors of the hotel, in the spandrels of the arches, portrait busts of famous Victorians of the age can still be seen. The Queen, herself, is over the front door with Albert next to her, and Palmerston, Derby and Lord John Russell represented among many others. For some reason, Baron von Humboldt, a 90 year old German explorer is also there. The canopy is much later, but otherwise the hotel exterior looks very similar today to the way it did when it opened.

As a contemporary account described the new wonder: "No object in the Metropolis strikes the provincial Englishman with more astonishment than the first sight of this huge building. From the dip of Piccadilly he sees it looming in the distance, far over the head of the royal palace, as he gets nearer it seems to grow into the air; and as he debouches full upon it from some side-street, it towers up like a mountain before him - a mountain chiselled from pavement to garret with clustered fruit and flowers, all wrought in enduring stone."

Within a very few years of its launching, the hotel had new management, a new chairman and a new secretary, as expenses got out of hand. Nevertheless, the company made sufficient progress for some years to pay reasonable dividends and was a success story quoted when others considered building hotels as well. The Grosvenor was one of the first hotels to have a lift, or a 'rising room' as it was known at the time. It was a hydraulic lift, powered by water, and worked with a rope which had to be hauled on to get the contraption off the ground, but it made the upper floors as easy to reach as the lower. That could put up the tariff for the rooms at the top of the building.

At the other end of Victoria Street near Westminster Abbey, the *Illustrated London News* reported in 1860 on the progress of the Westminster Palace Hotel: "This monster hotel is in the course of being erected at the East End of Victoria Street by a company of noblemen and gentlemen, for affording accommodation to members of Parliament and to gentlemen frequenting the law courts, as well as to foreigners and the public at large. To make the hotel as perfect as possible, the architects were directed to inspect various continental hotels and their investigations extended to upwards of 30 of the principal ones."

Paris would have been one of their stops, with the enormous Grand and Louvre Hotels. The Louvre could accommodate 500 guests and the Grand only a few less. The inspection did not result in a particularly inspiring edifice in London. Inside, though, the coffee room was 98ft (30m) long, 30ft (9m) wide and 18ft (5m) high and: "the internal furnishings of all the principal parts will be on a scale of magnificence more generally to be found in palaces rather than in hotels." For once the architect was filling the area as economically as was reasonable and leaving the glamour to the rooms indoors. "Reasonable", of course, meant that allowances had to be made in the width of the corridors for the necessity for two ladies in crinolines to pass each other. The "One Way Street" idea for hotel corridors was not an option. The shareholders, the noble-men and gentlemen, had chosen a fine location near the new House of Commons and nothing better than a very unpleasant selection of slum property had to be demolished to provide the site.

The restrictions on forming public companies were eased gradually during the late 1850s, but the pioneering years needed their noble and gentlemen shareholders; their aristocrats to build hotels as a harmless peccadillo for some surplus funds or to further their immense interests, and the railways to bring the traffic or build their hotels, for these were the lines of development for the industry in those early days. Smedley was an exception, because he would probably have flourished without the railway, though not to such an extent.

As the Queen went into her long mourning for her beloved Albert, dead at 42 after only 20 years of happy marriage, Britain entered into that dazzling period when she dominated the world,and the Liberals introduced a new Companies Act which was to revolutionize British business and, with it, the size of the hotel industry.

3
A pause for Albert Smith - the Critic.

Nostalgia for the "Good Old Days" is too often one of the great confidence tricks we play upon ourselves; the past is seen through rose-coloured glasses, the rough edges of reality conveniently blurred in the mists of time. For a vocal section of Victorian opinion this was the way they looked at the inns of bygone centuries; a time when writers would have had you believe all British landlords waited upon their guests with unfailing concern, civility and charm, compared to the disgraceful behaviour of continental hotelkeepers who were, to a man, rude and uncooperative. Undoubtedly English inns did have a high reputation in the Middle Ages, but the mid-Victorians, dissatisfied with the existing hotels, would have found the inns of 200 years before a great deal rougher than they were led to expect, and quite naturally so.

It was true that the reputation of continental hotels was growing steadily in the 19th century; this was due to the superiority of French cuisine and the higher status of hoteliers in the European community. At the same time, the development of the railways came later on the continent, so that the downfall of the coaching inns in Britain after 1837 did not have a parallel in many countries abroad for some years.

While it is possible with hindsight to see this period as the start of a new hotel age, to the Victorians who had to put up with the hotels they had inherited until something better appeared, the choice looked grim. For five months in 1853-4, *The Times* included every day "a melancholy and monotonous array of hotel bills" as an avalanche of complaints grew out of the correspondence columns. In one period of three days more than 400 letters were received, all saying that hotel bills were too high. There was a famous jingle at the time about a small hotel near Newbury in Berkshire, which summed up their feelings:

The famous Inn at Speenhamland.
That stands below the hill,
May well be called the Pelican
From its enormous bill.

The fact was that most hoteliers had lost their confidence; they would not take the risk of expensive refurbishing when they

52

might find their business destroyed overnight by a newly constructed railway. Investors who had happily put capital into booming stagecoach inns were now saving it for a rainy day, or waiting to see exactly what would happen. They could point to the unhappy condition of the hoteliers in Exeter who did wonderful business when the railway first reached their city; the passengers who wanted to travel further often had to wait for the coach, and that usually meant staying at the hotels overnight. Everything seemed rosy until the railway was extended to Plymouth and thence to Barnstaple, at which point the Exeter hotels barely managed to survive. It was not true that new hotels would automatically make money; a sizable hotel was built at Cheltenham and proved a white elephant. As did another large one at Sydenham in South London. Hoteliers had to be men of real vision to know whether they were at the nadir before eventual extinction or at the darkest point before the dawn.

The public were not concerned with the problems of the hotelkeeper; the inn had been part of their landscape for so long that it was regarded more as an institution than a part of a profit-making industry; they considered poor inns were as much a national disgrace as any examples of scruffy seamanship or sloppy drilling by the Guards. The public's complaints were crystallised in a little pamphlet produced in 1856 by an author and humorist named Albert Smith and entitled *The English Hotel Nuisance*. It was only 28 small pages in size and yet it reverberated round the catering world for well over 50 years.

Smith had a number of complaints and a number of suggestions, the majority of which were, astonishingly enough, later accepted by the hotels. Frankly, there was very little that Smith actually liked about English hotels. He objected to the ambiance of the average hotel, to: "the chilling side-board with its formal array of glasses......the empty tea-caddy and imperfect backgammon board; the utter absence of anything to beguile even two minutes, beyond a local directory, a provincial journal of last Saturday, or *Paterson's Roads*....in the majority of country places, the dreariness of the look-out; the clogged ink stand and stumped pens; the inability to protract a meal to six hours to get rid of the day; and, above all, the anticipations of a strange bed, with curtains you cannot manage, and pillows you are not accustomed to, and sheets of unusual fabric".

One suspects that Smith would have welcomed a fly crawling

up the wall.

It is in that mood, of course, that every little irritation gets out of proportion and he now took exception to the demand for a tip that seemed to follow the smallest service provided by the staff. The word 'tip' comes to us from the coffee-houses in the City of London where merchants gathered to conduct their business in the 17th century. If they needed a note taken to a colleague or client, they could place it in a box provided for the purpose near the table and then ring a bell which would attract the attention of a messenger. In the box they would put a coin as payment, together with the note, and on the lid were the letters 'T.I.P.' - To Insure Promptitude. Albert Smith liked such organized arrangements and there is an impassioned plea for: "all travellers, if the choice is offered, to patronize only those houses which advertise 'a fixed and moderate charge for attendance'. The practice is already extending, and as the railway scared away the tribe of hostlers, porters, coachmen, guards, postboys and other vultures, who fluttered about inn doors and yards, so we may be sure that the more we travel and insist on these changes, the more rapidly will the old system blow up and decay."

As the years went by, an attendance charge of about 1 shilling and 6 pence (71/2p) did become part of the bill, but as a later writer pointed out: "the result of this change we all know. People began to pay twice for service instead of only once, as before, and consequently started that interminable growl against 'tips' which rises and falls as regularly as the tide."

The extraction of tips is still with us 150 years later, but at least the new hotels did try to do more to entertain their customers and fill those long hours of frequently reincite day.

Smith also objected strongly to the compulsory charge for wax candles which was invariably a stiff 1 shilling and 6 pence (71/2p), for "we are content with Price or Palmer or a moderate lamp, or gas". Until electricity, it was common practice in hotels to have to guide the guest to his room at night by the light of a candle and to use candles for illumination in the rooms. Gas was available, but expensive and, to the uninitiated, potentially dangerous. At first too many people blew out the lamp without turning off the gas and a number went out like the light. Most hotels preferred to charge for candles and to play safe and cheap for as long as possible.

There was one case many years later in Switzerland when a

guest decided that, as he felt he had paid for the candles, he would pack them in his luggage when he left. The hotelkeeper sued him for the return of the stumps, insisting that the guest had paid for light and not for candles, and the court found for the hotelier. There seems to have been no British case of a similar nature.

In the better hotels it became the practice to include the cost of the candles in the charge for accommodation, though not until very late in the century was this a standard procedure; the poorer hotels continued to take the opportunity to fatten their bills with this item; in 1884, for instance, the Waverley Temperance Hotels in Liverpool, Glasgow and Edinburgh, still charged a penny (1/2p) a night for them.

The condition of the stagecoach inns brought particular condemnation from Smith because of their outworn practices and shabby furnishings. "The rooms have old forgotten names painted on them - the Chatham, the Portobello, the Ranelagh. The passages are dark and intricate, and on different levels, with obtrusive sills every now and then to trip you up; and the grand characteristics of the bedchambers are bad soap and four-post bedsteads, and inconvenient three-cornered washstands."

Four-posters were particularly unfortunate because of their size. Originally, they had been considered a luxury, as the drapes which hung around the sides kept out the draughts at night. There was privacy in a four-poster, outside noises were muffled, and you were not woken up in the summer by the light streaming in at an early hour. Well kept up, the four-poster had all this to recommend it but, when neglected, the drapes faded and gathered dust and the bed always dominated the room. If the room was small, the other furnishings would so constrict the open space available, that the guest would have to find somewhere else to use as a sitting-room. There had to be a chest of drawers for the clothes, when unpacked, a wash-hand stand for the jug of water, and a portmanteau stool to pile the luggage upon. Two chairs in the room took up space as well, and the bedchamber was, therefore, strictly an area for sleeping: "How great the contrast here presented to any foreign hotel you please to remember, with its airy, comfortable simple bed - its half sitting-room bed-chamber, with tables, chairs, bright chimney ornaments, and convenient escritoire."

As Smith had asked, the four-poster disappeared during the

century and bedrooms became more like sitting-rooms; this, in turn, led to the vogue for the studio-type bedrooms in our own time.

The variety of food in the hotels was limited too, and Smith pleaded for "something beyond 'Chop, sir, steak, boiled fowl' " to find its way onto the menu. Sure enough, a wider selection did follow.

The *English Hotel Nuisance* became celebrated, because it combined intelligent recommendations for improvements with a light, though caustic, touch. Few complaints about inattentive staff, for example, hit the spot as well as Smith's meeting with the waiter in the coffee room:"I arrive in the coffee room about 10 minutes before my time. A superb waiter - a Jeames in mufti - was reading *The Globe*; he scarcely raised his eyes as I entered, so I sat down, in awe and trembling, by the fire. No body was punctual that day, and when he had quite finished, in about a quarter of an hour, he brought the journal towards me - said 'evening paper' in the same tone that he croaked 'sherry' in my ear, at a later period; and then, placing it on the table, walked away with the proud consciousness of having done a charitable action."

To his complaints about hotels one addition was made about the customs of the day; a plea for:"the recognition of ladies in the coffee room, as in the *salle à manger*." The humour of all-male gatherings had palled on Smith after too many evenings of enforced attendance at such functions, and he felt that the presence of ladies would brighten up the surroundings as well as the conversation. He also objected to the fact that if a lady was not admitted, there was no alternative for her husband but to hire a private room in which to eat at considerable additional expense.

A few high class hotels did introduce coffee-rooms in later years where families could sit and dine, and menus did improve considerably, though choice did not, necessarily, have anything to do with quality. The cost of hotel services was always very difficult to find out before a guest got his final bill - which was another practice to which Smith took exception. This was eventually clarified by the production of printed hotel tariffs, at which point the guest was reassured and prepared to stay longer. Until tariffs were printed, long-term visitors would usually only stay at hotels until they found suitable lodgings, and permanent residents were extremely unusual.

While the abuses and shortcomings continue in some areas

to the present day, The *English Hotel Nuisance* proved to be a remarkably effective piece of propaganda for hotel guests.

4
All aboard the band wagon - 1862 - 1880

1862 was the year of the International Exhibition at Brompton in London, which was a little bigger than the Great Exhibition of 1851. It has failed though to live in our memories as vividly as the Crystal Palace and Prince Albert's patronage of the great spectacle in Hyde Park. Again, well over 6 million visitors poured into the capital, and again Thomas Cook worked day and night to transport his excursionists and look after their comfort. But this time Cook was offering a new idea; not just to take a day trip to London, but actually to stay in the capital overnight. There were to be two classes of accommodation and nothing illustrates more clearly the continuing lack of hotels in London than the fact that neither type involved a hotel. For the richer people Cook arranged lodgings in private homes, while the artisans were housed in brand new blocks of flats, called Peabody Buildings. Some rather harsh things have been said about Peabody Buildings in the 20th century but it is unfair to judge by the standards of later generations. In his time George Peabody made a commendable effort to reduce the number of people living in London in dreadful slum conditions, and he sits in his large Victorian Chair near the Bank of England looking as righteous as every statue to a Victorian humanitarian should. The flats that Cook used had just been completed and he took them for the Exhibition season.

Such hotels as London possessed had another field day and it was the last bit of encouragement the investors needed, for the Liberal government had that spring announced a new Companies Act. It was to make limited liability companies much easier to float. For the next three years the number of new issues averaged a vast £120 million a year. Said the British Almanac: "Among the results of the Limited Liability Act, none have been so beneficial to the architect as the proceedings of the hotel companies".

Twenty five major London hotels were built between 1838 and 1905, 16 of them between 1860 and 1890. The country's wealth had increased dramatically because of its industrial lead over Europe, and there was plenty of money to invest. Always a nation of punters, the British supported all kinds of flotations, and a number of hotel companies were among them.

One of the fastest off the mark was the Langham opposite

All aboard the band wagon

what is now the BBC. It was one of the best in London until a bomb cracked the water tank and flooded the hotel in 1940. It was only in 1991 that it was reopened as a hotel. The building stands at the top of Portland Place, which was the widest London street of its day and had been started by the Adam brothers in 1774. A large mansion called Mansfield House was demolished and the new hotel was constructed on the site of the house and its adjoining garden. By any standard it was a major undertaking and the prospectus which was issued in June 1862, was for £150,000 in £10 shares. The Earl of Shrewsbury was the president of the company and Lord Bury was vice-president. Both men were in advance of their time, for the aristocracy did not usually accept office in commercial ventures which could be described as 'trade'. It took three years from the prospectus to the opening and this is not surprising in view of the size of the hotel. It was half as big again as the Grosvenor at Victoria and could accommodate 500 guests. There were 10 floors from the labyrinthian basements to the roof, and the directors took the precaution of sinking an artesian well so that the guests could have their own water supply. Cholera could break out in epidemic proportions at this time and 50,000 Londoners died from it in the 1860s, even though the connection between the disease and water-borne sewage had been discovered in 1854 by Dr. John Snow. So although this was the first well under a London hotel, it was an eminently justifiable expense.

As the months went by, the original estimates could not be sustained and the company had to ask for a further £30,000. To obtain it, the investors were offered a preferential dividend of a very handsome 8% on the new capital, and there were naturally protests from the existing shareholders. At a meeting held in November 1864, when the opening was still many months away, there was a call for a shareholders' committee to investigate the accounts, and it was only after a long discussion that the proposal was dropped. To investigate the accounts of a company headed by an Earl of the Realm was an extreme step for any shareholder to propose and it indicates the lack of confidence in the successful outcome of the venture which was echoed in many comment columns.

At last on June 10th 1865 the doors were opened and from noon till seven in the evening 2,000 visitors, headed by the Prince of Wales, inspected the new wonder. *The Times* reported with impeccable fairness that the hotel was smaller than the St. Nicholas in New York or the United States Hotel in Saratoga, but it found the Langham superior in decoration, planning and comfort. Taking the optimistic view, the correspondent remarked that new hotels had "when well conducted, proved as remunerative as successful mines" and complained that up to 1860 the available hotel accommodation had provided: " at the best the comfort of a public house at the expense of a palace."

The language seems rather extreme and generalised for a newspaper of *The Times'* reputation but there was no doubting the writer's enthusiasm. He was enchanted by the hydraulic lift "which is little less than a well furnished room" and found the plumbing wholly exceptional: "Apart from the great saloons set aside for balls, wedding breakfasts, etc., there are no less than three main dining rooms, 14 lavatories and nearly 300 water closets." The significance of the last improvement can be seen from the advertisement for the Exeter Hotel in the Strand in 1856 announcing that there was a water closet on each floor.

If Victorian hotel architecture looks excessively ornate by modern standards, the extravagance was irresistible to the clientele for whom it was designed. There were three basements at the Langham where you could get lost among the bake houses, laundries and packing offices. The 'servants hall' could seat 260 and the kitchens were enormous. The ovens would hold between 1,000 and 2,000 plates and, some years later, communications were improved in the kitchen by installing a:"quaint little tram-way, which runs from one end to the other, with basket cars that look quite unique when laden with dishes destined to be sent up to table." It also had a: "hydraulic roasting jack capable of coping with 50 - 60 joints at any one time."

When the hotel was finally well established, there was between two and three tons of meat maturing in the stores, 210,000 eggs to buy a year and 25 women needed to operate the laundry. Yet for all this expenditure, the beds on the upper floors fetched as little as 1 shilling and 6 pence (71/2p) a night.

The hotel was advertised as being 95 feet (29 metres) above the Thames high-water mark, on a gravel soil in the healthiest part of London, presumably in contradistinction to the peat bogs of Belgravia. As you came into the Langham, you passed into a hall 50 feet square and: "close at hand is a Truffit's tonsorial establishment, then a newspaper and current literature stand, an office for railway

All aboard the band wagon

tickets, then a ladies' drawing room prettily furnished with a piano, elegant writing tables, shaded lamps, with flowers in vases dotted prettily about."

The hotel was also the first to have a Palm Court, which would become a favourite Victorian innovation; a conservatory to keep out the cold but let in the sun in the winter. The corridors in the hotel had gleaming white tile walls from floor to ceiling and £50,000 had been spent on furnishing the building. There were only 116 staff at the beginning, but as the hotel prospered, this number rose to 250.

The original manager was a German, Charles Shumann, from the Great Northern Hotel at Kings Cross. He was succeeded by an American, Captain James Sanderson of the Confederate Army, who had built up a considerable reputation in the United States. This was the beginning of that close association between the Langham and its American clientele which was to be its reputation until it was blitzed. In its size the Langham reminded Americans of similar hotels in their own country and an American manager must have been a reassuring sight. As they all sat together round the large restaurant tables or took their ease in the hotel courtyard, where the band played between 6 and 8.30 in the summer evenings, it was the epitome of European civilization. As the band cost £1,200 a year, such an impression was dearly achieved. About the same time, in 1865, the Evans Hotel restaurant offered the attraction of a choir singing at dinner-time, which gave rise to the fashion for musical meals.

The influx from the New World was to grow in importance, particularly when the end of the American Civil War enabled the United States to devote its attention to overseas trade rather than internal problems. Americans came on business as their exports and, in particular, their cheap food, grew in demand. They came also as tourists visiting a continent whose elegance and sophistication contrasted with their rather simpler ways, or coming back to the countries from which they or their parents had often sprung. Yet while American dress or theatre, society or cuisine might have been less fashionable, their standards of hygiene and their expectation of technical efficiency were often in advance of their European contemporaries. When they came, they were likely to stay for a considerable time. The hotel which proved popular with them had a useful buffer against the harmful effects that an economic slump could have on the home market.

Ritzy

Once the Companies Act was passed - and indeed a few flotations like the Brighton Hotel Company (1859) and the Westminster Palace (1857) had taken place as soon as conditions were made less stringent - the Bristol City Company was launched in 1863 and the Bristol College Green Company in 1864, in the same year as the Adelphi in Liverpool and the Great Western Hotel in Birmingham. The Gresham Hotel, Dublin, was registered in 1865 and companies to build new hotels, like the Alexandra Hotel in London, were launched as fast as the prospectuses could be run off at the printers.

A typical example, and one where fortunately the early records are more complete than most, was the Grand Pump Room Hotel Company in Bath. Originally the hotel was a small one, though very gracious and built adjoining the baths themselves. Bath had always been short of hotels during the season, and as Jerom Murch, the first Chairman, told the shareholders in 1867: "What can be thought of more likely to restore Bath to the position it once held..." By comparison with the Langham, for example, the money involved seemed quite modest; a total investment of £20,000 and Mr. Murch made full use of his reputable board, which included the Mayor of Bath, to advance the undertaking. The initial estimate had to be raised to £25,000 because: "it had been ascertained that the total cost of the building - including lifts, grates, chimney pieces, papering and Architect's commission - cannot be less than £13,000. This with £6,000 for the site, £4,000 for furniture and £1,000 for extras, would require a capital of £24,000".

The shareholders weren't quite so sure of the venture by this time, and only stumped up another £1,000 towards the extra £5,000 needed, but the directors pressed on and opened the hotel two and a half years after the original decision to form a company.

At the initial meeting after the hotel was opened, the directors presented the accounts for the first nine months' trading and, on a capital which had by then reached just over £29,000, the turnover was £4,408 which produced a profit of £715; £450 was then paid out as a dividend and a further £150 as Directors' fees. The idea of putting money away for a a rainy day in any quantity was quite foreign to the early Victorian hotel companies. The investors took the attitude that they invested their money in order to get a decent return and, if profits were made, they expected to have the vast majority paid out straight away to the shareholders. It will be necessary to examine the effect of this in some detail at a later stage.

For the first full year, which covered the period from March 1870 to March 1871, the turnover exceeded £7,500 at Bath and a profit of £1,652 was made. This represents a 20% profit before tax and there wasn't much tax! As income tax was well under 5p in the £, the dividends were practically tax-free as well, so that a company's profits could benefit the shareholders almost without deduction.

It had cost nearly £6,000 to run the hotel during the year and of this only £895 was paid out in salaries and wages. The percentage of wages to turnover was, therefore, about 11% which would compare today to a figure of around 30%. The staff were not paid well, though the directors pocketed £200 for their trouble. The cost of wines, spirits and food was over £3,600, almost all of which was used during the year and, therefore, would account for well over half the turnover. Even so: "not only are more and better rooms constantly required, but the working of the hotel is less profitable in various ways than it might be." So said Mr. Murch as he endeavoured to raise still more money for an extension.

One of the items which does not appear today is the cost of carriage hire for the guests' enjoyment and to bring the visitors from the railway station; carriages cost £316 in all. A considerable proportion of that sum would have been recovered, however, as visitors would also hire the carriages, in the same way as taxis or sightseeing buses might be used now. Washing for the hotel came to £227, but repairs and alteration were a minimal £95. Coal and gas were nearly £300 and nearly £200 was spent on advertising. The promotional cost is quite similar to the percentage approved nowadays by major British chain operations, but far in excess of the figure the average hotel would accept. The directors' fees would appear very high now by comparison with both turnover and profit, but substantial bonuses for successful operations was the Victorian method of achieving the desired results.

Only one thundercloud had marred the sunshine of that first full year for the Grand Pump Room. This was on the occasion a visitor had reported that money had been stolen from his room. Although the hotel protested that he had been negligent in leaving a very large sum unattended, the case went to court and the hotel lost. The damages, including costs, were nearly £600, over a third of the profits for the entire year. Although we shall look at hotel law separately, in brief a hotel was classed as an inn under various Inn Keepers Acts and there was extensive liability for damages, as this case shows. To make matters worse, the views of the judges differed in cases up and down the country so that the criteria for negligence did not have, at this time, nationally accepted yardsticks.

At the same time that the Pump Room directors were wondering how to raise their £20,000, the directors of the Midland Railway Company were considering a far greater project, the construction of an enormous hotel at their London terminus, St. Pancras.

The railway company hotels had continued to proliferate; the Charing Cross Hotel had been designed by Edward Barry for the South Eastern Railway at its West End terminus and opened in May 1865. It was one of the first buildings in London to use extensively white glazed terracotta as a cladding material. Inside it: "contained 264 flues from the multitude of fireplaces - a remarkable feat of smoke extraction." The hotel was an achievement which gave Barry, who also designed the Royal Opera House, great pleasure with its mixture of Renaissance motifs and the same roof construction as graced the Louvre in Paris. The *Illustrated London News* pointed out that: "the rising room is fitted with seats if visitors are indisposed to use the staircases" and noted with wonder on the opening day it was: "more than half occupied by the evening."

Barry used the artificial stone again when he designed the Cannon Street Hotel for the S.E.R's City terminus and the hotel was even more embellished, but neither could compare with Sir George Gilbert Scott's Midland Grand Hotel at St. Pancras.

Scott was a great architect, but a controversial one. His designs had not been chosen for the new government offices in Whitehall. He was an enthusiast, a devotee, even a fanatic for the Gothic style and he was very fashionable. The directors of the Midland Railway had decided to hold a competition among architects for the prize of building the hotel and 11 architects entered, including Scott and Barry. While the winner would get his usual fees, there would also be three consolation prizes of £200, £100 and £50. The directors had specified the maximum number of floors they wanted and the maximum bill they wanted to foot, but Scott gave them a design which added another two floors and an extra £500,000 to the cost. As you would expect, the result was a more imposing design and the directors couldn't resist it, even though their decision made nonsense of the competition. The architect who came second complained bitterly and justifiably that Scott hadn't kept to the rules. Scott said later, with his usual modesty, that he thought his design was: "possibly too good for the purpose it is to serve", but initially he set to work with enthusiasm to create what one modern traveller has described as: "to its admirers a place that restores romance to travel, to its detractors a wildly inappropriate Victorian extravaganza."

That the building was extravagant can hardly be denied. To take only one small example; high up on the facade, Scott wanted carved figures; not just busts like Knowles at the Grosvenor, but full-length statues which would have cost £100 each (about £7,000 today) and could hardly have been seen. The Midland directors settled down to some sizable rows with their architect. Yet they had deliberately agreed to a mammoth set-piece of a hotel, not only because Sir James Allport, their General Manager, was determined to improve the amenities for passengers on the line, but also because: "if the provincial Midland Company was to set up for itself in the capital, it must do so on the grand scale." There was one standard economy, though; the station booking office was on the ground floor of the building. .

Few things in Victorian commerce lent themselves to the "grand scale" as well as hotel design. The government of the day could put up their own splendid buildings and the town councils could erect solid and substantial town halls, but hotels could be more impressive than either. To see a new hotel dominating the skyline and dwarfing the hotels in its vicinity was far more imposing in Victorian times, as we have seen, than in our own days of tower blocks and skyscrapers. As the *Quarterly Review* said of the completed Midland Grand in 1872: "the building inside and out is covered with ornament, and there is polished marble enough to furnish a cathedral. The very parapet of the cab road is panelled and perforated, at a cost that would have supplied foot-warmers to all the trains for years to come".

Of course, such exotica did not lack for critics and it was suggested that: "to be consistent the directors should not confine their expression of artistic feeling to these great buildings alone. Their porters might be dressed as javelin men, their guards as beefeaters and their station masters don the picturesque attire of Garter-king-at-arms."

It is very hard to know whether to condemn the extravagance or cheer the courage of the men who created the Midland Grand. It was conceived at a most difficult time for the railways; the London, Chatham and Dover Railway went bankrupt in 1866 and the Great Eastern in 1867. Investors were shaken when one of the biggest city discount houses, Overend and Gurney, closed its doors in 1866. A number of major railway contractors, like Peto, failed as well. Bank rate soared to 10% for three months. With the worst outbreak of cholera in London since 1854, the approval of a budget of over £300,000 for the largest hotel in England was as much a vote of confidence in the future as anything else. It must have influenced the Midland directors that their hotel would overshadow the neighbouring and competing hotels at Euston and Kings Cross; the main frontage was 565 ft (170m) long and the two towers 270 ft (82m) and 250 ft (75m) high. Even within the company there was opposition, for Edward Baines, M.P. was the chairman of the railway's Shareholders Consultative Committee and against the hotel project, if for no other reason than because he was a prominent teetotaller.

The extra items of expense were certainly not confined to the outside fabric of the Midland Grand. Ten pianos were needed for the best sitting rooms, ranging from a grand piano in the finest suite to a cottage piano in the least expensive; but all in walnut cases. In the best suites the clocks cost the company £25 but in the poorer bedrooms only £8. The final cost of the Midland Grand was in the region of £450,000, but dinner, bed and breakfast was only 14 shillings (70p). There was accommodation for about 400 guests, though this figure included the clientele's servants for whom the tariff would be lower. It was a luxury hotel and expensively constructed. The passenger lifts which could hold 10 people, cost £710 each, while the luggage lifts could carry eight hundredweight and cost £340. These were some of the earliest luggage lifts and made the life of the porters that much easier.

Of course, the new inventions of today become the standard equipment of tomorrow and guests expect to find them in hotels. One such expense was the installation of the telephone and Alexander Graham Bell came to London in 1876 to try to get people interested in his new invention. He stayed at Browns Hotel in Mayfair. James Brown and his wife had worked in hotels and bought 23, Dover Street in 1837 and three more adjoining houses by 1845. Brown happened to have a telegraph line from the hotel to his home in the suburbs. Along that four mile line the first telephone call in Britain was made. Of course, the telephone soon made the same kind of impact as the first TV sets.

The Midland Grand used 9,000 tons (9.1m kilograms) of iron, six million bricks and 80,000 cubic feet (22,656 cubic metres) of dressed stone. As Lord Stamp, the chairman, said in 1939: "it is impossible to put in a new piece of heating apparatus or anything of that kind without meeting with the same obstacles that would be encountered in modifying the Rock of Gibraltar."

Yet even after the hotel was finally opened in 1873 there was still expense. The horses trotting over the cobblestones outside the building disturbed the guests and an arrangement had to be made with the local council to allow the Midland Grand to pay for the street to be covered with sound-absorbing rubberised material!

Could the Midland Grand pay a fair return on capital? Although the Midland directors had pointed to the Grosvenor's 8% dividend to justify their decision to go ahead in the first place, they refused to divulge any of their own profit figures for many years after the Midland Grand opened. The excuse was that it might give useful information to their competitors and although in the accounts they would use phrases like: "a very handsome net revenue" (1878) a later chairman declared his own position categorically when he said in 1889 that he was not prepared to disclose any details of the workings or management of the hotels, other than to say that they made a profit. In 1895 the board relented and did announce that the hotels as a whole gave a return of 51/4% on the capital invested, but they would go no further.

The termini in Euston Road - Euston, St. Pancras and Kings Cross - brought in vast numbers and many did need hotels. Much of the nearby land was owned by the Duke of Bedford and he didn't want his estate filled with hotels. So he only permitted the Bedford to be put up. In 1863 Thomas Walduck bought the hotel for £290 and £90 rent and started a family tradition. The resistance of the Duke was worn down and today the fifth generation of Walducks own a hotel empire in Russell Square, which includes the Bedford, Royal, National, Imperial and President Hotels. Indeed, the combination of the nearby stations, the City and the West End has led to hotels all over the area.

The early 1870s saw government trying to tackle the problems of drunkenness, in which the sheer availability of alcohol was important. So the expanding hotel industry provided new outlets politically. The Tory party had most of the land-owners who made a substantial part of their profits out of the sale of barley for beer. The Liberals believed in Free Trade and, therefore, disliked the concept of restricting the number of licences by law. On the other hand the Temperance Movement was growing more powerful and wanted not only additional licences refused but the total in the country substantially cut. The leaders of the Labour movement were almost all strong supporters of temperance, believing that drink was one reason why the poor remained poor. The law was clear, though. The holder of a licence to sell alcohol could only be deprived of it through misconduct, if he had gained the licence before 1869. The magistrates could refuse new licences but the existing ones were secure. To alter this, to actually have a pro-active policy of reducing the total number of licences, was a temperance ambition. The battle to achieve this objective would continue for many years.

Outside London the provincial cities often possessed at least one new large hotel, so that Peterborough had its Great Northern, Hull its Royal Station, and York and Derby also had their railway hotels. Indeed, Queen Victoria stayed at the Station hotel in Hull in 1864. (Hence the "Royal"). 10,000 Sunday School children turned up outside the hotel to sing God Save The Queen

In launching the projects the individual efforts of local businessmen were more important than the sheer size of the town, as can be seen from the construction of the Victoria Hotel, Sheffield. The Tontine Hotel had been the most famous in Sheffield before the coming of the railway, but this had disappeared as the town had altered and grown, and it had not been replaced. The time came, however, when the Mayor of Sheffield was also the chairman of the directors of the Manchester, Sheffield and Lincolnshire Railway, a line which got into such financial difficulties eventually that it became known from its initials as the "Money Sunk and Lost", and when combined with other railways into the Great Central, as the "Gone Completely". During his term of office the Mayor was asked for his support for the construction of a hotel on part of the station site, and he was fortunately able to decide that his duty as Mayor and his duty as chairman of the railway's board were absolutely compatible. There had been previous sites suggested for a new hotel, but negotiations had always broken down over the price the landowners wanted for the ground, so that the cost of the station land was apparently a good offer.

There was, however, a good deal of opposition from the townsfolk, firstly because the situation was in a poor part of the city, and secondly because there were a number of small local hotel proprietors who did not want more competition. The promoters therefore appealed to the local Lord of the Manor who was the Duke of Norfolk, and His Grace announced that while he would not speculate by investing in the project, he would be "honoured" if they would accept his donation of £1,000 and let him know if he could be of any further service!

It was the sort of gesture which illuminates not only how the aristocracy retained their position as men of enormous influence, but also the gulf which existed between the few rich and the numerous poor; how many people could afford to make a grand gesture of the modern equivalent of £60,000 or £70,000 without even bothering to collect any dividends which might come due? After the Duke had donated, the majority of the money for the hotel was forthcoming, but it was still necessary to find someone with the necessary knowledge and capital to run the Victoria. From a number of applicants, the directors selected Mr. George Mayer. Mayer was not a Sheffield man but he brought with him: "a large capital to the Victoria Hotel in order to fit it up in the first style of convenience."

At the opening banquet in the summer of 1862 one of the Sheffield aldermen agreed that Sheffield had needed a good hotel, but he suggested that they also needed a good town hall, a good, main thoroughfare and a more complete system of drainage; so much for priorities and town planning. Mayer was obviously more of a shareholder in the enterprise than a tenant and, after his death, the hotel continued in his family for a few more years until arrangements were made for the railway management to take over.

Many provincial cities had to wait until the late 1870s for their first 'grand' hotel, but a combination of the Companies Act and John Smedley's success with the pilgrims to Matlock made the development of the hydropathic institutes much more rapid. Smedley, himself, continued to be highly successful and became a very well-known figure. On a hill outside the town he built himself one of those grotesque Victorian mansions which look like Ruritanian castles and are constructed, it appears, to enable the owner to resist a formidable siege. He called it Riber Castle, 850 feet (260 metres) above the sea and, like the West wing of the hydro, it was battlemented: "in accordance with Smedley's romantic notion of mediaeval splendour." Success never altered Smedley's non-conformist outlook, and he continued to preach regularly in All Saints Church, which sadly was used after his death as the engine house for the hydro, just as Riber Castle eventually became a zoo in the 20th century. Smedley also kept well within the bounds of Victorian propriety at all times, providing, for example: "a shower bath for administering baptism to adults with proper decency" and when he died in 1874 the craze for hydros was in full swing.

Among the earliest imitators was the Rev. Shore whose chronic rheumatism was cured at Smedleys Hydro and who, perhaps a little ungratefully, thereupon started his own at Matlock, as did a number of other people. The competition must have been fierce, however, for in 1866 Rev. Shore moved to Buxton and started a hydro there. He died in an accident soon after, but his heir H.R.P. Lomas, built the business up well. Within 20 years there was accommodation for 200 guests and, in the peak season of August and September, the hydro would be completely full.

As Smedley had emphasised the importance of exercise and relaxation, the more secluded parts of the country seemed to many entrepreneurs to be particularly suited to the construction of hydros and in Scotland they started to mushroom. The hydro at Pitlochry cost £93,000, Craiglockhart £60,000 and Callander £54,000. There were hydros at the Bridge of Allan, Dunblane, Melrose and Crieff. In the South of England at New Barnet, Torquay, Upper Norwood and on the Isle of Wight. With Scarborough, Ilkley Wells and Hexham among others in the North, an immense amount of money was poured in, but it was over-production on a mistakenly heroic scale.

Mary Baker Eddy, the founder of the Christian Science movement, was obviously quite sincere when she said that the cure for cancer included a sip of pure water every half hour, but the sufferers still died. The famous Scottish doctor, Jonah Horner, insisted that patients in asylums should not have the water cure withheld from them, but it would have had little effect on their mental state. What's more, there were only a limited number of patients who would suffer the rigours of the: "medical head who used to keep patients in order like children and soldiers."

For a time a number of the hydros did make reasonable profits, but as a means of combating competition, many of them tried eventually to attract holidaymakers rather than just the unfortunate sick, and then it was said: "the hydro is a high class *hotel-pension*, generally situated in some quiet, breezy place, surrounded by lovely scenery, which tempts the inmates to take solitary walks on hillsides and down valleys in pure air."

Not only were they catering for invalids and people who needed a rest but they also tried to provide much more entertainment. While the Athol Hydro in Pitlochry was considered to have gone too far when it applied for a licence to sell drinks, the Callender Hydro offered its visitors fishing on Loch Vennacher, and the Coombe House Hydro at Kingston Hill staged out-of-doors theatrical performances. The Scottish hydros at Christmas would have fancy dress balls, readings and concerts, and there would be plenty of skating and curling. Lomas at Buxton staged informal dances, music in the drawing room, billiards and *tableaux vivants*. There were also concerts and shows in the hotel's 'recreation hall' and a little of the 'marriage market' crept in.

No matter how hard they tried, however, the hydros could not survive the glut of competition and they held an untenable position halfway between nursing home and hotel. Even as late as 1886 it was reported that: "The Edinburgh Exhibition has taken away visitors from the Scottish Hydros."

While the holidaymakers preferred the exhibition:"it appears that large numbers of tourists still believe that by staying at Hydropaths, they will have to submit themselves to a system of treatment." This was very often so in England but the practice had declined in Scotland, so that the hydro world had many heads but no recognisable face.

Profits started to decline or disappear and a little price cutting appeared even on the published tariff. At the Bridge of Allan Hydro at Ochil Park there was a seven shilling (35p) a week reduction for the clergy, and a 5% reduction if your bill was over £10. In many instances it was to no avail; the £60,000 Craiglockhart was offered for sale by the Receiver at £28,300. Callander, from an initial cost

Ritzy

of £54,000, failed to achieve its reserve at auction of £30,000, was offered again at £25,000 and was finally sold after another 4 months on the market for £12,000. The gloomy news constantly recurred that "still another of the Scottish hydros is in financial difficulties....having succumbed to what appears to be almost the universal fate."

Dunblane, near Edinburgh, closed. The Mont Dore at Bournemouth, whose foundation stone was laid by the King of Sweden and which was supposed to be the last word in hydros, never made a profit and quickly collapsed.

The 1880s saw the bankruptcy of many hydros and, at the same time, more new ones being built or extended as the lesson failed to sink in. In Harrogate in 1884 a prospectus for a new hydro advised investors that: "Experience shows that modern hotels combined with Hydropathic establishments, well placed, well built, and well conducted, pay a very high rate of interest on the sums invested in them. The Queens Hotel which immediately faces the proposed Lancaster Park Hotel pays 10% on the purchase of £58,000. The Swan Hydropathic is paying large dividends and Smedleys last year showed a profit of upwards of 20% and the undertakings in Southport, Tunbridge Wells and other places are also paying well....besides as more than 90 hotels in Harrogate are always full during the season and yield notoriously handsome profits, and as visitors increase in number every year, there is ample room for others without in the slightest degree militating against the existing ones." They could have added that it was said of Harrogate that: "Queen Victoria could have held a cabinet meeting in the town any day in August."

Strangely enough, the authors of the prospectus did not feel the less profitable events at Craiglockart or Callandar would be of interest to prospective investors!

In 1891 it was the turn of the Scarborough Hydro to be extended, at a cost of a handsome £25,000, which paid for another 120 bedrooms, a grand floral hall and many other public rooms. But at Scarborough the establishment was at least under the care of Professor Wells, just as Dr. Gully and Dr. Wilson had made Malvern a Mecca for the sick without the trimmings of a full social life. As some of the hydros failed to stay the pace, practical hoteliers moved in to pick up bargains, like Mr. MacDonald who got the Athol Hydro for £25,000. Where the medical attention at the hydros meant something, they survived much better, particularly as more was being learnt all the time about the methods of treatment which were most effective. Massage could be very helpful and inventors came up with new types of therapeutic bath almost as regularly as the annual Paris fashions. At the Imperial Hydro in Blackpool in 1885 there were 10 different varieties: Turkish, Russian, Sitz, needle, spray, rain, plunge, warm, cold or sea water. The hydros were a world where there was room for the genuine healer and the quack, the professional and the amateur, but like a casino, the majority of the players lost.   D o w n at the seaside the twinkling star of fashion, which was leaving the spas, had apparently come to stay. At Bournemouth, for instance, the railway finally arrived in 1870 and the town grew a great deal. Where before only the Exeter Park and the Lansdowne had made their debut since the Belle Vue and the Bath, the next decade saw the emergence of the Criterion, Pembroke, Queens and Highcliff Mansions. Because the town had been exclusive, it had attracted a rich clientele, and also one rich amateur hotelier, Merton R. Cotes, who arrived in 1876 and bought the Royal Bath - Royal after a visit by the Prince of Wales - spending £100,000 on refurbishing it in 1880.

It was soon after Japan had emerged again from the seclusion of centuries, and Japanese decor was becoming all the rage. It is, of course, very dangerous for a hotel to go overboard on the fashionable decor of the day because once the style is *passé*, the hotel looks equally old fashioned. Cotes was, however, wealthy enough to be unconcerned, and apart from his private collection of Japanese curios in the Mikado Room, he turned the old smoking room into a Japanese drawing room; there were birds, hand painted on the soft yellow walls, peacocks, herons, flamingos and storks, with heraldry in between and a dado of Japanese matting. Some of the furniture was imported from Japan but most was manufactured in the oriental style in England, including the piano. Branches were hand-painted across doors, walls and windows and bamboo light fittings were made to look like oil lamps. Whether a visitor from Tokyo would have felt at home is doubtful, but the novelty certainly attracted the custom of such eminently desirable guests as the Queen of Sweden and the Empress Eugenie. Even so it seems very unlikely that Cotes ever saw a return on his investment which had any meaning, except in terms of prestige. It was, however, prestige that Cotes sought. He had made his money in "trade", selling insurance in Northern Ireland. Initially he was, therefore, not acceptable in Bournemouth society when he settled in the town, but his hotel clientele after the redecoration changed all that.

Bournemouth did not have the racy reputation of Brighton or Margate, but its hotels attracted visitors who wanted a quieter setting and, in many seaside resorts, a hotel's own reputation was more important than the town in which it was situated. A town could flourish and a predominant hotel decline, as with the Brighton Hotel Company, which was established as early as 1859, in a most popular resort, and yet the board ran into considerable debt and it took many years to put matters straight. Even when the dividend had reached a respectable 6% the memory of those bad days kept the shares hovering at par, for there were high-flyers like the Queens at Hastings which had opened three years later in 1862 and managed 15% very regularly. The Queens had a highly successful management team in William Glade and his wife. Glade started as a waiter at the hotel, stayed over 40 years, and eventually finished up with a large slice of the equity. The Alexandra in Hastings was also paying more than 10% when the Brighton Company was struggling to reach its 6% and, not unnaturally, the best hotel shares became difficult to buy, with the lucky holders unwilling to sell and a restricted market emerging as a consequence.

For the seaside hotels who depended on a good summer season, the weather was important - a hotel like the Grand at Scarborough would only open for July and August. Admittedly there was, effectively, no continental alternative, for the numbers of people who were prepared to venture abroad on the international resort circuit was minute, even if very high-powered. Nevertheless, in a wet British summer, profits would slump badly as visitors cut short holidays or simply stayed at home. In 1882 the manager of the Granville, St. Lawrence-by-Sea in Ramsgate, took one look at the hitherto elusive sunshine, and telegraphed the Royal Exchange in London: "We have at last splendid summer weather. Come in your thousands and stop till Monday morning."

The seaside towns increased in size, importance and wealth as Britain itself grew greater during the '60s and '70s. The number of houses in Eastbourne more than tripled between 1861 and 1881, though as late as 1868 *Murray's Guide* told prospective visitors that: "for those who seek rational recreation and health-giving pleasures, East Bourne is altogether a very enjoyable place, but they who expect bustle and gaiety must go elsewhere." Yet within another 15 years there were many thousands of visitors, a string of new hotels and boarding houses along the Marine and Grand Parades and a growing reputation as the: "paradise of the lawntennysonians."

Where the original seaside clientele had been either the very wealthy or the day-trippers, now the growing Victorian middle class came, and the new hotels which were built for them were, at their most luxurious, modelled on the new city hotels and aped the continental fashion. Each seaside town wanted to have a show-piece in terms of a luxury hotel, and so Scarborough got the magnificent Grand in 1865, Southport the Palace in 1866 and Eastbourne the Cavendish in 1873. The Palace in Southport could advertise that it was only half an hour away from Liverpool by train, a boast which no longer holds true; today it's 42 minutes!

The names were selected to give the hotels an often spurious connection with royalty, so that Victoria Hotels abounded, as well as Imperials, Royals and the ubiquitous Prince of Wales. The local noblemen were represented by names like the Cavendish in Eastbourne and the Zetland in Saltburn, and famous royal residences were commemorated not only by simple plagiarism like the Palace, but also by the use of the word "Carlton" which derived from the old home of George IV when he was the Prince Regent; Carlton House.

Although the period after the Companies Act saw a massive expansion of hotel construction, the idea that building a hotel was a licence to print money was very far from the truth. Hotel companies did crash, directors and managers were thrown out, debts were amassed and shareholders complained vociferously. In 1881 one chairman reminded his shareholders of the £40,000 worth of debts he had inherited from his predecessors. The Washington Hotel, Liverpool, failed to survive the competition of a largely reconstructed Adelphi and became Temperance. The Metropolitan Hotel in the City of London was offered for sale only months after opening. The Hotel Continental in the West End went bankrupt, and there were many other examples every year.

The penalties for poor planning and inefficiency were exacerbated by the bad slump which hit British industry in the latter half of the 1870s. For over 20 years there would be deflation and rates of interest dwindled. Most commodity prices fell by a third due to cheap food imports from North America but in Europe there were a string of bad harvests and the French, in particular, suffered from a crippling outbreak of phylloxera which killed vast areas of their vineyards. Though cheap imports helped hotel expenses, the slump in the '70s affected the number of free- spending visitors and British hotel profits and dividends tumbled at the end of the decade. The Victoria Hotel, Bradford, went from 8% in 1877 to 4% in 1879, the Grand in Scarborough from 3 1/2 % in 1877 to nothing in 1878 and only 1% in 1879. Even the Langham went from 20% to 10%. The trade magazine, the *Caterer, Hotel Keeper and Refreshment Contractors' Gazette* which had started publication in 1878, prophesied at the beginning of 1879 a very gloomy commercial and industrial outlook. This was attributed partly to the alternative attraction of the Paris Exhibition to overseas visitors, but mostly to the stagnation of trade and a decreasing number of commercial travellers.

Few industries develop smoothly without setbacks and the overall picture for hotels in the '60s and '70s remains one of expansion on all sides. Sections of cities became known for their hotels, for just as the railways provided the communications to many seaside towns without building the hotels themselves, so whole districts round many of the major city termini became centres for small hotels and boarding houses: "In London a small group of hotels grew up in Pimlico associated with Victoria Station. The same thing occurred, on a larger scale, in Paddington and Bayswater, near the main arrival point for travellers from the West Country. In Liverpool the hotel quarter also redistributed itself over the same period, from the old town to the neighbourhood of Lime Street, the main terminal for overnight passengers."

There were occasions though when the ground landlords were not pleased to see the way their property was developing and: "the functional influence of the three large trunk railway termini was still reflected in the Bedford Office's losing battle to restrain the conversion of houses in the Bloomsbury Estate into private hotels and boarding houses during the late 19th century."

By the beginning of the 1880s the slump had done its worst and economic conditions were once again improving. A new boom for hotels started, but the state of the economy was not the only condition which affected the health of the industry. As important in many cases was the effectiveness of the staff and so far they have remained in the background of the industry's development. By 1880 we have a reasonably full picture of what life was like behind the scenes of a hotel.

5
A pause for the commercial traveller - the cornerstone.

While the hotels in the spas and seaside towns depended on the custom of the people with leisure and the money to spend enjoying it, the hotels in the commercial towns and cities were primarily supported by the salesmen who travelled round the country on behalf of their firms. As the Penny Post only started in 1840 and the telephone and typewriter were invented towards the end of the century, business was conducted much more on a face-to-face basis than it is today. The commercial traveller with his samples not only called on wholesalers and retailers, but often took the place of the mail order catalogue as well. Before the railways, he would load up his pony and trap and be sure of a warm welcome from the innkeepers he patronised, for part of the stock-in-trade of the commercial traveller was hospitality and the local hotel was convenient for showing his wares and entertaining his prospective clients. For the small hotel the arrival of a high spending traveller was a great day, and the manager knew he had to play his own part, ensuring that the people who were to be entertained were suitably impressed.

The coming of the railways made it easier to move goods around the country, but the cost was high compared to the pony and trap and, in addition, there were many small towns and villages which waited a number of years for the railway line to arrive. The travellers remained one of the lubricants of commerce and of hotel customers, though it could be a lonely life and the men relied to a great extent on the conviviality of their landlords and fellow guests to break the monotony. Or, at least temporarily, to take the place of wife and family. A hotel which catered for commercial travellers kept this in mind and many made a considerable effort to offer the small services which were particularly needed by this kind of visitor.

Landlords might get the 'boots' to meet the train to help the traveller move his samples to the hotel and, once installed, a room would be set aside for displaying them. When a retired commercial traveller, Mr. Wynn, took over the Dumfries Hotel in Cardiff and called it Wynn's, he changed more than the name. He installed new writing desks, as the travellers had to write out orders for Head Office and also reports on the progress they were making. Everything would

A pause for the commercial traveller

have to be done by hand, nothing could be telephoned through and, in the evenings, there would be the scratch of many pens as the last piece of drudgery was completed. Wynn produced a new stock-room for the samples and a luggage-room with a separate entrance from the street, so that the goods did not have to be carried through the main lobby but could be put out of sight as quickly as possible. The hotel manager might be stocking a warehouse but he didn't want to appear to be running one. There was also to be a new strong-room with a: "Hobbs patent fire and burglar proof door". This was a wise precaution as, on the one hand, the goods were often highly inflammable and, on the other, the hotelier did not want to finish up in court trying to stave off a large demand for compensation if they were stolen.

Wynn was also aware of the importance of communications and advertised the fact that as the post was not delivered before the departure of some of the convenient trains from Cardiff, the hotel would pick up the mail for the visitors from the local Post Office very early in the morning and would distribute it before 7.30.

Although few hotels would have been as well-geared to the needs of the travellers as Wynn's, all the hotels which hoped to attract this type of clientele had to make the attempt, for there was a considerable grapevine, and no real shortage of alternatives in a reasonably sized town. Each hotel would have a sort of working lounge called the Commercial Room, and one traveller who specified the ideal facilities, listed, besides writing desks, the need for blotting paper pads, telegraph forms, pen racks, timetables for railway trains, a twine box and gum bottle, a post box, a message slate and a morning call-board. The inconvenience created by waking up late, failing to receive messages from office or client, missing connections or ransacking the hotel for a piece of string, must have produced a good deal of frustration for the methodical salesman.

Much as the hotel manager relied on his "Commercials", the travellers were likely to be tightfisted when their customers were not involved. Their expenses would be scrutinised when they returned home, and if they could pocket some of their allowance they were likely to do so. Money might be no object to the clientele at the Langham, but it meant a great deal to the commercial traveller. He expected the tariffs of the hotels in which he stayed to be formulated with this in mind. He did not expect his bedroom to cost him much and if he had to pay for his horse as well, he would want this to be taken into account when settling the price for his own accommodation. A horse put up in a hotel stable in the latter part of the century cost six pence (2 1/2 p) a feed and another 6 pence if he stood on a pillar rein. One shilling and six pence (7 1/2 p) a night was the average for stable room and while the horse was in his care, the hotel manager was responsible for any harm that befell it.

Low bedroom tariffs meant the hotelier had to rely on the profits from food and drink in the restaurant and bar to see him through; the mark-up for drinks was therefore high. A bottle of sherry which cost the hotelier three shillings (15p) would be sold for six shillings (30p), but a bottle of wine which cost a shilling (5p) would also be sold for 6 shillings, or very nearly. Many of the bigger hotels were associated with wine merchants as shareholders and this sometimes meant that the stock was not purchased at the most economic price, so that complaints about the cost of drinks was a continuing theme among the customers. Hotel managers would often bottle their own wines and indulge in every kind of malpractice, but then there was also nothing to stop beer being adulterated for much of Victoria's reign and salt could be put into it as well to give the clients a still greater thirst. In view of the fact that the price of bedrooms had always been quite low, a custom had grown up, no doubt studiously fostered by the hoteliers, that guests should buy drinks: "for the good of the house" and this only died out very slowly. Sheridan, the 18th century playwright, had summed up the situation succinctly a long time before when he announced: "I call for a bottle of wine that my landlord may live, and I abstain from drinking it that I may live too."

When the commercial travellers assembled for dinner in their hotel, there would be one large table with the manager at the head, and during the meal the drink would flow freely. The only trouble for the abstemious was that there was another 'custom' - at the end of the evening the amount consumed would be totalled up and then divided equally between all present. Under these circumstances any manager anxious to improve his profits and careless of the condition of his liver, was likely to be at the very least half drunk by the time he got to bed every night. Apart from the fact that the system was unfair, it was also expensive and to counteract it many commercial travellers decided to 'Box Harry'.

A pause for the commercial traveller

Boxing Harry involved the traveller in returning to his hotel at teatime and consuming sufficient to last him for the rest of the evening. Then, as dinner time approached, he could sneak out of the hotel and thereby avoid paying for wine he hadn't drunk. The importance of eating sufficient tea is explained by the absence in most towns of any form of restaurant open in the evening. For although we now take it for granted that Indian, Chinese, Italian and steak houses will flourish on every corner, only the major Victorian cities could offer any alternative to a hotel. Having 'Boxed Harry', the traveller, on his return, had to contrive a facile excuse for his landlord who, deprived of his profit, would have to accept stories of relatives who had to be visited, a private assignation with a young lady, or a client who could only be seen in the evening.

Both hoteliers and commercial travellers were following the tradition that tariffs would be lopsided, because providing a bed for the night had, for so many years, been a sign of Christian hospitality rather than a profitable occupation. Furthermore, the cost to the hotel of a meal was comparatively high because the Victorians expected large quantities of food, and this made profits, once again, difficult to come by. In many cases the hotel manager was reduced to augmenting the meagre returns with comparatively extravagant charges for the morning newspapers, the ubiquitous candles or a cup of coffee.

For the majority who remained for dinner, the event followed the well-trod paths of stag dinners through the centuries; the conversation would be boisterous, getting steadily more animated as the hours passed and, after dinner, the old stories would be trundled out in an atmosphere growing steadily more blue with the smoke from the pipes and cigars, as well as the subject matter. Here were manufactured, or, at least retailed, that legion of tales about the Englishman, the Scotsman and the Irishman which have tickled such assemblies ever since. Politics, religion and business were discouraged as topics, but there might be music at a piano, poems recited and lengthy discussions on sporting or domestic subjects while the drinks continued to be passed around. This would be the fate of the traveller night after night from town to town.

The temperance hotels, like the Shaftesbury in Liverpool and the Trevelyan in Sunderland hoped to win the commercial travellers away from this type of atmosphere, but the numbers of men on the road could keep both types of hotel, licensed and temperance, reasonably full. One of the attractions of the travellers as a clientele was that they were not confined to one season or one event. As regular business, they were worth cultivating, even though they might not mix too well with the upper crust. Even at many of the best hotels there was a commercial room, with desks side by side and the travellers equally identical in their uniforms of sober suits and bowler hats, which they seldom removed. This was hardly for security reasons, though there were many court cases about lost umbrellas, hats and samples. On occasions the hotel would try to keep their two different clienteles apart, so that when the Queens Hotel, Hanley, in the Potteries, was redecorated, there was: "a new smoking room, a bijou restaurant bar" and a new Commercial Room in one wing, but the Coffee Room was carefully situated on the other side of the house and reported as such. Miss Elliott, the manager, felt that this was more fitting for everyone concerned.

Little changed over the years in hotels catering primarily for commercial travellers; it was not here that the private bathrooms were installed, or the elaborate *à la carte* but, nevertheless, it was just this type of traveller without whom the hotels would have been impoverished in many towns and who furnished the first excuse when things were bad; "not as many Commercials" was the cry, but, thankfully, they always came back with the return of better times.

6
Behind the scenes.

During the 19th century in Britain the hotel industry expanded out of all recognition and, as a result, there was a great shortage of trained staff, though this was alleviated to some extent by continental labour coming in to fill the gap. Although they never exceeded 10% of the work force, the welcome influx has continued to the present day and there are really two questions to answer: why were the continentals so much better at hotel operations than the native British, and why were they so keen to come to Britain.

There is no doubt that the training of hotel staff on the continent was at the time very much better. A senior chef was asked in 1893 in *Caterer*, to explain the difference between France and England in this respect; he pointed out that in France a father would pay a good head chef to teach his son, who would start at the very bottom and then, having learnt one part of his profession, would be transferred to another specialist chef in the kitchen, who would also expect to receive a fee. In this manner the boy would go right round the department over a period of years. As the chefs were being paid for their trouble, they were likely to teach the boy reasonably well and, at the end of his apprentice-ship, the young man should have received a thorough grounding. Even then it would only be the start of his career, but the foundations at least would have been well laid.

In Victorian Britain, where there was a shortage of labour in the kitchens, a boy would be paid to start work as a dishwasher. If he was enthusiastic and showed a modicum of intelligence he would be promoted to cook, but he would have little knowledge of the art of cooking except for what he had been able to pick up. There was no incentive for the head chef to train him or to get others to do so. Furthermore, the language of the Grand Hotel kitchen was French so, if he couldn't speak it, he'd have to learn quickly in the frenetic atmosphere. The French chef also pointed out that there was a great deal of difference between an ordinary cook and a chef, who was expected in France to be a leader of cooks. To be a chef on the continent was an honoured profession and there were whole families of them, going through the generations from father to son. Eating was more a part of French culture and chefs could acquire more the status of pop stars than cooks. In England, by contrast, a chef would hope that his son would grow up to do something 'better' because of the relatively low social position awarded a man who made his living in a kitchen.

The great French chefs would teach many young men during the course of their careers and these pupils would always be proud to say that they had received their original training from one of the masters. When Adolphe Dugléré died at 79 in 1884, he was still described in his obituary as a pupil of Carême, and Eugene Herbodeau remained till the end the man who had been taught by Escoffier. Moreover, he was proud of it and did all he could to perpetuate the memory of his boyhood hero. None of this really applied to the English chefs, though many were excellent and ran great kitchens, like Thomas Jordan, who was head chef at the Langham for many years.

More than any other nation, it was the French who dominated *haute cuisine*, made their language its own, and their employers proud to have a French chef working for them; men like Pierre Lecomte who controlled a staff of 50 at the Grand Hotel in Trafalgar Square in 1881 and who had been *chef de cuisine* in turn to Napoleon III, a Russian Ambassador, Baron de Rothschild and the 1st Life Guards.

Many of the chefs have been immortalised by the dishes and culinary expressions which still bear their name; Dugléré, for example, created the sauce which garnishes Filet de Sole Dugléré. Laymen got into the act too; Anthelme Brillat-Savarin, a lawyer, invented the mould which is used for making savarins.

The great reputation of French cooking is attributed to the influence of Catherine de Medici in the 16th century. This Italian-born Queen of France brought in her retinue Italian chefs who were greatly superior to their French counterparts. French cuisine had been as unimaginative as English up to that point, but the Italian Renaissance had fostered many skills and the French developed the culinary art from then on. Even so the development of the cuisine was a spasmodic process. In the 19th century its reputation stemmed more from the general French predominance in so many cultural and aesthetic areas, since the time of Louis XIV, than anything else. French was the language of diplomacy and what the French did fashionably today, the English were likely to do tomorrow. In the 18th century the French nobility entertained lavishly and employed chefs who were expected to live up to their masters' pretensions, as we've seen. Some of these chefs found their way to the homes of the British aristocracy, particularly after the French revolution had decimated the number of potential French employers.

After the Napoleonic wars, the political conditions in France were stable for a time, but the 1830 revolution had some French chefs on the move again. Notably, Alexis Soyer who had a couple of his staff murdered before his eyes and decided that the Duke of Cambridge's home was likely to be more conducive to the undisturbed preparation of haute cuisine. Soyer was only 21 when he came to England to work for the Duke, an indication of the high esteem in which French chefs were held, and he became the greatest name in British cooking before Escoffier, writing many books, working to relieve the famine in Ireland when the potato crop failed, and helping to feed the troops in the Crimea. Indeed the British army still has in its equipment the Soyer oven, created for cooking on the battlefields of Russia. Soyer achieved his fame without ever working in a British hotel, but instead spent 13 years as *chef de cuisine* at the Reform Club.

When it came to hotel managers, the British held their own with their continental colleagues a good deal better than in the world of top chefs. Even so there were a considerable number of foreign managers, particularly in the best London hotels. The attraction of Britain lay partly in exactly those circumstances which had driven Soyer to this country. Europe was often not a very safe place to be in the 19th century; wars and revolutions were commonplace as the 'haves' fought to keep the 'have nots' out of power. The purges of the enemies of the state were inclined to be indiscriminate, and many foreign workers came to Britain to escape political or religious persecution. The British attitude to Europe for much of the century was summed up in the famous newspaper headline: "Thick fog in Channel. Continent isolated". To emigrate to Britain from the middle of the century onwards was to live in the richest, most politically stable, most powerful and most inventive country in the world. It was peaceful and while it is true that there were four attempts to assassinate Queen Victoria during her reign and two demonstrators were killed in disturbances in Trafalgar Square in 1887, the latter event was so exceptional that it went into the history books. In Central and Southern Europe it wouldn't have been noticed, but in England the vast majority of the nation considered itself above political violence. The police were unarmed and the troops were very seldom needed for other than ceremonial duties, except overseas. You had no conscription, unlike the continent, where many an intelligent man fled the country rather than serve in the army of a sovereign he considered a despot; my grandfather for one.

There was also the simple fact that you had a good chance of getting a job in England in the catering trade. Mario Gallati was one of the great mid-20th century London restaurateurs. He ran both the Caprice and L'Ecu de France in the West End for many years. He recalled in his autobiography his own reasons for coming to Britain at the turn of the century: "At this time there was considerable unemployment in Italy and many other Italians had left their home country to work in England. I wanted to learn English....and I also wanted to widen my experience in every possible way. One advantage of being a waiter was that you could, with luck, travel the world, working in any country in which you happened to find yourself, A smattering of French and English was enough to get by in most restaurants. French being the international language of the cuisine and English the language spoken by most of the diners and tourists."

The Italy that Mario Gallati left he remembered with little affection: "My memories of Milan in the 1900s are mostly of the tremendous political and industrial strife, with long hours and poor wages driving the people into making continual demonstrations." He was working as a commis at the age of 10 and was lucky to have a job at all.

Whether it was Italy in the 1900s, Hungary after 1848, France in the days of the Commune, or Russia at almost any time, there were good reasons for emigrating. Coincidentally, while the continental hotel staff came to Britain, the British were emigrating as well. There were 6.8 million people living in Ireland in 1820 but only 4.4 million in 1900 and, between 1880 and 1910, over 81/2 million people emigrated from England in all. In spite of the fact that real wages rose 57% over a 25 year span, life was hard in the industrial towns and unemployment stalked the declining countryside. Hotels were not Blake's: "dark satanic mills" though and, for hotel workers, there were no industrial diseases to be caught from the dust under the bed.

The number of German staff in British hotels grew steadily over the years. Joseph Zeder, the manager of the   in London at the end of the century, said that: "a head-waitership was the recognized apprenticeship for a hotel manager in Germany and I believe it is here". In the hysteria of the first world war it would be suggested that Germans had dominated the catering industry and should not be allowed to do so again.

To really appreciate the condition of most of the British people at the time, it is only necessary to remember that a high proportion of the volunteers for the Boer War were rejected on medical grounds. Seebohm Rowntree's devastating report in 1901 concluded that 28% of the inhabitants of York could not afford a diet adequate to sustain a normal day's work". Charles Booth, another famous reformer at the time: "found that over 30% of the population of London was living at a level below that necessary to maintain mere physical efficiency."

By comparison, the servants' hall of a good hotel served breakfast at 8 or 8.30, dinner at 12, tea at 4.30 and supper around 8 in the evening. In a large hotel there would be cold meat for breakfast, though only bread and butter in small ones. Hot meat and potatoes would be served every day for dinner, green vegetables twice a week, and pudding on Sundays. There would be a plain tea, but cold meat and cheese for supper. The smaller hotels would be likely to give meat for supper only on alternate days and cheese otherwise. Beer would either be provided at a low price, or an allowance would be made of about two and a half pints a day for men and one and a half pints for women. For the staff in the kitchens and restaurants who had access to leftovers, there was even more to eat, and while the idea of people keeping up their strength on scraps from a rich man's table is anathema to us today, it was obviously preferable for the Victorian and Edwardian hotel worker to going hungry.

While the staff wages appear low, they did not compare badly with other industries. Typical salaries in 1883 were about £5 a month for a cook, £4 for a head waiter, £3 for a cellar man, 2 guineas (£2.10p) for a head porter or head laundress, £2 for a head chambermaid and £1.10 shillings (£1.50p) for a still-room maid. Waiters, though, were hardly paid any wages and had to subsist on tips.

The Attendance Charge made by the hotel seldom went to the staff. Guests soon got used to paying twice for service. If they did not, the *Daily Telegraph* in 1882 warned them of their fate when they left : "passing through scowling faces to an unhonoured exit". Charles Dickens *Dictionary of London* in 1880 offered one solution: "Attendance is now usually included in the bill. When this is the case, the servants invariably expect very much the same gratuity as when it is not included. But unless you propose to make a long stay, or a very speedy return, it is by no means necessary to meet their views in this respect."

Pocketing the Attendance Charge was a terrible example for management to give the staff. To cheat the guests in this way suggested that the guests were fair game. If management could rip them off, why shouldn't the staff try too? There arose a rational defence for theft. In a notorious court case (Chapter 12 - Spokes vs The Grosvenor Hotel 1898) one of the directors, trying to defend his fraudulent behaviour against the shareholders, pleaded that everybody behaved in the same way. The choice was wide; watering the gin, charging tipsy guests for items on the bill which hadn't been ordered, chefs accepting bribes from suppliers to pay more or to accept short weight deliveries. Restaurant managers demanding substantial tips for a good table in the restaurant or a popular night for a banquet; the opportunities to "fiddle" were always there, but the management were recognized as being equally liable to succumb to temptation. Incidentally, "a fiddle" was stock exchange slang for a sixteenth of a £. The staff were often supposed to augment their wages by receiving gratuities. These could be so substantial in a cloakroom or as a commissionnaire that a proportion of the tips could be demanded by the company as a condition for employment to do the job.

Management could retreat behind the strict letter of the law if necessary. Asking for tips was officially frowned on and when a waiter at the Royal Forest Hotel, Chingford, did so in the 1880s, he was dismissed on the spot. He promptly took his employer to court for a day's pay but he lost the case.

We have seen that in the early years of the Grand Pump Room Hotel, Bath, the wages were about 10% of turnover and the same was roughly true throughout the better hotels. The Langham in 1889 paid out about £8,000 from a turnover of £80,000 and the Prince of Wales Hotel, Southport, £1,877 out of about £18,500. In Switzerland in 1884, a national survey produced figures of 16,000 employees in the industry costing £200,000 out of a gross revenue of £2,112,000, a very similar percentage. This continued until after the Catering Wages Act in 1943 in Britain. From then on it moved up slowly to around 30% of turnover at the end of the century.

Staff turnover depended on the reason for working in the

hotel in the first place. Not only could a skilled craftsman travel if he wished, but many continentals came to Britain in order to learn the language and then return home. British and American visitors were an important part of the tourist market in many European countries, but they seldom had mastered a foreign tongue and expected the senior staff of the hotel they patronised to cope with English. The English supported the Swiss economy, as Professor Hunziker gladly acknowledged in his official history of 100 years of Swiss tourism, calling Thomas Cook's tours in the 1860s: "the foundation of the Swiss tourist industry". They had also been among the first to popularise the French Riviera, as the Niçoise charmingly conceded by calling their main beach road the Promenade des Anglais, and their hotels by such names as the Westminster, the Royal and the Cecil.

So the continental staff with ambitions obligingly came to Britain to learn the language and, as they came from countries which regarded hotel work as an honourable occupation, they were able to raise the craft standards of the hotels, and were acknowledged as superior to the British themselves. The palatial Highland hotels upheld their status by employing continentals: "typically a French chef, German waiters and an Italian or Swiss Manager". The *Globe* in 1880, commenting on the improvement in British hotels, said that the guests': "comfort (is) enhanced by service in the public rooms being performed in great measure by foreigners. English staff are not as good."

Continental staff were to be found all over the country, but they were, of course, still far outnumbered by British employees, and in a good, successful hotel the staff were likely to stay on year after year. At Buxton Hydropathic in 1888 about half the staff of 30-50 had worked for Mr. Lomas for between 12 and 20 years, and in 1879 the night porter at Hummums in Covent Garden had been receiving 15 shillings (75p) a week for the past 14 years. Growing old was not normally a problem in the industry. If the member of staff was capable of doing the job, nobody asked their age. One Porter who started at the Grosvenor Hotel in Victoria in 1915, finally retired in 1981.

While the continental men travelled and worked, the women seldom did and the female staff in hotels were usually English or Irish. The private houses of the well-to-do, hotels and boarding houses, would all have been in chaos without the dogged efforts of the enormous numbers of young women who went: "into service". Between 1890 and 1910 a third of the girls between 15 and 18 in the country were employed in this way. It was the largest single occupation open to women and over a million accepted it. While other areas of a hotel might have become the province of the continental worker, the housekeeping department was dominated by the British, unless the Head Housekeeper was the wife of a continental manager. One of the chains of promotion to management lay through the chambermaids, promoted to housekeepers and eventually to manager. It was also often the case that a husband and wife would be taken on as a team and while the husband looked after the accounting, the reception department and the restaurant, the wife undertook the wide range of housekeeping responsibilities.

Competition was fierce for the better jobs. The advertisement for a manager for the Marine Hotel in North Berwick in 1890 brought no less than 400 applications. The position was finally given to Mr. and Mrs. Ranhart, with Mrs. Ranhart specifically designated as manageress and housekeeper. The Ranharts came from the Palace Hotel, Hastings. It was accepted by the hotel owners that good managers would have had varied experience rather than be able to produce evidence of their ability to settle down for many years in one job. Joseph Gams, the manager of the plush Alexandra Hotel in Hyde Park in 1883, was Viennese, had worked for Delmonico's in New York and then come back to manage the Imperial Hotel in Vienna. He went on to manage his own hotel in the spa town of Marienbad, gave that up to become a wine salesman and eventually settled down at the Alexandra.

In a Britain starved of top hotel management, the successful Europeans could often take a tough line with owners. Robert Etzensberger had been manager of the Victoria Hotel in Venice and in charge of the commissariat for Thomas Cook's excursions by steamer up the Nile. He was offered the job of manager of the Midland Grand at St. Pancras but he said he would only take the position if the hotel were completed according to Sir Gilbert Scott's original plans. The Midland Directors, who had been hoping to economise in some additional directions, eventually agreed to this and Etzensberger stayed 13 years until he drowned on holiday in Switzerland.

He was succeeded by a man who was to be the most

Behind the scenes

prominent British hotel manager of his age. This was William Towle, later knighted, who had started his career at the age of 15 at the Midland Hotel in Derby and, by the time he was 22, had been made the manager. During his time in Derby he pleased his directors by introducing the concept of lunch baskets for train travellers. There were no dining cars at the time and the lunch baskets were good profit-makers, besides providing the passengers with an additional service.

The general manager of the Midland Railway, Sir James Allport, having decided that the best way to overcome competition from other lines was by improving the service on the Midland, was prepared to consider any ideas to this end with enthusiasm. The combination of Allport and Towle created the conditions for a group of railway hotels which became prominent in the '80s and '90s as Midland Railway Hotels and which, by the 1920s, was the largest chain in Europe. Both William Towle and his two sons, Francis and Arthur, occupied very senior positions in the industry over a long span of years.

As hotels grew in importance, a number of hoteliers achieved prominence in civic affairs, particularly in towns where hotels were an essential factor in the prosperity of the community. Merton Cotes, for example, became Mayor of Bournemouth more than once, and in the cities there was Philip Matthews, who ran Harkers and the North Eastern Hotel in York and who also achieved the highest civic office; unfortunately Matthews failed to last the course, dying of typhoid soon after his election. Members of Parliament included Spencer (Jabez) Balfour, the owner of the Victoria Hotel near Trafalgar Square, James Bailey, the proprietor of Baileys in Kensington, Sir Isidore Salmon of Lyons, Sir Bracewell Smith of the Park Lane in London, Sir Blundell Maple who created Frederick Hotels and a number of others.

Pride of place, however, goes to Sir Polydore de Keyser, who overcame many of the prejudices of his time to become Lord Mayor of London in 1887. Sir Polydore was born near Antwerp in Belgium and, although he was educated in Fulham, he never lost his continental accent. His father ran the Royal Hotel at Blackfriars, which prospered sufficiently for the family to build a new hotel at Blackfriars Bridge on a site which is now Unilever House. This was the de Keyser Royal Hotel, which was opened in 1874 by the

Ritzy

King of the Belgians and aimed to look after the passengers using Blackfriars station on their continental travels. The destinations you could reach from the station were chiselled in stone on the portico and, dismissing Leningrad, it still proclaimed late in the 20th century that transportation was available to St. Petersburg. Polydore was naturalised in 1866 and elected to the Court of Common Council in 1872 without much trouble. In 1882 he was elected an alderman for the ward of Farringdon Without, defeating an ex-Sheriff called Waterlow, and it was at this point that he had to face some very dirty political skullduggery. Waterlow tried to overturn the result by digging up an ancient ordinance which said that no tavern licence holder could become an alderman, a rule that went back to Richard II and Henry V. As Polydore was not only a licence holder, but also a Catholic and foreign born, there was plenty of fuel for prejudice to feed on, and Waterlow must have felt reasonably certain that his position would be upheld by the city fathers.

When the election was discussed, it could not be denied that the ordinance definitely existed, but while it was confirmed exception could be made in de Keyser's case and the election result should stand. This was a good day for the men of goodwill, and when de Keyser was eventually elected Lord Mayor, he became the first Catholic to hold the office since the Reformation.

It was, of course, more likely that an owner-manager would be elected to office by his fellow citizens than an employee- manager, but there were at least useful financial rewards in salaries and kind for the latter. A top position like Mr. Devine's at the Metropole in London in 1886 brought him £500 a year, and many managers had a bonus written into their contracts, payable if their hotel made sufficient profits. At the Victoria Hotel, Southport, for instance, the accounts for 1885 were sufficiently good for the directors to declare a 4% dividend, free of tax, and the manager got £96 as his bonus.

In a first-class hotel the manager would have a large staff. His main assistants would be his sub-manager, head day porter, head night porter, head chef and head housekeeper. All the female staff would be under the head housekeeper, except the book-keepers, the barmaids and the kitchen maids, who would be responsible to their respective heads of department. There would be a superintendent for the public rooms of the hotel - such as the lounge and billiards-room - and four separate head waiters. One for the coffee-room where the general public would be welcome, one for the *table d'hôte* room, one for the ladies room where families could eat together, and one for the private banqueting rooms. There would also be an engineer, a head cellar man and a head plate man; the cellar man would look after the stocks of wines and spirits and the head plate man the crockery and cutlery. The size of these latter tasks can be visualized by the racks of wine at the Metropole Hotel, Brighton, which accommodated: "a duty paid stock of 185,000 bottles." When the Grand Hotel in London re-ordered plates in 1889, they bought another 12,000! Then there would be an usher for the servant's hall, a timekeeper, linen-room, still-room, and laundry staff, as well as a large contingent of chambermaids.

In the kitchen the head chef would be equally well supported. His second in command would be the kitchen clerk, so that while the chef drew up all the menus and examined each dish before it went to the client, the kitchen clerk would take the orders from all over the hotel and check everything to see that it was correct. Normally, the second chef would look after the ovens and then there would be a roast chef, sauce chef, pastry chef, cold larder chef and a number of apprentices. Auguste Escoffier would introduce the Partie system in the 1890s at the Savoy. In luxury hotels today the kitchen jobs are not divided between men and women, but in Victorian times there would be a head kitchen maid, a fish maid, a head and under vegetable maid and a couple of 'scrubber' maids. The kitchen porters and washers-up would be men and, when the hotel was particularly busy, the manager would hire extra chefs: "of which there are always plenty seeking employment and who are paid by the day." Quantity, of course, did not necessarily equate with quality and when the porters, page-boys, lift men and receptionists were included in the complement, it can be seen that labour had to be cheap to keep the wages cost low, as they invariably were.

There were three types of people to be fed in a hotel; the staff themselves, the servants of the guests and the guests. The servants of the guests were looked after in the stewards' room which was usually 'below stairs' and they were looked after well. It was generally agreed that a servant who was dissatisfied with the hotel would very soon ensure that his employer was equally unhappy. It was, therefore, prudent for the hotelier to see to it that, though the tariff for servants was below that of other guests, the quality was very similar. The second housekeeper or the linen- keeper would be present at all meals to keep an eye open for any problems and one of the head waiters would carve. A few of the senior staff in the hotel would also eat in the stewards' room and it is a telling comment on the position of children in Victorian society that they would often eat there with their nanny, who was usually not allowed in any public room if she was in uniform.

There always had to be one milk sweet on the menu for the children, but such light eating did not apply to anyone else. For breakfast the menu would include fish and meat, and for lunch it would be soup or fish on alternate days, followed by a choice of joints with two vegetables and then a dessert and cheese. There would be tea, jam and toast for tea and cold joints and cheese at supper together, perhaps, with something which had proved unpopular on the *table d'hôte*. Some hotels gave a pint of beer to the guests' male servants and half a pint to the female, but others charged extra.

The Victorians travelled with a considerable retinue and, as we have seen already, a large number of the bedrooms at the best hotels were designed to be used by the servants. Indeed, before the invention of lifts, the rooms at the top of the hotels would be most easily sold to them and, of course, there was a good deal of residential accommodation for the hotel's own staff as well. Both sexes might be provided with living-in accommodation but the *Engineer* journal observed approvingly about the Midland Grand Hotel in 1867: "male and female departments having no communication with each other and approached by different staircases."

In many hotels both staff and guests were likely to meet in the morning for prayer. Morning services were attended by guests and staff alike. To this day, the Manager's meeting in the morning with his senior staff to discuss the day's events, is known as 'Morning Prayers.'

Hotels were an ideal stage on which to display the elaborate etiquette of staff seniority, and woe betide any hotel which failed to give the visiting nanny her last jot and tittle of status, or any junior staff member who didn't 'know his place'. Retribution would be severe and it must never be forgotten that to lose your job could be an unmitigated disaster, far more terrible than today. There was no social security to draw if you were unemployed, nothing to do except pawn your last belongings and then go to the workhouse or starve to death. If you had a wife and children to support or if your relatives were as poor as you, the threat of unemployment and the fear of being unable to work through sickness, were constant worries.

Mario Gallati was once accused unjustly of stealing a piece of steak worth two shillings and six pence (12½p) at the Russell Hotel where he was a waiter. When he refused to pay for it, he was dismissed. As he wrote later: "This was a mistake due to pride; in 1905, to be out of work in October meant you would be out of work all the winter.. " Only another waiter falling sick after Christmas produced a job after he had looked fruitlessly for a post for three months. Not surprisingly, he stayed with his new employer for years.

It is with this background in mind that the dangers of trade union membership become clearer. If you were labelled a troublemaker by the employers, you might never work again in the industry and the grapevine was pretty effective. If you had a job in a hotel, you were able to keep body and soul together and there was always the chance of a fat gratuity on which to pin your hopes. Rosa Lewis was tipped £100 when she cooked a dinner for a private hostess who was entertaining the Kaiser and, although this was exceptional, if you were earning a couple of pounds a month, it was the stuff of which dreams were made. The hours were very long and, even when the Edwardian Shop Act made the maximum week 74 hours, most hotel staff didn't come within its scope. Hoteliers met the legislation with indignation. Many felt anything up to 100 hours was perfectly reasonable.

Even so, the conditions weren't so bad that your friends died of them, as they might in a match factory, building a railway or in the mines. The incentive to join together to form a union was missing, and it was particularly difficult if a proportion of the prospective members didn't speak English well, only stayed the season and equated membership with revolution. To be a member of a union in many continental countries could lead you into direct conflict with the state and most immigrant workers were concerned only to earn a living. Of course, the British government's attitude was less repressive. Workers would not have to face deportation just because they had formed or joined a union, but this was beside the point; the scars of their experiences in their home countries led migrant workers to leave well alone.

Ritzy

While there was little interest in forming a union, there were a number of hotel societies; in 1877 the Hotel Employee's Society was founded and in its first seven years it paid out over £1,000 to sick members. There were branches of the society all over Europe and, during the same period, employment was found for over 4,000 people. This combination of assistance against the twin evils of sickness and unemployment could be supported by both management and staff, and the annual functions of the Society were always supported by managers from the best hotels. The Hotel and Tavern Keepers Provident Association was also a charitable institution, looking after a number of old and infirm members, who in 1885 shared £215 among 24 applicants. It was a small gesture, as was the £133 given from the Sick and Pension Fund of the City Waiters Provident and Pension Society in 1883. At the annual dinner that year a whip-round produced £180, but anybody contemplating his own future would have been well advised to adopt the Victorian ideal of self-help, rather than depend on the slim handouts available from such organizations.

If employees made only relatively puny efforts to band together, the same was also true of management. Attempts to form an English Hotel Association fell on stony ground as soon as the question of money came up. An attempt to form a British Association and Defence League in 1886 got no further than a meeting at the Westminster Palace Hotel. Five years later a movement, sponsored enthusiastically by the *Caterer and Hotelkeeper,* did little better. Editorial support was given in the form of articles and lists of prominent hotel managers who had pledged their support, but after gatherings at which people were solemnly elected to the chair, the minutiae of meetings and procedures carefully thrashed out and endless talking, there was no money to speak of actually forthcoming. The idea faded away for another decade. The former medical student and now the owner and editor of the *Caterer*, Frank Bourne Newton, was not discouraged, however and lived to fight successfully another day. In fact he lived until 1943 and died a nonagenarian, no doubt reflecting that the journal had come a long way since it first appeared in 1878 carrying an advertisement for a sure-fire hair restorer.

While this situation existed in England there were better results in other parts of Britain; a Hotel and Restaurant Proprietors' Association of Ireland was created and also a Scottish Hotel

Proprietors' Association. In Scotland the basic reason was the one which would eventually bring into being the Incorporated Association of Hotels and Restaurants (later the Hotels & Restaurants Association, later the British Hotels, Restaurants and Caterers Association and now the British Hospitality Association). Legislation was hurting the Scottish hoteliers. It was in 1881 that the first meeting was held at the Waterloo Hotel, Edinburgh and the grievances aired. Afterwards these were placed before the Lord Advocate of Scotland by a deputation. The hoteliers started by objecting to paying house duty on their entire premises when the guests occupied a good part of it. House duty was paid by every home owner and the hoteliers held that, as visitors had paid their own where they lived, the tax was being paid twice if the hotels paid as well. Stores were exempt, so why not hotels?

The amount involved was 5% on the rental for the hotel and, not for the first time, the hotel industry was trying to find out where it belonged; there surely had to be a difference between a private house and a business where the product was bedrooms for sale. Many hoteliers also took strong exception to paying the licence to run a carriage for the whole year when Highland hotels only needed the licence for the few months of the season; the same applied to the bar licence in a seasonal hotel. Finally, the hoteliers wanted to know why so much competition was allowed. Clubs, they felt, should not open at hours when hotels had to be shut, and railway companies should stick to running trains rather than venture into the hotel business. If only hostelries were legally allowed to receive travellers, then the Scots held that hydropathic and temperance institutions were illegal. The Lord Advocate said that he would look into all these complaints, but the whole exercise did very little good, except that an association came into existence, which was more than resulted from the efforts of the Sassenachs. In many of the battles the IAHR would have with government, local authorities and licensing justices, the same pain of hitting your head against a brick wall would be experienced.

As hotels became more complex structures, larger and better, the tasks and skills of the manager became greater as well. The host of the Staging Inn was a long way removed from the controller of the 'giant caravanserai', as the big hotels were lovingly labelled. To start with, the managers had to tackle the large number of new inventions which were often of fundamental importance; gas cooking apparatus was produced by E.D. Owen in 1849 (though solid fuel ovens were still preferred by many chefs 100 years later), lifts were coming in by the late 1850s, Edison perfected the incandescent lamp in 1879 and there were major improvement in drainage, fireproof floor construction, soil and waste disposal, ducted ventilation, water supplies and refrigeration. Ice had been imported from the United States at first, but by 1880 the main supplier was Norway, which shipped 30,000 - 50,000 tons a year. Boats carrying 500 tons or more would unload at Surrey Docks and although half the original weight would melt in transit, at two shillings and six pence (12½p) a hundredweight, (55 kilos) there was still a fair profit to be made.

While today we would pick up a telephone - which were now beginning to be installed - and get a plumber, engineer or electrician to solve the problem, the good manager in those early years would want to understand the technicalities involved to a much greater extent. While the *Caterer* would still be running a series of articles in 1891 on the correct way to look after stables, there were also, cheek by jowl, complicated expositions on laying drains and installing electric bell systems. Managers faced a long list of problems which they expect to delegate today.

The new inventions were costly. It was easy enough to carry out the necessary work for a hotel as you were building it, but exceptionally difficult when you had an existing hotel, with the solidity of construction which has been seen already. Although the courtyard at the Langham was lit by electricity in 1879, the directors did not readily provide the money to fit up the whole hotel, as 10 years later the bill for this was £5,000, or about three months profit. Sometimes the cost of the invention itself was unnecessarily expensive; the Electric Light Act of 1881 made it very difficult to get a supply for private houses, into which category the hotels were put again, and consequently many hotels had to install their own dynamos. Now, as a result, the effects of a power strike are not felt by some of the Victorian hotels who invested in this way and simply use their own generators. Although the cost of electricity could eventually be a half-penny (about 1/5p) a unit, the right to sell it was originally vested in private companies who charged extortionate rates, but: "through wells and dynamos, hotels can be independent of water and electricity companies with their exacting arbitrary conditions."

Of course, the public's only concern was to obtain these wonderful new facilities, and if a new hotel could provide them

98

where an old hotel could not afford the expense, then the guest's loyalty was likely to switch quickly. Decisions on heavy capital expenditure must have given many managers sleepless nights, as they contemplated the technologically advanced newcomers. When the Metropole in Brighton opened, the Grand suffered badly, and eventually a shareholders' committee investigated the management, but it found nothing to complain about - except the existence of the Metropole! As building programmes grew, more and more managers had to fight new competitors for the business they had carefully nurtured over the years.

It was also true that the new inventions themselves could get old-fashioned, as hydraulic lifts, for example, were overtaken by electrically operated ones. The guests preferred the smoother ride, and with lifts there was originally some of the fear among the public that characterised the first passenger rides in an aeroplane years later; were they safe, would they crash, wasn't it more sensible to take the stairs rather than tempt providence? Gas could be lethal and there were a number of fatalities with gas water-heaters, which were introduced around 1880. Thomas Cook's only daughter was tragically one of the victims.

A death in a hotel has always been one of the nightmares that haunts a manager, but fire is even worse and many hotels had their own fire-fighting teams; there were two resident firemen at the de Keyser Royal Hotel who did nothing else but wait for a blaze. There were day and night firemen at the Langham and there would be regular fire practices at new hotels like the Cecil. As late as 1960 there was a night fireman employed at the Piccadilly Hotel, though he never had to put anything out. In the country areas, of course, the problems were much worse; the Railway Hotel, Sandown, was burned to the ground in 1879 because the fire-engines at Sandown were out of order. When fire broke out at the George Hotel, Axminster in 1881, the local fire engines were not enough and two extra appliances had to be sent by rail from Exeter, a distance of 27 miles. By the time they got to the blaze it had a good hold, burnt for 10 hours and did £10,000 worth of damage. Even at short distances, with only horses to pull the machines, the fire brigade could easily arrive too late or have insufficient water power to stem the conflagration.

The hydros were particularly vulnerable as many were situated high on the hills because of the panoramic views. The luckless Calla nder Hydro was practically destroyed in 1893 and the Cairn Hydro was completely burnt out. The fire engines could not get up the hills or provide the necessary water pressure.

Hotel managers, like airlines in the future, did not know whether to talk of their safety records in terms of fire precautions and the fireproof construction of the building, or to keep quiet about the whole thing. No doubt the manager of the Wheatsheaf Hotel in Manchester, which was said to be Britain's oldest, gave the matter careful thought as well, but in the summer of 1882 his hotel was destroyed anyway - struck by lightning - and it was to be some years before the solution to that hazard also appeared.

By the beginning of the 1880s the pattern of management was becoming clearer; with the growth of large hotels it was more difficult for a hotelier to own his business, and the divide widened between the board of directors and the manager they employed. There would still be those who would successfully jump the gap, but the manager, as just another employee, was a growing trend, and there was often friction between board and manager. There was no prejudice against employing women in that position, though. The names of able Victorian ladies adorn the letterheads of a large number of hotels of the time and, in addition, the manager's wife was very often the real power in the operation. If none of these ladies has achieved a place in the Industry's Hall of Fame, they nevertheless stood comparison with their male colleagues in every respect. It was true then, though, as it is today, that the larger the hotel, the more likely it was to have a man in charge. You have to think hard to find exceptions. Rosa Lewis ran the Cavendish in Jermyn Street, Marie Ritz served on the board of Ritz Hotels in an active capacity after Cesar Ritz's death, Lady Honeywood had her own chain of hotels and Lady Towle had an important role in the running of Midland Railway Hotels. But rarely were women made managers of large hotels.

Life behind the scenes in a hotel towards the end of the century involved long hours, only moderate wages and demanded the capacity to accept a degree of servility, but it was also a warm roof over tens of thousands of grateful heads.

7
A pause for the winner.
Frederick Gordon - 1835 - 1904.

Unfortunately for the researcher, Victorian hoteliers were not public figures in the sense that their lives and actions were faithfully recorded for posterity in immaculate detail. On the contrary, their origins were often in doubt, their private life a mystery, and they were forgotten almost as soon as the obsequies had been pronounced. They would have had hundreds, or indeed thousands, of acquaintances during their lifetime, as they welcomed guests, paused in a lounge to enquire whether all was well, or settled minor disputes in the sanctity of their offices. What they were really like, though, behind the face the public saw, or behind the beard and moustache which so often hid even the surface of the Victorian hotelkeeper, remained to all, but their most intimate friends and relations, almost totally obscure.

This was even true of the greatest of the Victorian hoteliers and the head of by far the largest hotel company the world had ever seen up to his time. In the *Caterer*, it said: "there are few persons who know what manner of man the head and forefront of the business is." His name was Frederick Gordon.

The founder of the Gordon Hotel Company is too important an influence and a prototype to be allowed to remain merely a footnote on the Register of Companies, the name of an avenue in Stanmore in Middlesex, or the occupant of a massive but overgrown grave in the same parish. Consequently, although it is not possible, or even desirable, to study a large number of Victorian hoteliers in depth, we can examine the life of this one extraordinary individual, a man who started with practically nothing and, in the best tradition of all Cinderella stories, finished up with a Royal, not to mention a Grand, a number of Metropoles and a Burlington.

Frederick Gordon was born in Ross-on-Wye, Herefordshire, a small West Midlands market town in 1835. His father, Charles Gordon, had gone there in the early 1830s from London in order to take a job with a local house decorator. The Gordons were a large family and Charles Gordon's wife was the daughter of a well-known local man, Thomas Minett. Her brother, Henry, was a solicitor and when Frederick grew up, he was articled to his uncle. In 1843 Frederick had a brother, Alexander, and in 1846 a sister, Lizzie.

Ritzy

Charles Gordon did not stay in Ross. It is quite possible that the local agricultural community may have fallen on harder times, and he went back to London, where he carried on as a decorator, but began to specialise in 'principal dining rooms'.

These dining rooms we would call restaurants today, and they were springing up to cater for the vastly increased business community which London was spawning, as the city grew ever greater in importance and magnitude. The prosperous new middle classes needed somewhere to eat, somewhere respectable, and Father Gordon was kept busy. Decorating dining rooms was not, however, as lucrative or as physically untaxing as managing them, and Father Gordon decided to obtain a job as manager of some dining rooms, with daughter Lizzie as cashier.

It was about this time that Frederick qualified as a solicitor and started up in business in Holborn. In the summer of 1864 he married 21 year-old Emily Warman in Chigwell, Essex, where they set up home. Frederick had not entirely lost touch with Ross and, after his first son was born, Emily had their first daughter, Ellen, at the family home in Herefordshire in the spring of 1866. There is no evidence that Frederick, a short, cheerful man, was a very successful solicitor, but he managed to garner a living from his practice in Holborn and made a good friend out of his new brother-in-law, a 25 year old engraver called Horatio Davies, who had married Lizzie in 1867.

How long Frederick would have struggled on with his practice is academic, for his life changed course completely when he was 34 years old, with a wife and two children and making little headway. At that point he suffered a blow which would have been the last straw for many men; two days before Christmas 1869 Emily died of pneumonia, only 26 years old.

For Gordon it was a watershed, and his phenomenal rise to fame and affluence dates from this time. To start with, he decided to submerge himself in city politics and managed to get proposed and seconded for the Bishopsgate Ward of the City of London Common Council. Sometimes these elections are uncontested, but in 1870 there were 15 candidates for 14 places so that a ward vote was necessary and, on a show of hands, Gordon came last. A few years before he might have accepted the defeat, but he was tougher now, he had the two motherless children to fight for, and so he demanded a poll. In the short time at his disposal he lobbied furiously for support. When the count ended and the result was announced on the first anniversary of Emily's death, Frederick had come top.

It was just the beginning and Gordon knew it. In the charmed world of the city magnates, a small solicitor from an artisan background with little money and few contacts, had a long way to go. For the rest of his life, Frederick kept his origins deliberately hidden; he never gave an interview to the press, and even his grandchildren were to have no knowledge of the identity of his first wife, for Frederick did marry again, a lady called Harriet Philips, who was 11 years his junior, and might well have been a widow herself. She bore him 8 sons and a daughter and, surprisingly for the age, they all survived.

Why Frederick decided to go into the catering business we do not really know. In his obituary in the *Financial News* many years later it was written: "many will remember the buffet in Milk Street which he founded." This must have been one of his earliest investments. Of course, his father was in the industry and his brother-in-law, Horatio Davies, gave up engraving some years later to take over a restaurant in Poultry, in the City, called the London Tavern. In time Davies bought other restaurants, like Pimms, and, of course, made a fortune from the spirit-based drinks named after the restaurant. There is a story in the family that one day when Gordon was starting his legal practice, he was looking for a cheap lunch and couldn't find anywhere for a snack. So he decided to start a restaurant to fill the gap he saw in the market.

Business must have been brisk for soon Gordon took a lease on a famous city landmark, a former home of Richard III, called Crosby Hall. Since 1466 it had been known as a place for eating and reference can be found to it in Shakespeare. Incidentally, it was also in 1466 that we find one of the first recorded examples of creative banqueting - a dish on a menu which re-emphasises the theme of the event. It was at the dinner after the installation of the new Archbishop of York in that year, that the guests   ate for their dessert a marzipan model of St. George and the Dragon.

By the time Frederick started to restore Crosby Hall, all that remained of the original palace was the great banqueting hall, the council room and the associated chambers. It was very dilapidated but Sir Thomas More had lived there, as had Erasmus, the great

Ritzy

Humanist, and every caterer knows the value of a large slice of history if you want to create atmosphere. Gordon decided that he would try to suit all pockets and, by the time he had finished, you could have a stand-up snack at the counter for five pence (2p), or: "a recherché dinner in the Throne Room" for two guineas (£2.10.) The latter was: "a place set apart for higher-priced dinners than those served in the Banqueting Hall and specially intended for the benefit of ladies." Crosby Hall was restored with stained-glass windows and historical wallpapers and Gordon obviously backed his judgment with all the finances he could muster.

Gordon was a strong innovator but, if inspiration failed him, he was always an excellent plagiarist. He was a stickler for cleanliness and a feature of Crosby Hall was the: "40 neat and civil waitresses.....The crowd between 12 and 3 seem to fill the building, ample and commodious as it is." There was, surprisingly, no smell of cooking and the dining rooms were supplied with: "pure, filtered water" as Frederick characteristically cashed in on the publicity attendant on the cause of the cholera deaths.

The restaurant was a tremendous success and the city fathers and sons started to flock to it. Soon he was able to open a second restaurant in a building which had been known as the Holborn Casino. Originally the word casino was associated with music and dancing rather than gambling. The new venture was simply called the Holborn Restaurant.

Whilst discussing the origins of words, the start of the word restaurant is complicated. It begins with a particular recipe for a fine chicken soup in 18th century France which was nicknamed 'the divine restorer'. The ingredients were, however, too expensive for the poor people and so a bright chef created an imitation and sold it in shops. The 'restorer' could be sold by people who were unable to offer set meals, for to do that a licensed victualler needed a charter from the Society of Rotisseurs. Those who possessed such charters were called Traiteurs - Charterers. Eventually the 'restorers' got together with the 'traiteurs' and became restaurateurs. I told you it was complicated.

The Holborn opened in 1874 and this time Frederick was able to take advantage of the burgeoning banqueting trade. The Holborn had its own Masonic Temples, which were well patronized as the Craft expanded, but there were also many other social functions, like the

A pause for the winner

Oxford and Cambridge Boat Race dinner and regimental gatherings. The latter had been confined to a few cavalry regiments up to 1860, with the dinners held in June and concentrated on Derby Week, but now they were becoming more and more popular. Again, Gordon provided a new facility for a growing demand and flourished.

Just as Frederick built his catering expertise, so he also constructed a following in the City. The papers wrote: "He had the great quality of inspiring liking in all whom he met". "Nothing escaped him and nothing was left to chance. He was an indomitable worker." "Always of a cheerful disposition, Frederick Gordon went through life in an atmosphere of contagious optimism". "Few men have had a wider circle of personal friends and still fewer are in his position of having no enemies." Even on his tomb there is a deep-cut inscription: "Till we meet again". The optimism is reminiscent of John Smedley and, if Gordon was no teetotaller, he was, like Smedley, properly prepared to turn down business of a dubious and perhaps immoral nature.

Throughout the 1870s he worked on the Common Council for Markets, for Orphan Schools, Coal, Corn and Finance, Law and City Courts. He sat as a Commissioner for Sewers as Bazelgette completed his great work and was on a number of other committees as well. He met and worked with important figures in the powerful city guilds, and by 1877 he was ready to rely on the support of his twin pillars - a City reputation and a successful catering business - to enter into a new and potentially dangerous venture; to build a new hotel in Trafalgar Square, at a cost of £85,000, to appeal to the middle classes, and led not by the aristocracy, but by other businessmen like himself. The site was excellent, as Trafalgar Square was relatively new and a great attraction for visitors, while neighbouring Charing Cross was both central for entertainment and for government offices and transport.

What was potentially dangerous was the state of the country's economy as once again the Victorian world dipped from boom to slump. The competition of newly emergent nations like Germany was threatening British exports. In 1876 the slump started and by 1879 11% of the work force was unemployed. Obviously this led to a serious drop in demand and there were many bankruptcies, most seriously the City of Glasgow Bank in 1878. In spite of so many flotations, the bank was still not a limited liability company and the

Ritzy

debts had to be paid by the shareholders.

An optimist always, Gordon probably felt that the economic ills would right themselves in good time, and the economy would recover. But it was still 300 rooms, £85,000 and a tremendous undertaking for a man who was, in hotel terms, a complete novice.

Building started in 1879 on the site of Northumberland House, the old ducal mansion of the Percy family in Trafalgar Square, and a board was created for Gordon's Grand Hotel with a membership designed to appeal to the widest possible section of the investing public. The City was represented by John Pound, a highly respected name and a future Lord Mayor. The brewing industry was taken care of by Alexander Johnstone on behalf of Bass, Ratcliff, some of whose directors had large share holdings, and the men-about-town investors by Francis Cowley Burnand, probably the most famous editor that *Punch* has ever had. Flair, probity, proven success and the strength of the brewers were all there, and Frederick also invited Horatio Davies onto the board to see that the family were well represented. It was a young group, with Pound the oldest at 49 and Davies only 36.

On May 29th 1881, the Lord Mayor of London opened the hotel, which was reported as: "providing luxury and comfort to which the travelling public had hitherto been little accustomed." Architecturally speaking, the building was a mess, built on an irregular, semi-circular, half-triangular site. It was called: "A shapeless pile, but one is amazed at the richness and magnificence of its interior. All that marble, mosaic, meralis, alabaster and gilding can do has been done. Reds, greys, whites and golds are admirably harmonized and blended. There is no barbaric profusion of gilding. The typical gloom and mustiness of English hotels is dispelled. The arched roof of stained glass over the dining room gives a flood of daylight. The fittings of the dining room are gorgeous. A spectacle almost distressing in its magnificence. There is soft and diffused electricity, A smaller dining room and a general Reception Room which is a sumptuously fitted, lofty, spacious apartment with marble pillars and with walls and chimneys of carved walnut."

Not only was the hotel successful: "contrary to many predictions" said *The Times,* but the efforts of the nearby Charing Cross Hotel to hold back the tide and its clientele by cutting prices was of little avail. A new hotel was too great an attraction unless a management had earned exceptional loyalty. It was difficult to compete for feminine custom, for instance, when the ladies' drawing room at the Grand was so exotic: "the walls above the dado of black and gold are covered with green silk damask, the ceiling is full of gold stars, and the fireplace is adorned with enamelled plaques by Elkington."

Gordon also had an idea to obtain a strong male clientele. It so happened that the Conservative party had at last recovered, thanks to the efforts of Disraeli, who had led the first majority Conservative administration for 30 years. The two Conservative clubs were the Carlton and the Junior Carlton, packed to capacity and with no hope of becoming a member except through dead men's shoes. Tired of waiting, a group of 100 men under the Marquis of Abergavenny got together to create a new club, the Constitutional, and one of them was Gordon. Having formed it with Robert Cecil, the Marquis of Salisbury, as president, (Prime Minister, Arthur Balfour, was his nephew; hence "Bob's your Uncle"), membership swiftly grew to 5,000 and Gordon was elected to the committee. Where to build the new club premises? Gordon persuaded his colleagues that 28, Northumberland Avenue would be ideal, right next door to the Grand! With his brother, Alexander, a member of the club and manager of the Grand, the country members of the Constitutional were unlikely to look further; it was a great coup, and well justified the decision to extend the Grand by a further 70 rooms.

Gordon was 45 when the Grand opened and he immediately set to work to raise the capital for another new hotel, the First Avenue in Holborn, so named because Frederick approved of a movement which wanted the streets of London to be numbered like New York for the sake of simplicity. When the First Avenue opened in 1883 Gordon started yet another new one down the road from the Grand at the corner of Northumberland Avenue and called it the Metropole. Throughout the '80s he was expanding and for the year ending November 1888, the 3 hotels showed a profit of over £210,000. This was the rock-solid foundation on which he intended to base the biggest flotation the hotel industry had ever seen.

The aim was to raise no less than £2,201,000 and the package the shareholders were to purchase included all the most fashionable investments in hotel terms; in addition to the famous London hotels, there were some good seaside names; the Burlington in Eastbourne and the Metropole in Brighton were very fashionable resort hotels

Ritzy

and the Royal Pier Hotel on the Isle of Wight was not far from Osborne, Queen Victoria's favourite home. To add the last touch of glamour, the company was also to own the newly built Metropole Hotel in Cannes and the Metropole Hotel in Monte Carlo.

Gordon was one of the few English hoteliers to invest in the Riviera which was then in the middle of a get-rich-quick boom similar to that which would be experienced in the 1960s by the West Indies. It was a fabulous world of almost unlimited tourist wealth, attracting crowned heads and millionaires during the season, the mecca of the aristocracy and the *nouveau riche*. For a few people it was an immense gold mine; men like Camille Blanc who had the concession for the Casino in Monte Carlo, and a handful of really expert hoteliers.

It was a four months season from December to April and, like London, the stories of boom business attracted so many new hotels that the market was soon flooded. There were 50 first-class hotels in Monte Carlo at the turn of the century and, as a consequence, the available business was spread too thinly for more than a few to be successful in the long term. It was a totally international clientele and, therefore, affected by the vagaries of European politics to a considerable degree; a royal assassination or *coup d'état* would keep the aristocracy affected at home awaiting developments; a diplomatic row between France and another nation could cause a temporary boycott; the area was primitive in many ways and outbreaks of cholera or smallpox would frighten off the visitors or could ruin a season. The whole operation was as risky as the roulette tables, which provided one of the main attractions. The casinos operated in Germany during the summer, like the one at Baden-Baden at which the Blanc family had flourished originally, and the balmy winter weather on the Riviera complemented the German social round.

Gordon had two splendid locations for his Riviera hotels; the Metropole at Monte Carlo still stands in its sub-tropical grounds adjoining the casino, while the Metropole at Cannes had a magnificent panoramic view over the bay, high above the little town. As it was a winter season, the attractions of sea bathing did not interest the visitors and the remoteness of the town made the hotel equally distant, hopefully, from any plebeian epidemics.

As Cannes changed its character between the two World Wars, the setting of the Metropole became a disadvantage and it was sold in the 1930s to the Bishop of Nice as a seminary. It was demolished 50 years later and a splendid block of apartments took its place. The wonderful grounds are still there though; the cactus plants and palm trees, the great ornamental gates at the front and the plaque to commemorate the opening by the Prince of Wales. You couldn't fault Gordon's planning. He could hardly be blamed for failing to see the way habits would change 40 years hence, and if he had satisfied those future generations, he would have done little business in 1890. It was the everlasting dilemma of the resort hotelier.

With his successful record, his London, seaside and Riviera hotels and his own persuasive charm, even the immense issue of over £2 million was a success. In 1890 Gordon, the house-painter's son, found himself the chairman of an enormous hotel company, happily selling beds to his clients, and retiring in the evening to his country mansion, Bentley Priory at Stanmore, just outside London, where William IV's Queen Adelaide, had died. He hadn't exactly planned to live there; he had bought it to convert into a country hotel but, for once, he'd backed a dud.

For it was Gordon who stated most clearly the core of hotel profits:"We think it is very nice, of course, to get visitors into our *Table d'Hôte,* but we do not go in, as some of the other large hotels in London do, for making - I will not say the chief business, but at any rate a very considerable proportion of it - restaurant business. We prefer if we can to let our apartments, and you may rely on it that the backbone of hotel business is the letting of apartments."

From a man who made all his early money in restaurants, this was a very clear-sighted viewpoint.

The progress of Gordon Hotels after 1890 cannot be seen separately from the development of the whole industry, which we left as the slump of the late 1870s was coming to an end, but whatever the future might bring, Gordon epitomised the Victorian ideals of self-help, courage and determination leading on to fame and fortune.

8
The pleasure of your company
1880 - 1889

Visitors to London in 1880 could obtain the advice of the greatest living British novelist on all their problems, by purchasing Charles Dickens' *Dictionary of London*. On the subject of hotels he wrote: "One of the latest changes in London, during the last score or so years is in the matter of hotels. In proportion to its size, London is still worse provided in this respect than most of the great Continental or American towns. Almost every great railway, however, with the exception of the South Western, has now a handsome hotel in connection with its terminus....None of these hotels are at all cheap for people who do not understand hotel life, but they are very convenient for the new arrival, especially at night, and will probably prove quite as economical in the end as hunting about in a cab for a cheaper lodging. Indeed we may go further, and say that it is possible, with judicious management, to live almost as cheaply at one of the large hotels as at any of the ambitious second-class houses."

Dickens lists the well-known hotels, like the Langham, Westminster Palace, and the: "Buckingham Palace Hotel just opposite the great ballroom window of Buckingham Palace" but also discusses the cheap ones: "There is also a large class of comfortable and more old fashioned hotels, such as the Bedford, Covent Garden, for families and gentlemen; the Tavistock also in Covent Garden for bachelors where bed, breakfast and attendance costs seven shillings and six pence (37½p), and which has one of the best smoking rooms in London. Among the cheap hotels, special reference should be made to the Arundel on the Embankment....but it is of very little use to look for rooms there, unless bespoken beforehand."

"Nearly all the streets from the south side of the Strand are full of small private hotels, a sort of compromise between hotels and lodging houses, where the casual visitor will find himself comfortably, if perhaps a little roughly quartered, and where he will be in a thoroughly central position, even for business or pleasure. Hotels on the "temperance" principle will be found at Shirleys', 37, Queen Street, Bloomsbury; Fithians, 17, Great Coram Street....Foreign visitors will do well to bear in mind that the continental custom of taking all, or the great majority of meals out of the hotel does not obtain in England, and that a London hotel-keeper under such circumstances will consider himself ill-used."

Dickens was a good judge of hotel life and had travelled widely. London was still under-hotelled, particularly as the capital was becoming more and more the centre of the world's business and was the core of its greatest Empire. By 1880 the railway network was all but completed, though there were still additions to be made in some remote areas. Non-railway hotel operators had long realised that railway hotels constituted very difficult competition. The profits of the railway hotels were not important in terms of the performance of the whole railway company. If they lost money but made the railway's major freight customers happy, then that was an additional benefit. They could be perks for senior railway management looking for reasonable holidays. They could be impressive locations in which to deal with bankers. The hotels could, in fact, be loss leaders and, if the parent company didn't want to announce their financial performance, that could be arranged by creative accounting as well.

The development of rail travel, with its side benefits of additional customers for hotels, was also being augmented by the increasing number of passengers on liners. The first steam-propelled passenger ship to cross the Atlantic was the *Savannah* in 1819, though nobody would actually pay for the journey and she, therefore, arrived in Liverpool with her new cabins still unused. The second steam ship was the *Royal William* in 1833 which did little better and only managed to attract seven paying customers on her inaugural voyage. For many years after, the growth of transatlantic travel by steam was very slow. The sailing boats were long established but they were at the mercy of the winds and could lie becalmed for days or even weeks. Travel by sea was dangerous, and until the middle of the century it was quite usual to hold religious services and take leave of your friend as he prepared to board a ship, very much as if he was on his death bed.

There were also some very costly failures, like Brunel's *Great Eastern,* a mammoth ship which bankrupted the company originally set up to build her. She lost her reputation in a disastrous voyage in 1861 when a violent storm left her drifting helplessly for days. It was a terrible blow to Brunel who died shortly afterwards. "For a few short unprofitable years....the *Great Eastern* was a *bona fide*

Ritzy

transatlantic liner carrying thin lists of hundreds, in space prepared for thousands of passengers." But from the hotel industry's point of view there *were* hundreds, where there had been scores on smaller boats, and some lines were expanding successfully. There were more people travelling on the ships operated by Samuel Cunard, for instance, a Canadian whose vessels could proudly boast that they had never lost a passenger.

In the effort to make transatlantic ships pay, there were three main sources of business: freight, immigrants and travellers. It was a long time before the travellers were more than the icing on the cake. Much depended on new inventions, like the principle of screw propulsion instead of paddle wheels, and then twin screws, so that one could fail without disabling the ship. Speeds increased, so that journeys which at the beginning of the century could last a month or more, were steadily brought down to under a week at the end of it. Business started to improve, particularly after the end of the American Civil War.

By 1880 there were many fine liners on the Atlantic, fitted out more luxuriously than all but a handful of hotels, and ferrying passengers quickly and safely. In 1875 the Inman Line's *City of Berlin* took the Blue Riband for the fastest crossing of the Atlantic in 7 days, 18 hours and 2 minutes. Together with the White Star Line and Cunard, the 3 companies dominated the market.

The ships still carried sail in case anything went wrong, and indeed the first two Cunard ships to jettison that safeguard had cause to regret it. Both the *Umbria*, launched in 1884, and the *Etruria*, in 1885, broke down in mid-ocean and floundered about. There were still disasters, like the *City of Boston,* which sailed in 1870 and was never seen again. A worse tragedy, in terms of lives lost would, of course, occur in 1912 when the *Titanic* went down but, once the American Civil War was over and the United States began to play a larger part in economic affairs, the call of Europe drew increasing numbers of American visitors.

It was a two-way traffic, with Thomas Cook leading tours to the States and British businessmen and holidaymakers surveying the vast continent. The methods of American hoteliers, too, were studied by men like Richard D'Oyly Carte, the creator of the Savoy Hotel, a theatrical impresario deeply involved in the presentation of Gilbert and Sullivan operettas, but with a passion for hotels as well.

The pleasure of your company

The American visitors, meanwhile, brought with them their own standards of taste and hygiene, as well as habits of eating and living which differed in small ways from the Europeans. They enjoyed, for instance, their native tomato, and eventually this was introduced into England by the Savoy. They expected the technical achievements of their inventors to be available, such as smoother lifts, electric light and better plumbing. Hotels which wanted their custom badly enough were prepared to invest in these advances more quickly than might otherwise have been the case. Of course, a slump in America would reduce the numbers prepared to spend the considerable sum involved on a trip to Europe, but the trend over the years was steadily upwards.

The Americans did not restrict themselves to London. They could be found in the Hydropathic institutions, tramping the Scottish Highlands and visiting relatives from whom they or their parents would often have been separated for only a small span of years.

Those who reached Edinburgh were among the first to see the effects of over-optimistic and unplanned hotel development, as the demand for accommodation created in the 1840s had long since been fully met by the extra bedrooms built. Any form of state control to prevent over-capacity would have been anathema in an age where *laisser-faire* was the economic religion, but many hoteliers must have wished the situation was different, and in Edinburgh the expansion of hotels was not always a simple question of whether they would pay or not.

As the North British Railway Company was in competition with the Caledonian Railway Company, the North British Hotel was a weapon to get more business for the former's trains, but when the remodelling and reconstruction of the hotel was mooted in 1885, a number of shareholders opposed it vigorously and even went to court to try to stop it. They pointed out in a manifesto that the city's hotels were nearly empty for much of the year, and even at the peak of the season only a few sold all their rooms. Hadn't the Douglas Hotel, which was even patronised by the Prince and Princess of Wales, recently been converted into offices? Hadn't the Cafe Royal Hotel, which had been valued at £16,000, been sold in desperation for £9,500 and wasn't the Rainbow Hotel now business premises as well? Within 200 yards of the North British, they said, there were no less than 16 hotels including the North British, Waverley, Cockburn,

Star and Imperial, while another 5 minute journey would take the visitor to a further 14.

Of these the Caledonian, Roxburghe and George can still be found but there were a number of others at the time which failed to survive. The court listened but held, quite naturally, that the railway company had a perfect right to take whatever action it felt fit if a majority of the shareholders approved. There can be no question, however, that the dissenting shareholders were right and that the overall wastage of capital invested in Edinburgh hotels continued to be considerable.

The lessons of Edinburgh, predictably, had no effect on the investors in London, and the 1880s saw the beginning of that flood of new hotels which was eventually to create exactly the same result in the English capital. As early as 1880, the new magazine, the *Caterer*, was warning of the dangers of rank amateurs entering the industry. The occasion was the establishment of an ex-Army and Navy cooperative to run a hotel. The *Caterer* warned the prospective investors that no matter how glowing the prospectus, bankruptcy was bound to follow the operation of a hotel by people who understood nothing about the business. The journal also went as far as it dared by saying of the prospectus that: "the art of puffery has been used to the maximum." *Caterer* was proved right and the hotel, which opened in 1883, swiftly failed. It was sold in 1886 to a group headed this time by a professional, J.R. Cleave, who renamed it the Windsor and did very well with it. Cleave had worked for seven years as a cashier at the Langham and this training, together with the fact that his backers were able to buy the hotel for a fraction of its cost, gave him a good start. The hotel was also freehold, unlike many of the other newcomers, and within four years Cleave was the joint owner.

Disaster also befell Hatchetts, a hotel in Piccadilly opened in 1886 by a company headed by Frederick Gordon's highly successful relative, Horatio Davies, but which turned out to be one of his few defeats. Together with the land, the initial cost of Hatchetts was no less than £120,000, but in 1887 it went for £65,000. Even worse befell the Northumberland Avenue Hotel which had first been announced to a gullible public in the summer of 1882. The prospectus modestly suggested that a 19$\frac{1}{2}$% dividend would be nothing untoward and a mere £200,000 would be needed to build a 500 bedroom gold mine from which the directors would only take £2,500 a year - plus 5%

of any dividends over 15%! Isaacs and Florence, who had been responsible for the Holborn Viaduct Hotel and were to design the Coburg Hotel in 1896 (now the Connaught), were the architects in charge, and Viscount Pollington headed an imposing list of directors. Nevertheless, by the spring of 1884 the £9 shares had fallen to £2.17.6. (£2.871/2p) and when Judge Chitty put in the liquidator in the November there was precious little to salvage. The hotel building site was taken over by a Croydon contractor called J.W.Hobbs and a new company was formed under the chairmanship of Spencer (Jabez) Balfour, of whom we shall hear more later. Even so the hotel was not opened until 1887 at a final cost of £520,000. It was called the Victoria.

Failures were, in fact, quite commonplace. Like the conversion of the Cannon Street Hotel in Manchester into a vegetarian restaurant, and the fate of the Royal Hotel, Birmingham, which at one time was the best in the city. By 1881 it was: "regularly going bankrupt". Building and investing in hotels was becoming a fashion, giving numerous municipalities status, architects a method of advancing their theories, investors a stake in the equivalent of a Stately Home, and directors a business which combined glamour with luxury. It was a heady mixture but if: "where there's muck there's brass" then alternatively where there was glamour there might only be dross as far as profits were concerned.

About 300 receiving orders a year were made against publicans and hotel-keepers throughout the country, but the hotels which failed were, of course, only part of the story. More bedrooms were genuinely needed for the increase in business in many towns, so long as the hotels were constructed and run on a sensible basis. If the cost of servicing the capital was too great, if they were poorly situated or extravagantly managed, then there was trouble ahead. The same applies today. Many were well run and could offer the new guests higher standards than ever before.

Frederick Gordon's Metropole Hotel was built at the corner of Northumberland Avenue, next to the ill-fated Northumberland Avenue Hotel. Like his Grand Hotel nearby, architecturally it wasn't perfect. The Royal Institute of British Architects called: "the design commonplace and the detail coarse." They asked for changes, but the regulating authority, The Metropolitan Board of Works, decided not to put the tenant to the expense. So it remained, according to the RIBA:

Ritzy

"unworthy of its site." The Metropole was one of the newcomers in 1885, and set out in its 88 page brochure - of which 45 were paid advertising! - to bang the drum: "Particularly recommend it to ladies and families visiting the West End during the season; to travellers from Paris and the Continent, arriving from Dover and Folkestone at the Charing Cross Terminus; to Officers and others attending the levees at Buckingham Palace; and to Colonial and American visitors unused to the great world of London." Not in the brochure was reference to the suite on the first floor with a small private staircase to a discreet exit. It was often occupied by the actress, Lily Langtry, and it was widely believed that her appointments were "By Appointment". The hotel was ideally located for the palace. The Metropole wisely chose not to echo the complaint of the chairman of the Charing Cross Hotel that business had fallen off because of the: "dynamite outrages in Trafalgar Square", These were Fenian explosions because the problems of Ireland have been with us for a very long time.

It was during the summer that trade was at its brightest, but there would be plenty of businessmen at other times of the year, as well as the revenue from banqueting. At the height of the season accommodation would be hard to find and it was those brief periods which encouraged entrepreneurs to believe that London and the other cities could support more hotels. So they built them; the Central in Glasgow in 1883, with wine cellars sufficient for 60,000 bottles, the St. Ermins in Westminster in 1887, the Hyde Park Hotel in 1888, full of glorious period furniture, the Park Hotel, Cardiff in 1884, and many others. In the face of so much new competition, some of the older hotels started to decline. For example, when Claridge died in 1882, his hotel business was in poor shape.

So much building, so much capital invested, at least provided a gold mine for the furniture companies granted the contracts for furnishing and fitting out the new establishments. Foremost among those who benefited was Maple & Co., with its two guiding lights, John Maple and his son, John Blundell Maple. John Maple (1815-1900) opened his shop at 145, Tottenham Court Road in London in 1841, and by the time his sons, John Blundell and Harry, joined him in 1862 the store had grown and was well known as a drapery, furnisher and carpet supplier. Such a combination was particularly useful to companies putting up hotels, for the alternative was to deal with a number of suppliers, which was costly in terms of time and made it more difficult to get the best wholesale prices. Comparatively few organisations were equipped to handle large orders, but John Maple had the resources and could see what a wonderful opportunity this was to expand his business. The company already had a reputation for quality and though Harry had died by the 1880s, John Blundell had established many firm friendships with developers like Fred Gordon.

The contract for the Grand in Trafalgar Square went to Maples and after the press had acclaimed the results, Gordon also gave the firm a £70,000 contract for the First Avenue Hotel, where: "In the sleeping apartments and sitting rooms, the upholsterings are of a superb richness and exquisite delicacy." In 1882 Maples handled contracts as far apart as the County Hotel, Newcastle, the New Hotel, Preston, the Queens, Birmingham and the Royal Spithead, Isle of Wight. It seems likely that Maples were prepared to wait on occasions for their money, as there was a widespread habit during the period of hiring furniture, very much like the system we now call Hire Purchase. If a hotelkeeper fell into arrears, the company could apply to repossess the furniture, though this was a desperation measure; guests seldom took any more care of their bedrooms in Victorian times than they do today, and there was the usual excessive amount of wear and tear. Maples, of course, did not have the field to themselves by any means, but they were the most popular company and had the added cachet that they were also engaged by hotels overseas and thus had an international aura.

Although the public watched eagerly for the opening of new hotels, many of the older hotels continued to maintain their special place as long as they filled a particular niche; such a hotel was Andertons in Fleet Street which looked after generations of newspapermen at very reasonable charges and produced sufficiently good results to try to go public in 1884, though with-out success. 100 bedrooms, a coffee-room where lunch cost two shillings (10p), a Masonic temple and a thriving bar produced a turnover in 1883 of nearly £24,000 for a 9% profit after depreciation. Although it wasn't glamorous enough, it was really a sounder proposition than many which did float successfully.

The best hotel in London was reputed to be the Bristol which was small and very select, but the Clarendon ran it close. When Lord Chesterfield retired as Master of the Buckhounds in 1880, the

Ritzy

banquet in his honour featured a menu for which the hotel charged six guineas (£6.30), a sum which would have kept one of the chefs and his family for a month. Amazingly, in today's money, that would be about £350 a head.

Most of the new hotels in London followed the same pattern of architecture and management that had been pioneered by the early railway hotels 20-30 years before, but one was very different and that was the Savoy.

It is difficult to see the Savoy through eyes clear of the smoke screen put up by generations of their excellent professional publicists. From the very beginning the Savoy was in show business, a hotel built by Irishman Richard D'Oyly Carte in the heart of the theatre district where he had made his fortune producing Gilbert & Sullivan operettas. The building was started in 1884 and finished in 1889; it wasn't at all like the type of building put up by a Barry or a Gilbert Scott. D'Oyly Carte had been influenced by the quality of the American hotels and tried to incorporate the best of the two transatlantic traditions; the Savoy was the first hotel to have a really substantial proportion of its bedrooms equipped with private bathrooms, an eccentricity which led the builder to enquire whether it was anticipated that the guests would be amphibious! There were 80 private bathrooms originally. Then the whole building was constructed of concrete, encasing steel joists, to make it entirely fire-proof. Apart from the doors and window frames there was very little wood used. D'Oyly Carte had no less than 6 lifts installed, though it was still necessary to point out that they were : "perfectly safe, their movement smooth, rapid and pleasant." The building was: "faced in Doulton Carrara Ware, that is a white, matt, glazed terracotta" and it was far simpler in appearance than the Gothic or Italian Renaissance designs which were fashionable before.

As was natural with a showman, D'Oyly Carte set out to attract his friends in the arts and, through them, the high society who enjoyed their company. His Board included Michael Gunn, the manager of the Gaiety Hotel, Dublin, the Earl of Lathom, who was Lord Chamberlain, Hwfa Williams, a sportsman friend of the Prince of Wales, well known in fashionable circles, and two financiers, R.B.Fenwick and A.H.Weguelin. It was a powerful board, financially and socially, but it had little knowledge of running hotels.

There is a major difference between constructing a hotel with the most modern facilities and trying to run it to a high standard. It was an excellent marketing gimmick to have a Restaurant Committee, composed of cool gourmets like Reuben Sassoon and Arthur Sullivan, and a nice piece of stage dressing to have: "a seneschal wearing a silver chain" usher you into the dining room, but this did not mean that the food would be cooked well, the waiting immaculate or the wines well selected.

The hotel was designed with great care; there was electricity throughout and you could turn the lights off when you were in bed without crossing the room. Twenty four hour service was the proud boast, with no extra charges for attendance, and the upper floor rooms were just as large as the lower ones. So there were plenty of attractive features for the brochure, but the hotel had taken five years to build and the lavish outlay on the seven storeys, the artesian well 500 feet, (160m), down, the Genoese lounge and all the other exotic public rooms, had built up a large capital outlay. Yet the type of knowledgeable guests who D'Oyly Carte wanted to use the Savoy were not going to come more than once if the hotel was run less than perfectly.

D'Oyly Carte had already tried to get one of the great professionals on the continent to manage the Savoy. This was Cesar Ritz, who had built a reputation on the Riviera and in Switzerland and Germany, which gave him a fan club of important guests, second to none. He was a perfectionist and a true expert but he was also deeply involved in many other undertakings and was hard to persuade to join D'Oyly Carte. Only after a lot of cajoling and the promise of a massive fee, did he agree to even visit the Savoy, so that D'Oyly Carte could proclaim his connection with the undertaking. When he first arrived it was announced discreetly that he would be the restaurant manager, but within a few days he had agreed to run the hotel completely.

At the time the hotel was not doing well; as reported at the time: "Directors and management are by no means in perfect accord", and the story of Ritz's arrival and the prosperity he brought has been one of the best known happy endings in the industry's folklore. It was not quite that simple though, and it was not to end happily at all. To start with it was necessary to get rid of the incumbent manager, William Hardwicke, and he had a perfectly valid three year contract. Dismissed by D'Oyly Carte with a lordly wave of his magic wand,

Ritzy

Hardwicke refused to vanish like the Demon King and instead issued a writ for £3,125 which the Savoy, according to the *Caterer*, had to settle out of court for the full amount. Even so, the career of a man who had risen slowly and painfully to a high position in his profession, suffered a setback from which it was impossible to recover and Hardwicke sank to managing a relatively insignificant seaside hotel on the South coast.

With the Hardwicke problem out of the way, Ritz could settle down with his established and memorable team of departmental heads, starring Auguste Escoffier, his great chef, and including Autour, his No:1, Agostini to look after the accounts and Echenard, a *maître d'hôtel* deeply steeped in experience as a connoisseur of wine. The clients could now be guaranteed to come, but as the expenses involved in opening the hotel had been great, and as Ritz did not like to economize, it was difficult to make substantial profits from the investment for some years.

The Savoy not only spearheaded the changes to come in constructing and running a luxury hotel, but also catered to the family hedonists as they won their battle over the forces of restraint. The Victorian ideals of self-help, hard work and Christian virtues, and the rather wide definition of sin, had been fundamental in building the nation to its preeminent position by the 1880s. But now there was a growing desire to enjoy the fruits of father's labour and instead of building companies by leading from the factory floor, there appeared a numerous class of share-holders only interested in collecting dividends and letting hired managers get on with the job of keeping the wheels in motion.

The constraints were under fire and some of those attacked affected the hotel industry; D'Oyly Carte, for instance, wanted to encourage people to dine in hotels by choice rather than eat in a hotel only if they were staying there. He also wanted them to be able to dine later, for his restaurant, like all others, was most heavily patronized between 6 and 8.30 in the evening. Others felt the same, for at this time banquets would start with a reception at 5 o'clock in the afternoon and would usually have finished by 11 at the latest. This was understandable in terms of the early days of the century when to be out late at night in ill-lit streets was to invite trouble. Sounds familiar? But there were no highwaymen left at Hyde Park Corner, even if mugging with a sandbag was a risk the unwary pedestrians were warned about; it was called sandbagging. Street lighting had improved and being home early started to seem dull and prudish to many perfectly respectable people. It was a long road to the 20th century but the hotels, for totally selfish reasons, were eager to support any liberalisation of laws or customers, affecting dining out.

One area of catering which improved a good deal was that at exhibitions. This was largely due to a new firm, called J. Lyons & Co. It was the brainchild of Montague Gluckstein, who had a cigar making company. He saw the opportunity presented to caterers by exhibitions which regularly attracted audiences running into the millions. He, therefore, decided to compete for the catering contracts, together with his brother, Isidore, and his brother-in-law, Barnett Salmon. They didn't fancy risking the reputation of their tobacco business by associating the new company, initially, with either family name. So they asked a mutual friend, Joseph if they could use his name. The company was formed in 1887 and the Newcastle Jubilee Exhibition in that year was its first venture, followed by Glasgow, the largest since 1862, in 1888. The first exhibitions were a great success and a second J.Lyons & Co. was formed in 1889. There were 5,000 shares and if you had more than 1,200 you could be a director. Many of the directors and all of the power thereafter remained within the Salmon and Gluckstein families.

The seaside hotels also did well unless they had to face some luxurious newcomer across the road. The Brighton Grand, for instance, having got over the inefficiency of the original board, was able to pay a 9% dividend in 1886 and 1887, only to find its good work undermined by the arrival of Frederick Gordon's new Metropole Hotel. Any idea that lavish expenditure was confined to the capital could be instantly dismissed by looking at this new wonder. The Metropole was designed by no less a luminary than the President of the Royal Institute of British Architects, Alfred Waterhouse, who had a passion for red brick and terracotta. A lot of his work is still extant.

As this was a Gordon Hotel, Maples were responsible for the furnishings and one of Gordon's Riviera friends was also involved: " the fine statuary marble place is from the chisel of Prince Victor of Hohenlohe." There were 700 rooms and: "the decorations are in a warm rich golden brown, graduating to ivory white." The Metropole had three dining-rooms which could be divided by glass walls or seat

Ritzy

500 guests at a time. There was a grand staircase of finely polished marble, a library, smoking-room, lounge, billiard rooms, iron wine bins: "sufficient for 20,000 dozen apart from wines in the wood" and many different varieties of bath: Turkish Baths, Russian Baths, plunge baths, Apodyterum and Moorish divans. It was suitably exotic for a town which could boast the flamboyant Royal Pavilion, and from the back windows you could see: "the beautifully terraced Italian garden which is one of the beauties of the hotel."

The grounds adjoining hotels all over the country were a greater part of the attraction for visitors at this time than they can be today when land is so very expensive. There were tennis courts adjoining the Midland Hotel, Derby, gardens in many of the London hotels and, at the seaside, winter gardens were often constructed as well. The winter gardens were a determined effort to avoid the vagaries of the English climate. Roofed-in with glass and heated with pipes, they were apparently impervious to the weather and it was hoped that guests would be happy to wander through the floral displays, write letters at the tables provided, read, knit, crochet, embroider, smoke cigars, sip wine or just quietly snooze. The idea was sound enough but the upkeep of the buildings was an added overhead to hotels with only a short high season.

The railways tried hard to get visitors during the quieter winter months and by 1880 they were already running weekend, bargain-priced, packaged holidays. You could depart first-class from Liverpool Street Station in the City on Saturday after lunch and be met at Harwich by a porter from the town's Great Eastern Hotel. Then, your luggage having been carried to the hotel for you, tea would be served and, until Monday morning, you would have all your meals and accommodation provided. You would leave for London again after breakfast on Monday and pay a total of 35 shillings (£1.75) for the weekend. That would be about two weeks salary for a chef. Many seaside hotels offered special weekend terms and twelve shillings and six pence (62½p) was a popular tariff for full board from Saturday till Monday morning at smaller places like the Grosvenor Hotel, New Brighton, in 1884.

In spite of seasonal difficulties and greater competition, hotels in the 1880s fared pretty well because there was an increase in the size of the middle class prepared to use them, and in tourists and businessmen, but at the same time expenses remained very stable. The chairman of the Langham announced in 1881 that:"the undertaking has now arrived at a point when its progress would be most marked, and money would be literally coined by the company." Birmingham was so short of hotel accommodation that shops were converted into bedrooms!

An examination of the dividend performance around the country during the decade helps to explain the ready support for new ventures; the Midland Hotel in Birmingham paid 121/2% from 1882 onwards, the Queens in Harrogate 12% in 1884 when the £5 shares stood at £8, the Alexandra in London 9% from 1884, the Queens in Hastings over 10%, while with Gordon's Hotels, as one shareholder ruefully recalled in less palmy days in 1912: "ordinary shares went to a 50% premium. They originally paid 121/2% and could have paid 20%." These high dividends still have to be compared with gilt-edged government stocks paying 31/2%.

Gordon was aiming for a new market at the Grand, believing that there should be hotels offering luxury surroundings at prices that would attract the middle classes, and this proved extremely sound. As the standard of living improved over the next 50 years, this concept would be applied by Lyons to the less affluent still, and Sir Billy Butlin at his holiday camps to an even less well-to-do strata than that. Hotels, as we have seen, did seek out particular sections of the market, as they had done in the earlier part of the century, for the class barriers of Victorian society made mixing a problem. At the Metropole, London, for example, porters would deliver letters to guests staying in suites but, if you only had a bedroom, you would have to collect your post from the porter's desk.

Life in a good hotel at this point was getting steadily more opulent. Your three shilling and six penny (171/2p) breakfast at the Metropole now included: *"Beefsteak au beurre d'Anchois*, grilled devilled legs of chicken and fried soles." You could also have grilled ham, porridge, cold meats and various other snacks with your tea, cocoa or chocolate. The basic price of your bedroom changed very little over the course of the decade. At the Grand it was three shillings and six pence (171/2p) throughout the period for a single room. On the other hand, the Grand was one of the few hotels which would tell the guest from the start what he was letting himself in for, as there seemed to be some polite reluctance to tackle the manager on this score and tariffs used the word 'from' when listing room prices.

Ritzy

Baedeker's famous guide pointed out to its readers that the cost varied according to the floor, and advised them to ask about the exact amount soon after they arrived.

It appears likely, however, that prices also varied in many establishments according to how much the client appeared able to pay, and how busy the hotel was at the time. The tariff for bedrooms was usually raised if the guest did not accept *demi-pension* but this was an accepted practice. At the Grand: "The policy was to get a lump sum. A man likes to know when he enters what he has to pay."

To modern eyes it seems strange that the cost of a meal was often as much or even more than the cost of accommodation. At the Empire Hotel, Bath, for example, the cost of a single bedroom was 'from' four shillings and six pence (22 1/2p), a double bedroom 'from' six shillings and six pence (32 1/2p) but dinner was definitely five shillings and six pence (27 1/2p). In fairness, it was quite a dinner. "The Empire dinner is served at separate tables in the Dining Room from 7 to 8.30 and consists of Hors d'oeuvres, Soup, Fish, Entrée, Joint, Poultry or Game, Sweets and Dessert, also Coffee served in Lounge." Portions were smaller than today, but not by that much and the diners lived in blissful ignorance of the penalties of excessive overeating. Lunch was another heavy meal, usually served between 1 and 2.30, and breakfast was really equally substantial. The Empire hotel's breakfast was three shillings (15p) but an additional shilling (5p) was charged for guests who wanted poultry - and they didn't mean eggs!

Apart from eating, and presumably resting after eating, the guest at a good hotel also expected a considerable amount more help with his entertainment than he receives now. The best tickets for theatrical performances were available and sightseeing tours would start from the hotel. Carriages and horses would take visitors to the races and in the spas you could, of course, hire invalid chairs. Frederick Gordon, always one to try to offer that little bit more, had the idea that visitors might like to spend time not only in a central hotel but also in a country mansion. To that end he purchased Bentley Priory, a splendid stately home in Stanmore. As communications were difficult - the railway line ended at Harrow - he also built a railway from Harrow to Stanmore for his prospective guests! Gordon was never one to let trifling problems stand in his way! The pretty little station in Gordon Avenue is now an attractive private house. The idea was not a success, though, so Gordon sold the railway and moved into the Priory, with his wife, 11 children and the usual brigade of servants. Obviously needing a small hotel for such a ménage.

In the 1880s hotel bills recalled the saying that big trees from little acorns grow. Wherever you turned, there seemed to be more money to pay. A fire in the bedroom in the evening cost a shilling (5p), and if you were extravagant enough to have one for the whole day during the winter, it would cost as much as two shillings and six pence. (121/2p) A sponge hip bath would be six pence (21/2p) and up to two shillings (10p) if you took one in the public bathroom. When you took an ordinary flat bath, the chambermaid would come staggering along the passage, humping a large jug of hot water and another of cold, so that a tip would be almost obligatory. The bath itself would be under the bed. When this element of hotel bedroom furnishing finally ended its useful life many years later, one wonders what happened to the vast number of surplus hip-baths dotted around the country. It was also not unusual for guests to bring their own baths with them and, in addition to trunks, the porters might have to manhandle metal bath-chairs or rubber tubs into the bedroom. It was not surprising that porters needed wheelbarrows to transport the guests' trunks and impedimenta from entrance to bedroom.

The battle between staff and guests for tips to add to the attendance charge was waged on many fronts. It had been the custom for years that guests eating in the dining-room would pay their bill to the waiter, rather than sign the account and have it placed with the rest of the charges. But: "paying at the time gives the waiters too favourable an opportunity for exacting fees" and Gordons at least introduced signing. The guest was definitely at a disadvantage otherwise, trying to argue with a waiter in a room filled with other diners, all of whom, in the better hotels were, of course, in full evening dress.

Even in the 1880s the visitors had little choice but to eat in the hotel: "In those days there were very few respectable restaurants in which to dine out. Lord and Lady Randolph Churchill when they first married, could only find the St. James Hotel (where the Bristol now stands) where according to her memoirs, there was a dingy dining room lighted with gas and an apology of a dinner". At the hotels there would be an ample choice, but the small touches you expect as a matter of course now, were almost completely unknown:

125

Ritzy

"If cooks could only be induced to garnish their dishes and serve them up daintily" complained the *Caterer*: "they would be far more appetising. For example, a few sprigs of parsley around a dish, a little chopped up and sprinkled over fried potatoes or a beefsteak, makes all the difference in the world to their appearance....a few fried onions helps out a beefsteak immensely....a handful of watercress greatly helps the look of a roast of beef."

The major complaints against the large new hotels were not, however, in the realms of cuisine or charges for the small extras; the main complaint was the way in which guests had become items on a conveyor belt. Well within the memory of the experienced hotel client were the days when the guest would be greeted by the manager on arriving at the hotel. He was now shown to his room by a receptionist. Guests missed the magisterial word of welcome, the personal touch which could still be found on the continent. It was bad enough being away from home in a strange town without losing that personal reassurance that the manager knew you were there and was anxious to see that you were well looked after.

Many of the wealthy guests were much more accustomed to personal attention in their own homes than we are today. It rankled that ringing the bell for service in the bedroom did not result in the almost immediate response from the chambermaid that would be forthcoming from their own servants. A wife who selected her own staff from the countless applicants available did not take kindly to a waiter who was less impressive, and consequently complained that: "the down-at-heel, shabby-genteel, grey whiskered grandfatherly personage who reeks of gin and invariably says 'comin' sur' as he goes away, still survives in the hotel world."

In hotels in the 21st century guests do many things for themselves without thinking; turning on the taps, pushing lift buttons, switching on the light and, therefore, need help from hotel staff less frequently. If, however, you had to wait for hot water to wash, for instance, the speed of service would become a matter of greater urgency. In a small hotel where there were fewer guests to look after, the problem was not so acute, but in the large units it was a constant source of irritation.

Many guests had by now decided to make the hotel their permanent home; the residents might include well-to-do young men, middle aged bachelors who couldn't be bothered to keep a home, childless couples and wealthy widows, but these regular guests soon learned how to cope.

The danger for the hotels in the future could be seen in the ingenuous comments of one contented commentator in 1887. "And yet with all this luxury and splendour - we refer particularly, of course, to gastronomy - it is pleasant to note that the prices for procuring the same have not increased in anything like the same proportion. A good dinner can now be procured, served in a magnificently upholstered and otherwise fitted-up dining hall, resplendent with gilt carving, statuary, mirrors, stained glass and first class pictures, accompanied by high-class vocal and instrumental music, for from three shillings and six pence (171/2p) upwards, and courses in the menu numerous, and the whole well-cooked and well-served."

All of which was splendid except that the prices had not risen in keeping with the quality of the product. When they had to, it was going to come as an unpleasant shock to the clientele who would react by looking elsewhere.

As the industry expanded, new areas for cooperation emerged. To improve standards 1889 saw the creation of the Universal Cookery & Food Association which would be responsible for many years for the industry's great exhibition - Hotelympia. Another society was founded in the same year, which would also stand the test of time. This was the Reunion des Gastronomes, devoted to improving the standard of British haute cuisine, even if it wouldn't take women members - and continued not to do so long past the end of the period this book covers.

Which brings us to the not always so Gay Nineties.

9
The nine day wonders 1890 - 1899

"The Gay Nineties" is so familiar a sobriquet that it comes as something of a shock to discover that the gaiety was not so apparent to the Victorians who were alive at the time; the decade ended with the Boer War and started with a particularly nasty financial scare, as Barings, one of the most solid pillars of the banking establishment, came within an ace of crashing due to South American loans of the utmost recklessness. Oddly enough, a hundred years later, an executive in their Singapore office was even more culpable and the company did collapse. In 1890 confidence in the City was badly shaken, Bank Rate went temporarily to the then crisis level of 6% and the middle classes pulled in their ample belts in just such areas as spending in hotels. Frederick Gordon was lucky enough to see his enormous flotation of over £2 million successfully completed just before the trouble broke and: "within two or three weeks of the issue, the debenture stock was quoted at four-and-a-half to five-and-a-half premium and the ordinary to one and a quarter." Part of the reason lay in the restricted market in hotel shares. Punters wanting a ticket for this glamorous expanding industry could best participate by buying some Gordons. And it *was* expanding still. Marie Ritz recalled that it was a time when London couldn't get enough new hotels and the *Caterer* reported that: "in regard to London hotels, the cry is 'still they come' ".

For a dispassionate view of the architectural merit of later Victorian hotels, it was necessary to wait for the promotional hype to die down. Then in *Caterer's* 1928 Golden Jubilee issue, the boot really went in: "whose title to remembrance rests on their structural deceits and interior conceits....On rubble filled pillars....were imposed inferior brickwork structures....internal discomfort....only ended when the shabbiness from the green dampness of the external walls, crumbling of stuccoed reliefs and pediments, heralding the complete decay which set in a few years after their opening, made it very soon good business to close them."

Well, in fairness, a considerable number of the structures are still with us today but, true, there was often a good deal of jerrybuilding. Artistically, hotels remained one of the areas where new ideas could be displayed to advantage. The Pre-Raphaelite movement with its ability in: "staining wallpapers with poetry", was coming into fashion. Rococo, French Baroque and, in a few years time, Art Nouveau, all produced examples of their styles in British hotels.

Each new hotel was hailed as the most wonderful ever, but there was no question of which would be the largest, for Jabez Balfour, the owner of the Victoria Hotel, had purchased from the Cecil family a site on the Embankment which was going to be large enough to build a 1,000 bedroom hotel and work was progressing on this immense development. Frederick Gordon saw both this venture and the Victoria, which was situated next to his Metropole in Northumberland Avenue, as serious local competitors. The Victoria had been completed in 1887, 2 years after the Metropole, and Balfour was as important in the City and as respectable as Gordon himself.

Since 1868 when Balfour's Liberator Building Society had first been launched, the public had flocked to place their savings in his organization, promoted in many instances by non-conformist ministers endeavouring to augment their stipends. The Liberator offered the splendid return of 8% interest a year and successive stock issues of new Balfour offerings were always over-subscribed. With buildings like the Victoria as tangible evidence of the prestigious uses to which the investors' money was being allocated, Balfour's reputation flourished and he was elected Mayor of Croydon and the member for the constituency.

Although Balfour was almost a dwarf in stature, he had a tremendous personality and radiated confidence. He was also one of the cleverest and most heartless crooks of his age and he had built his empire on the purest sand. It was the old trick of paying the 8% dividends out of the new capital the public subscribed, for the only profits his companies made were diverted into his own pockets and those of his cronies. In September 1893 the bank he had founded to handle the flood of money he was lent, suspended payment and, as he was fleeing to Chile, a yawning abyss of £12 million opened up under his unfortunate supporters. Unluckily for Balfour, he was recognized by a visitor to South America, extradited and sentenced to 14 years in prison. The liquidator of the wildly complicated mess he left behind found a partially completed monster hotel to deal with as well as the Victoria. Frederick Gordon stepped in to buy the Victoria and: "Gordon Hotels have got rid of a formidable rival by swallowing it whole."

The price was £417,433, a snip compared to the cost of building it in the first place, and the price included not only the lease, the four bathrooms, the furnishings and the stock, but also such trifles as the dinner contracts for the 9th Norfolk Regiment, the Buffs, the Grand Masters Chapter and the Institute of Civil Engineers. There was also an income of £1,500 a year from the sale of showcases to no less than 32 companies; Liberty's had a year for £50, Cadbury's for £10, the U.K. Tea Company for £83.10.0. (£83.50), and Grierson Oldham, the wine company, three years for £25 a year. Many of the Victorians were extremely able when it came to selling advertising space in their hotels and it is doubtful whether any British hotel today has a comparable income from showcases, in real money terms.

The manager of the Victoria at the time was George Reeves-Smith, who was to go on to be the most important British hotelier in the first half of the 20th century. He reminisced about the primitive Victoria plumbing many years later. "There were hundreds of flat baths, capable of holding a few inches of water, one under every bed; a few Sitz or hip-baths were available for anyone who wanted a greater depth of water. The corridors were cold during the winter and a coal fire was necessary in every room occupied. There was no central heating, no hot and cold running water in the bedrooms." And the Victoria was a luxury hotel.

It was not by any means the only new venture for Gordons during the decade. The Cliftonville Hotel, Margate came in the same year, the Burlington, Eastbourne was enlarged in 1895, the Lord Warden in Dover in 1896 and the Metropole in Folkestone opened in 1898. It is a stunning building overlooking the sea and was a great asset to Folkestone as a resort. In the early stages, however, it was refused a provisional liquor licence by the Justices in 1893. Only after considerable difficulty was the decision reversed, without which the whole concept would have foundered.

Finally the Grosvenor at Victoria was leased from the London & South East Railway. To pay for all the acquisitions and improvements, more ordinary and debenture stock was issued until the company had to service a capital of approximately £3 million. Raising money in the market to finance expansion was - and remains - a perfectly normal method of expansion, but having to raise money to keep the existing assets in good shape *was* dangerous. Efforts could successfully be made to disguise the truth by suggesting that the new cash would help to produce greater profits by improving the hotels, but this was only the case when tariffs could be increased accordingly, and often they could not.

Gordon had every incentive to pay high dividends, for any distribution above 8% meant that an additional payment had to be made to the holders of a class of stock called Founders Shares. There were 100 of these Founder Shares and a 1% distribution over 8% cost the company between £5,000 and £10,000, distributed to the lucky holders. To give an indication of what this was worth to Gordon, the split in 1893 would have brought him £2,560 personally, apart from the declared dividend on the ordinary and preference shares he owned. It was not surprising that the *Statist*, a highly regarded commentator on economic affairs, reported to its readers: "there is nothing for depreciation from the enormous £2,841,000 at which purchase price the properties and business and capital expenditure stands in the balance sheet. The transfer of only £17,000 to general reserve gives an idea of the disposition to divide profits up to the hilt, which is referred to in the Board of Trade Committee's report, as usually characteristic of Founders Shares companies." The criticism had no effect on the price of the Gordon Hotel Company shares which continued to rise to the general satisfaction of all the shareholders.

Gordon Hotels were by no means alone in arriving at the situation where most of the profits had to be distributed. The investors wanted high dividends, the founders benefited even more from the same policy, the hotels when new needed little spending on them and tomorrow's problems could be taken care of by hoping that they would not materialise. But tomorrow's problems could only be minimised if there were two favourable factors; stable prices and a lack of meaningful competition. The Victorian business community at the time was cocooned by the pre-eminence of the belief that nothing would ever change, and for a number of years there actually was deflation and all was well. But it really couldn't last as far as the hotel business was concerned, if only because of the expense of repairing dilapidation and fighting the envious competition which did spring up.

Gordon Hotels was only one of the incipient chain operations. Another was the group of Midland Railway Hotels which from 1885 had been the day-to-day responsibility of William Towle.

Ritzy

The Midland had decided to develop the hotel operation in order to strengthen its position in the major provincial cities along its routes. As a consequence, together with the Midland Grand in London, the Midland, Derby and the Queens in Leeds, William Towle found himself involved in the building of the Midland, Bradford - which was needed to compete with the hotel of the London and North Eastern - and in controlling hotels in Morecambe Bay and Normanton. By 1890 he was believed to be taking home the largest salary of any hotel manager in Europe. In the same year the company bought the Adelphi, Liverpool, to further increase his responsibilities. The Adelphi went for £105,000, so that the original shareholders got their money back with a 5% bonus, but in view of Radley's initial achievements, the outcome says little for the efforts of his successors.

Towle was a great champion of the industry and a prolific writer on the unfair treatment he felt it received from successive governments and official bodies. In the Jubilee edition of the *Railway News* he wrote: " the nation owes a debt of gratitude to the Railway companies for the provision of many good hotels which would certainly never have been built by other capital." Another writer in the same magazine in 1925 suggested: "In more recent years the Midland Railway developed its hotel building plans to an abnormal degree, erecting big hotels at great expense at Manchester and Liverpool, catering mainly for relatively wealthy travellers. It had over £2,366,000 sunk in hotel ventures." It wasn't, in fact, a lot of money by comparison with the total capital involved in running a railway.

The philosophy of the railways hadn't changed over the years. Hotels were a natural partner to trains because when the journey was over, a lot of passengers needed somewhere to stay. If there was nowhere suitable, they might not travel. Pan American Airways would adopt exactly the same policy after the Second World War, building hotels in cities which lacked fine hotels, and the InterContinental Hotel Corporation emerged as a result. The railway hotels were also used as regional depots for the catering needs of passengers. They supplied refreshment rooms and dining cars in their area. Towle's initiative with the lunch baskets in Derby had grown into a massive catering operation.

The railway companies wanted the hotels to attract customers onto the trains. They would, on occasions, leave them open during the winter to encourage rail traffic, when it would have saved their hotel division money if they had closed the hotels. The competing demands of the trains and hotels were usually an in-house problem for the railway company. What would happen though if a hotel company leased the hotels from the railway? That came about with Gordon Hotels who leased the Grosvenor at Victoria from the London & South East Railway and additional South Coast properties thereafter. In a position to referee would eventually be the Earl of Bessborough, as chairman of both companies. He definitely had a conflict of interests on occasions with the seaside properties.

While Gordon Hotels made most of their money from their London operations, Midland had to pay much more attention to the provincial hotels. Much of the control of the hotels was the result of an endless stream of memoranda from Towle, setting down in great detail every minute policy he wished to have followed. The memoranda were mounted in each hotel in special reference books, called Guard Books, and at the end of each missive was the command to: "Acknowledge Receipt." Having done so, a manager could hardly excuse any failure by saying he was unaware of the policy; it was a very effective, if cumbersome, approach to a problem which concerns every hotel chain chief to this day.

In each hotel there was usually both a superintendent and a secretary. While the secretary dealt with business matters the superintendent was responsible for discipline, staff management, the reception of visitors and the maintenance of standards. The supplies the hotels needed were bought in the open market and the superintendent could personally select them without reference to his head office. The hotels blended their own tea and coffee, and bottled their own wine. Mrs. Towle, apart from having two sons, Francis and Arthur, also took responsibility for 600-700 female staff and was undoubtedly a very strong personality.

Compared to their father's humble upbringing, Francis and Arthur had the best, both being educated at Marlborough and Francis going on to Trinity College, Cambridge. Arthur worked in hotels overseas until, in 1896, the two young men joined their father in the company. From 1898 onwards they were joint assistant managers. They were only 18 and 20 but they were under the paternal eye of their father and continued in that role until 1911 when all three became joint managers, prior to William Towle's retirement in 1914.

Ritzy

The Towles can lay fair claim to being the most distinguished family of British hoteliers until the Fortes, as William and Frank were both eventually knighted and Arthur came to run the largest hotel company in Europe, when all the Midland Railway Hotels were put together under his control in 1925.

There were about 1,500 staff engaged in running the seven hotels during the 1890s, with the chief clerk in London supervising 25 staff and the accounts department in Derby mustering 30, but this was not overstaffing at a time when so much of the work had to be done in laborious longhand. William Towle certainly did run fine hotels and he did not skimp on the quality of the employees; chefs like M. Mestivier at Liverpool or M. Briais at the Midland Grand at St. Pancras could turn out work comparable to any other luxury hotel restaurant.

The standard of British cuisine rose steadily and the leader of the crusade was Auguste Escoffier, together with Cesar Ritz; the most famous hotel names to come out of the whole century. Escoffier was married to a French poetess named Delphine Daffis but the lady played about 12th fiddle to his beloved kitchen, and when she decided that the London climate was not to her liking and returned to France, Escoffier only felt it necessary to visit her on very rare occasions. Otherwise he was left to devote himself entirely to the propagation of a cuisine which enshrined not only *his* good ideas but those of many of his less literary colleagues, and also to the evolution of of a new method of running a kitchen.

Escoffier came to the Savoy in 1890 at Ritz's request and soon realised that British methods of cooking could use a little refining. The tradition of Carême had been primarily a search for ever better displays of food; to serve 40 guests at a meal with the Prince Regent, Carême once produced well over 100 dishes. The food looked magnificent but it would be tepid when you were finally allowed to eat it, and you could only take what you wanted from the platters within your reach. Etiquette would not permit a guest at the time to ask for a dish to be passed along the table. The manner of service changed during the next 70 years and, in the late Victorian quality hotel dining-room, the guest could order from a lengthy *table d'hôte* menu.

Escoffier improved on the prevailing system of cooking in three ways. He improved the speed of service by producing an assembly line; previously, when a chef received an order, he would be responsible for putting together all its ingredients. For an *oeuf poché Florentine*, for example, one chef would produce the spinach, the cheese sauce and the poached egg. In Escoffier's system the vegetable chef would prepare the spinach and the egg and then the saucier would provide the cheese sauce. The dish could be prepared quicker and the finished product would be checked by Escoffier, himself, before it left the kitchen to ensure that it was correct. There would be seven *parties* (fractions); larder, soup, sauce, fish, roast and grill, vegetables and patisserie.

When Escoffier moved with Ritz later in the decade to open, first the Ritz in Paris and then Ritz's Carlton Hotel in London, the kitchen operation had been made so smooth that it was possible to offer the guests a new style of menu; *à la carte*. Here the guest would order his dinner hours in advance and he could choose anything he liked, within reason, though often with the help of the restaurateur.

Escoffier also simplified the number of dishes for banquets still further so that, by comparison with Carême's 100 dishes, he might only have 40 for a menu for Edward VII.

To Escoffier, and indeed to many of the great chefs, the kitchen was more a temple than a factory. He spent much of his life within its walls, and there grew up a meticulous ritual, with Escoffier as high priest. Working for the high priest was not only a great honour but an awesome experience for the new chef until he had settled in. Unlike many chefs, Escoffier was not a bully; he did not lose his temper and, when angry, would retire to his cubby-hole until he had cooled off. He allowed no drinking in his kitchen except for an unlimited quantity of a barley drink which was always available. The heat in the Victorian kitchen was fierce, for although gas cooking had been patented by Robert Hicks as early as 1831, most hotel chefs still preferred to work with wood and coal. Consequently most managements allowed their chefs large quantities of beer, just like the steelworkers of the time, in order to replace the body's liquid loss. Beer was safer than water, anyway, unless a good drainage system was available, though public plumbing had been much improved and the Savoy did have its own well. Even so there was a severe typhus epidemic in London in 1905.

Escoffier is, of course, famous for his *Guide Culinaire*, a comprehensive recipe book which was to be the 'bible' of chefs for most of the next 100 years. If there were any arguments about the correct preparation of a dish, the last word on the subject would be Escoffier's decision in the *Guide*. The great man spent hours, not only in setting down the recipes, but also in inventing new dishes. To a public which had been accustomed to a limited cuisine for most of their lives, this new world of exotic tastes had unlimited fascination. Escoffier was constantly called upon to create something new and even more exciting. This was his great joy, though he grumbled, with a good deal of justification, that he was the only type of artist who could neither patent nor copyright his inventions, for though the new dishes might take him many hours to create, any chef could then copy them, down to the last detail.

The influence of Escoffier was not only in the *Guide Culinaire* but also in his great reputation among his fellow chefs and in the number of men he trained during his long period in London; his disciples looked on him with awe and affection and, like any first class leader, he earned their respect, both by being able to do anything in the kitchen better than they could, and by being prepared to work longer and harder than anybody else. Long after he retired to Monaco, he would occasionally accept invitations to visit the kitchens of great hotels where he would be received as a venerable sage by his admirers.

It was Ritz's belief that a great restaurant was vital to the success of a great hotel and this Escoffier provided, without either of them apparently being too concerned with the cost as the years went by. Both the maestros wanted to go further by creating the all-embracing, perfect hotel. Any restrictions which came from the board of directors proved increasingly irksome, as they realised how much the clients came to the Savoy specifically because of their professional ability. Ritz worked for hours on selecting the right shade of bulb for his innovative, concealed lighting in the Savoy's bedrooms. He eventually settled on a shade of apricot pink which he insisted: "reduced the appearance of a woman by 10 years." In Ritz's garden in the country at Golders Green he and Escoffier would create new ideas; like the brilliant marketing concept which finally brought ladies into the hotel's public restaurant. Solution? Name dishes after the leaders of society. For example, the Duchess of Aosta loved Escoffier's pears in chocolate sauce, so that dish is still known as Poire Belle Hélène after her Grace. Nellie Melba, the famous diva, liked thin, crisp toast. That's now Toast Melba. It attracted the ladies to the Savoy restaurant and, where they went, their acolytes were not far behind. At the end of the day, though, the Savoy directors had the final say. Yet Ritz knew there were plenty of very rich men prepared to back him if he wanted to break away and form his own company and this eventually he agreed to do.

For many years the circumstances of the departure of Ritz and Escoffier from the Savoy were hushed up. Marie Ritz blamed their departure on the impossible behaviour of a housekeeper who, she said, had the support of a director; by implication, because of something more than friendship. Everybody said the parting was amicable, though nobody explained why, if that were the case, Ritz's belongings were turfed out of his apartment at the Savoy, so that he found it necessary to accept an offer of accommodation from a friend who ran the Charing Cross Hotel The degree of amicability is also undermined by a short paragraph in the *Caterer* for April 1898 which stated quite simply and categorically: "Actions are pending against the Savoy at the instance of Ritz, Escoffier and Echenard for wrongful dismissal and breach of contract." The whole story is told in Chapter 10.

Only a hotelier with the fanatical following of Ritz could have survived such a dramatic departure from his previous company. The fact that the reputations of both Ritz and Escoffier were unaffected over the years was due to a cover-up, acceptable to both sides. It would not have helped Ritz to have a lot of dirty linen washed in public when he was trying to raise money for his hotel developments. From the Savoy's point of view, Ritz had powerful friends who could withdraw their patronage.

Sir Henry Burdett, the Vice Chairman of Gordon Hotels might well have had this and the Spokes-Grosvenor Hotel case (Chapter 12) in mind when he told his shareholders in July 1898: "I am impressed, as you must have been impressed with what has appeared in the newspapers about other hotels, and I have asked myself how it is, and why it is, that the Gordon Hotels have escaped these scandals." Sir Henry was being economical with the truth.

Resignations had been in the air at Gordon Hotels barely a year before. Business had been good for some years and the shares had more than doubled. The £10 ordinary had reached £24 while the dividend remained a steady and luxurious 10%. Then, in April

Ritzy

1897, Sir Blundell Maple decided that he wanted to go into the hotel business and approached Frederick Gordon to chair the board of a new hotel company to be called, confusingly for us, Frederick Hotels. From Sir Blundell's point of view this move made sound sense for if, as his own publicity trumpeted: "whenever one finds an exceptionally well appointed hotel, it may safely be premised that Maples have been concerned in its development" then why not collect the resulting profits as well?

Gordon was not averse to the idea of joining Sir Blundell, for they were good friends and he had cheerfully accepted a seat on the Maples board already. Agreed, there had been a certain amount of friction because Sir Blundell had not invited any other Gordon Hotel directors to join Maples and they, for their part, had insisted - quite rightly - on going out for competitive tenders for furnishings and fittings, rather than automatically give the new business to Maples. From Sir Blundell's point of view, though, two tenders were no different from two hotel companies. Why shouldn't Gordon then chair both companies? His view was not accepted, however, and when Sir Blundell launched Frederick Hotels, the board of directors at Gordons voted to refuse to deal with Maples any more. It was a difficult situation for Gordon himself and a war of conflicting statements quickly broke out within the Gordon's board. One faction held that Gordon could not adequately serve two masters, in the same industry. Gordon, himself, said that his action was in the best interest of Gordon Hotels. His opponents then called an extraordinary general meeting to ask him to resign from the board of Maples though there was no effort to get him to resign from Gordon Hotels. By the day of the meeting on October 14th 1897 Gordon shares had plummeted to £18.10 shillings (£18.50p) and Gordon had a lot of explaining to do.

The main attack came from one of his oldest friends, Alfred Holland, a first class professional hotelier who was to be a Director of the Ritz Hotel in London for 20 years. Gordon had a great name in the hotel business, but much of the day-to-day work was Alfred Holland's and he complained that: "Mr. Gordon in one of his circulars, has belittled the part I and my colleagues have played in bringing the business of the company to its present successful position." He tried to excuse Gordon by making Sir Blundell a sort of Svengali: "inviting Mr. Gordon to join Maple's board was the start of an attempt to unload their untried ventures on this prosperous

138

company."

Unfortunately for Alfred Holland the Gordon magic was much too strong and Gordon had a unique ace in the hole because his brother-in-law, Horatio, was being installed as Lord Mayor of London in one month's time. Gordon won easily enough but three of the six directors resigned, leaving him with a pyrrhic victory. It was pyrrhic because he replaced the defectors with influential city friends who knew nothing of the hotel business, and then himself became involved with other companies, as chairman of Ashanti Goldfields and of Apollinnaris and Johannis, the principal bottled water company, and as a director of Pears and Bovril.

From this time onwards Gordon Hotels started to decline: "Experts have been replaced by non-experts, and instead of three hotel specialists, we have an ex-secretary, a brewer, a beef juice manufacturer and a statistician." The retiring directors were missed. There was also major additional competition in the Strand area from the new Hotel Cecil.

The Cecil was the name given by the liquidator of Jabez Balfour's companies to the monster hotel he had been constructing on the Embankment. It had been six years in the building and was opened in the spring of 1896 with 800 bedrooms and great fanfares. It was a very splendid hotel indeed, and the liquidator had done an excellent job in getting the original shareholders to put up the necessary additional money to finish it off. Making it profitable was another matter again. Inevitably the overheads were enormous, with Mr. Bertini, the new manager, controlling in the catering department alone a staff of 200 in three separate kitchens. The facilities were exceptional and there was no more imposing room in London than the Grand Ballroom, which was over 100 feet long, 66 feet wide and a vast 46 feet high. It says much for the skill of the architect that there were no pillars at all in the room, so that the 600+ guests had an uninterrupted view. When the first set of accounts were produced they showed a handsome turnover of nearly £250,000, which can be compared with, say, the Langham's figure of about £100,000; unfortunately, the operating costs were very high at the Cecil which meant that less profit was made out of each pound received. As the financial analysts were not slow to point out, where Gordon Hotels spent £70 out of every £100 they took, the Cecil spent £90. Consequently Bertini, the accepted ideal choice of 1896, became the

Ritzy

great mistake of 1897 and disappeared from the scene. It might have been the largest hotel in Europe but, as with so many of the new hotels: "each was a nine days wonder and then fell back to become an accepted part of London life". The managers who were dismissed usually fell back to become an accepted part of the life of small country or seaside towns, far from the scenes of their former glory in the capital. It is sad that so many careers, which were painstakingly built over 20 and 30 years, could be destroyed in such a short space of time. In this hotel and football management still have much in common.

The overbuilding in London was taking its toll even in the '90's. Berners Hotel was only one to go into Receivership in 1895. D'Oyly Carte stepped in to buy Claridge's quite cheaply and the year was a bad one for the industry everywhere. *Caterer* reported: "The depression in general business of the country and the hotel trade in particular, is emphasised by the reports of hotel companies which have reached us since the beginning of the year. Never were the number of non-dividend and shrinking dividend concerns greater. For the first time in 28 years even the White Hart, Salisbury, is paying no final dividend."

Amid all the gloom there was still a growing desire to live it up. Banqueting and eating out grew more popular and clubs of every description were formed and flourished. There was even a London 13 Club with many members from Lloyds, courageously dedicated to ignoring every form of superstition. A hundred and sixty nine was the quorum which gathered for drinks, and dinner was announced by the head waiter, who gained every-body's attention by the simple - if expensive - expedient of smashing a large mirror on the floor. The guests then went under two ladders into the dining room where all were seated at 13 tables of 13. After the meal came speeches, with the chairman inviting the members to spill salt with him and then to break their own little mirrors, which were thoughtfully provided.

There were less eccentric groups than the 13 Club and, overall, for those who could afford it, there were more opportunities for entertainment. One minor obstacle remained, which was the habit throughout the country of early nights, and the major problem here was the law which closed restaurants at 11 o'clock. Ritz was particularly keen to get this amended and, with a great deal of lobbying in the right quarters from Edward's Marlborough House set, Parliament relented and allowed restaurants to remain open until half past midnight. Many restaurants, notably the Savoy, benefited and it became extremely fashionable to take after-theatre suppers.

Licensing hours for hotels generally continued to be the same as for pubs, the licence itself the same for both categories of business. In the days of the stagecoaches, this was fair enough, but there was little similarity between a large hotel built after the Companies Act and the local hostelry. Hoteliers wanted a separate licence because the application to the Magistrates was often seen as another opportunity for the locals to get drunk, rather than a chance to improve the social amenities of a town for its visitors. This was the Justices' original position with the Metropole in Folkestone. There was a Royal Commission on the Sales of Intoxicating Liquors in 1899 and it recommended different licences but nothing happened for many years.

Because it is still one of the finest hotels in London, the opening of the rebuilt Coburg Hotel in December 1896 deserves to be recognized. The Coburg was owned by Auguste Scorrier and loyally named after the Royal House to which Prince Albert had belonged. Its position, just off Grosvenor Square, could not have been better. During the Great War, however, when German names became very unpatriotic, the Coburg became, first the Carlos after its location in Carlos Place, and then the Connaught. The high standards set by Scorrier continued after him.. The first manager of a hotel can usually set the tone for good or ill for years to come. The Coburg was fortunate to have Kossuth Hudson, after Scorrier, a good hotelier whose previous experience had been on the Riviera with one of the top Gordon managers, and who was able to translate that excellent training into London terms. To be saddled with the name Kossuth can be likened to a child today being christened Che or Mao, but Hudson survived without noticeable ill effects.

In the countryside there were a number of developments. The invention of the bicycle had provided the first sign that the wheel of fortune was at last turning in favour of those hotels which had survived the passing of the stagecoach. The bicycle provided a cheap means of transport compared to a horse and trap and fitted in well with the new emphasis on exercise and sport, of which the growth in leisure activities like football, cricket and rugby were other manifestations. In 1878 the Bicycle Touring Club first made a

Ritzy

register of approved hotels for the benefit of its members, long before the RAC undertook the same task for motorists in 1897. By the 1890s there were sufficient cyclists to make a substantial market for the country hotels, and the cyclists were not only likely to need overnight accommodation, but were customers for packed lunches as well as for drinks. While the motor car remained a luxury until well after the First World War, the cyclists were able to discover the beauties of the English countryside peacefully and economically. The road system was more than adequate for the amount of traffic and the dangers of horses drowning in the 18th century potholes of the A1 or holdups by highwaymen had passed into history.

Golf was another sport which had grown in popularity, and among the first of the hotels built specifically to cater for this type of visitor was the Golf View Hotel at Nairn in Scotland which was opened in 1897. It was a brave venture but the Lord Provost, in wishing the proprietress good luck, drove well into the verbal rough when he anticipated: "getting well away from the tee, might find an easy course, and loft off to the green of prosperity and there land on the green of success." Perhaps the Scotch had flowed a trifle freely before he started his address.

By the end of the century the seaside resorts had their characters fully formed. The small villages had developed into thriving towns, though this was not always beneficial to the hotels. Some towns had been adopted by the factory workers, so that when the Wakes Weeks were created in the North, the inhabitants, through the medium of saving with Holiday Clubs, were able to go to stay at boarding houses in nearby resorts. Young resorts like Blackpool, which had only five hotels in 1856, boomed, but the upper crust looked for fresh horizons. A town like Brighton could uniquely mix the two types of clientele, but a number of other resorts lost their carriage trade to an increasing extent. The wealthy turned to those of the seaside towns which emphasised the quieter life. Bournemouth began to publicise more intensely its convalescent qualities and the town council discouraged the more plebeian attractions. It was a question of parks versus amusement machines or, in Folkestone, a question of whether the Metropole Hotel could block the access for the general public to the green sward of the Lees in order to make their hotel more exclusive. The answer eventually was that they could not. The big spenders started to search further afield for their holiday homes and more twin towns, like St. Annes for Blackpool, emerged. The Isle of Wight was very popular because of Queen Victoria's love of her house at Osborne and, of course, the journey across the water helped to keep the island remote.

There was now a much larger tourist industry at the seaside towns and a proliferation of boarding houses and private homes as well as hotels. The old picture of a quaint fishing village trying to become a small town was becoming steadily more out of date. The power structure in these towns had a major effect on the influence of the industry nationally. In most seaside towns there was a small coterie of influential families, mostly landowners, who had a vested interest in the expansion of the resort, like Jervis in Bournemouth earlier in the century. As we've seen, to expand the town meant using more agricultural land for housing and this was more valuable to the owner than farming or grazing. It was inevitable, therefore, that these families were in the forefront of the effort to get investors to put up money for those big hotels which would give additional status to their towns. Indeed the families contributed themselves and often occupied seats on the boards of directors.

These men were never professional hoteliers and yet they came to represent the hotel industry in their locality, because of their financial stake and local prestige. Most other industries retained a strong leavening of professionals in places of power but a lot of major hotels were controlled, when it came to the crunch, by part-time amateurs. The local MP, who would be unlikely to be adopted by the constituency if he were *persona non grata* with the great families, would certainly understand *their* interests, but he did not represent hotels as the Labour MPs would represent the workers in the next century.

Occasionally, as we have seen, a hotelier broke into the charmed circle, but the industry was shackled right across the country from the beginning in terms of political influence. The professional hoteliers had neither the education nor the grievances to spur them on; they were spread thinly across the country, composed of many nationalities and, being nomads by nature, they could not take a long term view. Only a threat of the utmost severity would unite the two sides and that was not forthcoming in the '90's. It would arrive with the Liberal Government in 1906.

As the decade drew to a close the rumblings of war rang

ominously in the hoteliers' ears. Lord Kitchener's handling of the Fashoda Incident in 1898 had inflicted a humiliating defeat on the French and it became unpatriotic for them to holiday in Britain. The outbreak of the Spanish American War had reduced the number of United States visitors - as it would with Suez in 1956, the Yom Kippur War in 1973 and many other international events which scared the American travellers. The Boer War was to have an even worse effect on trade. Nevertheless, for the 3 months season which London enjoyed, there was still a great demand for accommodation, as there was for the even shorter seaside peak.

Sir Blundell Maple had managed to float his Frederick Hotels with the aid of Frederick Gordon as chairman and totally without the assistance in his prospectus of any details of the past trading of the operations involved; the issue was oversubscribed and raised nearly £11/2m from the public. It said much for the reputation of both Sir Blundell and Gordon that this was possible, but once the public has faith in a section of the stock market and in entrepreneurs with good records, it often tends to support them unquestioningly. Frederick Hotels did have some nice properties, including the new Majestic Hotel, Harrogate, the Royal Pavilion, Folkestone and the Great Central Hotel at Marylebone Station, which the Great Central Railway had been unable to afford to run itself. The Great Central Hotel managed to find one new attraction for its visitors by offering a cycle track on its roof for guests in need of exercise, but this hardly compared to the improvements first provided by earlier hotels at termini.

The Carlton had been opened by Ritz in the last year of the century without too much in the way of publicity. First, because a new hotel was no longer news and second, because there was some question of whether a management so recently in serious disagreement with the Savoy would be effective on its own. (The Savoy Company, for their part, had expanded by rebuilding Claridge's.) Ritz soon proved himself anew by producing a really lovely hotel whose frontage was an exact duplicate of the present Her Majesty's Theatre and which contained many special Ritz touches. The walls were painted because Ritz considered wallpaper unhygienic and there was a clever system of double windows to reduce traffic noise. Every room had a bathroom and the selection of fixtures and fittings showed Ritz at his best. Ritz was such a perfectionist that the day he opened his Ritz Hotel in Paris at about the same time, he sent the chairs back to the manufacturers. He had decided they were two inches (5 cm) too high and had them all cut down. He was, however, satisfied with the amazing 200 showcases he had installed in the lobby, which provided the hotel with a profit from that source which has never been exceeded. It was in the Carlton restaurant, however, that Ritz and Escoffier triumphantly achieved their finest results with the new *à la carte* menu and the promotion of after-theatre dining. The restaurant became one of the favourite rendezvous of London's society and, as the ladies swept down the staircase which Ritz had considerately planned for the purpose, the scene was set as surely as on the stage next door.

The Victorians had to experience gracious living to want it and the hotels were one of the shop windows. It certainly was not just a question of new recipes or fashionable decor; it was far more the opportunity many guests had of using a bathroom for the first time, switching on an electric light or turning on a tap. Better systems of drainage could be devised for a hotel, so that the domestic market benefited from the improvements which started with hotel construction. The Prince of Wales once moved house because he couldn't stand the stench of the drains. Hotel management had to demand a far higher standard of hygiene than existed in many a wealthy private home, and these standards had to be good enough for foreign visitors as well as British. Consequently, the home country was influenced - as it had been in its cuisine by French chefs 100 years earlier - by American inventions, by Italian grace, Swiss organisation, and German efficiency. Though Britain was the most powerful country, it still learned from its foreign visitors and its foreign staff, and these lessons were disseminated throughout the land through the agency of the hotel industry.

Unfortunately for the hoteliers themselves, the cost of an old hotel continually modernising its plant was exorbitant and the public's demand for new inventions made life difficult for the older established companies. If the cost of living had continued on an even keel it would have been easier, but at long last the situation changed. The reason was the Boer War. The significance of this conflict to the British economy has been overshadowed by the far worse effects of the First World War, but this comparatively minor action in South Africa dealt two severe blows to the hotel industry; it created inflation

Ritzy

and it cut down the amount of business the hotels enjoyed. From the time of the war onwards, British hotels operated under much greater strain than before, and after the vast expansion which had been seen between 1860 and 1900, the growth of the industry slowed down.

Fred Gordon, the Hotel Napoleon.
Caterer.

John Smedley; his Hydro paid 20% dividends for years.

Sir Polydore de Keyser, the first Catholic Lord Mayor of London since the Reformation.

Sir William Towle started catering on trains.
Caterer.

Richard D'Oyly Carte brought show business to the hotel industry.
Caterer.

Sir Joseph Lyons lent his name to the Salmon and Gluckstein family creation.

Jabez Balfour, probably the greatest Victorian con artist; only peripherally a hotelier.

Sir George Reeves-Smith dominated the Hotel Association for 30 years.

Cesar Ritz, a great hotelier who drove himself much too hard.

Auguste Escoffier, a great chef who, unfortunately, backed very slow horses.

Rosa Lewis proved that it didn't matter if you were poor and a woman; you could still make it if you had the talent.
Caterer.

Sir Isidore Salmon built the first great food empire.
J.Lyons & Co.

Sir George Gilbert Scott, whose Midland Grand Hotel at St. Pancras is the grandest of the Victorian Grand Hotels.

Frank Bourne Newton, who made The Caterer – and a large number of hotel industry organizations – actually work.
Caterer.

Norman Shaw, one of the great architects, who built the Piccadilly Hotel in his "Imperial period".

The Earl of Bessborough, who balanced the conflicting demands of his train company and his hotels with great skill.
Caterer.

Guests were there to be waited upon, not to haul on ropes to get the lift to move.

The Rising Room sounded very much more impressive than a lift.

Most Victorian quality hotels had a Billiards Room – but no television.

TRANTER'S

(Private, Family, & Commercial)

TEMPERANCE HOTEL

7,8,9, Bridgewater Sq., Barbican, London, E.C.

RECENTLY ENLARGED.

VISITORS to London will find many advantages by staying at this quiet, clean and home-like Hotel

MOST CENTRAL FOR BUSINESS OR PLEASURE.

Near St. Paul's Cathedral, G.P.O., and all places of interest. 3 minutes walk from Aldersgate Street, and 5 from Moorgate Street Metropolitan Railway Stations; Terminal of the Great Western, Great Northern, Great Eastern, Midland, L. and N.W., L. C. and Dover, and in connection with A.L.L. Railways. 15 minutes walk to the Law Courts. Trains, Cars, Buses, every three minutes, to all parts of London and Suburbs. Highly recommended. Established 1859.

Write for "VISITORS' GUIDE," showing "HOW TO SPEND A WEEK IN LONDON." (Regd.) With Tariff and Testimonials, post free on application to C. T. S. TRANTER, Proprietor.

⇥ TARIFF. ⇤

APARTMENTS, Etc.

Clean and Well Ventilated Bed-rooms.

Bed-room for one person	... ... 1/6, 2/-, 2/6 per night.
,, two persons	3/-, 3/6, 4/- ,,

According to the size and position of room taken.

The above charges include use of Spacious Coffee, Smoking, and Reading Rooms, Fire, Lavatories, &c., &c. Electric Light in Public Rooms.

PRIVATE SITTING ROOMS, from 4/- per day, including Gas and attendance.

BREAKFAST OR TEA.

Plain, with Preserves, &c., &c.	1/-	Plain, with 2 Eggs Poached on Toast	1/6
Ditto with Cake	1/3	Ditto with Rump Steak, Chop, Fish,	
Ditto with 2 Eggs or Bacon	1/4	or Ham & 2 Eggs	1/9
Ditto with Cold Meat	1/6	With choice of Tea Coffee or Cocoa.	

LUNCHEONS AND SUPPERS.

Chop, Steak, or Cold Meat, with Potatoes, Bread, Butter, and Cheese 1/6
Basin Bread and Milk, Gruel, or Oatmeal Porridge .. .. .. /6

DINNERS.

Weekdays, as per arrangement. Sundays, at 1.30 consisting of
Soup, Joints, Vegetables, Sweets, and Cheese.. .. .. 2/-

Hot or Cold Baths, Hot 9d., Cold 6d.

SPECIAL INCLUSIVE TERMS TO AMERICANS AND OTHERS DESIRING IT.

Visitors are received at a fixed charge of 5/6 per day, to include First-class Bedroom, Boots, Breakfast and Tea with Chop, Rump Steak, Ham and Eggs, or Cold Meat at each Meal. (Special Reduced Weekly Terms during the Winter.)

PERFECT SANITARY ARRANGEMENTS. NO CHARGE FOR ATTENDANCE.

TELEGRAPHIC ADDRESS: "HEALTHIEST" LONDON.

The Tranter Temperance Hotel was jut one who served a moral, as well as a commercial, purpose.

If you dare not drink the water, there would have to be plenty of room to store the wine.
Caterer.

The Drawing Room at the Cecil Hotel. One of the biggest Victorian hotels, it didn't survive the Slump.

The Winter Garden was designed to improve off-season occupancy by enabling guests to take advantage of the winter sun.

An expensive depictment of peace, plenty, industry and science on John Thomas' pediment of the Great Western Royal at Paddington in 1853. Still in the Graeco-Roman style.

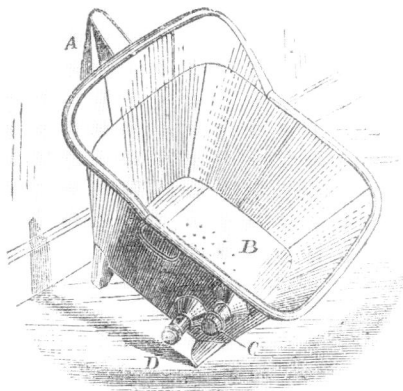

When there was little effective medical help for illness, the belief was that baths were beneficial – hence the Hydropathic Institutes.

The London – Brighton Rally was one of the first Victorian special events and was probably copied from the Monte Carlo Rally by Fred Gordon.

William Claridge had many different levels of bow, depending on your rank.

The lounge at the Russell Hotel was a respectable location for meeting family and friends.

The dining-room at the Metropole Hotel in the early 1900s.

The dinner-dancing craze was a very profitable sideline for hotels – and still is.

10
A pause for the great cover up.
Ritz and Escoffier vs. The Savoy Hotel

The Savoy Hotel's archives are, without question, the finest in the hotel world. From the beginning of the enterprise, nothing seems to have been thrown away and among the records, the Guard Books, the press cuttings and the memorabilia of great occasions at the hotel over more than 100 years, there are four large box files. These record the story of the great cover up; the facts behind the departure of their second manager, the greatest hotelier in the world - Cesar Ritz - and the greatest chef in the world - Auguste Escoffier - from their positions as general manager and head chef of the Savoy on March 7th 1898. They explain why the great barrister, Sir Edward Carson, told the Savoy Board that: "it is the imperative duty of the Directors to dismiss the Manager and the Chef".

Cesar Ritz has undoubtedly been the greatest influence on hotel management in the history of the industry. The ultimate accolade - the conversion of his surname into the adjective, Ritzy - only emphasises his importance. The ambition of tens of thousands of budding hoteliers, during his heyday and since, has been to equal the standards of the great man. Even today, many of the British hotel colleges are teaching the ways of the master. With single-minded, total application over a long period of years, Ritz sought to refine and refine again his concept of how the perfect hotel should be furnished, staffed and managed. Escoffier was, equally, a perfectionist, and it was a mutual bond between them.

Ritz was a stickler for cleanliness - at the turn of the century his Carlton Hotel was really the first in Britain to be built with all the bedrooms having private bathrooms. He was a great showman. Other hotels might have Palm Court ensembles. He had Johann Strauss and his Orchestra. Others might have finger bowls; he flooded the courtyard at the Savoy for a function. Both Ritz and Escoffier fully deserved their high reputations.

Ritz took enormous care to keep his personal clients happy. He would write to his hotel managers just to tell them that some countess liked three pillows rather than two. He flattered his guests and they loved him for it. One client invented a new liqueur and asked Ritz

Ritzy

what he should call it. Ritz suggested Grand Marnier and M. Marnier considered that a brilliant idea. Stories about Ritz and Escoffier have been retold countless times. The double booking which resulted in a hot and ugly room being pressed into service for senior aristocracy; royalty had the original room. Ritz filled the eyesore with foliage and put blocks of ice behind the branches to keep the room cool. Or his famous saying that the client is always right but the client always pays. As for Escoffier, he used to be called on to cook when there were state visitors - for example, Prime Minister, Raymond Poincaré of France.

In spite of the overwhelming legend and the universal praise, however, there remains a real question of whether Ritz was either a brilliant businessman or a good influence on the industry. After all, the primary duty of a businessman in a public company is to make the maximum profit for his shareholders and the evidence seems to be that, by that criterion, Ritz was only a limited success and unnecessarily extravagant during his time at the Savoy.

The record speaks for itself. When Ritz took over control in 1889, the hotel was not paying its way. There was a very considerable burden of debt from the opening and construction expenses. They had nearly bankrupted the fledgling company. At the end of five years of Ritz's management, both ordinary and preference shares were still below par and the hotel was only paying a 5% dividend. This was less than both new companies, like Gordon Hotels, and the old established firms like the Langham and the Westminster Palace. Ritz certainly made better profits in 1895 and 1896 and he paid off the debts he inherited, but with his clientele and the brilliant team he had carefully nurtured, he should have produced a much healthier balance sheet.

There were three main reasons why he didn't do so. First, it is very doubtful whether this was ever his sole aim from 1890 onwards. In his early days on the continent he had to submit to the disciplines of owners who wanted the best possible returns on their investments. Their constraints. combined with his professional ability, enabled very good results to be achieved. As his reputation grew, however, he was subject to far less control. His employers and backers knew they needed him more than he needed them. He knew it too. As he was a perfectionist, his main aim was to run the perfect hotel. If extravagance in reaching that objective reduced the profits, then there

148

was always the possibility of more jam tomorrow. The directors, who were not hoteliers might be able to veto his plans but they knew they were normally wiser to leave him to get on with running the business

The second problem was that there were too many businesses for Ritz to run. In the 1890s, apart from the Savoy, he was involved in hotels or hotel projects in such cities as Rome, Paris, Frankfurt, Cairo, Johannesburg and Biarritz; 11 in all, at one time or another. The Savoy was content that, out of season, he should follow other interests. In an age before flying this meant, however, that he was away from London for long periods and he relied on his management teams to keep the flag flying when he wasn't in town.

In that lay the third problem. In London he was particularly proud and fond of his team; Escoffier, Echenard, Agostini, Baumgartner, the personnel manager, Collins, his secretary, and Elles, the restaurant manager. He knew they would be a strong management team for any hotel and Ritz wanted to have his own hotel; it was always his dream. So in 1896, he formed the Ritz Hotel Development Company. All the London team, except Elles, were founder shareholders.

Of course, in forming the company and devoting so much of his time and energies to non-Savoy projects, he was letting down Richard D'Oyly Carte, the chairman of the Savoy company. D'Oyly Carte, grappling after 1895 with the purchase of Claridges, didn't know of the Ritz Hotel Development company for a long time after its formation. He didn't know that meetings to raise money for the syndicate from potential backers were held in the hotel, at the Savoy's expense, including the entertaining. As they noted when the scandal broke "The intention...in forming such syndicate being, as soon as their agreements expired, and without letting their intention be known previously, to leave the employ of the Defendants (The Savoy), taking Mr. Escoffier with them, and ....start a business opposition....to the injury of the Defendants." The opposition eventually being Ritz's planned Carlton Hotel.

What Ritz probably didn't know was that when he, the hotel lion, was away on his travels, the mice were going to play with a vengeance. If the general manager was going to cheat the Savoy, then why shouldn't they all do it? The clients were cheated too. Any number of corrupt practices began to flourish. Nine foolscap pages in

Ritzy

the Savoy's archives written by an anonymous: "One Who Knows" spells them out in great detail. He quotes one catering supplier who said it was difficult to allow 5% off his tariff for the Savoy, give 5% to Escoffier and supply Ritz and Echenard's private homes for nothing. The solution for the suppliers was to deliver short weight; sometimes as high as 40% less than Escoffier had his minions sign for. The identity of the whistle-blower was never identified.

Ritz was paid £24,287 between 1890 and 1896. (A rough guide is to multiply that figure by 40 to get 2003 prices). D'Oyly Carte gave him 2,000 shares as well, which by 1895 were worth £30,000 (£1.2 million). Even so, Ritz had the hotel pay £80 (£3,200) over 6 months for his washing in his Hampstead home.

Keeping up with the gander, the restaurant staff had the sauce to insist on buying all the fresh fruit, including that for banqueting. The hotel paid the restaurant manager 2p (80p) for each table d'hôte meal taken and 3p (£1.20) for each banqueting cover, whether the guest ate the fruit or not. Elles, who earned £720 a year (£28,800), also charged £1 (£40) to clients who wanted a table in the restaurant and £2 (£80) on Sundays. He also had the right to authorise credit for his clients. Ritz's doctor was allowed to sign cheques for cash for £200 (£8,000). In June 1897, the outstanding credit totalled £13,000 (£520,000). Of course, if the restaurant staff granted credit, where credit wasn't due, the resulting tips might well be substantial. To get a comparison, the hotel's coal-porter might earn £36 (£1,440) a year.

"One Who Knows" is probably the only contemporary critic we have of Ritz as a hotel manager, per se. He wrote:"Ritz, Echenard and Escoffier are all masters and they have no power over one another. The Savoy Hotel is like a house without any master. Escoffier has climbed to such a height that nobody dares approach him, not even Ritz, when it is a question of the supply of food to the kitchens; in fact he does what he likes, and does it how he likes and when he likes......Messrs. Ritz and Echenard seem afraid of Escoffier."

It was the same pattern overall. D'Oyly Carte needed Ritz because, as Gilbert and Sullivan's impresario, he was far more involved in putting on shows, and in 1897 he fell seriously ill anyway. Ritz needed Escoffier because the reputation of the Savoy rested, to a considerable extent, on his wonderful food.

A pause for the great cover up

Why did Escoffier need the bribes from the suppliers? He was earning £1,000 a year (£40,000) and yet in 18 months in 1897/8, he took £8,000 (£320,000) in bribes. He certainly maintained a lavish private life style which he probably couldn't afford, and there was a rumour that he consistently backed very slow horses. For whatever reason, he stole from the Savoy. To make matters worse: "He who knows" wrote: "there is no doubt...that the Chef....does insist upon and extort commission all round. This is notorious. " Which meant that, if the greatest chef in the world considered it acceptable to steal from his employer, then his adoring acolytes would conclude that it was alright for them as well. It's the same situation as those head chefs today who take drugs and, by their example, suggest it is the done thing. Their juniors are led astray.

If Ritz had countless admirers, he also had one determined adversary; Helen Couper-Black who was D'Oyly Carte's second wife. She had previously been his assistant and she was an able woman. According to one friend, George Edwardes, the famous London theatre manager: "The whole foundation of the Savoy business rested upon her" at the beginning.

The impact of Ritz's arrival must have bruised Helen D'Oyly Carte's ego considerably. Ritz would not consult her on anything, would not tolerate any interference, but made it clear that he was perfectly prepared to listen to his own wife, Marie Ritz. She was only 23 in 1890, much younger and less experienced than Mrs. D'Oyly Carte. Marie Ritz recalled: " 'Your taste is good' Ritz said to me 'so go ahead and choose colours and fabrics at once. I trust you' " The energy which Helen D'Oyly Carte was to show in investigating Ritz's management record in 1897 was probably fuelled by that lengthy period of perceived humiliation.

Ritz's self-esteem grew apace. He was surrounded by sycophants and was always being offered large sums of money if he would become involved in this or that hotel project. For the 13th son of a poor Swiss peasant, it was a heady transformation. At the best of times, he had been difficult to control. In January 1892, at a board meeting, D'Oyly Carte said: "a very unpleasant and unsatisfactory scene occurred" and Ritz apologised in writing later: "having lost control of myself in a moment of excitement, a thing which will not occur again."

During the summer of 1897 the profits from the Savoy's

151

kitchen had fallen disastrously. The gross kitchen profit in previous years had been between 32% and 36%. It fell to 24.5% in the first half of 1897. It could have fallen more, but one element of the kitchen costs was the staff wages. Escoffier was able to keep these low by conning his staff with the idea that kitchen work was an art form rather than a job. He explained that long hours and dedication were necessary to master the art. The rewards would not be in larger wage packets, of course, but in increased artistic ability. It was a convincing argument for the naive and it has been used to keep down the wages of junior chefs ever since.

In the Autumn of 1897 the Savoy directors had had enough. They resolved to have a full investigation, which Helen D'Oyly Carte had been advocating since the end of 1896, and she joined in the lengthy examination enthusiastically. The studies undertaken were exhaustive. They even included full reports on the daily movements of Ritz and Escoffier. It all became rather melodramatic. At one stage a private detective met one of Escoffier's business partners, Charles Liddell, at a railway station, to find out if he was acting as a go-between with the wine and cigar companies supplying the Savoy - the suppliers selling their goods to Liddell, who sold them on to Escoffier at a higher price and shared the profits.

In the first six months of 1897 the Liquor Stock losses - the difference between what the drinks revenue should have been and what it actually was - amounted to over £3,400. (£136,000). This was serious larceny. It is perhaps significant that, under Ritz's regime, the stocks were only checked twice a year. (Today it's normally done every four weeks.)

Ritz made many excuses when confronted with these malpractices in early 1898. He said that competition had forced down the selling price of wines. It hadn't. He said the contrast in kitchen profits was with the highly successful Diamond Jubilee year, but the turnover hadn't, in fact, declined that much. He said he had to pay the waiters more to keep them from being poached by other hotels, but the money the waiters received hadn't gone up much. The auditor's work was not made easier by the fact that Ritz had told the head checker to destroy the invoices when there were too many to fit into his box! He was asked to explain why some suppliers sold their goods to him and then he sold them on to the Savoy. He couldn't.

Ritz was told at one point: "You have latterly been simply

152

using the Savoy as a place to live in, a pied-a-terre, an office, from which to carry on your other schemes." That seems a pretty fair summary.

The Savoy directors were faced with a terrible commercial, if not ethical, dilemma. Ritz and Escoffier had a tremendous following, both among the monied public and within the industry. This was illustrated when D'Oyly Carte tried to replace Escoffier. An able French chef accepted the post on February 27th and retracted on March 4th. He said it was "impossible for me to be so ungrateful to M. Escoffier. I should lose the esteem of all my friends." The public included its leader, The Prince of Wales, who loved Escoffier's food. Would anybody believe the directors if they took action.?

Never a man to do things by halves, D'Oyly Carte retained a team of barristers, headed by the eminent Sir Edward Carson. The advice the directors received on February 28th 1898 was crystal clear. They had to fire the chef and the manager. The directors still wavered. They asked Sir Edward if they could give Ritz one last chance to explain the deficiencies. Sir Edward said: "Certainly not."

So the directors did as they were told and they issued a statement: "A matter, however, of greater importance became apparent to the Directors in the autumn (1897) and that was, that there was a much less percentage of profit on the sale of food and wine than in previous years. Upon this, of course, the diminution of the gross receipts has no bearing. The Directors accordingly considered it necessary to institute a searching enquiry into the causes of this diminution of profit, an enquiry which conducted practically day by day, by and under the direction of a committee of investigation, has been a very laborious task and has occupied many months. The Directors have ascertained the principal causes of the deficiencies. They further have ascertained that other abuses have sprung up prejudicial to the business in many ways and calculated to alienate customers." "Acting under the advice of eminent counsel, the Directors have found it their imperative duty to dismiss the two managers and the chef from the service of the company.....the shareholders may rely that the earnest and continuous efforts of the Directors...." etc etc.

When Ritz, Escoffier and Echenard were fired, many less senior staff went with them: "On Monday the 7th, (March) after the changes had been effected, the kitchen staff agreed to do their duty that evening but expressed their intention of leaving after midnight....Of course, their leaving our employ thus was wholly improper and illegal, but we found it impossible and useless to argue with these Foreigners who take the quaintly humorous view that they are the servants of the official under whom they serve and not of the Proprietors who pay their salaries."

Nevertheless, the kitchen staff were replaced by 8 o'clock the next morning. When there is a conflict of interest, loyalty to the manager rather than to the company, remains the biggest challenge to the chain hotel board room to this day; foreign or British.

The dismissals were the talk of the industry and the glitterati. Ritz, Escoffier and Echenard denied doing anything wrong and *Caterer* tersely reported that the managers had: "issued writs against the Savoy for wrongful dismissal and breach of contract." The Savoy counter-claimed for damages. The legal proceedings were to go on for the best part of two years. Profits for 1897 were eventually, £15,585 (£623,400). £11,000 (£440,000) down on 1896. The directors couldn't save the dividend which slumped to 7 1/2%.

In the following months the Food and Beverage profits improved dramatically. Kitchen profits went up from 24 1/2% to 45% in 1899. The 1898 dividend was 10% again with profits of £20,276 (£811,040) in spite of a disastrous first quarter.

The key player among the guests was, of course, the Prince of Wales. When HRH heard that Ritz had gone, he said: "Where Ritz goes, I go." He was as good as his word and cancelled a small party at the hotel. On February 28th 1899 D'Oyly Carte wrote to HRH and explained his side of the story. He quoted Carson's advice that there had been: "Gross negligence and breaches of duty and mismanagement". There is nothing to show that HRH ever replied.

The main defence of Ritz and his colleagues was that the Savoy had known about their actions all the time and, as they hadn't taken any action before, they had waived their right to do so thereafter.

As the months went by, however, the case for dismissal grew ever stronger. The suppliers admitted they had been bribing Escoffier and that many had delivered short weight. The egg supplier took the precaution of hiring Rufus Isaacs (Later Lord Reading and Lord Chancellor) to represent them. Isaacs managed to settle out of court for the modern day equivalent of £132,000. And that was just for eggs! The total recovered from the suppliers reached £8,087 (£323,480) by the end of 1899. Other illegalities were easily proven. Ritz and Escoffier must have realised that they had no chance of winning in court, and that their reputations would be ruined by the evidence which would be produced. They gave in. On January 29th, 1900 their solicitors agreed a settlement. They signed a long statement admitting their guilt to all the charges which had been made. They appealed to the Savoy to agree that their confessions should go no further.

The position of the Savoy directors was very delicate. They had been put to enormous cost over the past two years and had suffered a much greater loss of profits that they were ever going to be able to get back. They had also been attacked by Ritz, Echenard and Escoffier ever since the dismissals, as heartless and ungrateful employers. Much damage had been done to the hotel's reputation among their clients. On the other hand, both Ritz and Escoffier remained famous for their skills and were surrounded by powerful friends. Furthermore, if all the sordid details emerged, what would that say about the competence of the directors to run the shareholders' business? In modern times many similar scandals have been hushed up to protect those who should have been minding the shop. Sometimes millions of embezzled pounds finishes up in company accounts under some such heading as: "Extraordinary expenses"!

On the whole, the board decided, as long as their former management stopped criticising the Savoy, the directors were best advised to lock the door on the whole sorry mess. Nearly 40 years later Marie Ritz was still trying to keep the bargain, blaming Ritz's departure on "Mrs. W", the housekeeper with friends in the board room. The lady, Mrs. Willis, appears, in reality, not to have been involved at all.

The settlement with the Savoy enabled the company to recover a lot of money. Ritz and Echenard agreed to pay the company £4,173 (£169,200). In addition there was a solution to the dispute concerning the over-ordering of wines and spirits. For example, the original £576 (£23,040) stock supplied by Messrs Strauss and Lestapis, two of Ritz's friends, didn't sell very well. Nevertheless, Ritz had bought another £960 (£38,400) worth a few months later. Under the settlement, Ritz bought both the very substantial bin ends of those wines and a large amount of other vintages and spirits from the Savoy. The total bill for all that was £6,377 (£255,080). A massive grand total of £10,500 (£424,280)

Escoffier agreed that he owed the company £8,000 but his solicitor said that he had no funds at all. His friends had clubbed together to give him £500 but that was all he could offer. The Savoy agreed to take that in full settlement...£4,173 from Ritz and Echenard, £500 from Escoffier, £8,087 repaid by the suppliers and £6,377 for the wine. Total: £19,137 (£765,480.) In 1898 the total profits of the company for the year had been £20,276.

In April 1901 Richard D'Oyly Carte died, aged 56, from dropsy and heart disease. On June 24th 1901, Cesar Ritz collapsed at his Carlton Hotel after announcing the cancellation of the lavish programme of celebrations to mark Edward VII's coronation. He never fully recovered and died at 68 in 1918 in: "a sanatorium for the mentally deranged" in Switzerland, just before the end of the war.

Escoffier eventually retired in 1914 and then had: "fallen on bad times" according to a minute of a meeting of the directors of the Ritz Hotel in London on December 17th 1924. As a consequence, it was agreed that a pension would be provided to which the Ritz in London donated £60 a year, the Ritz in Paris £100, Marie Ritz £50 and Baron Pfyffer in Switzerland £50.

Escoffier died, an "eminence blanc", in 1935 at the age of 88. Francois Latry, the head chef at the Savoy at the time, said: "M. Escoffier was one of the greatest chefs who ever added glory to our profession." So he was - but he seemed to do a lot for the bookmakers as well.

The gang of three were undoubtedly great professionals but they also condoned, and took part in, the malpractices that have bedevilled the industry before and since. Which just makes them human beings, rather than gods.

The Savoy directors kept their word. The true story of the scandal was buried in the Savoy archives for a lot longer than the 30 Year Rule on State Secrets and, while there might have been a lot of gossip where hoteliers gathered, nothing more ever appeared officially or in the press.

11
The law and hotels.

The position of hotels at law has often been obscure. Sir Henry Kimber, who was a solicitor himself, wrote a memorandum on the subject for the newly founded Incorporated Association of Hotels and Restaurants in 1914. He said "the legal position of an innkeeper today is complicated and uncertain. It is founded on unwritten laws of the realm, and can only be ascertained by a lengthy reference to decided cases dating back to the reign of Queen Elizabeth."

The root of the problem was that a modern hotel was not really an inn. A classic example of this was the law regarding the billeting of horses where there was not an adequate barracks nearby. In such cases the hotelier in 1890 had to accommodate them for two and a half old pence (1p) a night and provide stabling for the horses. If he didn't have his own stabling, he had to hire it elsewhere and then give it free of charge to the military. He also had to provide each man with one and a quarter pounds, (half a kilo) of bread, a pound (just under half a kilo) of meat, a pound of vegetables and two pints (about a litre) of small (weak) beer for 10 old pence (4p). It wasn't just small country hotels that were affected; even the hoteliers of fashionable Hastings had to accept 100 soldiers in the summer of 1890, and a hardly modified system continued during the First World War. There were, during the war, constant complaints from the industry about the prices paid by forces personnel in hotels and restaurants.

Another nonsense was the law on gaming which was designed to keep the pubs from deteriorating into gambling dens, but also resulted in a hotel manager being liable to a fine if he played cards with his own guests in his own apartment. The licensee of the Coffee House Hotel in Carlisle was fined £2 for this in 1879, yet at Beverley in 1890 only costs were awarded in a similar case and the Bench said it was: "a very harsh and abominable law." The definition of gambling was wide, and though the Victorians loved the turf, played cards for high stakes at their country house parties and were very welcome visitors to casinos all over Europe, the official policy was to pretend that gambling was frowned upon by all intelligent and law abiding people; particularly when the poor were involved, as they were in the pubs.

Ritzy

The Gaming Act also prohibited the playing of billiards outside licensing hours in a hotel, even by resident guests, although it was alright to play in a licensed Billiard Hall. Also, the billiards room could not be opened in the hotel: "on Sundays, Christmas Day, Good Friday and public act of thanksgiving days" and, again, there was a case in 1876 when a fine was imposed for the offence. The first half of the 20th century would see a number of bills introduced into parliament by the IAHR to try to get hotels a separate and different licence from pubs.

Much of the law was decided by precedent rather than by legislation for, by 1914, there had still been no attempt to define by statute the rights and liabilities of either an innkeeper - and, therefore, a hotelier - or of his customers. Such enactments as had been passed dealt with subjects like the enforcement of the common law right of lien. There were also laws about the limit of liability and the sale of drink.

The right of lien is the right to hold onto the luggage or valuables of a guest until the bill he owes you has been paid, and this a hotelier was entitled to do. The only way the law had changed over the years was on the question of whether the hotelier could sell the goods to settle the debt: this had been illegal until it was permitted by the Inn Keepers Act 1878. The property had to have been left with the hotelier for six weeks and an advertisement to say the innkeeper was going to sell it had to be put into the local newspaper a month before he did so. After all that, the goods could finally be sold without the owner's approval.

Before 1863 the hotelier, under common law, was responsible for the full cost of any loss or injury to property in the hotel belonging to his guests. It was not necessary for the property to be put into a hotel safe, nor for the guests to tell the hotel manager what valuables he had brought with him. As a consequence, the liability was extremely onerous and there were ample opportunities for unscrupulous guests to indulge in sharp practices. Indeed, many hotels made it easy for thieves as well. Keys to bedrooms were either on a board in the lobby or hanging up in the service area on each floor. A thief could wait until the coast was clear and pick up the key or even walk into unlocked bedrooms. It was only after the Grosvenor Hotel guests in London had been robbed of more than £500 worth of valuables in the 1850s that simple security procedures were introduced and the concept of

The law and hotels

master keys and doors with safety locks came to be adopted. After 1863 the law was changed so that the hotelier was only liable for up to £30 as long as he complied with certain conditions. These included the exhibition of a notice reproducing the appropriate section of the Act, so that the guest was aware of the law. It was also necessary that neither the hotelier nor his staff were guilty of neglect. Even so one hotel keeper complained that some guests: "seemed to stay in hotels to lose valuable jewellery." If the valuables were expressly deposited with the hotelier, the liability was for their value. The Act further altered the law by releasing the hotelier from responsibility for the guests' carriages or animals.

The part of the Act which caused the judiciary the most headaches was the question of neglect and, unfortunately for the hotels, different magistrates and juries gave different decisions on very similar evidence. When Mr. Jones, for instance, went to bed at the Norfolk Square Hotel in London in 1878, he put his watch and chain on the chest of drawers. It was not there in the morning. The manager said that the hotel had not been guilty of any form of neglect but the guest sued and got £27 damages. Other similar cases, however, were dismissed. Guests who left umbrellas on the appropriate stand outside the hotel restaurant might get damages if they were stolen, or they might not. As we saw at the Grand Pump Room Hotel in Bath, however, a lost case could be very expensive indeed.

Damage to property was only one aspect of the results of neglect. Sometimes the argument concerned damage to life and limb, particularly as new inventions created dangers to which the general public were unaccustomed. Mr. Jones only lost his watch, but Mr. Smith lost his life when he wandered into a service area near his bedroom in the middle of the night, presumably looking for a toilet, and went straight down the lift shaft. The Midland Grand Hotel in 1883 could well have done without the subsequent publicity, but when a lower court awarded damages of £3,500 they decided that they must appeal and they won in the higher court by two votes to one.

Any guest who asked for accommodation was entitled to receive it, so long as there was a room empty and that he paid a reasonable deposit, if required. Up to 1914 the hotelier was not entitled either to ask the name of the guest if he wished to remain incognito, nor for any other personal details, and the manager had to accept the guest even if he believed him to be bankrupt. What is more he had to accept not only a man, but also his wife and children and, within reason, his companions and servants. Admittedly, if you had a large and unwholesome dog, you could be turned away (R vs. Rymer 1877). The law to make registration compulsory came in during the First World War, primarily to keep track of foreigners.

It was in 1899 that a case occurred which established that dress could be a factor in providing service or not. Viscountess Harburton was in cycling clothes and the proprietress of the Hautboy Hotel, in Ockham, Surrey, refused to serve her in the Coffee-Room. The bar, yes, but the Coffee-Room, no. The Bicycling Touring Club financed the court case that followed, but the jury found for the hotel. This was in spite of an impassioned plea by the plaintiff's counsel, who told the jury that such a verdict would result in future generations considering them: "purblind and perverted". Viscountess Harburton's case was that she had felt that it was improper for her to be asked to take refreshments in a room where gentlemen were smoking and where there were even one or two members of the 'working class' present, but it was to no avail. (R. vs. Sprague).

Failure to provide goods and services or trying to cut corners could, however, be dangerous as there so often seemed to be solicitors or their clerks on the receiving end. In 1891, for example, Mr. Philpot, a solicitor's clerk, took a room for his wife and himself, together with his three children, in a hotel in Bournemouth where he proceeded to contract rheumatic fever from, he alleged, damp beds; that cost the hotelier £150 damages. A solicitor in Birmingham in the same year stayed in a hotel and was charged for five breakfasts he had not eaten. He sued and got his money back.

The case, however, which epitomised the difficulties between admitting guests and also accepting liability for them, concerned two electoral workers who returned to their hotel at two o'clock in the morning and were refused admission by the landlord because of the lateness of the hour. This case was eventually decided by the Lord Chief Justice, who held that the licence given to a hotelier was in the nature of a monopoly, and that, therefore, he had to receive guests at any time. Admittedly, there was obviously a danger in opening a locked hotel door at dead of night when you were responsible for the belongings of everybody in it, but that was just unfortunate.

Cases came to court on the most unlikely points of law; it was

The law and hotels
held that a hotelier was responsible for damage to his guests' property occasioned by a fire which *didn't* start on the premises, but had no liability if the fire broke out in the hotel. Also that if you signed on behalf of a guest for a registered letter, you were responsible for its contents. (Whalley vs. the Washington Hotel, Liverpool, 1885). That if you left your trendy bicycle with an ostler who had contracted the yard from the hotelier, the hotelier remained responsible for your machine if it was damaged. (Briggs vs. the Angel Hotel, Leamington, 1886.) The vast majority of the cases and most of the law didn't really worry many hoteliers during their careers, but there was one area where they were constantly concerned and that was licensing.

If a hotelier lost his licence, he lost an important source of his profits and it would , invariably, put him out of business. Yet the Licensing Laws were interpreted differently and there were many new Licensing Acts during the Victorian and Edwardian periods and agitation for changes all the time.

We have seen how the Temperance Movement began in the 1830s and it grew and flourished for well over 70 years. There were many different societies representing slight variances of viewpoint, but as far as hoteliers were concerned, the battle was over Local Option. The idea behind Local Option was that the inhabitants of an area should be able to vote on the question of whether they wanted licensed premises in their locality or not. If a sufficient proportion voted that they did not, the justices would be able to withdraw the licences that existed and make the area 'dry'. The supporters of local option had decided that the path to total prohibition in the country led along this winding subsidiary road, rather than down the main highway of outright prohibition, which they realised was unlikely to be constructed by Parliament. In 1864 a bill was moved: "to enable owners and occupiers of property in certain districts to prevent the common sales of intoxicating liquors" if there was a two thirds majority in favour. The voting in the Commons was 292-35 against and although the bill was introduced annually in slightly modified forms for some years afterwards, it never looked like being passed. Indeed it even failed to get support from some areas where it might have expected the most enthusiastic reception; many churchmen were against it and Dr. Magee, the Bishop of Peterborough, provided the rallying call for its opponents in the debate in 1872, when he said: "it would be better that England should be free than that England

161

should be compulsorily sober."

"Better free than sober" had a splendid ring to it, and the battle might have seemed to be over until the leader of the Local Option lobby, Sir Wilfrid Lawson, changed his tactics and in 1879 brought in a resolution rather than a bill. While the Commons would not pass a bill, a resolution in favour of a temperance measure was not an immediate attempt to create a law. It could be supported by many members whose constituencies had large numbers of temperance voters and who wished to curry favour with them. The resolution was at first defeated by 252-164 but passed 229-203 in 1880. Although a witness before a Select Committee, who was himself a prominent teetotaller, said in 1878: "the hotel system is one by itself and it may be fairly conceded that while a traveller is residing at a hotel, it is as though he were in his own house", nevertheless, the hoteliers were convinced that once the pubs had been destroyed, they would be next on the list. Certainly Sir Wilfred kept his eye on hotels as well. In 1879 he told the House that the magistrates at Aberystwyth had been attending a function at the Lion Hotel, and as they did not want to go home, they granted an extension of the licence on the spot. The Home Secretary gravely agreed that this was very wrong, though it is doubtful whether Sir Wilfrid was mollified or the magistrates unduly perturbed.

With the resolution passed, the Local Optionists waited for a bill, but the government, under Gladstone, did nothing. In 1883 the resolution was carried by a larger majority, 228-141, and still the government did nothing. The political climate was now right, however, for licensing justices to refuse new applications and, on occasions, to refuse to renew licences. The most famous case at the time was Sharp & Wakefield (1891) where Miss Sharp, the licensee, was refused a renewal because her public house, said Mr. Wakefield and the Mendal, Westmoreland magistrates, was surplus to the requirements of the locality. Furthermore, as it was remote, it was too difficult to supervise. Four years litigation later, the House of Lords held that licences were only given at the discretion of magistrates and nobody had an inalienable right to renewal just because they had obeyed all the rules and their livelihoods depended on it. So it became something of a lottery, because the way in which this decision affected a locality depended entirely on the views of the local justices. In one year in Birmingham 50 licences had to be surrendered and the local brewers arranged compensation for the dispossessed licensees among themselves.

The hotel industry watched with disquiet the whole question of compensation, as it was agreed from the beginning that any official compensation fund for dispossessed landlords would have to be provided by all the remaining licensees and these included hotels. Because of the compensation clause the 1888 Local Government Bill had to be dropped and bills failed to pass the Commons in 1893 and 1895. In 1899 an opponent of the Veto Bill stood at a by-election at Osgoldcross, Yorkshire, specifically on the issue. He won by a margin of 2-1, but still the agitation continued and, although Lawson died in 1906, the rout of the Conservative party in that year enabled Asquith, the new Home Secretary, to bring in a bill to get rid of no less than a third of the 100,000 public houses in the country. This had a galvanising effect on the efforts to form a body to speak for the hotel industry, a project which had almost sunk without trace, through almost total apathy, in spite of regular attempts to get it to float over the years.

The compensation which Asquith's Act required from the hotel industry was very large indeed in total, and there seemed no hope that the bill could be stopped, because the Liberals had a 356 majority in the House of Commons. In spite of frenzied efforts by the whole catering world, the bill passed all its stages in the Commons; the third reading by the enormous margin of 350-113. But then, at the last gasp, the legislation was overwhelmingly rejected by the Tory dominated House of Lords; 272-96. For the hotel industry the Conservative equivalent of the US Cavalry had turned up in the nick of time. It was the final piece of major legislation that the Lords were ever to block, for the constitutional crisis concerning reform of the Lords followed almost immediately. When the dust settled again, the Lords were never the same power in the land.

Sir Wilfrid Lawson introduced his first Local Option Bill in 1864 and Asquith introduced his Licensing Act in 1908; 44 years during which the hotel industry was constantly aware of the growing power of its enemies and their determined efforts to deprive part of the industry of its business. Of course, hotels would have survived even if, in Britain as in the United States, there had been a parliamentary majority for prohibition. Even so, British licensing laws were to be far more restrictive than the continent for most of the 20th century. This

Ritzy

did have an adverse effect on tourist arrivals, though it's impossible to measure by how much. When the hours of opening in Scotland were relaxed towards the end of the 20th century, the effect was not to increase the level of drunkenness. The "evils of drink" are genuine enough, as the number of alcoholics in the country can always testify to, but then excess is never wise. As far as the hotel industry, as a whole, was concerned, selling alcohol was a small element of their real business. They, therefore, felt that they should be separated from the pubs. The Brewing interests, which were considerable in Parliament, did not. They valued the extra element of respectability that association with the hotel industry brought. They were always against a separate licence for hotels.

Prominent hoteliers did their best to get successive governments to approve the separate licence. Sir William Towle, writing in 1914, with a lifetime of experience behind him of all the problems of running the Midland Railway Hotels, summed up his own feelings with resignation: "The genius of the English people is not in the direction of hotel keeping. In addition to this, the extraordinary want of sympathy displayed by so many of the justices in connection with these enterprises, and their persistent endeavours on every opportunity to treat large hotels and their representatives as common public house keepers in their dealings with them, seriously militate against private enterprise being directed to hotel keeping in England."

It was a baton which would be taken up by, among others, Towle's contemporary, Sir George Reeves-Smith, with a dogged determination which achieved almost nothing in his lifetime either .

The mid-Victorian licensing laws were less onerous than they were for most of the 20th century. It was only after 1872 that children under 16 were forbidden to drink alcohol in hotels, and the Licensing Act of that year made opening hours five in the morning to midnight; a 19 hour trading day. A Leamington case had also established that guests staying in hotels could entertain their friends outside licensing hours. The shorter hours were really the result of the First World War legislation which was designed to produce a more sober and industrious war effort. Victorian Britain depended heavily for its tax revenues on drink. As the *Caterer* commented in 1885: "Not only are we, as a trade, under greater legislative control than any other country in the world, and our intoxicants are also more heavily taxed than those of any foreign nation, but we pay more than one fourth of the whole national revenue."

The Victorian problem was to stop excessive drinking without reducing the revenue to the Exchequer, just as today there is still a somewhat schizophrenic attitude towards smoking when the Chancellor sees his income from it. Legislation was passed in the 1870s to prevent short measures and to provide inspectors, but Victorian hoteliers really had little to complain about except being lumped together with the meanest drinking house.

The value of a licence was well illustrated by Rudd & Blackford in 1886. The owner of a Bournemouth hotel offered £1,000 (about £75,000 today) to the plaintiff if he could get the hotel a licence, but when the plaintiff did so, the owner refused to pay. He was taken to court and judgment was found against him in full. If a licence was worth such a vast sum it is no wonder that the hoteliers were frightened of the Local Option lobby.

12

A pause for the court case.
Spokes vs. The Grosvenor Hotel Company and others.

Throughout the history of hotels, most accusations of malpractice have been against the staff; watering the gin, stealing from hotel bedrooms, fiddling the bills and defrauding the tax man. The malpractices of the owners have usually been concealed, even from a press always keen to criticise the industry for its shortcomings. There was, however, one occasion when the whole story came out. It couldn't have been typical in its entirety , but elements of it probably occurred quite frequently. We are talking of Spokes vs. the Grosvenor Hotel Company and Others in 1898. It is also interesting because, thanks to the extensive law reports in the newspapers at the time, we are afforded a first hand glimpse into Victorian hotel operations.

Richard Drew's Plan One was quite simple. First you had to pack the Grosvenor Hotel Company board of directors with pliable, supportive friends and relatives. Then you needed to enter into contracts with suppliers you controlled. The contracts would be at prices well above the lowest comparable ones available. If you didn't control a company capable of supplying certain items, you had two further options. You could get the suppliers to deliver to the hotel, but to invoice one of your companies. Then you just increased their prices when you billed the hotel, as if the supplies had originated with you. Or you could give introductions to the hotel and take bribes for doing so, particularly if the introductions would almost certainly guarantee the supplier getting the contracts.

Plan Two sprang effortlessly from Plan One. When the hotel paid lower - or no dividends - because of the effect of Plan One on profits, the shares would drop in value. Then you made sure that whatever stock came onto the market was bought up by you at the depressed prices. You could pay for the shares with part of the profits of Plan One. Then when you owned the hotel, you could let it trade normally and when the profits rose, so would the value of your shares. Another illicit fortune beckoned.

It was fraud on a majestic scale and on a 20 year canvas. The Grosvenor was a substantial business. From 1884 - 1895 it looked after 713,000 visitors and employed 190 staff. It also has to be remembered that among the 713,000 there were many permanent residents.

To pack the hotel board, you had to get rid of the old one. In the Grosvenor's first 20 years, the hotel's profits were, of course, affected by economic slumps and booms and by the speed at which the demand for bedrooms kept up with the growing supply of new hotels. Early in 1876, however, a serious economic slump started and for three years England's industry bore the brunt of a great depression. The Grosvenor was unable to pay a dividend to its shareholders and its £10 shares slumped to £7. There was a call by shareholders, including Dick Drew, for a Committee of Inspection. On June 20th, 1878 the committee reported unfavourably and the directors all resigned.

There followed an Extraordinary General Meeting and Messrs, Artis, Hale, Davis and Grogan were elected directors. C. T. Artis had been on the Board which had resigned and he was Drew's father-in-law. In July, William Hale, a member of the Committee of Inspection, was elected chairman at a salary of £200 a year. He was an old friend of Drew, who had put enough shares in Hales' name to qualify him as a director. Drew continued to own them and took any future dividends. A director had to have 50 shares, then at £7, so this was an expenditure of £350. Hale was an accountant who had been the secretary of a Public Company at a salary of only £175 a year. So the share purchase would have involved him in expending two year's salary otherwise. As he stated in court in 1898: "£100 a year is useful to me." Another close friend, of Drew, Edward Newitt, became a director in 1881. Drew's brother in law, Owen Reynolds, joined the board in 1882. Then Mr. Davis disappeared and Mr. Grogan died. The board was satisfactorily packed and Drew's nephew, Joseph Drew, was appointed a director in 1892.

Now for the contracts. Drew had originally been employed in a counting house at £150 a year. By 1878, though, he was: "a member of the firm of Cowell and Drew" who were butchers in fashionable Knightsbridge. And in 1878 the Grosvenor board decided to give its meat contract to Cowell and Drew at a price of 5¼d a lb (450 gr.) This was about the going rate. Maybe the Board could have got 5d but what's a farthing! Well, not much today, but to bring 1878 prices up to 2003, you have to multiply by somewhere between 30 and 50 and hotels buy a lot of meat. Between 1879 and 1895, the court was told, the Grosvenor Hotel paid Cowell and Drew £110,565.50 - that's for about 860 tons of meat, say 378lb a day (172kg), but then the Victorians ate a great deal of meat. For breakfast as well as lunch and dinner, and then there was the banqueting consumption as well, plus staff feeding.

That makes the overcharge on the meat contract alone - at 1/4p - £5,528. There is another consideration, though. During the 16 years of the contract, meat prices dropped. This was due to the vastly increased imports of cheap American meat. Through-out the period there was deflation. The contract grew more valuable to Drew as he bought cheaper but sold at the same price. If you multiply by 30 for today's money, you get about a £165,000 fraud on the meat contract alone.

In 1882 Drew: "carried on the business of Grimmond & Co, who had a greengrocery shop" in fashionable Belgravia. Grimmonds got the contract for greengrocery for the Grosvenor in 1882 and from 1882 - 1895, the Grosvenor paid Grimmonds a total of £41,658 for greengrocery. They also paid them £11,319 for coal!

How could a greengrocer's shop supply coal? Very simple. Coal Merchants, Charrington, Sells and Co., provided the coal and delivered it to the Grosvenor. They then invoiced Grimmonds and Grimmonds invoiced the Grosvenor. For example, Thomas Potter, manager of Charrington's Kings Cross depot, declared in court that in 1890: "they were supplying Messrs Grimmond with Welsh Coal at 22 shillings (£1.10p) a ton and kitchen coal at 17 shillings (85p) a ton." Grimmonds then charged the Grosvenor £1.42 a ton for the Welsh coal and £1.32 for the kitchen coal. That's a mark-up of between 30% and 55%. The Grosvenor bought, on average, 600 tons of coal a year.

In 1886 Drew bought shares in Rush's laundry. In 1887 he bought up all the rest. The contract price for the Grosvenor's laundry was fixed at £3 for 1,000 articles. An accountant, called by the plaintiff, said that - based on the price at important hotels like the Langham and Westminster Palace - the contracted rate should have been £2.

The secretary at Rush's from 1882 - 1887 was Owen Reynolds, the Grosvenor director who had married Drew's sister and been introduced to Rush's directors by Drew. Drew had provided Reynold's qualifying shares at the Grosvenor as well. Originally a land agent in Ireland, Reynolds became the manager of Rush's in 1887 at a salary of £174 a year. To this could be added his £100 director's fees at the Grosvenor. Mr. Reynolds had also been given nominee shares in the St. James Hotel by Drew, of which he also became a director. So Reynolds was unlikely to disagree on any fundamental point with Drew. As Mr. Reynolds told the court: "he took only a minor part in the discussions of the Board of the Grosvenor Hotel Company when he joined. He left matters to the senior members."

He also confirmed in court that his client, Longs Hotel, paid £2.10 per 1,000 articles to Rush while another client, The St. James Hotel, paid £3.15 per 1,000. Between 1879 and 1895 Rush's received nearly £24,000 from the Grosvenor.

These examples of fraud on the shareholders of the hotel were not a full account of the offences, though. The eventual plaintiff's counsel, Arthur Jelf, Q.C., said in court that he didn't want the case to go on for months!

The pace of innovation in Victorian times was very fast and keeping luxury up to date gave Drew more opportunities for making money. There was a cosy arrangement with a company called R. C. Cole. The hotel needed a piano. Drew bought it for £50 and sent it to Cole, who sent it to the Grosvenor and charged £85. When the question of electric light for the Grosvenor arose, there were richer pickings. Cole recommended Crittalls. That company got the contract at a figure of £10,500. Cole got a commission from Crittall of £4,000. What percentage of that did Drew get? He said on oath in court: "I will not swear it was not £2,000, because it was with other payments."

As the hotel's profits suffered, some of the shareholders bailed out. That often brought them into contact with a Mr. Pertwee, a stockbroker in the City of London, who did a large business in hotel shares and, yes, he was related to Drew too!

According to Mr. F. Thornton, who worked for Pertwee, Drew decided what the shares were worth and then Pertwee sent out the circulars. If the shareholders decided to sell, Drew normally was the buyer. Robert Webb, the Company Secretary, also testified that dissatisfied shareholders might approach him to help sell their shares. They hoped to get the best price in this way but Webb only contacted Drew and then told the shareholders the price he was prepared to pay: " There was no competition."

There was, of course, one other person who had to be bribed

Ritzy

to stay quiet about all that was going on. Joseph Zeder had been a head waiter at the Alexandra Hotel before he saw an advertisement for the job of manager of the Grosvenor in 1878 and applied. In Germany this was the traditional route to the manager's chair and the British hotel industry benefited greatly from its able German staff.

Zeder had known Drew at the Alexandra and met him again at the Grosvenor. The terms of his employment at £300 a year, included stipulations that he was to own no shares in the company and was not to earn any money beyond his salary. Zeder never did earn shares but he got £100 a year: "as a Christmas Box" from Cowell and Drew from 1879 - 1895. "He had received other similar gratuities." Mr. Zeder, officially, only earned £300 a year but he declared in court that his own Christmas present to Mrs. Drew never cost him less than £20. Nearly a month's salary. He also said that he had absolutely no say in who supplied the hotel. That was entirely up to the directors: "When he had once volunteered some advice on the subject, the Directors told him it was their business and not his." "He was allowed to spend petty cash at the rate of £2 a month."

To add insult to injury, it was also suggested that the goods invoiced to the Grosvenor at the inflated prices, didn't always arrive. Short weight and falsified invoices were alleged. Cowell & Drew employees, like Clarke and Fry, agreed there were malpracticies. Other employees were produced by the defence to deny it. The jury found for the directors in these matters. It does seem, however, significant that a man called Alfred Clements was the storekeeper and cellar man at the Grosvenor for some years. Clements had previously been Company Secretary at the Grosvenor from 1875 - 1878. Then he had joined Cowell & Drew and, subsequently, Grimmonds. How convenient for Drew it must have been to have a trusted ally in such a crucial post

If you were a member of the charmed circle around Drew, you could expect lots of tidbits. Like many others, the company solicitor, George Rolfe, Robert Webb, the Company Secretary, and Mr. Clavell, the Chef, would get a joint of meat from Cowell & Drew every week and it would be entered into the Day Book, but never paid for, according to witness Clarke. Drew lent his fellow director and nephew, Joseph Drew, £100 to set up a Butcher's shop in the 1890s, but he was never repaid. Hale had no business other than his directorships,and admitted owing Newitt about £350, Drew £150, and there were other debts outstanding to him as well. Drew had friends running a couple of boarding houses at the seaside in Bournemouth and the charmed circle were invited on occasions for free weekends. Zeder went several times. The directors would also gather in the back room of Grimmonds for discussions with Drew and were offered lunch or tea. There was even a direct phone line between that room and the board room at the Grosvenor.

In return the charmed circle would expect Drew to arrive towards the end of board meetings and, as Hale told the court: "I demurred to his presence on several occasions." It was true that, by the middle of the 1890s, Drew owned 75% of the shares in the Grosvenor. That meant that the largest shareholder was present at board meetings, but he was also the principal tradesmen used by the hotel.

Although the court case was about the Grosvenor Hotel, Drew's tentacles spread much wider. Hale was a director and chairman of the St. James Hotel till 1897 and Drew had provided him with the qualifying shares for that post as well. Hale agreed Drew was the largest shareholder. Newitt was a director of the Salisbury Hotel. He agreed in court that this was through Drew's influence too. The circle had infiltrated Longs Hotel as well. As the contracted rate for laundry alone at the St. James was also about 50% higher than usual in the trade, it seems likely that their directors were equally corrupt.

Nemesis arrived in the shape of Henry Kimber, M.P. for Wandsworth, a prominent solicitor and a shareholder in the Grosvenor for 16 years. Kimber finally got fed up with the dividends he received from his investment in the Grosvenor. Mr. Kimber was the vice chairman of the Cecil Hotel, a director of the Westminster Palace Hotel and Chairman of the Bedford Hotel in Brighton. So he knew the business. He protested that there was: "no rivalry between the Grosvenor and the Westminster Palace Hotel" but this was received with laughter in court.

In 1896 Kimber circularised the shareholders to get them to agree that more information on the company's trading was needed. He tried to stop the balance sheet being passed but Hale didn't let him speak. He tried to get elected as a director but Rolfe, the company solicitor, told him he had no chance as Rolfe had ample proxies to block him. Drew had divided some of his share holding into blocks

171

of 10 and then put them into the names of at least 50 nominees. This ensured that if there ever was a vote at a meeting of shareholders, he would always win on a show of hands. Leonard Hatchard from Cowell & Drew gave evidence that one of his responsibilities was to collect dividend warrants from at least 12 of Drew's nominees.

There was only one remedy available for Kimber. He created a "Reform Committee" and got up a petition among the minority shareholders for a Board of Trade Enquiry. Russell Spokes, a fellow director at the Westminster Palace was the nominated injured party.

The enquiry was granted and the directors were called to give evidence. Hale declined to talk to the enquiry. He said his counsel advised him that he might incriminate himself. After being threatened with prison, he eventually came up with the documents which Mr. Whinney, the Board of Trade Inspector, wanted. Drew was also ordered to disclose documents and refused, on counsel's advice. They might incriminate him as well. He asked the Court of Appeal to overrule the order but the Court of Appeal decided against him. They held that Mr. Whinney was only doing his job. Zeder testified that he had answered 1,400 of Mr. Whinney's questions.

In court, Mr. Whinney's clerk, Ernest Gundry, showed exactly why there was such resistance from the directors and Drew. He testified that the cost of provisions had risen since 1875 from £4,000 to over £10,000. (This, in spite of the fact that there had been deflation.) The expenditure over 20 years on provisions had been £336,120. In the first 9 years, there had been a turnover of £113,000 and a profit of over £26,000. In subsequent years, on a much larger turnover, there was a loss of over £9,000.

When the report of the Board of Trade Enquiry was published, Mr. Kimber agreed to underwrite the costs of a lawsuit by the minority shareholders against the directors and on February 10th 1898, the case opened in the High Court before Mr. Justice Ridley and a special jury.

It is extremely unusual for a body of minority shareholders to sue the directors of a Hotel company for fraudulent conspiracy, which is a criminal offence. Russell Spokes was the official plaintiff because Kimber was in India when the action started.

Now Drew and the directors had to produce a defence. When the possibility of a Board of Trade enquiry emerged, the inflated prices were suddenly reduced. Then some of the potentially damaging witnesses disappeared. Nobody could find the chef, Clavell. Drew consolidated his shops into a new company and burnt a lot of the old books at Rush's laundry. The salary of two potentially crucial witnesses increased substantially. The company secretary, Webb, had an increase from £150 a year to £225. Zeder's went up from £300 to £400.

In addition, some very fine barristers were employed for the defendants; Sir Edward Clarke, Q.C., and Joseph Walton, Q.C. for Drew. Lawson Walton, Q.C., and three other barristers for Hale and Reynolds. Mr. Witt, Q.C. for Newitt and Joseph Drew. The latter didn't appear in court at all, but he had admitted at the Board of Trade enquiry that the malpractices had occurred.

How did the directors find the money for their QCs to represent them for 9 days in court? Did Drew pay the bill? Hale was asked the question in court and said he had borrowed some money from Owen Reynolds. As we have seen, Reynolds was the Manager of Rush's on £174 a year. Never mind lending money to Hale, how had Reynolds managed to pay his own barrister? It might also be asked what qualifications Joseph Drew had for the Board? When he wasn't considering the problems of the Grosvenor he was an assistant butcher at Cowell and Drew.

Mr. Justice Ridley had little doubt of the correct result and pointed the jury in that direction. Two of his comments were especially damaging to the defendants. When Hale testified that he thought it was in the interests of the Grosvenor Hotel that Drew should be present at board meetings, Ridley said: "I really think you do not want any more from this witness after that answer. What better evidence can you have of conspiracy than that? "

He also totally undermined Drew's credibility. Drew said he couldn't remember if the chef had been sent a Christmas Box by Cowell and Drew: "I do not remember the amount or I would tell your Lordship". Ridley commented: "I am not so sure about that." Sir Edward Clarke protested that this was not a proper observation but Ridley replied heatedly "I do not expect to be lectured by you, Sir Edward Clarke." There were elements of a Kangaroo Court.

The main defence was that the high prices were justified because the hotel always had cash flow problems and Drew helped them with extended credit and loans. There were unexpectedly high items of expenditure. For example, in 1881 several thousand pounds had been spent on a new restaurant. In 1885, when there was no dividend, £2,000 had to be spent on sinking an artesian well. There was that installation of electric light for £10,500 in 1892. In 1896 when there was no dividend, £10,000 had been spent on rebuilding.

All the directors denied knowledge of individual malpractices. Hale said he didn't know for a long time that Drew owned Grimmonds. Newitt and Reynolds said they only learned of Zeder's Christmas Box at the Board of Trade enquiry.

For the plaintiffs, expert witnesses were produced from within the hotel industry. Gordon Hotels were the largest chain in the country. R.C. Hambro, general manager of their Metropole Hotel in London, testified that 4 1/2p a lb would be the right price for meat over the past 12 years. George Brinkworth, manager of the Westminster Palace, said they were paying £1.80 per 1,000 articles to their laundry.

When the dust settled and the jury retired to consider their verdict, it only took them 65 minutes to find the defendants guilty. This left the court with two problems. The first was that the main sufferer from the actions of the directors was the principal defendant, Richard Drew. As he owned 75% of the shares, he had been deprived of 75% of the lost dividends. Over the years other shareholders may have been deprived but that was the position in 1898. Secondly, there was the question of the Statute of Limitations. If a crime is committed in Britain and goes undiscovered for seven years, the criminal cannot be prosecuted, except for offences like murder and treason. The frauds had been going on for 20 years. Did the Statute of Limitations apply if the defendants had, themselves, made sure the offences were not discovered? Mr. Justice Ridley said he'd think about it.

There then was the question of what to do about the directors. They were still in place at the Grosvenor and, therefore, the interests of the minority shareholders were not being protected. The prosecutor, Arthur Jelf, wanted a Receiver appointed. Ridley decided he couldn't do that as the company wasn't in financial difficulties. The case went back to the Court of Appeal before Lord Justices Smith, Chitty and Collins in March. At this point the defendants gave in. They didn't object to whatever was proposed. Kimber, Spokes and General Frederick Fitzwygram were then appointed receivers and managers of the hotel: "without salary and without security" for six months.

1898 was not a good year for the image of British Hotels

with the Ritz and Escoffier dismissals coming only a month before the Spokes case. As Sir Henry Burdett, the vice chairman of Gordon Hotels told his Annual General Meeting in July 1898: "I have asked myself how is it, and why is it, that the Gordon Hotels have escaped these scandals." He found the explanation in the character of his chairman, Fred Gordon. By 1900 the Hotel Napoleon had reached agreement with the London & South Coast Railway to operate the Grosvenor. What happened to Drew and the directors? Certainly, the directors lost their positions on the boards. Hales testified that he was unemployed and had resigned from his position as chairman or director of the Grosvenor, St. James and Salisbury Hotels. The company into which Drew had amalgamated his interests went into deficit, due to the bad publicity the trial had brought. The fact remained, however, that Drew had 70% of the shares of the Grosvenor and counsel suggested a figure of £700,000. Even after the costs of the trial Drew would have been a very wealthy man. Of course, the trial was a considerable strain. On 'Doctors orders' Drew had disappeared to the country for a long time. Sometimes, however, guilty people make remarkable recoveries from all kinds of illness when being ill ceases to benefit them.

The prosecution had demanded a £120,000 (£3.6 million) refund on the £300,000 (£9 million) Drew enterprises had been paid over 20 years. Yet if that had been the decision, three quarters would have gone to Drew as the main shareholder. And when the hotel was sold, Drew would have got the lion's share of the proceeds.

There is one last question that remains unanswered. Where did Drew get the money to start the fraud in the first place? To buy the shares for his nominees, to give the puppet directors the cheerleading they needed to qualify and to buy into Cowell and Drew. Logically, the plan would have been drawn up with his father-in-law, C.D. Artis, the sitting director in 1878, who could make sure the board of directors at the time were condemned. A man with his own companies, in a substantial way of business, who could provide the seed corn money. Artis was a director of the company who supplied the Grosvenor with wine.

It was a brilliant scam, thought out and executed in great detail. When reviewed from the vantage point of 2003, you'd have to say that, on balance, both Plans One and Two really did work.

13
After the ball was over
1900 - 1914

"Profits have been adversely affected by the high price of provisions and supplies and by the ever increasing public demand for the maximum of convenience and luxury. The wave of temperance and the tendency of customers to economise have helped to sap a one time profitable source of income - wine consumption. The burden of taxation increased by the Compensation Act which came into operation with the year, is now exceedingly onerous." To make the best of a poor situation, the *Caterer* told its readers that what was needed was: "enterprise in advertising, close buying, stopping leakages, adopting improvements, keen personal supervision and a quick appreciation of ever developing public requirements."

This was in 1906 and neatly sums up the difficulties which had arisen or worsened since the old Queen died. It had not been a happy 5 years. Where the hotel industry had been accustomed to dropping food prices, stable fuel costs and deflation, the Boer War had changed the picture for the worse. Now prices were beginning to rise and interest rates were climbing too. This had a serious effect, not only on the cost of overdrafts, but also on the reserve funds of a number of existing hotel companies.

What happened was this. When times were good, every company put a small part of its profits aside in case there was a rainy day in the future. There was often another reserve fund for future refurbishing of a major kind - new boilers, major roof repairs and similar items. These reserve funds had to be invested safely and, indeed, when Gordons put money into more speculative securities, like New Zealand Loan & Mercantile, their shareholders complained. And with cause because Gordon had not chosen wisely. Consequently, Gordons, like most of the other hotel companies, put the bulk of the money into Consols, that great British government security which gave you a fixed 3% on your money with total safety and which had the strength of the whole British Empire behind it. After the war, though, you could get more than 3% on your money equally securely from other investments, and therefore Consols fell in price. Although you still got your 3%, the value of the reserve

After the ball was over

funds diminished if your business needed the money for the purpose for which it was originally intended. If Consols fell from 100 to 90, your reserve fund would finish up worth 10% less.

As these funds were usually much smaller than the more prudent management of today would demand, the effect was greater and shareholders who had welcomed the distribution of large dividends in the past, now found their companies short of reserves. If it became necessary to raise more capital as a consequence, the interest charges were up as well, and life for the directors grew even more difficult.

Almost all the goods needed for refurbishing and running the hotels became more expensive; carpets and curtains, plates and cutlery. Wages went up as well; a chef who had been earning £1 a week in 1880 was by 1914 earning £2 a week and a kitchen porter £1 a week instead of £2 a month. One chef who would have benefited was employed for a time at the Carlton Hotel in London - Ho Chi Minh - the future Vietnamese leader. Escoffier apparently promoted him from dish washer for saving the scraps left by guests for the poor people. The new salaries were, of course, still very low and the inflation puny, but where we have been used to rising prices, the Edwardians were shocked by them.

The public's disposable income was reduced as well. During the war it had been necessary to levy additional taxation, and when the conflict ended the government was not able to put it back to the prewar levels. Instead income tax at one shilling (5p) in the £ remained at an all-time peak, and after 1909, if you earned more than £3,000 a year, you had to pay super-tax. Don't fret for them; it didn't stop the rich getting into the fashionable habit of drinking champagne with every meal.

With staff costs doubled, food costs up 50% and additional taxation, the results should have been a higher tariff for the hotels, but in many cities there was now much too much competition for this to be possible. The Midland Grand which charged 14 shillings (70p) for dinner, bed and breakfast in 1873 was only charging 12 shillings (60p) in 1912. Prices simply could not rise with so much spare capacity in the industry, and with still more hotels being built. In London alone the decade saw the opening, among others, of the Piccadilly, Ritz, Waldorf, Imperial and Lyons' Strand Palace Hotel, the latter charging only 6 shillings

Ritzy

(30p) for bed and breakfast and attracting large numbers of guests as a result. A less imposing newcomer was the Goring at Victoria in 1909, but it was among the very few who offered a private bathroom in every bedroom. The Goring family, in the person of George Goring, still run it today.

When hotels ran into such difficulties, the arguments raged fiercely about who was to blame, and all too often these arguments eventually finished up as inquests. Was it the fault of the manager accused of taking commission from suppliers, stealing the food and wine in conspiracies with his heads of department, overcharging customers and turning a blind eye to the visits of prostitutes, so long as they were well paid to do so? Or was it the directors, forcing the managers to buy uneconomically from friends of the board, thus cheating the shareholders but feathering their own nests? Those directors who invested the reserve funds unwisely, also might insist on unprofitable capital expenditure, on retaining inefficient staff because of their personal relationships, and persisting in interfering where they should have left the control in professional hands.

The truth differed according to which company you were studying. The best generalisation is that it depended on the strength of both directors and management, for good or evil, whether a hotel prospered, rather than the excuses which economic conditions provided. Certainly there were abuses on both sides but then hotels were close to the sources of Edwardian sin and there were many who would take advantage of the situation. One potential additional cost Gordons did fight successfully for the whole industry. It occurred when the Westminster Council wanted to charge the Metropole Hotel for removing refuse in 1906. Gordons went to court and the judgment was that hotels were akin to homes and, therefore, the refuse had to be removed free.

In 1900 Spiers and Ponds went into the hotel business with Empire Hotels in Lowestoft, Bath and Buxton. As young men Felix Spiers and Christopher Pond had started with railway station refreshment rooms and, by their peak in the 1920s, they would have 200 of them. By 1908 they also had 12 hotels and an unusual tariff; you could stay in them, on full board, for £168 a year, £95 for 6 months or £60 for 3 months.

Of the new London hotels both the Piccadilly and the Ritz added poignant footnotes to great traditions. The Piccadilly was

After the ball was over

the brainchild of the nephew of Sir Polydore de Keyser. He was also called Polydore and he had taken over the de Keyser Hotel after his uncle's death. Young Polydore was determined to write a new and even greater chapter in the family annals and sunk his personal fortune, as well as that of many of his friends, in creating: "the most unashamedly Baroque piece of stage design, a thickly rusticated ground floor, and above, colossal columns." The architect, Norman Shaw, had reached a period in his work when he wished his buildings to epitomise the grandeur which was Imperial Britain, and in Polydore he had found a nincompoop who would agree to foot the bill. Although the Piccadilly was in the perfect spot, almost on top of Piccadilly Circus, the initial outlay was far too great; the hotel opened in May 1905 and called in the Receivers in July 1905.

The astonishing thing about the Piccadilly to modern eyes was the speed of construction. The Egyptian Hall on the site had to be demolished, the foundations went 80 feet (25m) into the ground, there were 300 bedrooms and colossal decoration. Yet it only took 18 months to build! Mind you, it had taken the de Keysers 50 years to build up their business and young Polydore took less than 10 to lose it. He died in Montreal at only 42, victim not of a broken heart in exile, but of scarlet fever as general manager of a major hotel. The de Keyser Hotel passed into the hands of Lever Brothers and became their headquarters. The accounts department moved into the Grand Ballroom, the executives into the bedrooms and the precursor of many other takeovers had reduced the competition for the London hotel industry by one. Meanwhile the Piccadilly, with its fine Masonic Temples, the dining room panelled exquisitely in Australian Oak of a quality unobtainable today, and its labyrinth of public and private rooms, was taken over by a new company, headed by H. Mallaby-Deeley, M.P. The member for Willesden installed Fritz Heim, a hard working German manager, and he quickly made the operation profitable. The factor which made all the difference, of course, was that the company no longer had to service the original capital; only the money involved in buying a failed enterprise.

Quite different in concept was the Ritz Hotel, which was opened some years after the successful creation of the Ritz Hotel in Paris and which incorporated the same ideas which had made the Carlton so popular. There was one major change and that was the absence from command of Ritz himself. In 1901 he had been working like a beaver to ensure that the Carlton would outshine every other hotel in celebrating the coronation of his greatest client and most most cherished patron, Edward VII. Indeed, Ritz owed a very great deal to the man who had supported him blindly when he left the Savoy. Among other favours, Edward had also broken the conventions by actually coming and dining in public at the Carlton. The hotel, of course, benefited enormously from this open expression of his approval. The Carlton was to be host to a shining array of famous guests and Ritz might well have seen the great day as the absolute peak of his career. On June 24th, however, just two days before the coronation, Edward had to be operated on for appendicitis and, much to his disgust, he had to postpone a coronation for which, in all conscience, he had waited an almost record number of years. The departure of the offending, if useless, organ and the majority of the capital's visitors could have been synchronised, so rapidly did the one follow the other. As Frederick Gordon told his sorrowing shareholders: "Well, I won't say that all the visitors in the hotels, but a very large proportion of them, immediately the announcement was made, left bodily."

While Gordon was no doubt cursing his luck which had been turning sour of late, poor Cesar Ritz collapsed. He had a complete nervous breakdown brought on by driving himself too hard for years and culminating in endless hours of labouring towards a royal anticlimax. Though he rallied after a while for a couple of years, he had a relapse in 1903 and thereafter sank slowly into both public and mental oblivion. Today he would probably have been brought back to near normal with modern drugs, but such progress lay many years in the future, and there was no cure for the finest hotel craftsman of his time: "Do what you like" became the stock answer of the man who had taken such delight in helping and supervising and by 1908 he had resigned from all his companies and was an invalid.

Building started in 1904 on the hotel which would be named after him. It was built on the sites of the old Bath and Walsingham Hotels and had a steel frame, one of the first of its kind in London, though the Waldorf soon followed. Since the Ritz is also faced with Norwegian granite it must be one of the most solid structures in Mayfair, and with its covered colonnade it rightly merits its present position as a protected building. The decor was entirely Louis XVI, unlike many others who borrowed from the styles of Louis XIV and

XV as well - known as Tous les Louis. Though Ritz never managed the Ritz, its grace and charm, its lightness and spaciousness and its thoroughly elegant taste, all bear witness to the man it helps to immortalize. True to his teaching, the hotel had no dust traps, like the tops of wardrobes or heavy drapes, and was painted rather than wallpapered. When you wanted Room Service you rang a bell. To monitor how quickly you received attention, there was a set of bells in the room service department and a duplicate in the manager's office. The board was fortunate to persuade Alfred Holland to join them some years after his resignation from Gordons, which was exactly what was needed after Ritz succumbed. To the end of his long life in 1937 Holland served the Ritz and the Carlton.

Frederick Gordon had found the going rough after the Boer War was over. The 10% dividend, which shareholders had been told after the Holland fracas they might expect to improve, had in fact declined to 8% and the shares had slumped near to par. In the last full year of Gordon's chairmanship, however, he had been able to report: "the improvement is a very satisfactory and substantial one but it is not as great as the directors would have liked to put before you."

It is very likely that Gordon could have pulled the company round if he had been in his prime, but now he was an old man and in the summer of 1903 he fell ill and was advised by his doctors to go to his hotel in Cannes to recuperate. On March 22nd 1904 he went to the opera at Monte Carlo and suffered a heart attack late at night which proved fatal. The man who had earned the title: 'Hotel Napoleon' as surely as Ritz was called: 'Hotelkeeper to Kings and King of Hotelkeepers" left the scene at almost the same time as his rival but, unlike Ritz, Frederick Gordon had never been seriously under attack. The business he had founded was still sound and his own reputation still intact. The disappointing results of the last few years were almost universally regarded by the public as a regrettable, but temporary, pause after the 20 years of unbroken prosperity he had given his supporters. He left £500,000.

Many of the hotels were freehold, the Gordon Hotel wine stocks alone were worth £180,000 and 1903 had been a better year. Gordon probably felt that the economic conditions in the '70s when he started were much more difficult than the post-Boer War period, and we shall never know whether he would have triumphantly overcome the industry's malaise. Or whether, like Henry V, for instance, he died at the right time for his fame to remain untarnished. There were, however, even in his lifetime, two significant and disturbing factors; in the 10 years since 1893 the number of nights when Gordon beds were occupied had declined by 11% and this was a direct result of the new competition. Second, the sale of wine had dropped 10% in 1902 alone and this was because money was so much tighter.

The *Caterer* had suggested that advertising could help, and Gordons were well to the fore on this front and even employed their own advertising manager. Robert Donald gave an interview to the *Advertising World* and they were able to elicit full details of his carefully worked out marketing strategy: "We use the society papers regularly" explained Donald "as well as the Ladies' Weeklies and some of the dailies. We want to get to the travelling public. The quantity of circulation is not everything. We advertise in the half-penny dailies to keep on the right side of the newspapermen." It was easier to obtain favourable editorial coverage in Edwardian times than it is now, but Donald also knew how to provide the right stories: "Look at the large number of dinners, dances and other gatherings held at our hotels; they each mean a certain amount of publicity for us if managed properly." This use of public relations operated side by side with heavy media purchases: "It is nothing out of the ordinary for us to run a dozen pages in *Bradshaw*, and we are large advertisers in the other guides as well. We supply all the leading steamship companies with literature as well as producing tariffs and souvenir books."

All of which was potentially very sound, but how did Donald measure the effectiveness of his advertising? Donald parried: "We are not like the proprietor of an ordinary article. For us to the present it has been found impossible to systematically check the returns afforded. Until this is overcome we are totally dependent on our judgment. We have found that advertising as a whole pays very well." So the classic defence of the advertising manager wandering around in a fog of unsubstantiated judgment had been formulated as early as this. More should have been learned about this important subject, for Gordon's advertising was expensive and the occupancy had dropped by that 11%. In fairness, what Donald couldn't anticipate was the serious effect on business in the Trafalgar Square area, caused by closing Charing Cross Station in 1906 when the roof collapsed.

In the countryside the economic downturn was not the

prime consideration. The revival of the country hotel, left to rot by the departure of the stagecoach, was now a greater possibility than had ever seemed likely in the past 70 years. We have seen how the bicycle, and later the motor car, brought new traffic onto the roads. Unfortunately, the provision of a new market did not automatically provide the necessary capital to revive the near derelict hotels. Many were in the ownership of the local gentry, but leased to the brewers, and there were a lot of complaints that the only item of any quality obtainable was the drink. Food was usually either of a poor standard or unobtainable, while the bed-room areas had often not seen a lick of paint for years, far less any refurbishing.

Where was the money and the drive to come from to alter the situation? The answer, in part, was Albert Henry George, 4th Earl Grey, a former Governor-General of Canada and yet another example of that apparently endless supply of Victorian humanitarians. Grey wished to bridge the gap between the out-and-out prohibitionists on the one hand, and the brewers on the other. He proposed that each English county should set up a trust to run country hotels. The original name chosen was The Public House Trust and the principle advocated was that the gentry should not renew the brewers' licences on suitable properties, but instead put them in good order and reopen them as decent hotels. It was a very ambitious scheme but Grey was a powerful and determined fighter and, with the help of a number of the Lords-Lieutenant, the idea slowly got off the ground.

The first hotel was at Ridge Hill, 16 miles from London, on what had been the mail road to Holyhead. It was called The Wagon and Horses and had exactly 3 bedrooms. The county trust found an ex-policeman to run it and this worthy was paid a salary plus commission on what he sold, except for alcoholic drinks. The basic wage was a slim 30 shillings (£1.50) a week, which had to cover not only the manager and his wife, but also one servant to help them run the hotel. Admittedly they had a coal allowance, but the normal commission on drink sales would have been more rewarding financially and there was also a deduction for living in the hotel. Perhaps a policeman was chosen because no hotelier worth the name would look at the job.

The experiment, nevertheless, was a success as far as the move in emphasis from drink sales was concerned, and the Barnet brewer who had been sending the hotel its beer, soon found that he was supplying it with an equal amount of fresh water, so that the demand for tea could be satisfied. The Wagon and Horses was run by the Trust from 1903 and in 1904 it was joined by the Rose and Crown at Tring, another Rose and Crown at Tewin, also in Hertfordshire, and The Red Lion at Radlett. Although the efforts of other trusts were important, it was Hertfordshire which made the most progress and, when it was decided to amalgamate the trusts, it was the emblem of Hertfordshire, the hart couchant, which was adopted as the symbol of the new company. It was not until after the First World War, however, that the name Trust Houses was finalised. By then the non-alcoholic turnover of the company was 40% of the business, whereas in 1903 at The Wagon and Horses it had only been 9%.

There was plenty of opposition to Lord Grey because, almost uniquely, he managed to antagonise both the brewers and the temperance supporters. The brewers didn't like the way the managers were directed to any kind of sale except drink, and the temperance lobby objected to the fact that drink was sold at all. The magistrates did on occasions turn down the applications of the trusts for licences, and progress was slow in many parts of the country. Indeed Trust Houses was entirely confined to Southern England and the Midlands until after 1918.

If there was opposition, there was also powerful support. Lord Rothschild built The Rose and Crown at Tring for the trust and then leased it to them at a moderate rent. The Countess of Caledon owned The Wagon and Horses and was also generous in her terms. Many people bought shares in the trusts even though the dividend was not allowed to be more than 5% and was likely to be much lower, like the 2 1/2% paid in 1910. The limit was raised to 7% in 1914 but the supporters of Trust Houses were not investing for the sake of the return on capital. They were anxious that the supporters of moderation should win the drink war, and they also wanted to save as much fine architecture as they could. They took pleasure in rescuing such historic inns as the 15th century Roebuck at Broadwater in Sussex which was reopened in 1911, the 15th century Red Lion at Colchester which was bought in 1913, and many other buildings which were hundreds of years old.

The founders of Trust Houses sank their capital into an ideal. If they had known that their company might eventually be targeted to strengthen the asset position of a take-over bidder like Allied

After the ball was over

Breweries 60 years later, one can only imagine their indignation. Through their charitable efforts, by 1914, there were 32 hotels with accommodation, five more without it and Trust Houses was becoming a permanent part of the hotel scene.

Magistrates remained under pressure from the Temperance movement to reduce the number of liquor licences. The Brewers fought back. Lord Burton, was assured by the Lord Chancellor in 1903 that a licensee should not lose his living simply because of a policy of reducing licences. To further ameliorate the licensee's position, in the 1904 Licensing Act there was legislation to make the justices refer a licence refusal to the Quarter Sessions for a final decision. If a licensee *was* refused a licence for any reason, other than misconduct, the brewers had had a special Compensation Fund for some years, set up to reimburse him for the loss of his livelihood.

Parliament now decided that compensation would come from a levy on the licensees who survived. The hotels which had licences had to pay their share, even though the turnover of most hotels only included a small proportion of revenue from the sale of drink. Now enough Hoteliers realised that they needed a different form of licence to differentiate them from the common pubs and avoid the compensation levy. The brewers were equally determined to keep the hotels on side as part of the world of publicans. They knew that hotels weren't going to lose their licences, so only the brewers would get the benefit of the compensation levy. It was a battle that would rage for the next 60 years and it led to the formation of the first English Hotel Association in 1910.

The figure for compensation could be much higher than the now licenceless pub was really worth, so the Brewers were pleased that the hotel industry were going to help to make the necessary funds available. The Brewers had a strong parliamentary lobby and they were powerful financially.The Brewer, M.T.Bass, MP., once told Sir Wilfred Lawson, the head of the Temperance movement in the Commons, that: "for every £1 you could put down, the Trade could put down £100."

The temperance issue reached a climax, as we have seen, after the Liberals swept into power in 1906 and Herbert Asquith, the Chancellor of the Exchequer made it clear in his first budget that he was going to honour the election pledges and take steps against the licensed trade. He could count on the support of the official Labour

185

Ritzy

party as well. Keir Hardie, their leader, was a strong temperance supporter believing, as so many of his colleagues did, that drink held back the working man from outgrowing his lowly status. The Conservative MPs were reduced to a rump, just making up the numbers in the Commons, and some members of the hotel trade could see that they needed a voice, as they had never done before. One commentator compared their lot with the Israelites in Egypt and decided that the Israelites: "were really in a happy position compared with the licensed trades under the partisan control of Campbell-Bannerman, Asquith and Co."

The industry would have been unsuccessful in fighting many of the provisions of the proposed new Licensing Act in 1908 but the Lords threw it out anyway. Not for nothing were the brewing members of the House known as the Beerage.

What was passed eventually was the Licensing Consolidation Act 1910 which did affect hotels in a number of ways. It gave licensing justices the power to refer the renewal of a licence to a Compensation Authority. If the Authority decided to withdraw the licence, the licensee would, of course, be entitled to compensation. That would come from the levy on all licensed property, based on the rateable value, and the maximum levy would be £100 a year. So hotels had to pay for publicans who lost their licences, but investors in hotels knew that they too could be put out of business if, by any chance, they lost theirs. And the compensation would be solely for the loss of their liquor trade but not for any other losses.

Frank Bourne Newton, the publisher of the *Caterer*, seized the opportunity to try yet again to gather the hoteliers together in one body. Newton had become a partner of the *Caterer*'s founder, Frederick Barrett, in 1879 and took over from the editor within a year. In 1893 he bought the magazine for very little and launched it as a public company. The stumbling block in the 1880s when Newton had tried this before, was the £5 nominated as the annual fee but there was now the Compensation Fund to be contended with and £5 was the least of a large hotelier's problems. After canvassing for support, the *Caterer* was able to publish a manifesto in April 1906 calling for the formation of a national organization, though the support came almost entirely from the provinces.

Why the London hotels thought they could stay out of the association and still gain the ear of the government is obscure, though they might well have considered themselves superior to their country cousins and decided to place their confidence in the time honoured "word in the ear" of their influential clients. There was one exception, Dudley James, the owner of Morley's Hotel in Trafalgar Square, and he was made chairman at the association's inaugural meeting. By the end of the year, the Incorporated Hotel Keepers Association had been registered, and it had 3 declared objects:

    a. To encourage and promote the interests of hotel-keepers and hydropathic proprietors in general and particularly of those carrying on business in the United Kingdom.

    b. To collect and disseminate statistical and other information relating to hotels and kindred interests.

    c. To consider all questions affecting the interests of hotel-keepers and hydropathic proprietors and, if necessary, to petition Parliament to promote deputations in relation to Public and private legislation affecting the same.

To the modern eye there are many interesting points about these aims. They specifically apply to Hydropathic Institutions, so that these operations, which had originally a medical *raison d'être*, were now accepted completely as a form of hotel. It was ironic that a body devoted to fighting licensing laws should also represent operations originally devoted to teetotallism, but the hydropaths had themselves often given up abstemious principles. The association did not represent restaurants in the beginning and there was a case to be made for this. Hotels are, basically, in competition with restaurants for the patronage of the public. The fact that people nowadays primarily think of eating in restaurants and sleeping in hotels is, as we have seen, a considerable change from the early days of the 19th century, when the hotel flourished on the revenue from eating and drinking, and the bedrooms were less important.

It is desirable that hotels should be known equally for sleeping and eating, but the present connection of hotels and restaurants in one association has made it impossible to have a hotel industry campaign along the lines of: "Next time you eat out, eat in a hotel." The original members of the association did, however, object to one type of restaurant, and that was the late-night members club, which

Ritzy

was able to serve food and drink after the hotel restaurant had had to close. If you were a member of a club, the licensing laws didn't apply to you. Hoteliers protested vociferously against these clubs, but with little initial success.

What the association was able to deal with successfully were more minor items concerning the price of champagne and a questionnaire on wages and insurance rates. In 1909 when swingeing increases in licensing duties were introduced, the larger London hotels were forced to close ranks with the association, and in 1910 the restaurants joined with the hotels in a renamed Incorporated Association of Hotels and Restaurants. Delegations called on ministers as important as Lloyd-George and Asquith and these were the first occasions when hotels had lobbied government as an industry. They lobbied to stop legislation that would have adversely affected hotels. Stopping things happening was always where the association would be at its strongest and most effective. Its attempts to get new ideas adopted - the separate licence for hotels from pubs, stopping supper clubs serving guests later than hotels, more hotel schools - were, all too often, unsuccessful for many years.

Sometimes the IAHR wouldn't act at all. In 1902 the Hotel Employees Union tried to incite strikes. There was a peace conference at the Savoy and Reeves-Smith made heavy concessions. A weekly half day off was granted and it was agreed that the staff would be paid in future for the time they spent eating meals when they were on duty. Fines for things they accidentally broke were abolished and the Cooks' societies settled their dispute in return for much better pay. Now, ten years later, the IAHR refused to negotiate with seven Friendly Societies who had formed an organisation called KARTEL to improve pay and conditions for its members in the industry. The IAHR said it couldn't speak for its members in this area and there were minor strikes of hotels and restaurant workers as a consequence.

Organising foreign workers is a union organiser's nightmare and there were a lot of them in the major hotel centres. There was no need to have a passport in those days and in 1904, it was reported that 75,000 aliens had arrived in Britain. Balfour's Conservative Government were concerned. They introduced the Aliens Act in 1905 for: "the exclusion of destitute aliens". The Aliens Act restricted migrant entry to eight ports where there were Immigration Officials.

These could turn back those they considered unwelcome, but if you had a job and you weren't going to be a burden on the state, you were likely to be allowed in. London had clubs and associations to help those who wanted to come; the Geneva and Austrian Clubs, the Geneva Institute, the International Association of Hotel and Restaurant Employees and the International Ganymede Club. All enabled German and Austrian hotel staff in particular to find jobs

Lord Bessborough, who had taken over from Frederick Gordon as chairman of Gordon Hotels, agreed to act as president of the association which gave it the right aristocratic cachet but was hardly a dynamic choice. Bessborough also took the credit, which was rightly Newton's and James', for the formation of the association and passed it on to the London hotels who didn't deserve it at all. In writing to new members Bessborough said: "Unfortunately, there was at that time no authorised society in connection with hotels and restaurants, with the result that a committee had to be, and was, hurriedly formed by the Directors of the principal London Hotel companies and the position of hotels in relation to licences and taxation was put before the government."

It is quite possible that the original association carried little weight without the London companies, but ignoring the 1908 association was very petty. Bessborough's task was to unite the hotels throughout the country, and he might have looked at his own performance when he said at the Annual General Meeting in 1914 : "A publicist (for hotels and restaurants) cannot expect support from men which until a few years ago they declined to give to their own representative body, and which, as this report shows, they even now only render half heartedly." *The World*, which was an influential magazine, put it all down to a rampant jealousy: "Jealousy is the blight of their industry - for hotels and restaurants are in truth today a great and growing industry. The industry is honeycombed by jealousies. There is jealousy of rival concerns, jealousy of personal ties, jealousy of administration and management, jealousy of caste, jealousy of race between British born and foreigners and between nationalities."

This was the murky undercurrent which seldom broke surface but which prevented the industry from fighting together and from sustaining its development as a: "great and growing industry". It was a paradise for snobs in a narcissistic age and few hoteliers could cope when supply exceeded demand. What excuse could they give for the practice of writing to visitors in other hotels and asking them to cut short their stay and move to the writer's hotel? It was hardly saving a guest from a fate worse than death and, not unnaturally, the average hotel manager started to look warily at letters addressed to visitors on plain envelopes which arrived at about the same time they did. Yet the hotels continued to publicize lists of their expected guests in order to see their hotel's name in print, and if the competition got valuable information, the manager at least had had his ego inflated.

Amid the increasingly difficult economic rapids, the Midland Railway Hotels steamed on and at the beginning of the decade they had started to build a hotel in Manchester. Cottonopolis, as the Victorians nicknamed the city, had not been noted as a good location for building hotels. In 1886 the 350 room Victoria had opened at an initial cost exceeding £100,000. It had a dome on each corner of the building and an enormous one in the middle, so that it looked rather like a child's sand castle. No effort had been spared to make its decoration as elegant as possible. The designers had used Burmantoft's Faience - a type of porcelain - Minton Ware, Lincrusta Walton - which was a mural covering - marbles, cathedral glass and Tyneside tapestry. There was a steam laundry at the top of the building, a 10 table billiards room which was much admired and, within two years, a large overdraft and bankruptcy for the original company. The Manchester Corporation, who were the Landlords, found the hotel back on their hands and were bailed out by a London brewer, Sir Alfred Kirby.

Where there were very successful hotels in other provincial centres, like Birmingham and Liverpool, there was no comparable operation in Manchester. William Towle intended to put this right by building the Midland in the heart of the city. Like the builders of the Westminster Palace in earlier days, Towle and his architect, Charles Trubshawe, travelled round Europe and America looking for the best of the new ideas, and when the hotel finally opened it had more rooms than the Manchester Town Hall. It also had at least one major improvement on its predecessors in the shape of an elaborate ventilating system to keep the air in the hotel fresh. The atmosphere in the big cities was polluted to a considerable degree and the choking yellow fogs descended in the winter and stayed for days. Now at the Midland: "a series of filter screens of linen and coke which receive 80,000 cubic feet (2,265 cubic metres) of air a minute remove impurities."

To keep out the street air on the ground floor, revolving doors were introduced. By ducting through grids into the bedrooms, the air was kept circulating and the atmosphere must have been a great deal pleasanter than the customers were used to finding.

There were many little touches at the Midland which showed Towle's thorough and meticulous attention to detail. Every bedroom had a clock on the wall synchronised from a central point in the hotel and electrically illuminated from the bed by the press of a switch. There were, of course, telephones in every room and Towle built nearly 100 bathrooms as well. This was an exceptional number for a provincial hotel, but in Canada the Canadian Pacific Railway Hotels were always built with a complete set of private bathrooms, even though they were often in quite small towns, like Calgary and Banff. Towle might well have taken note of this on his travels.

The hotel opened in 1903 and became extremely popular almost immediately. It was well run and much needed, but the fact remained that the investment was large and the tariff that could be charged comparatively moderate. There was the immediate difficulty that the hotel was half empty or worse at the weekends, particularly during the winter, and consequently the hotel was not likely to make even a reasonable return on capital. It was the old story all over again. In these last years of Towle's hegemony before handing over to his sons, it would have helped if they had at least appreciated the results of this type of extravagance, but the lesson they actually absorbed was that quality was all that mattered. That the hotels reflected the importance of the railway company and could be justified on that ground alone.

As the decade wore on, the hotel industry became steadily less profitable. From 1904 - 1914 the Cecil, for instance, paid no dividend and yet had to sink fresh capital into keeping the hotel up with the times. The owners spent up to £40,000 on the creation of large palm courts within the hotels, where visitors could enjoy their afternoon tea and bask in the sunshine under great domes of glass. One court was 93 feet (29m) long, 45 feet (14m) wide, and 32 feet (10m) high. The other was 110 feet (33m) by 28 feet (9m) by 28 feet (9m). When they were opened, the public flocked to see them but what profit could be made from such a costly investment?

191

Ritzy

By 1910 most of the hotel shares were standing below par again. The Savoy £10 shares, which had been as high as £20 in 1896, now varied between £4 and £6, and even the Carlton £1 shares sank to 10 shillings (50p). At these prices the return was still over 8% but the shareholders were losing capital, pressure was constantly on the hotels and the public continued to be offered a wider and wider choice.

There were exceptions, of course, in the prevailing gloom, but they were usually on the periphery. The great success story was the growth of J.Lyons & Co., whose tea shops were all the rage and who distributed to their fortunate shareholders, on four successive years, the stupendous dividend of 42$_{1/2}$%. Where Gordons in their heyday had struggled to achieve profits of £250,000, Lyons notched up figures in excess of £1$_{1/2}$ million only 10 years later. The Salmons and Glucksteins opened their first hotel, the Strand Palace, on September 14th 1909 and it had 470 rooms but not a single private bathroom. It contrasted with the first American hotel to offer every guest that attraction, which was the Mount Vernon Hotel in New Jersey in 1853.

Lyons' philosophy was: "pile it high and sell it cheap". They made a fortune out of tea shops and they became a national institution and a major public company. But the business, from its inception was run by the Salmons and Glucksteins. A lot of the major decisions were made, not at divisional management meetings, often not at board meetings, but at meetings in the homes of the family directors. To really run the company it was a great advantage to have been born into one or other of the two families and bear one of the two specific names.

Meanwhile, in Wales, the ability of Richard Jones, whose company, R.E.Jones, had many catering establishments as well as the Mackworth Hotel, Swansea and the Carlton Hotel, Cardiff, produced 20% dividends. When Jones, the founder, died in 1923 his successful company ran the Piccadilly and many other hotels. A printing worker originally, Jones had found he had difficulty in getting anything to eat on the night shift. So he started Great Western Coffee Taverns and went on from there. These were situations, however, which depended on the genius of the original entrepreneur. Gordons declined without Frederick Gordon and Frederick Hotels without Sir Blundell Maple, who died young.

After the ball was over

At the seaside the public remained fickle and chose whatever was newest and most fashionable. The entente cordiale with the French, fostered by Edward VII, led to a growing tourist traffic from Britain to towns like Dieppe and Deauville and the big hotels on the coast lost a further section of their upper crust clientele. The tourist centres still suffered from a short season and this was well illustrated by the manager of the North British in Edinburgh who protested about the new valuation which had been placed on his hotel by the local rating authority. He suggested that the building should be regarded as a monument, but that it certainly shouldn't be rated as a hotel. In the summer season, which only lasted nine or ten weeks, he needed 145 staff, but that number could not be too heavily reduced when the hotel was not full, and there were times in the winter when he had "three servants for each guest." He suggested that a rate of £4,000 a year would be far too high, but in the end he had to pay £10,000.

What to do with the seaside hotels in the winter was a very vexed question. There were certain towns with mild climates, like Torquay and Bournemouth, which attracted permanent residents during the period, but these were exceptional. In most coastal towns there was little business, but to close was often as costly as to stay open. Where the railways owned hotels they wanted them to stay open in order to get more travellers on their trains. For the small numbers involved it looked like an unnecessary expense, but if one railway did it, the competition often stayed in line. Gordon Hotels on the South coast stayed open in spite of vigorous protests by many shareholders, and Bessborough's dual role as chairman of railway and hotel company as well, was bound to be considered an important factor in this decision. If Gordons had shut the seaside hotels in the winter it would have saved money, but made the railway journey less attractive by removing the best hotel at several destinations.

There were still hoteliers who would place principle above the crying need for custom, and in one of the earliest examples of an attempted colour bar, the managing director of the St. Ermins Hotel in Westminster took a firm stand. At the time of the Ecumenical Methodist Conference in 1901 the hotel put up a: "a number of eminent coloured divines" and American guests approached the director, Harry Richardson, to ask that the ministers be told to leave. If the hotel was not prepared to abide by this wish, not only would the Americans leave, but they would also spread the word back in

Ritzy

the States. Richardson angrily refused and the general consensus of opinion was that it was thoroughly bad form for the Americans to interfere, they should leave their primitive habits at home and the British would accommodate whoever they pleased.

By the time George V came to the throne, the great Victorian hoteliers had all but vanished into eternity. The showbiz arena of the spas had changed into less romantic, but slightly more effective, medical centres. Or alternatively, achieved a precarious existence as holiday homes for the genuinely idle rich. The Celtic fringe of the country was still undergoing development which never seemed to produce the hoped-for results. The only major resort in Devon was Torquay and nothing much existed in Cornwall. Wales, as a whole, was poorly provided with hotels. Scottish hotels there were in profusion, but many of the follies were still going bankrupt whenever the economic situation took a turn for the worse. Oblivious to all the facts, the Scottish railway companies were again putting up hotels. The completion of Turnberry by one company was only the signal for the building of Gleneagles on a competing line. Both of them are jewels in the crown of British hotels today but took many years to justify their cost in terms of profit.

In Ireland, the efforts to bolster the country's economy with the benefits of tourism were only partially successful. During the terrible years of the potato famine in the 1840s the population had been decimated and when massive emigration followed, the country seemed to develop an air of doom. Some hotels were built in Ireland by the railway companies and, as in England and Scotland, the Irish landowners encouraged investment. There were many scenic views and leisure activities to enjoy. Even so, apart from a few elegant hotels in Dublin, the Irish hotel industry remained rustic in the extreme. The local labour was untrained, there was not the same influx of continental staff that helped the rest of Britain and, again, there was only a very short season.

In all the peripheral areas of the country it was more difficult to take advantage of the new inventions because products like gas, electricity and telephones took longer to reach them.

The new generation of top management faced a very different situation from their predecessors. William Towle bowed out after the building of the Adelphi in Liverpool in 1914 and his sons, Francis and Arthur Towle took over Midland Railway Hotels as war loomed.

After the ball was over

George Reeves-Smith at the Savoy had to fight far more competition than Ritz, and Bessborough at Gordons, with infinite *sang froid*, went down with the profits ship.

One small step in the right direction was the creation of a Hotel School at the Westminster Technical College in London. It was strongly supported by Isidore Salmon and Lyons and offered scholarships because nobody wanted to pay for the tuition. It struggled for many years to get a respectable number of students but academic hotel education had at least been born.

It might have been possible for the hotels to have over-come their problems of over-production if the world had remained at peace. The number of tourists was increasing both from America and the Continent and, slowly but surely, the habit of staying in hotels was growing and coming within the financial compass of more people. The bicycle and the motor car were helping to make travel easier and holidays at the seaside were becoming more popular. A realistic hotelier in 1913 might have accepted that there had been mistakes, over-enthusiasm and over confidence, but he could reasonably have looked forward to a sounder future. Like so much else, however, the dream was shattered by the reverberations of that fusillade in Sarajevo.

14
The First World War - 1914-1918

War with Germany had been feared and anticipated for many years. Building great empires and fierce competition in foreign markets, together with misplaced chauvinism, are factors always likely to lead to areas of conflict with other countries. By 1914 Germany had backed off from the threat of war on two occasions already in the infant century. Yet in the summer of 1914 the British government was more concerned with possible civil war in Ireland than with European events. The Austrian Archduke was assassinated in late June but it wasn't until July 24th that the Cabinet was told by the Foreign Secretary that there was a major potential crisis as a result. By August 4th Europe was at war.

Britain hadn't really been involved in a war in Europe since the Crimea, 60 years before. Normally, despite occasional sabre rattling, Britain didn't go to war with Germany. The Germans had, historically, been our allies against the French, the Royal Family were members of the House of Saxe Coburg and their predecessors had been of the House of Hanover. When Queen Victoria died in 1901, the grandson supporting her in his arms in Osborne House was the Kaiser.

For the hotel industry, the World War, commercially, was a lottery. If you lost, the hotel was requisitioned by the government; the Metropole in Folkestone to house Belgian refugees fleeing the German invasion in 1914, the Grand Hotel, Broadstairs for convalescing Canadian Officers in 1917, the Great Central at Marylebone for convalescing British officers. The Metropole Hotel in London was commandeered for the Ministry of Munitions in 1916 and the residents had to be booked out immediately. The great hall of the Cannon Street Hotel became the Insurance office for the Government War Risks (Insurance) Department and the Inns of Court Hotel a recruiting station. London hotels were obviously the most likely to be requisitioned to house the vast numbers of additional civil servants running the war. Twenty nine London hotels were commandeered in all. One consideration was the proximity to the government offices in Whitehall. The nearer you were, the more likely you were to be commandeered. The government did consider evicting people from their homes instead, but you can empty a hotel quicker than you can throw citizens onto the street.

If your hotel was taken over, the government took a long time to agree the rent it would pay. In principle, it initially took the view that it was within its prerogative not to pay at all. Although acceptable terms were often reached with the hotels, it was not until the Master of the Rolls ruled in the hotel industry's favour in the Appeal Court in June 1918, that it was finally decided that rent and compensation *had* to be paid. The Court held that any other position meant that owners of property had no rights. If, said the Master of the Rolls, it had been the government's intention to abolish those rights, they should have made it clear in the bill, the Defence of the Realm (Amendment) No: 3 Act, 1915. (Known as DORA.)

Lost turnover was only one element. To agree the value of the goodwill you had lost took a lot longer; Gordon Hotels finally settled with the government's Compensation Court in 1924. You needed compensation because the customers who couldn't stay with you, were very likely to have settled down in other hotels before you got yours back. Even here, though, you could be lucky; the Goring Hotel in Victoria was one of the last to be taken over - this time for the Americans. The US Army took good care of the building, painted it before they left, settled the war claims immediately and paid for both the loss of goodwill and the need for additional advertising to start regaining the old clientele.

You could also be taken over for the billeting of troops; 600 soldiers were billeted on the Star & Garter Hotel in Richmond in 1914. There was also the question of maximum prices for servicemen in hotels. The IAHR would often take up the cudgels with the military authorities. The problem was that the armed forces wanted to set prices that were far too low to cover the hotels' costs. One excuse was the low pay of officers but, as the IAHR pointed out, the prices applied to Generals as well. Bed, bath and full board in Eastern Command in 1917 was set at a maximum of 52 1/2 p a day, while all the top price hotels could charge officers for dinner in London was 25p. If you didn't accept the prices you could be threatened with blackballing, being put off-limits for the forces and even with being closed. To stop the soldiers getting drunk, the General Officer Commanding had the right to close a pub near a camp. Several tried to extend this power into the right to shut down a hotel.

Ritzy

Even the hotels which remained in business were not going to enjoy the influx of tourists, as they had pre-war; the Americans soon recognized that the liners they travelled on were quite likely to be sunk by the German navy. The sinking of the SS Lusitania in 1915 was, indeed, a prime cause of the Americans entering the war on the side of the allies. European tourism, of course, came to a halt. In a surge of patriotism in 1914 - not, perhaps unconnected with the fact that hotels like the Cecil were seeing turnover drop 40% - many hotels offered bedrooms for wounded officers but, when business improved, the offers were often quietly dropped.

As far as their owners were concerned, another unfortunate effect of commandeering hotels was to undermine the hotel sector of the stock market. The market dislikes uncertainty and when a hotel company's assets are taken away by the government without any agreed terms of compensation, the investor is definitely left uncertain of future prospects. Hotel company shares crashed and often for other good reasons. The *Financial Mail* in 1919 plotted the performance of 52 hotel companies over the last 10 years. The dividends had averaged 5.29% a year. The Piccadilly Hotel, however, had done particularly well. Between 1910 and 1919 it paid dividends totalling 577%. Without its performance, the other 51 companies only achieved average dividends of 4.27%. The *Mail* pointed out that you could get 6% fairly easily in far securer financial instruments. They also recalled that the Savoy had averaged 2.5%, Gordons 1.6% and the Waldorf had never given a dividend at all.

If you were lucky, your hotel wasn't taken over. Then it was possible eventually to make substantial profits in many towns. There were to be vast numbers of soldiers on leave and fewer hotels in which to house them. In addition, with the increasing shortage of servants due to war service and casualties, more houses were closed up and their owners moved into hotels permanently; this improved turnover still further. There was also no necessity - and indeed it was very difficult - to spend money on refurbishing the hotels, which, at least temporarily, reduced that large item of annual expenditure. It also gave hotels an excuse to avoid an expense highlighted by the *Economist* in 1914 before the war: "Ostentation is part of the stock-in-trade of the high class hotel. The keenness of competition...which consists not so much in price cutting as in presenting lavish and costly luxuries to attract customers."

The First World War

Wine and spirit sales were affected by the earlier closing time enforced by the 1914 Intoxicating Liquor (Temporary Restriction) Bill - all licensed houses in Folkestone, for instance, had to shut at 8 o'clock in the evening - but higher room occupancy eventually helped to make up for the loss of bar profits for hotels there. When a new kind of normality had been worked out, business started to improve.

It took time to adjust to the demands of wartime. Initially, all the horses were withdrawn from the streets, anticipating that they would be needed at the Front in France. Horse-drawn buses in London were allowed to continue operating and took over the responsibility of delivering milk and bread for a short time. Hotels found their supplies disrupted but, of far more concern in the long term, was the steady rise in prices over the next 4 years. Prices in 1914 were actually lower than during the Napoleonic wars; better farming methods and cheap American food had forced down prices. If you took the Retail Price Index as 100 in 1837, it was only 74 in 1900, but hoteliers probably didn't study the RPI that often. Food and drink, china and linen, everything a hotel needed was likely to cost a lot more. Most foods doubled in cost but initially competition made it more difficult to increase prices. Then, in the latter years of the war, if hotels considered raising prices, they knew they were likely to be accused by the public and press of profiteering; a serious charge in wartime.

The vexed question of the Compensation Levy was a constant source of conflict. It was based on the Annual Licence Value of all licensed premises and this had been settled with the authorities after the Act of 1910. The Value was based on the turnover of the business but this was affected during the war by the increase in the price of alcohol. It was also affected by the reduction in hours when drinks could be served. Up and down the country hoteliers appealed for lower levies, sometimes successfully and sometimes not.

In August 1914 business at the seaside collapsed as everybody headed home but later, during the war, hotels by the sea generally did very well. The Grand in Eastbourne paid its shareholders a dividend of 13% in 1915 and that was even better than the average of 10% it had paid over the previous 10 years. The Metropole in Brighton did consistently good business and the short summer season was extended into the spring. The opportunity to get away from the

199

stress of normal life for a few days was very welcome. Again, luck came into it. Dover hoteliers were unlucky as the town was closed to maintain the secrecy of troop movements and the Western Highlands became a Prohibited Area. The main seaside problem for most hoteliers, though, was not to show a light out to sea. You could be fined £100 (£4,000) or get 6 months in prison for that.

There were sporadic Zeppelin raids but most parts of the country escaped these. Hotels started to advertise their concrete - and, therefore, they hoped, bomb-proof - roofs. Anxious Gordon Hotels shareholders were reassured at the company's 1917 AGM that all the hotels were fully insured against air raids. This was necessary; 15 were killed when The Midland Grand at St. Pancras was bombed in February 1918.

In February 1915 even reinforced concrete would have been inadequate when a squadron of German warships shelled Scarborough, doing considerable damage to the Grand and a number of other hotels. There was concern that this might become a regular occurrence, which obviously frightened off holidaymakers thinking of visiting the area. Sea attacks were, however, infrequent, though the East Coast was to suffer again.

Where the threat of the German navy did the most damage was to the Isle of Man hotel industry, which was only served by ferry. Here, the fear of submarine attacks meant that almost all the ferries were cancelled and this had a disastrous effect on the island's economy, which relied so much on holidaymakers. Over a million passengers had been carried in 1912 and now there were 20,000 hotel and boarding house beds resting idle. Seaside hoteliers didn't just have to worry about the Germans either. In the summer of 1914, the Hotel Bath in Felixstowe was burnt down by militant suffragettes!

Spa Hotels did good business as well during the war. Their "cures" were still popular as old habits died hard and many other, more effective forms of treatment, were yet to be invented. The most popular spas for the British before the war had been on the continent; Baden-Baden in Germany and Knokke in Belgium, for example. With so many continental spas out of reach, the British had to revert to visiting their own.

What didn't help seaside or spa hotels was the decision to suspend the usual cheap and excursion railway tickets during the summer. The reason given was the need to move troops by rail instead. The Country Committee of the IAHR almost ceased to meet as the prices of railway tickets soared. The Leisure market was adversely affected as well. A return ticket from London to Devon cost £7.50, easily the equivalent of £300 today.

Some hotel builders had got their timing disastrously wrong. William Towle's swansong, the Adelphi in Liverpool had been rebuilt at the enormous cost of £750,000. The hotel was opened in March 1914 and part of its raison d'être was to take care of tourists arriving in Liverpool from America. A few months afterwards, of course, tourism closed down for four years. Some hotel projects had to be halted as building supplies were no longer available. Among those was Gleneagles in Scotland and a proposed hotel in Piccadilly which would, many years later, be the Park Lane Hotel.

On the other hand, Lyons successfully completed the building of the Regent Palace Hotel at Piccadilly Circus and opened it on May 26th 1915. It had a monster 1,028 bedrooms and 1,000 staff. The tariff was very reasonable, tips were forbidden and the hotel was a success from the start. As you would often have to wait a fortnight before getting a room for the night at Lyons' other hotel, the Edwardian Strand Palace, it was not surprising that Lyons' hotel division made £28,400 profit in 1914, and £52,000 in 1915 when their Regent Palace was also contributing. Within the Regent Palace's profits were items like the rent of £3 a week from the hairdressing salon and the hotel got 12% commission on sales as well. As with Fred Gordon's valuable Founders Shares, a select group of the Salmon and Gluckstein families and friends had Deferred shares. There were only £5,000 worth of them, but they were entitled to the rest of the distributed profits after the Preferred and Ordinary shareholders had been paid their dividends. In 1914 the Deferred shareholders got £11,700 in all - a 234% dividend, and in 1915 they collected a 300% dividend. As other hotel companies were suffering, complaining Lyons shareholders who received 9%, were not thick on the Annual General Meeting ground.

The staff position in the hotel industry was particularly affected by French staff going home to fight, and the removal of all the German and Austrian personnel, who left for other countries or were deported home. That took time, though; the *Caterer* reported that, even two weeks after the outbreak of war, 10,000 German waiters remained in the country according to the Police Register.

Ritzy

All the foreign employment clubs - like the Geneva, Austrian and the International Ganymede - were suppressed during the war. This was somewhat embarrassing for the leaders of the industry, who had often, prewar, been the guests of honour at the social events of these organisations. The 1914 deportees were crowded together in camps before being sent home. These were called Concentration Camps; a name first coined by the British in the Boer War period to try to cut down the activities of Boer guerrillas by imprisoning their families and infamously corrupted by the Nazis after 1933. Hotel registration forms were also introduced during the war, primarily to keep track of overseas visitors. Under the Defence of the Realm Act, any guest over 14 years old had to register. For not having a register, one hotel in Truro was fined 5 shillings. (25p).

Even if you were naturalised it did not automatically protect you from the wrath of your neighbours. The popular press started an extreme anti-German campaign and many of those who had become naturalised still left for America or went back to the countries where they were born. A German name became a mark of Cain. As early as October 1914 Prince Louis of Battenberg was forced to resign as First Sea Lord and the family later changed their name to Mountbatten. As we've seen, the . became the Connaught. Hotel Managers took to announcing their changes of name in the trade press; L.Gumprecht of the Kings Oak Hotel in Epping wished it to be known that in future his name was Marden. The Royal Family became the House of Windsor in 1917.

The *Caterer* magazine also spoke of the influence which Germans had exercised in the industry pre-war. German waiters had: "long held sway in our chief hotels and restaurants". Their: "careful training, linguistic capacity, correct deportment and attire, self control and deferential attitude have all been factors in their success."

The *Caterer* always tried to be even-handed but political correctness lay far in the future. Commenting on one unsavoury incident, *Caterer* commented "Bad mannered Jews, as against gentlemanly, lead to closed doors." It didn't seem odd at the time that such barriers were not also specifically prescribed for, say, all ill mannered Calvinists or loutish Yorkshiremen.

The vacancies in the top hotel ranks, where they had been filled by Germans and Austrians, led to unexpected, but no less welcome, promotions for other Europeans. Italians, Scandinavians and Swiss nationals were much in demand. As the war dragged on, conscription was introduced and the number of male staff available to keep the hotels going diminished further. It had already been decided though that hotel managers and heads of department were Reserved Occupations, too badly needed to be recruited, though they could volunteer and large numbers did. After conscription was agreed, hotels could be fined for not disclosing all the names of male employees who were liable to be called up. The ages covered were from 18 - 61.

The industry turned to women to fill the gaps. The Savoy even employed them in the restaurant, which would have been unthinkable pre-war - and would be again between the wars. The uniforms were: "dark chocolate coat and skirt, a tinsel bodice and apron with tête de négre bow, biscuit coloured stockings and brown crocodile shoes." Hotel staff, realising that they were in short supply, were also happy to be poached by other hotels for higher wages. These factors led to the cost of staff doubling during the war.

To compensate, hotels tried to get more work out of the staff. This could be seriously contentious. Gordon's First Avenue Hotel was charged with a total of 25 summons for not giving its staff a half-day holiday every week. The 1912 Shop Hours Act had laid down that maximum hours were in future to be 12 hours a day for 5 days - and 14 hours on Saturdays. The question was whether this applied to hotels, who were accustomed to only allowing Sunday afternoons, or an equivalent number of hours, off-duty. Gordons asked the London County Council to: "defer raising this very important and far-reaching question" but they were turned down. It was decided in court that workers in kitchens and restaurants were covered by the Act and had to have the full half-day but on Appeal to the Kings Bench Division in May 1916, it was subsequently held that hotel employees were not the same as shop assistants and, therefore not covered. The hotel working week of around 80 hours continued.

In his time Fred Gordon may have concentrated on filling beds but the industry remained primarily interested in selling food and drink. This became increasingly difficult as the war dragged on. There were food shortages because cargo ships were sunk and many foreign ship owners avoided the conflict area. When the Americans entered the war, their forces had to be brought across the Atlantic which meant that the ships involved couldn't also carry

Ritzy

the food Britain needed to import. Many of the European countries from which Britain normally obtained food were cut off, occupied or hostile. Submarine warfare in 1917 took a heavy toll on allied shipping. There had to be rationing.

In the beginning, rationing was simply a question of who could afford the higher prices which inevitably emerged from war shortages. There were also increased taxes on coffee, tea and sugar. The poor, however, very naturally, objected to going without if the rich didn't have the same problem. Initially, the hotels dealt with higher prices by reducing the number of courses and the size of the portions the guests got for their money; there was ample room to do both.

The government helped in December 1916 by insisting on a maximum of three courses for dinner under the Regulation of Meals Order. Of course this didn't stop anybody from having two dinners in two different restaurants. The IAHR tried to get the government to see that general rationing was inevitable, but without success until near the end of the war.

Rationing only covered certain foods; primarily, meat, sugar, bread, flour, butter and fat. It never, for example, covered fish. Hotels had to keep records of how much they used of these commodities in a register. Failure to record them correctly resulted in hundreds of court cases, where hotels were fined anything from £5 - £100. One Liverpool Magistrate said: "A man to comply properly with the Order and fill up the forms properly, needs to be an expert accountant." The Piccadilly Hotel in London was not unusual in being fined £25 on 13 separate summons for using too much of the rationed items. On the other hand, hotels found that wastage was substantially reduced by the keeping of these registers, which became part of standard financial control practice thereafter. For once the government had helped.

Eventually, with rationed items, the amounts provided became minute. In 1917 bread rolls had been limited to exactly 2 ounces (55 grams). For breakfast in 1918 hotels could serve a guest no meat, use no sugar, only offer 3 oz (85 grams) of bread, no flour and only use 1/3 oz (9.5 grams) of butter or fat. For dinner you could serve 3 oz (85 grams) of meat, just 1/7th oz (4 grams) of sugar, 3 oz (85 grams) of bread, 1 oz (28 grams) of flour and 1/3 oz (9.5. grams) of butter or fat. If a guest wanted a glass of milk, a Doctor's certificate was needed to certify that it was essential for them to have it.

Later in the war the public were issued with food coupons. Then hoteliers had to collect the coupons and match them to the invoices of food they had used. They also had to record the names and addresses of the guests who had eaten the food. When you consider that in September 1917 the Cairn Hydro in Harrogate used 10,778 lb (4,889 kilos) of meat, 1,067 head of poultry and could accommodate 320 guests, the Food Register must have taken teams of clerks to produce. In working out what you were allowed to serve it was assumed that 25% could be added to the weight if the meat was delivered cooked. If cooked and without bones, then you added 50%. And you had to keep separate records for Salad Oil. When first applying for rationed goods, you had to complete: "A Preliminary Demand Note for butter and margarine (Form D15 in triplicate)". It was a practical hotelier's nightmare. Not surprisingly, the IAHR was constantly complaining of the form filling, on behalf of the members.

Meatless Days were introduced when no meat could be eaten at all. In London they were eventually Tuesdays and Fridays, and in the provinces Wednesdays and Fridays. In addition, on all the other days you couldn't serve meat during prohibited hours; like between 5.30 am and 10.30 am. Articles appeared in the trade press pointing out that the mushroom was the nearest thing to meat in food value. If there were insufficient potatoes, then parsnips were the next most nutritious vegetable. At the Mansion House in London, the Lord Mayor had whale meat on his menu and pronounced it: "not unlike a bit of tender beefsteak." The regulations were made under the Public Meals Order by the Food Controller, who took onto his staff two eminent hoteliers; Arthur Towle from the Midland Railway Hotels and Isidore Salmon from Lyons.

Alcohol was another problem. Lloyd-George said that the three worst enemies the country faced were Germany, Austria and drink. Drunkenness could now have a bad effect on the war effort. Munitions workers drank a lot and the supply of shells and bullets to the front was being adversely affected. The government dealt with the problem by reducing the level of Proof. Which meant they adopted the practice of all dishonest bartenders; they watered the drinks more. A lot of additional water was added to the bottles.

Prior to 1915, there had been 55% alcohol in whisky. At

that level it was described as 100% proof. The government wanted to halve the amount of alcohol; to make it 28.6%. The distilleries objected strongly. A compromise was reached at 37.2% instead of the former 55%. That level remains pretty much intact to this day; 70% proof. The tax level differed over the years. In 1928 it was £3.621/2p a gallon, (4.5 litres) for 100% proof. If you used 70% proof you paid £2.54. Other kinds of spirits had their alcohol content permanently lowered too and the effect of the licensing tax in 1917 was to double prices. To that extent, the Temperance Movement finally triumphed.

By 1915 hotel guests were banned from drinking after 9.30 in the evening, before noon, or between 2.30 and 6.30 in the afternoon. What's more, even when you could get a drink, only the guest who signed the register could have one. He couldn't treat his friends after October 1915. The penalty was a £100 fine. Even his family could only have a drink with meals, but not otherwise. The Ship Hotel in Grimsby was prosecuted in 1916 for serving drinks out of hours and allowing residents to treat their guests to a drink. The fine was £103, (about £4,000 in today's money).

In the early years of the war, the enjoyment of eating out seemed offensive when others were dying in battle. Only when the soldiers on leave started to look for entertainment, did eating out for enjoyment become respectable again. The attractions of the more expensive hotels were beyond the means of the poorer soldiers. They could, however, afford to rent a billiards table for an hour or so. One bright entrepreneur who spotted that niche market, rented derelict premises and created billiard halls, is said to have been Bracewell Smith, who would become a power in the hotel industry after the war. There were far fewer social functions during the war than usual and the London Season, with its debutantes and glittering parties, was largely cancelled. The newly fashionable hotel was the Piccadilly in London which attracted the subalterns on leave and the flappers.

Nor were food and drink the only area where shortages occurred. In January 1918 the Holborn Viaduct Hotel was commandeered for the use of the Coal Controller. The end of the war came just in time for the hotel industry's central heating systems; there was a Lighting and Heating Order restricting gas and electricity usage to 5/6ths of the 1916 or 1917 consumption (whichever was the greater.) Hotel bedroom fires were not the answer either; they were forbidden. South Coast hotels were fined for having dances during

206

prohibited hours; they used up too much heating and electricity. As the war dragged on, things got worse. In April 1918 a Curfew Order was introduced. No hot meals were to be served between 9.30pm and 5am. There was to be no light in the dining room after 10 o'clock. Guests were requested to walk downstairs, saving the electricity the lift used.

The hotel industry was often asked to help the war effort. The IAHR bought War Loan shares with most of their reserves. Hotels were also asked for old linen for bandages for the wounded. In 1918 there was a request for nut shells and fruit stones to be put into sacks (the government would provide them) and sent to help the war effort. Why they were needed wasn't disclosed.

During the war the small hoteliers decided they needed a voice as well. As usual, The *Caterer* was happy to oblige with publicity and editorial support. Frank Bourne Newton, its editor and major share holder, had always believed that you increased your circulation by being the voice of small bodies within the industry. The Residential Hoteliers Protection Society, later the Residential Hoteliers Association, was started in July 1916 and was triggered by the need to put up prices. By this time everything else seemed to have gone up, but not the tariffs for hotel bedrooms or hotel food. Nobody, however, wanted to be the first to break ranks. The RHA enabled hotels to act together. There were geographically based committees and they met to agree price rises.

Meanwhile, the IAHR, representing the larger hotels and the hotel companies, was still led by the Earl of Bessborough (Gordon Hotels) with George Reeves-Smith (Savoy) as the chairman of the Parliamentary Committee. It was that committee which negotiated with the government and was recognized as the authorised representative of the industry. The fact that they only represented the owners and not the employees did not come into it. The shopping list of changes the IAHR wanted was extensive. One of the longest standing grievances was that the Compensation Levy was still only paid by hotels which existed prior to the 1910 law. The Regent Palace would have been excused. The government agreed in London to reduce the levy by a third. It was also agreed in 1915 that for every hour or part of an hour when drink sales were voluntarily suspended, 1/15th of the Excise Duty would not have to be paid.

The IAHR was also prepared to use its financial resources to help members fight test cases in court. It provided funds to Gordons when the question of the Shop Act arose. They also supported Lyons in 1915 when they were fined for not paying Entertainment Duty when the diners at the Trocadero restaurant were entertained with music. The Appeal Court held that the public were, primarily, paying for a meal. It was a worthwhile victory, though the legal costs were a hefty £900.

It is also very expensive to finance a war. In 1918 the Chancellor of the Exchequer, Andrew Bonar Law, was looking for more ways to raise taxes and decided to introduce a Luxury Duty on certain goods, including hotels. It would be levied at 16.6% and the IAHR mobilised immediately to resist it. Fortunately for the industry, Bonar Law had decided that the method by which the details should be worked out was to appoint a Select Committee for the purpose. The House of Commons declined to approve an item in the Finance Bill which was so indefinite. It was eliminated at the Committee stage and never reintroduced.

Another proposal at the time was for the formation of an Interim Industrial Reconstruction Committee for the Catering Industry. Both employers and workers would be represented on it. The IAHR attended the earlier meetings but decided that continuing support was not likely to bring about the kind of reconstruction they hoped to build upon, so they opted out.

Amidst the terrible slaughter of the war, the passing of some famous names in the world of hotels was little noticed. Jabez Balfour died in 1916. Long out of the picture, but never forgotten, Sir Joseph Lyons died in 1917. Lyons is assumed today to have been no more than a figurehead, but his showmanship made an important contribution to the initial development of the catering company. Cesar Ritz died in 1918. Hoteliers mourned lost sons and the deaths in battle were tragically multiplied towards the end of the war by a massive outbreak of lethal influenza. Millions more died in the epidemic and one of the victims was Frank Bourne Newton, the secretary of the Residential Hoteliers Association and the son of the editor of *Caterer*. It was a crippling blow for his 68-year old father, who had now been running the magazine for nearly 40 years. He was buried in Manor House cemetery in London, which has since gone bankrupt. The only graves there which are still in pristine condition are those of General Booth of the Salvation Army and his wife.

Frank Bourne Newton Sen. soldiered on for a few more years, but then retired to Hove, leaving a trade paper as strong as any in the country.

All bad things come to an end. When the Armistice was agreed the hotel industry turned gratefully to the challenges of peace, which included the need to refurbish and upgrade as many hotels as possible. It was in 1918 that hot and cold running water was installed in the first Bournemouth bedroom. The pioneer recalled in later years: "I frequently had prospective visitors decline accommodation because the bathroom had a sink in it"! Better than an enemy shell.

15
After the War was over. 1919-1929

The Great War changed the lives of most of the wealthy people who used hotels. Their men had been among the first to volunteer for the carnage and the loss of life they suffered was correspondingly high. In the higher echelons of the hotel industry the Earl of Bessborough lost two sons and Sir Francis Towle had been bereaved as well; just two among a host of the grieving. Many of the upper classes with landed estates, now lacked heirs. They also experienced difficulty in recruiting large numbers of staff - and paying for them if they did find them. Many decided to sell up and they often moved into hotels as permanent residents. Some major private homes were converted into hotels by the new buyers.

Inflation and higher taxation had reduced the wealth of the middle classes too and the way of life of Edwardian times was far more difficult to sustain after the war. For example, the Aliens Act 1920 ensured that all hotel guests, wherever they lived, had to register when they stayed at a hotel; unheard of bureaucracy before the war when you hardly needed a passport to travel overseas.

There was upheaval further down the social scale as well. The man in the street had been promised: "a land fit for heroes" by the wartime government and wanted a higher standard of living than he had suffered pre-1914. Women from every class who had played their parts in the factories and on the home front, wanted more equality - and the vote. In addition, the country's export markets had, inevitably, been neglected while the nation's manufacturing was on a war footing. The whole dreadful experience of war had been a terrible shock to the British way of life and now life was full of new problems.

Naturally, the upper classes wanted a return to the 'good old days'; to pick up the threads of their pre-war lives and get back to 'normal'. Hotels were a recognisable part of that normality; the dress codes, the relationship of master and servant, the gastronomic culture of French menus (untranslated), the parties during the Season, the debutantes' 'Coming Out' balls, Henley, Ascot, - the luxury life. Where, however, the hotel product had originally mirrored contemporary times, it now started to petrify into a memorial to a bygone age. For example, where full evening dress for dinner had been de rigueur for the upper classes on every evening before the war, it would slowly decline into dinner jackets or even suits in the evening. The decline would be seen as dropping standards by the hoteliers and would be resisted as much by the majority of customers as the industry. Luxury hotels would insist on guests wearing full evening dress for years yet.

At the end of the Great War there was a short-term boom, as the survivors set out to enjoy themselves. Demand was so great the Ritz converted six suites into single rooms. But the boom only lasted about a year. After that there was a quite severe slump, albeit with a substantial drop in the cost of living. After a short period of stabilization, there was a further slackening in manufacturing exports. Business became very difficult, though the hotel industry in London benefited considerably from the enormous British Empire Exhibition at Wembley in 1924 and 1925. The General Strike in 1926 did it no good at all but, overall, most hotel companies then made steady progress for the next three years. If Gordon shares never came anywhere near the £24.50 they stood at in the 1890s, £3 - £4 was better than the pitiful £1.95 they had sunk to in 1922. Admittedly, the Piccadilly paid an average of over 90% from 1913 - 1919 but this was totally exceptional. On the periphery of hotel operations, the company that did consistently well was the *Caterer*. The trade magazine paid the preference shareholders 8% like clockwork for 30 years and the ordinary shareholders often did equally well. Not surprisingly a lot of the 160 shareholders in the 1920s were actually in the industry.

The change from a wartime economy with full employment, to one with millions of servicemen and manufacturing workers without jobs, created considerable hardship. The end of the Great War saw the main concern of the British Foreign Office switching from fighting Germany to the results of the Russian Revolution. With a world power advocating international class warfare, the British government was concerned that the concept would gain supporters in the UK. The industrial scene was fertile ground for the extreme left wing. Even hotels and catering were affected. Admittedly, in 1919 the minor strike of some restaurant workers could not be compared with the contemporary mutiny of the navy at Dundreary, but it still concerned the IAHR. Early 20th century industrial strife was far more violent than, say, the Miners' Strike in the 1980s. In 1911

Ritzy

50,000 troops were called out to back up the civil power. In 1919 the navy had sent warships to Liverpool to protect merchant shipping; 250,000 were on strike at the time.This number even included the police, 9,000 of whom were dismissed as a consequence. Rioters had been shot dead by soldiers. There was plenty of precedent for giving in to the unions or fearing the worst.

George Reeves-Smith, for the only time in 30 years at the helm of the IAHR, overstepped the mark. Fearing that the militant Hotel Workers Union would bring out their members on strike in 1919, on behalf of the IAHR he offered recognition and support to the less militant British and Allied Waiters, Chefs and Employees Union. He had no authority to do so but he thought the latter would be a counterbalance to the HWU and, after all, he was chairman of the IAHR Council. When that body was informed, however, a majority were horrified and it was only with difficulty that a motion of censure of his action was avoided at the next meeting. It was finally glossed over as a misunderstanding but, within a year, the promise to help the union had been withdrawn. From then on any union which wanted to negotiate wages on a national basis on behalf of their members was told that the IAHR had no power to do so; the same response as 1913. When the unions tried to deal with individual hotels, they were referred back to the IAHR. The buck didn't stop anywhere.

The hotel unions were not very strong and the guests were seldom socialists. When the staff came out on a lightning strike at Christmas in 1920 in Torquay, the guests supported the management by serving themselves. When strikes collapsed the workers would often not be rehired. Even Isidore Salmon, who was renowned for his charity work and public spirited actions, allowed a waitress to be dismissed for wearing a union badge. When over 500 of her colleagues struck in sympathy, they were all dismissed and replaced. Support for the unions was always weak. In 1924 only 100 members of the HWU turned up for a rally in Trafalgar Square. It was in this atmosphere that a trade unionist named Ernest Bevin decided that one day he would force the catering employers to pay their waiting staff a decent wage. It would take him 20 years to achieve his objective. The industry was more supportive of the Ministry of Labour's efforts to find employment for disabled servicemen. There were 720,000 of them in 1919 and it was feared that if they were not found jobs, it might be a cause celebre for voters to fasten onto. It was agreed to recommend that 5% of the staff in hotels with more than 20 bedrooms should be recruited from the disabled. Far more were, in fact, employed. In 1926 42% of the male staff at the Royal Bath Hotel in Bournemouth were disabled in one way or another. Ninety three per cent of their staff were British but there were only 8 British trained waiters and 6 British trained cooks.

The main problem for the industry throughout the 1920s was financing the improvements necessary to keep the hotels up to what were becoming modern standards. Worse, to pay for them out of the profits of what was still a relatively short season; in Edinburgh, for example, the season only lasted from June to September. The bedrooms at the new Park Lane Hotel might all be built with private bathrooms in 1927, but throughout the country a large number of hotel bedrooms in 1919 didn't even have hot and cold running water. Tin baths were still to be found under a host of beds, waiting to be filled by chambermaids; only a jug and basin were available if you wanted to wash your hands. Admittedly, there was only one private bathroom in Balmoral in the early 1920s and, when required, a tin bath had to be brought to the bedroom of the Prince of Wales. Even so, a larger proportion of rooms with private bathrooms did become a feature of luxury hotels, though Gleneagles, the great Scottish resort hotel, only had 25% of its rooms in that category when it finally opened in 1924. The process was not, in any way, uniform. In 1945 there would still be only about 50 hotel bedrooms with private bathrooms - in Wales!

The two choices for hotels were both unattractive. If they stood still, they might be overtaken by their competition. If they modernised, the investment could be very considerable and financing it might reduce the annual profits. The problem was, of course, that the cost of every item had to be multiplied by the number of bedrooms. During the decade radio would become extremely popular and that had to be installed. The public wanted to tune in on such new products as the Supersonic Heterodyne wireless. They also began to expect good hotels to have built-in wardrobes, lights by the bed and soundproofing. To make London's new Dorchester Hotel bedrooms soundproof in 1929, the cavities between the floors were packed by the builders with the natural material which is the worst sound conductor known; dried seaweed! As Reeves-Smith forecast: "In my opinion, silent windows and air conditioning will ultimately be

Ritzy

looked upon as a necessity in rooms subject to the noise of traffic."

Hotels were increasingly expected to have telephones and central heating as well and it all had to be paid for.

Of course, the poorer hotels didn't offer the same facilities - and then they were roundly criticised in the press for not doing so. Certainly, there were to be plenty of otherwise passable hotels in the 1950s where guests still had to put 5p in a gas meter in order to light their bedroom fire. Even more minor revenue producers were not neglected; the penny-in-the-slot lock to open a toilet was first introduced at the First Avenue Hotel in 1919. To use them, you had to open the door with a penny (1/2p).

Hotel bars could not have slot machines. These were illegal under the Betting Act 1853 and a hotel which tried to contravene the law in 1924 was fined £10. Change was gradual. In 1920 there was electric cooking in a hotel in Bradford but it was a rare exception. Improved equipment did enable Imperial Airways to replace the ubiquitous luncheon basket with a served lunch on the plane for the first time on October 27th 1925. The first hotel at a British airport, the Aerodrome Hotel at Croydon with 50 bedrooms, was opened by Trust Houses in 1928. Already in 1919, though, guests for the Birkdale Palace Hydro, Southport, were being flown from Blackpool to the beach outside the hotel. When it came to the need to upgrade the small hotels, successive governments were equally uninterested in helping. This contrasted with the French, who in 1919, set up a national tourist board and provided cheap money for small hotels to carry out refurbishment. This was through a government fund, the Credit National Hotelier, run by the Ministry of Commerce.

One major development in the hotels was the increasing number of dinner-dances and cabarets. The upper classes had held these privately in their own homes before the war but were now more prepared to enjoy them in public. Sir Francis Towle at the Metropole near the Embankment started the Midnight Follies for Gordon Hotels in 1921 and: "London is the only city in the world where you can see 500 or 600 people in a restaurant, all in evening dress." The Big Band era, if it did not match the current popularity of the silent films, certainly provided an acceptable alternative to millions. Band leaders, who would become household names, led from the front. Mantovani at the Metropole, Debroy Somers and then Carroll Gibbons and the Savoy Orpheans at the Savoy, Jack Hylton, the future impresario, at the Piccadilly and Henry Hall in the provinces. Geraldo, Harry Roy, Ted Heath and Eric Winstone would be along later. The first BBC outside broadcast from a hotel was to listen to the band at the Carlton in June 1923. The Frascati Restaurant orchestra had played at the BBC the previous March and been very popular.

The Savoy had tea and dinner dances every day except Sunday and other hotels followed suit. Cabaret was an all the year round entertainment in many West End hotels. These new fashions were not highly regarded by all the industry. Mallet, who had succeeded Escoffier at the Savoy, complained that: "the art of dining is being killed." He blamed this on the demand for faster service, the fact that fewer good chefs were being employed in private homes, a loss in interest and poor culinary education. Francois Latry, who came to the Savoy afterwards, agreed but added: "The jazz age is the greatest sinner."

The popularity of dinner dancing and cabarets led to problems with the Performing Rights Society. Protecting the composers, the PRS took many hotels to court for playing music without getting a licence from the Society to do so. As a consequence in 1927, various associations, including hotels, dance teachers and the musicians union, formed the International Council of Music Users. The object was to stand together against the increasing fees being charged by the PRS. Agreement was only reached in 1929 that if a hotel charged for dancing, then the PRS would get 2% of the first £1,000 revenue, 1% of the second and 1/2% of the balance.

The major hotel boardrooms in the land were split unequally between hoteliers and non-hoteliers. It certainly wasn't easy for a hotelier to get onto the board of a major company. Four out of the seven directors of Gordon Hotels in 1920 were barristers by profession. The caterers were represented by the Salmons and Glucksteins at Lyons, the professional hoteliers by Reeves-Smith at the Savoy and the brothers Towle - Arthur controlling the London, Midland and Scottish Railway Hotels from 1925 and Francis trying to make sense of an overcapitalised Gordon Hotels from 1920. While the private hotels were run by their owners, there were usually only a couple of token professional hotelier directors in any major hotel company who could talk knowledgeably about the details of the business.

There were only a few large hotel chains; 32 LMS railway

Ritzy

hotels continued to provide the best standards available in many of the major provincial cities throughout the country, although in the mid-1920s only the Adelphi and Gleneagles had hot and cold running water in every bedroom. Competing with the Adelphi in Liverpool or the Midland in Manchester was very difficult because the railways were prepared to subsidise them. They were the standard bearers; luxurious, imposing and reflecting well on a national icon. The British loved their railways as they loved their favourite car marques. The hotels were suitable settings for senior railway executives to meet and relax in, they were the necessary administrative back-up for railway catering and grand outposts of the railway empire. Whether they made money or not was a relatively insignificant factor at the end of the day, compared to the total financial performance of the railway companies. Of course, this meant that the hotels which were in competition with them, thought themselves unfairly treated. It made it more difficult to justify building other luxury hotels in the same provincial cities; hotels which would have to stand on their own feet without railway revenues to back them up.

Gordon Hotels still managed some of the country properties of the London, Brighton & South Coast Railway, but Lord Bessborough, who had been chairman of both companies, died in 1920. Gordons created a new top management team by hiring Sir Francis Towle as managing director for an immense £7,000 a year (about £300,000 today). The new chairman was General Guy Dawnay and the team set to work to re-establish Gordons as the major player in the industry it had been under Fred Gordon. British hotels were run down. There was plenty of business for the American Cockroach Company, whose advertisements warned that: "No hotel in the UK has a clean kitchen unless they are under contract to us."

Gordon's initial problem was to get their commandeered hotels back from the government and to get sufficient compensation to put them back into their pre-war condition. In May 1919 24 London hotels were still requisitioned. Agreement was only reached in August 1920 that the government would pay compensation, largely due to actions brought by the Debenture Holders of the De Keyser hotel. The final agreement was confirm-ed in the Indemnity Act 1920 which set up a Compensation Court to decide how much the government owed. The arguments dragged on. In 1925 there were still 15 cases nationally where the Compensation Court had not made

216

a final decision on the various hotel companies' losses. Inflation over the years, of course, usually made the sum finally granted inadequate. Gordons had to raise £250,000 in 1923 to repair the damage done through their properties having been commandeered. It cost them a massive 8% interest a year. This was a much more expensive exercise than it would have been pre-war, but the government believed hotel companies should look after their own financial problems.

Gordons under Towle was a more carefully controlled company. Towle very quickly identified the previous management's weakness: "large unexplained shortages existed in most of the branches of the business; the whole of the drink donated to staff from top to bottom was on much too high a scale. These matters have now been thoroughly and drastically dealt with."

Towle also took advantage of the drop in the cost of living in 1921: "It was, therefore, decided after most earnest consideration, to make a very drastic cut in the rates....the effect was instantaneous." Gordons made steady progress during the decade, paying a dividend of 5% in 1924 for the first time since 1914. Towle was also one of the first to try to create a distinct hotel brand, advertising: "Whatever service is to be found in one Gordon Hotel can be found in any of the others."

The major company in the countryside was Trust Houses, which had grown mightily since its Edwardian foundation. In 1919 it had a capital of £500,000 and made a profit of £42,000. It operated 71 hotels and this would grow over the next 20 years to 195. The hotels particularly benefited from the growing ownership of motor cars, though there were mixed opinions about the grading of hotels by motoring organizations. The RAC started the process in 1904 and the AA followed suit in 1909. In 1900 there had been 701 drivers. In 1910, 48,000. During the 1920s car ownership increased from 100,000 in 1919 to over two million in 1930. Their owners were largely in the hotel operators' market. They became more restless than of old and the weekends saw them heading for the countryside to enjoy their new possessions. The hotels in the major cities suffered accordingly. As Reeves-Smith lamented: "owing to the advent of the motor car, Saturday and Sundays are dead days in large cities throughout the world." Even during the week the hotel market's mode of travel was switching from trains to cars. Where 21 million first-class railway tickets were sold in 1924, by 1938 that number had dropped to 14 million. Another effect of the motor car was, of course, that they had to be kept somewhere. Hotels now had to provide garages and often couldn't charge for them. It was more capital expense.

If the hotel infrastructure was important, no less was the supply of a sufficient number of trained staff. Wages had gone up during the war because of inflation and the staff shortage, and their increase remained higher than the rise in tariffs. Competition still made it difficult to put up prices. Many of the hotel brochures referred to: "Prices on application". This was not a euphemism for: "We don't talk publicly about anything as common as money." It was far more: "We're prepared to haggle about how much you pay." It wasn't just maids or porters who cost more. According to Reeves-Smith in 1929, the cost of a Hungarian Band for the Savoy dinner-dances had been £80 a week pre-war but he now needed a band and a cabaret which cost him £650 a week.

Before the war the British personnel were augmented by a large number of continental workers: "During the last three decades British Hotels may be said to have been dominated by the German Manager and his alien assistants" reported the *Caterer*. Now it was agreed in 1918 that no further German or Austrian staff would be allowed to work in British hotels. Not only was this the policy of IAHR members but the government itself refused to provide work permits for continental immigrants from any country. Obviously, this was not antagonism towards any number of overseas countries but there was a large problem with unemployment at home. The government wanted the available jobs to reduce that figure.

The only exception was for a small number of continental exchange workers where, if British citizens took jobs in France and Switzerland, then an equivalent number of their nationals could come to work in Britain; they were called Voluntaires. The problem was always to find sufficient British youngsters to go abroad. Eventually 200 work permits would be given to the French if 100 Brits would cross the channel in exchange. Too often they couldn't be found. The Home Secretary reported in the House in 1927: "During the 3 1/2 years ending June 25, 620 work permits were granted to hotel employees and 167 were refused." It was a drop in the ocean of demand. The difficulty with the 'jobs for the Brits' policy was simply that there weren't enough British subjects who wanted to work in the industry. Arthur Towle, speaking of staff recruitment at a Hotel Association conference in 1928, said: "The hotel industry is not a business to look down upon. We don't want the scum. We want well educated boys and girls from nice homes."

Reeves-Smith was pessimistic about British potential at his company's AGM: "Suitably chosen and sensibly trained British boys make quite good cooks, though not for high positions." O.G. Goring, the owner of the Goring Hotel was even less hopeful: "An Englishman is not a cook and no amount of persuasion will make him one." Harry Yoxall, Chairman of the International Wine & Food Society said: "Outside London Britain was an absolute desert in the 1920s....it was a penance to eat away from London." He did, however, like the food at the Royal Clarence in Exeter, the Angel at Bury St. Edmunds and the Compleat Angler at Marlow.

Isidore Salmon, trained like all the Salmon and Gluckstein youngsters in the kitchens, felt that such an apprenticeship for future management was essential. Francis Towle, with a Cambridge degree, disagreed. The fact was that Westminster, the only British hotel school, still struggled to survive because of a lack of pupils and the IAHR had to raise £2,000 a year to prevent the London County Council closing the courses down: "Even free training and maintenance grants have failed to attract any adequate recruits to the waiter's calling".

The IAHR grimly compared Westminster - only training waiters and cooks - with Cornell, an American Ivy League University, boasting a full department of academics, headed by a Professor. In France there were about 20 hotel schools. A proposal for a Scottish Hotel School was floated in 1929 but it wouldn't become a reality for over a decade thereafter.

Many of those who had got their work permits before the war, continued to make progress. Italo Zangiacomi had come to Britain from Italy in 1897 and ran the Piccadilly Hotel restaurant with great success for many years. He was then the manager of the hotel for 12 years until the outbreak of the Second World War. Like many others, however, he never became naturalised, which was to have tragic consequences as we shall see.

One of the side effects of the staff shortage was that competent workers did not have to retire. As long as they could cut the mustard, they were assured of a job. M. Neuschwander, the manager of the Charing Cross Hotel had taken in Ritz and his family in 1898 when

Ritzy

Ritz was dismissed and they were turfed out of their rooms at the Savoy. M. Neuschwander, at the age of 85, was still managing the Charing Cross in the 1920s after 50 years at the helm. Longevity of service continued. Rudolph Richard, who had much to do with putting the Connaught on the map, managed the hotel from 1935 until he died at 75 in 1973. One English hall porter at the Grosvenor joined in 1915 and stayed in the job until 1980.

What the hotels had going against them was the public perception that they were not much better than pubs and that the hours were long - which they certainly were; In 1919 it was agreed that they would not exceed 72 hours a week for waiters. This had to be contrasted with an eight hour day in industries with official Trade Boards. In 1919 the IAHR had been asked by the Ministry of Labour to discuss the creation of such a body, together with workers' representatives. The IAHR delegation absented themselves after a few meetings and, as the union was so weak, were never pressured into having a board and so escaped the limitation on hours. The atmosphere in a hotel, until the unsophisticated worker got used to it, was much posher than a factory. A lot of workers simply didn't feel comfortable in the ambiance of a hotel. And, as if all this wasn't enough, the basic wages were at the bottom end of the national scale, hardly higher than the dole.

Usually, of course, there was the added reward of tips and the financial benefit of meals on duty. Many staff lived in the hotel and there were other sources of income to be tapped of a less respectable kind. When Bracewell Smith bought the Café Royal in London in 1929 he was amazed to find that there was no Wages Book. It was, however, pointed out to him that it wasn't needed because the only people who received a salary were the manager and a few accounts clerks. The chefs lived off bribes from suppliers and the waiters from tips.

Additional temptations were put before staff. For the waiters there was the attraction of corkage. Where today this is a charge made to clients who want to bring their own wines into the hotel for a function, it didn't start out that way. It began with champagne houses wanting to increase their sales over their competitors. Often the clients would take the advice of the waiter on which champagne to have with their meal. Some champagne houses, therefore, offered to pay the waiters a bribe, such as 50p, if they handed in 12 corks on which the champagne house's name was visible. In itself, this was no more than rewarding a recommendation, though the hotel might have preferred another brand to be promoted. What was more serious was that the cork and the label were the only way of identifying what was in the bottle. Labels could be easily forged and the cork was the vital ingredient if some crooks wanted to pass off an inferior liquid as champagne. The waiters were asked to deliver the corks to accommodation addresses and what happened to them after that was anybody's guess, but shady nightclubs would have benefited.

Suppliers also applied restrictive practices to the hotel industry. Wholesale grocers wouldn't deal with hotels, holding that they weren't shops. In fact it was true that the Shop Act did not apply to most hotel workers, but obviously hotels were in a special category of customer, buying far more than the average household. The retailers and manufacturers of products like crockery and glass also ran price rings to keep the costs to hotels artificially high. Gas, water and electricity were supplied to hotels at domestic rates but not business rates. Hotels were discriminated against.

In 1920 Bessborough was succeeded as president of the IAHR by his son. The association decided in that year that an executive of 10 members would carry out council resolutions. Five were to come from London, three from the provinces and two from the railway hotel companies. The association fought on many fronts. In the early 1920s the pubs - and, therefore, the hotel bars - were closed in London by the Licensing Magistrates at different times. In five districts at 11 o'clock and in the rest at 10.30. It was 10.30 in Marylebone and 11 o'clock in Westminster. It could mean different opening hours for pubs opposite each other in the same street. Indeed it had for years at the east and west ends of Princes Street in Edinburgh, under the Scottish Local Option Act 1910. The IAHR hired counsel to attend licensing sessions and protest; Marylebone was one chosen. When the IAHR counsel were refused a hearing by the magistrates to put the case for 11 o'clock, the association went to the Appeal Court, claiming such action by the magistrates was illegal. So it was, decided the Lords of the Appeal Court, and the magistrates had to go through the procedure again and this time hear the IAHR case. The court then retired for five minutes and returned to say they hadn't changed their minds and that was that. The costs of the case were a sizable proportion of the IAHR's annual budget, though the

Ritzy

London hotels did subsidise the action. It was like the charge of the Light Brigade; ill conceived, gallant and very costly.

They were even less successful in trying to get a separate licence for hotels from the one granted to pubs. One effect of this might have been to improve recruitment. As Reeves-Smith said: "Because hotels are pubs, middle class parents don't want their youngsters coming into the industry."

Another hoped-for result might be to stop Compensation Fund payments. These still only benefited the pubs who were denied a licence, whereas magistrates invariably renewed the licences of hotels. The size of the levy differed around the country. In 1919 the country was divided into 152 areas. Of these 28 charged no levy in that year, 44 less than the maximum of £100 allowed, but 80 charged the levy in full. It raised £643,000 for those who lost their licences. A lot of that money went to brewers who owned pubs. For that reason, the brewers were naturally very much against a separate licence for hotels. They would, however, advance an alternative argument that denounced proposed changes as: "class legislation" and governments would not find the parliamentary time to debate such a seemingly unimportant issue. The IAHR had to fall back on Private Members bills. Like today, it was a lottery whether an MP was successful in the ballot for these and usually the IAHR's nominee wasn't. On the one occasion in the 1920s when he was, the debate on the bill was cancelled at the last minute because of the 1926 General Strike.

The expenses for trying to introduce the bill came to over £1,000 when the subscription income of the association was under £2,000 a year. Subscriptions had to rise but this led to 40 resignations, leaving just over 500 members representing 700 hotels. It was a delicate balancing act for the association which wanted to grow, not decline.

The development of new hotels was often hampered by the refusal of the magistrates to grant them licences. When the Weston super Mare magistrates gave a a licence in 1924 for a project to build the Grand Central Hotel, it was the first new one to be granted in the town for 35 years. A licence to build the Central Hotel in Swansea in 1927 was the first new one granted in 45 years. In the same year, the building of a 300 bedroom hotel in Manchester was frustrated by the magistrates, as was a first-class hotel for Worthing. The local councillors often regretted the decisions, but the magistrates were

222

all-powerful and the temperance movement opposed new licences with dogged determination. Reeves-Smith correctly pinpointed the anomaly. In towns which needed to attract more visitors: "Hotels and restaurants were places which (magistrates thought) would be better to abolish rather than create."

The industry's amour propre was upset; their fight for respectability undermined. The thinking of the magistrates might have been influenced, however, by the IAHR's denunciation as: "tyrannical"of Lady Astor's: "Under 18" bill to stop alcohol being sold to such youngsters. It is not a good marketing ploy to insult the customer. In 1900 there had been 102,189 licensed premises in Britain. By 1925 these had been brought down to 80,420, a 20% drop. The consumption of alcohol had dropped steeply too. Since 1900 spirits were down from 32 million gallons to 10 million in 1928. 34 million barrels of beer had been drunk in 1902 but only 25 million in 1927. The brewers cursed the cinema and the wireless even more than the temperance movement. It was also pointed out in the House of Lords that there were 33,000 convictions in 1926 for drunkenness in London with a population of 7.4 million. There were 36,000 in 'dry' Philadelphia with 1.8 million.

An unsuccessful struggle to get a licence could have been a boon to many prospective investors. One major firm of contractors was asked about the probable viability of a new hotel in the provinces. They said it would be full from Monday to Thursday at a tariff of 75p for bed and breakfast. The contractor then pointed out that building costs were 17 1/2p a foot cube and, if the hotel was full on all 7 days a week, at a charge of 87 1/2p, it would still hardly pay. Pre-war costs for building hotels were about a third lower than the 1920s. As Reeves-Smith said: "The expenditure necessary for the construction of a first class hotel is, at present, so high as to make an adequate return on the capital outlay practically impossible in this country".

There were still other problems for hoteliers trying to operate their hotels efficiently. The size of the domestic market dwarfed that of hotels and there were insufficient products manufactured specifically for hotel use. So hoteliers had to try to make the machinery designed for a home, work in very different surroundings. As M.H.H.Wood, a small hotelier, told the Scottish Committee of the HRA in 1929: "The Food and Cookery Exhibition is held in London each year and there is a jumble of equipment exhibited, mostly suitable for private houses." He wanted: "the big cooking appliance firms to stage an exhibition....suitable to a small hotel." He asked in vain.

George Reeves-Smith and the Savoy Hotel company remained the major power in the Hotel Association which elected its first woman councillor in 1926. Mrs. Muggeridge served until 1934. She was the daughter of Sir William Towle and the sister of Sir Francis and Arthur. The election doesn't appear to have been contested. The IAHR became the Hotel and Restaurants Association of Great Britain in 1926 . By whatever name, George Reeves-Smith still made sure that it acted in the way he wanted. It didn't cost his Savoy much; the time spent on meetings, some financial support for the Westminster Technical College courses, a contribution when court cases of importance to London hotels had to be financed. Other senior executives - the Towles, Isidore Salmon, Bracewell Smith at the Park Lane, - were content to leave matters in such dedicated hands. Reeves-Smith normally got his way with the association, although achieving the results the industry needed was another matter. For example, the old and needy who had worked in hotels would have liked to rely for help on the Benevolent Association but the charity's income was very small. 1924 was a record year and they still only raised £2,000 from the entire industry.

There were always mutterings that the IAHR was run for the benefit of the large London hotels, rather than the industry as a whole. It wasn't true. When the chance came to help the country members, the IAHR never failed to give them their full support. If the country members didn't provide initiatives on which the IAHR could work, that was hardly the fault of the London hotels. What was more, when money had to be raised, Reeves-Smith and Isidore Salmon invariably contributed more than anybody else. The fact was that the only senior members of the industry ready to give the IAHR the time it needed were Reeves-Smith and Isidore Salmon. But it was Reeves-Smith who always chaired the most important committees; Salmon didn't enjoy the limelight.

Salmon was born in 1876 and left school at 15 to start work as an apprentice cook. All the family started at the bottom, but they always reached the very top after a few years. Salmon had been chairman of Lyons since before the First World War. He had been in charge of Canteen Administration during the war, controlling 14,000 women feeding the troops. He earned the rank of Major and was awarded the CBE. As a senior businessman, Salmon was a suitable candidate for many public roles after the war. He was the chairman of the London War Pensions committee between 1918 and 1922. He served on: "government and parliamentary committees on such diverse issues as transport, the employment of prisoners, the price of building materials and public accounts." He was knighted in 1933.

He also became MP for Harrow in 1924 and vice chairman of the London County Council. He was a quiet man, though, and hated flattery: "Say what you like about Lyons but please don't glorify me". He ran a hugely successful company and still, when it really mattered, seated in the kitchen of his home, surrounded by family directors like Alfred, Harry, Maurice, Julius and Barnett Salmon and Sam, Montague, Isidore and Barnett Gluckstein. In 1927 all 10 were on the Lyons board. Unjustifiable nepotism? Well, other companies might try to pay a 5% or 10% dividend. From 1919 - 1939, right through the Slump, the dividend on J. Lyons shares never fell below 22.5%. Under those circumstances, the shareholders were not about to rock the boat. The system showed no signs of being broken, so no-one was intent on mending it. That was also why it was tolerated by the City.

Throughout his life Salmon worked hard to help the hotel industry improve. For years he supported Westminster Technical College, badgering the LCC for more support and donating funds himself. He was intent on raising the standards of haute cuisine, even though his own company made its fortune from far simpler fare. He was one of the earliest disciples of decimalisation and: "used the shareholders' meeting of June 1937 to launch a £50,000 fighting fund so that the Decimal Association could carry out a programme of education, campaign for public support and convince the government of the need for change."

When it came to issues concerning the hotel industry, however, he achieved very little. He recognized early on the power of the brewers in parliament. It was they, through the Brewers Association, who were most likely to be called into discussions with government but he could still point to one advantage of being an MP. When the government was questioned about German waiters being given work permits in 1928, the response was that only 6 Head Waiters had been granted these. Why the exceptions? The shortage of good management of that kind in the country. All six were heading for Lyons.

Bills to improve the position of the hotel industry met with no success. Where Salmon did make a lasting impact was when Leslie Hore Belisha, the Secretary for War, recognized the inadequacy of the catering arrangements in the army in 1937. Salmon became the Honorary Catering Adviser to the War Office and, from his work, the Army Catering Corps emerged in March 1941. He called on his friends to help; Richard Byford, Catering Manager of Trust Houses, became Chief Inspector of Army Catering and, on the outbreak of war, many of the industry's best known managers became members of Salmon's team. Tom Laughton, who owned the Grand in Scarborough, met him early in 1940, just before Salmon's death. He said he was small, shrewd and dictatorial, with a hard exterior. Laughton was in charge of service catering in Scotland and when Salmon visited him, he: "picked up on everything" that Laughton was doing. He then sent Laughton a letter saying that he was performing a first class job. Rex Joseph, the last Managing Director of the Lyons hotel division, says that Salmon was always respected and regarded as the head of the family.

Salmon was an orthodox Jew in a mildly racially prejudiced Britain. As Bernard Levin commented in *The Times* 60 years later: "Decent society in those days was filled with people who had forgotten what Anti-Semitism *had* led to, and who could not guess what it *would* lead to."

The same myopia characterised the IAHR's view on colour bars. This was stated after a court case involving the refusal of a hotel to accommodate a black guest. The association pronounced in February 1925: "A hotelkeeper must work on the principle that his hotel is run for the benefit of his customers and if they object to a coloured guest, regard must be had to that objection. It is too much to expect a hotel proprietor to offend his regular customers by breaking away from a set rule and there-by losing business."

The IAHR continued: "The solution would seem to be in such guests (coloured) choosing hotels where they are likely to be welcome."The *Caterer* made the same point only a few years later when another black guest was turned away: "After all, we have known both American and English people to leave moderate size hotels because of the acceptance of Jews, and the latter being given tables in the dining room in the immediate vicinity."

After the War was over

In the very same issue of the magazine there was a eulogy on Isidore Salmon's commercial brilliance, as if he was totally unaffected by the *Caterer's* comments. Nobody could see the ambivalence. In fact, Salmon was the Chairman of the Board of Jewish Deputies, the official representative body of the community.

Bracewell Smith came to prominence in hotel circles when he bought the: "steel bird cage" on Piccadilly. This was a skeleton steel structure where development had stopped in 1914 and had never restarted because the owner died in the trenches. Bracewell Smith had been a headmaster in Yorkshire and had moved into hotels after the war by buying the Shaftesbury near the Strand. From the Shaftesbury to the Park Lane in Piccadilly was a massive move, though. It was announced that 90% of the cost of the hotel had been put up by Yorkshiremen. Well, technically, Harry Wardman, the major financier, had been born in Yorkshire, but he had emigrated and: "has built about half of Washington".

The hotel is one of the finest examples of Art Deco design in Britain. It is still plastered with Preservation Orders and deserves to be. When it opened in January 1927 it provided stiff competition for the other luxury hotels. Then Gordons opened a contrasting luxury hotel two months later down the road. The Mayfair was designed to offer its guests the archetypal British country house. Everything was to be British; built for £1 million by the British, with all the material manufactured in the UK and employing only British staff. The technical advice of the Swiss Manager at their Metropole Hotel in Monte Carlo wasn't mentioned. With the Mayfair opening, Gordons decided they could do without their first hotel, the Grand, and in 1928 it was converted into shops and offices.

Another prominent hotelier to come to the fore was Lady Constance Honeywood, in the chair at Honeywood Hotels. It wasn't just that she had a large number of prestigious hotels. It was the fact that a woman led the company and in a male dominated industry this was enough to get her a great deal of publicity. She was also married to Sir Courtenay Honeywood, a member of one of the oldest families in Kent. The HRA was delighted to invite her to join the council of management as another token lady member. It was a step up from the position, pre-1923, when the members couldn't even bring their wives along to the Annual Lunch.

International tourism grew in the Twenties. The Americans

Ritzy

were the favourite tourists to Europe because they stayed the longest; an average of eight days. They were, however, expensive to house because the majority always wanted central heating and private bathrooms. One of the major attractions for American visitors throughout the 1920s was that Europe didn't have Prohibition. You could still drink as much as you liked and what you would find in profusion were cocktails, an ever growing range of exotic mixtures. These provided a good profit as the sum paid for the whole was far greater than the sum of the several parts. There was, of course, a substantial movement trying to get the UK to follow America's example of Prohibition. There were four unsuccessful Temperance Bills introduced into Parliament in 1922-1923. The prohibition crusade in Britain was nicknamed the Pussyfoot campaign. The name came from a temperance advocate in America called William Johnson. He pursued law breakers in Indian Territory and from his cat-like tread, he gained the nickname. He gave over 4,000 lectures on the virtues of giving up drink and a non-alcoholic cocktail, called a Pussyfoot, can still be mixed by any good bartender. Between January and April 1920 the Anti-Prohibition Committee - mostly the brewers - spent a massive £60,000 (about £2 million) opposing any such measure in Britain. In view of the results of Prohibition in America, this turned out to be more than special pleading. Another attraction to the Americans was that Britain devalued sterling against the dollar. This happened often during the rest of the century and always proved a great boon to British tourism.

Britain's incoming tourism was far smaller than countries like France and Italy. Four times as many Americans visited France in 1928 - 1.8 million to France but only 412,000 to Britain. The reason was that both continental countries' tourist industries were heavily supported by their governments. The Italians alone spent £250,000 a year on international advertising. Mind you, much of that budget could be recovered by the revenue obtained from taxing the hotel bills of foreign visitors. The 5% taxe de sejour (daily tax) was implemented in many European countries. In Belgium it ranged from 15% - 20%.

When Sir Francis Towle decided in 1926 to try to set up a national body to compete, he called it the "Come to Britain" movement. This developed by the end of 1928 into The Travel Association of Great Britain and Ireland. It had the inevitable

228

aristocrat as its President - Lord Derby - and he advised the fledgling organisation that they needed a budget of at least £25,000 to start! The government, through Winston Churchill, Chancellor of the Exchequer, provided £5,000 as its contribution and this miserly figure was not exceeded for many years. The HRA warmly supported the building of a channel tunnel, but there was little light at the end of their own efforts to improve British tourism inflows. It also didn't help when Sir Francis started a practice that was to become a tradition with many senior officials in future years. He severely criticised the hotel industry, saying that: "the great bulk of English hotels are obsolete in design". It was probably true but it would have been the kind of negative comment expected from competitors rather than nominated supporters. Criticism was also apt to flow from the motoring organisations. Their ambition was to provide their members with more than the first aid of breakdown mechanics. So they extended their services to helping members settle complaints with hotels. They also graded the hotels, wisely concentrating on whether the hotels had - or didn't have - specific facilities. In spite of this, the HRA, who could stand anything but criticism, was in reasonably constant disagreement with both the AA and the RAC; to make matters worse, the motoring organisations frequently refused to discuss grievances with the HRA, ignoring the industry body. Criticism also came in 1927 from the Royal Society for the Prevention of Cruelty to Animals, objecting to the way in which lobsters and trout were cooked alive. The industry was never short of critics.

In 1927 it was agreed by the Come to Britain movement that hotels should pay 5% commission to Travel Agents. As both the Continental and American hotels were paying between 10% and 15%, it wasn't rocket science to work out in which countries the Agents would recommend their customers to take their holidays. The industry, however, had overwhelming confidence in quality but very little in sales promotion. That wouldn't change for many years.

By 1929 the hotel industry was in reasonably good shape. Hotel companies quoted on the Stock Exchange had increased from 29 - 113 in the past 50 years. It was, however, like the Titanic heading in a fog for an iceberg. The fog was economic planning and the iceberg was the Wall Street Crash on October 24th 1929. Sir William Towle was spared that, dying earlier in the year.

16
A pause for the leader
Sir George Reeves-Smith 1858 - 1941

For the last 25 years of his life Sir George Reeves-Smith was the most important hotelier in Britain. From 1915 he was vice president of the Savoy Hotel Company and from 1910 he was either chairman of the council or the executive committee of the IAHR, later the HRA. So, on the one hand, he ran one of the most important and prestigious hotel companies in the country and, on the other, he guided the employers' federation, always keeping in mind the interests of the Savoy Company.

Compared to hotel giants like Fred Gordon before him and Charles Forte and Max Joseph after him, Reeves-Smith was unusual in his eminence because he was always, basically, an employee. He looked after the family hotel in Sussex, inherited from his father in 1906 but, overall, he served the D'Oyly Cartes at the Savoy. They, for the most part, left him to get on with it. Richard D'Oyly Carte, who appointed him, because at the time he was a very sick man; Rupert, who succeeded his father, because he took over the reins as Chairman at 27 and Reeves-Smith, in post already, was far more experienced.

Reeves-Smith, according to his fulsome obituaries, was born in 1855 and died, aged 86, in May 1941. When he died his successor told the Savoy's Publicity Manager: "His first post as an hotel manager in London was at the Victoria Hotel in Northumberland Avenue in 1894." That went into the obituaries as well. The truth was that he'd got the job in 1891. Furthermore, his name was George Smith and he'd died at 83. The great man spent a lot of his life manufacturing a false image and a false record.

According to the records of Brighton College, where he was educated from 1873-1875, he was born on January 17th 1858 and his name was George Smith; his second name was Reeves but there was no hyphen and his death certificate says he died at 83. His father, also George Smith, was for some years the lessee of the Aston Lower Grounds in Birmingham. George Reeves Smith Sr. was, by profession, a licensed victualler; he ran pubs. He went on to own the Esplanade Hotel in Seaford in Sussex late in life, but when he died in 1906 he only left £1,368. Reeves-Smith's brother and sister were both on the stage, and neither catering nor acting were considered the most respectable professions at the time. All the indications are that Reeves-Smith always craved that respectability and felt that society did not give hoteliers the status which was their due. Certainly, he achieved his life's ambition when he was knighted in 1938 .

It's never possible to be completely sure why a character, long dead, chose to reinvent himself, but it is important if you're considering the life and career of Reeves-Smith. From the time he adopted the hyphen and increased his age, he was committed to acting a part and there is ample evidence that he was always on stage. A liking for the dramatic obviously ran in the family. Here was a man whose costume never varied. Throughout his life at the Savoy he wore a morning suit every day, unless he was in evening dress. It was reported that the day war broke out in September 1939 he caused a sensation among his staff by walking into the hotel in a lounge suit. It was like the Horse Guards giving up their breastplates and shining helmets for khaki for the duration of hostilities.

At the Savoy he had joined a hotel company which, as we've seen, was dominated by show business. By D'Oyly Carte, the great impresario, by a glittering good and great board, a company which had built, and was responsible for, the Savoy Theatre. What was more, a hotel company which was always designed to appeal to American guests, a glamorous market considerably removed from the staid English establishment. Throughout Reeves-Smith's career he continued to take a keen interest in amateur dramatics and was responsible for employing bands and cabarets at the Savoy which were among the most famous in the country. He loved show business; he even acted in amateur theatricals and he was, for some years, a member of the committee at the theatrical Garrick Club.

There was a second thread which ran through the life of Reeves-Smith; a determination to divorce the hotel from the public house. Year after year, in speech after speech at the IAHR, he advocated a different licence for hotels from pubs. He arranged for Private Members Bills to be introduced for that purpose. He lobbied government ministers. He got nowhere but he never stopped trying. In an obituary, Sir Francis Towle, a close friend, said: "he was never ashamed of being a hotelier". Not ashamed, perhaps, but ever anxious to improve the status. That was a telling comment by Towle, though. It suggests that there were many hoteliers at the time who *were* ashamed of their profession.

Towle obviously felt it was worth putting Reeves-Smith onto the other side of the scales, even in an obituary, to try to counteract the inferiority complex of hoteliers who felt that way. And Towle, managing director of Gordon Hotels, had been knighted at a relatively early age, for his services during the Great War, so he had little to be sensitive about himself.

The truth was that to be a hotelier was nothing to be proud of and this continued to be the case for many years after Reeves-Smith's death. If you wanted to be accepted into society during his lifetime there were strict, but unwritten, rules on admission to that select grouping. As we've seen, a background in trade could disbar you in Victorian times: Merton Cotes didn't get accepted by the Bournemouth establishment until royalty had stayed at his hotel. You could be disbarred if you lost your wife, either by divorce or premature death; Frederick Gordon never mentioned his first wife, even though it is difficult to understand today why it was a disgrace to die of influenza at an early age. Having a German name after 1914 didn't help either: so the Saxe Coburgs became the Windsors. Way after Reeves-Smith's death it certainly didn't help to be black; black guests were only accommodated at top hotels if they were very eminent, in one way or another - and not always then.

With Reeves-Smith, there are many possible scenarios. The age was: "class conscious and class driven" according to Winston Churchill. The nouveau riche sent their children to public schools and Father Smith no doubt wanted to give his son a better start in life than he had had. Social climbing would have been on the family's agenda, but the youngster could have been mocked by some of the boys at school for being the son of a publican. On his marriage certificate he still used the name Smith but it could be significant that his signature throughout his life had the Reeves running into the Smith rather than clearly separated with a hyphen. There is no evidence at the Public Records Office of a change of name by deed poll and his marriage certificate in 1888 gives his name as plain George Smith.

After school Reeves-Smith had been apprenticed, first to Spiers and Ponds, the railway caterers, and then to a wine merchant in Bordeaux called Jean Calvet, one of the largest in France. He was later said to have been Calvet's secretary, but a colleague on the IAHR, Henry Clark, who ran hotels in London and Norfolk, reminisced once that they had been apprentices together at Calvets. Reeves-Smith learned to be an expert on clarets. At the Naval Conference in 1930, when he was over 70, he used Château Lafite 1865 and broke the necks of the bottles himself with red hot tongs; old corks tend to break up if you try to remove them, so you avoid the danger of getting pieces of cork in the wine by simply breaking off the whole neck; it's a very skilful process.

After Calvet he joined his father at the Aston Lower Grounds, on the site of what is now Aston Villa Football Club in Birmingham. It was contemporaneous with Alexandra Palace in London and had its roots in the pleasure gardens of earlier centuries, in places like Vauxhall and Sadlers Wells in the capital. Aston Lower Grounds could boast a major exhibition hall, a theatre and an aquarium with an art gallery above. There were tea rooms and a boating lake, a skating rink and a football pitch. It was 31 acres (12.5 hectares) of primitive Disney. Technically, it was remarkable too; for example, part of the Great Hall floor could be raised. When Reeves Smith provided the Savoy cabaret audience with a raised dance floor to improve their view in 1929, it was considered a remarkable innovation. Reeves-Smith had, however, seen the self same mechanism at Aston Lower Grounds 40 years before. The Hall was 200 feet (60 metres) long, 90 feet (27 metres) wide and it was already lit by electricity.

In 1884 at the age of 26, Reeves-Smith became managing director of the complex. That was the occupation he gave on his marriage certificate when he wed Maud Hindle, a hop merchant's daughter, in a Lambeth registry office in 1888. They were to be married for over 50 years. Reeves-Smith's experience at the Aston Lower Grounds would naturally have affected his outlook in later life. Primarily, of course, it gave him first hand experience of many branches of show business. For example, William (Buffalo Bill) Cody's Wild West Show played Aston Lower Grounds in 1887. This theatrical management training would have been very much welcomed by Richard D'Oyly Carte; it would almost have been a meeting of fellow impresarios. Reeves-Smith's future views must also have been coloured by a crucial event, when the reputation of Lower Aston Grounds as family entertainment was ruined by the publicity following "The Aston Riot" on October 13th 1884. Radical Liberal party supporters broke up a Conservative Garden Party and there was a rough-house. A bunch of "Roughs" stormed the walls and broke up the furniture in the Great Hall. The family image of the Grounds was irreparably damaged and now Reeves-Smith had seen the destructive power of protesters at first hand. At the Savoy he was always scared of a militant union gaining any influence.

The market for Aston Lower Grounds was not the same quality as the Savoy would expect. It was more like the trippers on the Victorian pier but Reeves-Smith would still have been very anxious to make his first management role a success. It was not to be. Aston Lower Grounds was eventually a failure and the company sold out to Flowers, the brewers, in 1891. Reeves-Smith saw he was going to need another job and applied for the position of manager at the prestigious, 500 bedroom, Victoria Hotel in London in 1890. Perhaps he felt that George Smith, age 32, didn't sound as impressive as George Reeves-Smith, age 35. From that period comes the new image.

In March 1891 *Caterer* reported that Reeves-Smith had taken over as manager of the Victoria from Henry Logan. This was a major career progression. Only during the 20th century did the centre of London shift West to Mayfair, Belgravia and Kensington from around the Strand and the City, so the Victoria was very fashionably located. Of course, it is ironic that when Reeves-Smith altered his curriculum vitae to impress the Victoria's owner, he was conning one of the greatest Victorian con artists; Jabez Balfour, who you'll remember from Chapter 9.

As simply an employee of Balfour, Reeves-Smith wasn't in any way a participant in the Liberator Building Society scandal of 1893, but he must have feared for his new persona. Neither the failure of Aston Lower Grounds nor the criminal nature of the Liberator Building Society were his fault, but he had been involved in both enterprises. In later life, as we've seen, his official curriculum vitae said that he had become the manager of the Victoria in 1894, a convenient date *after* the crash. With the passing of the years, the story stuck. Reeves-Smith tried again, this time becoming manager and then managing director of the Berkeley Hotel in Mayfair. In 1897 a syndicate, organised by Reeves-Smith, was formed to take over the Berkeley. Reeves-Smith met Richard D'Oyly Carte at the opening of the rebuilt Claridge's Hotel in 1898 and the Savoy's chairman was impressed. They even had electricity in common, for the theatre at Aston Lower Grounds and the Savoy Theatre D'Oyly Carte had built, were early utilisers of the new invention. D'Oyly Carte invited Reeves-Smith to join the Savoy board but, as he was under contract to the Berkeley, he couldn't accept. So D'Oyly Carte bought the Berkeley to get Reeves-Smith.

When Reeves-Smith arrived at the Savoy there had been an interregnum after the Ritz and Escoffier debacle. He took over in 1901 when the dust had almost settled. The corruption did affect Reeves-Smith in one way though. He became in later years a stalwart supporter of the Bribery & Secret Commissions Prevention League.

If Reeves-Smith was always on stage, he wanted the cast at the Savoy to be properly dressed as well. That included guests as well as staff. He was rigid about the company's dress code. Even Lloyd George wrote to thank him for being admitted to the Savoy restaurant one evening when only wearing morning dress, rather than the prescribed dinner jacket. (He had come from the House of Commons, he explained.) Hedda Hopper, a syndicated film columnist of immense standing in the United States, was not admitted to the restaurant because she was wearing a hat. The London luxury hotel dress code continued rigorously long after Reeves-Smith passed away. If you had to hang on when phoning the Ritz in 2001, the recorded voice would speak not of the delights of the hotel, but of the need to wear a coat and tie, and certainly not trainers or jeans.

In his own life, he was the epitome of the type of guest a luxury hotel would want to attract. He had his cigars made specially for him in Havana and had his first after breakfast. He was keen on chess, philosophy and fishing on the Test. He was elegance personified, spoke French and Italian fluently and possessed great charm. He would have been delighted that his friend, the author Arnold Bennett, made him the role model for the hero of his famous book, *Imperial Palace*. He lived his part as managing director of a great hotel company.

His love for the dramatic also helped his company in that all hotels are in show business, to a greater or lesser extent. He once said: "if you ever build a restaurant, make certain that the entrance is down graceful stairs." If the Savoy was originally a show business hotel, par excellence, under Reeves-Smith it stayed that way. He was never happier than arranging the lavish dinner dances and cabarets. On one occasion he spent £60 (About £3,000 today) on artificial grass for a Derby dinner. Long after the other hotels had given up their evening entertainment, the Savoy was still in business. Their bands were famous, particularly that distinctive dance music pianist, Carroll Gibbons and the Savoy Hotel Orpheans. The future BBC radio icon Geraldo (Gerald Bright) was the second band for many years. The BBC would broadcast from the Savoy and the public listened in their millions.

Reeves-Smith had a dry wit. He would tell guests who complained about the prices: "The Savoy is expensive but not dear." He was once asked to define a bona fide meal: "One which is not taken as an excuse for getting drunk" he replied

When the IAHR was formed in 1910, Reeves-Smith was elected chairman of the council of management, the committee which ran the association on a day-to-day basis. When the executive was appointed in the 1920s, Reeves-Smith was elected to chair that body too, so he continued in the seat of power. He was always reelected and chaired the April 1941 meeting before he died the following month.

He was popular and he held an important post in the industry, but the final point in his favour was that he was always there. His attendance record at IAHR meetings was exemplary and better than anybody elses. The Communists taught the comrades that this was the best way to seize power in unions; get on committees and always be there when everybody else had retired exhausted. Then you could pass the legislation you wanted. Reeves-Smith saw to it that, if there were decisions to be made, he would always know what was going on. Only with the union negotiation in 1919 did he go too far and the system backfired.

The secrets of the Savoy's popularity were many faceted. During his 40 years at the helm, Reeves-Smith employed 32 chefs - and 31 of them were French. With Westminster College desperately trying to get applicants for its basic cookery courses, Reeves-Smith's ability to attract talented staff for the kitchen from across the Channel was very important.

He was a polite and courteous employer but he was also very knowledgeable, quite capable of arguing prices with the chef or spotting a glass out of place on a banqueting table. Rupert D'Oyly Carte would look after the furnishings and decor but Reeves-Smith ran the hotels. As there were Claridge's and the Berkeley, as well as the Savoy and the Simpsons-in-the-Strand Restaurant to control, he had senior managers dealing with day-to-day administration, but he was firmly in charge when it mattered. D'Oyly Carte was a: "shy, retiring man", "formal in manner but gentle and considerate." Just the right image for his job as a Secret Service courier in the Great War!

A compassionate man, Reeves-Smith was particularly concerned to help the victims of the First World War. He raised £300,000 to build a British Hospital at Montana in Switzerland after the war. He also raised enough money to build Preston Hall, near Maidstone for tubercular soldiers. He even had nail brushes fixed to the wall of the hotel cloakrooms so that one-armed soldiers could wash their hands.

It was a poorly kept secret that Reeves-Smith was desperate to earn a knighthood. Surrounded by the good and the great, he wanted his own recognition. Even within the Savoy company, his background credentials didn't match those of his colleagues. Rupert D'Oyly Carte had been to Winchester, as had Miles Thornewill, his right hand man. The board had Frank Goldsmith, who was a lawyer - Sir James Goldsmith's father - and Claude Serocold, from Naval Intelligence. This gave Serocold a common link to D'Oyly Carte, the former spy. It was all very cosy and Reeves-Smith was the outsider; indispensable but living in a very snobbish society and with his own plebeian secrets to keep hidden. He was finally successful; after he had been the chairman of the committee which dealt with the allocation of hotel bedrooms for the period of George VI's coronation in 1937, he finally received the accolade. He got the Legion d'Honneur from the French as well in July 1938. Both fully warranted.

Reeves-Smith's primary responsibility was to build up the profits of the Savoy Hotel company and he was in control from 1901 - 1941. Obviously, this period covered wildly different economic conditions. Everything from economic boom and expansionary periods to war and slump.

In Reeves-Smith's favour, the company survived all the bad times. It paid its shareholders a very respectable 10% throughout the 1920s and if it had difficulty making profits during the slump, the company was never in any danger of calling in the Receivers. On the other hand, it expanded very little. The core of its business was identical at the start and finish of Reeves-Smith's tenure of office. This might be put down to the difficulty the hotel industry had in raising capital from the City. This, however, didn't stop Trust Houses from expanding massively and newcomers, like Bracewell Smith, managed to get the necessary financial support as well. Reeves-Smith could have thought that it was impossible to run a large group of luxury hotels; that the necessary attention to detail was not possible if there were too many units.

If that were the case, why not experiment by increasing the size of the company one or two units at a time? Gordons owned hotels in France, Ritz was an international hotelier and the Savoy company had a hotel in Rome. The general approach to expansion seemed to lack dynamism. It is also possible that Reeves-Smith, who was over 60 in 1920, convinced himself that new hotels weren't viable investments.

There was little that could be done to increase profits during the Great War but the company flourished for much of the 1920s. For seven years between 1924 and 1930 the profits were consistent in the £164,000 - £186,000 range. The emphasis on building up the American business was constantly maintained and it was not possible to anticipate the enormous drop in that market which followed on from the Slump. The opening of a New York office and the support of the *Come to Britain* campaign were progressive moves. There was, however, a good deal of competition to the Savoy group in London, with the opening of new luxury hotels during the 1920s and the Slump which led to a great deal of price cutting.

Much of what Reeves-Smith hoped to achieve happened after his death. The growth of hotel education he had always supported. The recognition that hotels are different from pubs and the improvement of standards throughout the country did finally come about. A general appreciation that there was nothing to be ashamed of in being a hotelier was to be acknowledged. Today plain George Smith might have achieved as much.

17
The Slump years: 1929 - 1939

The image of the Slump which has come down to us is one of unmitigated disaster over a long period of years. Well, for the hotel industry, it wasn't quite that way. The Slump took time to develop; from October 1929 it took about 18 months for its full impact to be felt. It was devastating earlier on for hotels which depended on the luxury market and those beloved American tourists who stayed a week or so instead of the normal 3 days. Companies like the Savoy saw their turnover drop by up to 50% and their profits by even more. Where the Savoy's 1929 profits had been £183,000, they sank to £23,000 for 1930 and £10,000 for 1931. Total profits for the five years 1931 - 1935 hardly exceeded those for 1930 alone and the average for 1931-8 was £40,000. From 1930 - 1935 few of the large London hotels paid any dividend to either their Preference or Ordinary shareholders.

Hotels which did not depend on tourists - and that applied to most of them - were usually in a different position. Certainly, if they were in the manufacturing areas, like Liverpool or Manchester, the severe effect of the Slump on heavy industries was reflected in a very nasty downturn in their trading. Between 1929 and 1933 the LMS Hotels' net receipts dropped 44%. Between 1925 and 1938 the drop in profits in their Manchester and Liverpool Hotels accounted for more than two thirds of the total reduction the company suffered. In 1937/8 their tariffs were even lower than in 1932/3. Liverpool hotels were also affected by Transatlantic liners moving port to dock in Southampton. There were, of course, other smaller chains of railway hotels, like the Imperials of South West Railways and their hotel in Southampton which benefited as the Adelphi in Liverpool declined.

LMS also opened three brand new hotels before the war; the Welcombe in Stratford on Avon, the Queens in Leeds and the Midland in Morecambe. Yet by the outbreak of war they only classified six of their hotels as 1st class, with another six 2nd class and eight 3rd class. The Queens in Leeds in 1937 marked 100 years of continuous railway hotel building - from the beginning at Euston in London in 1837.

If Liverpool hotels did very badly during the Slump, up

The Slump years

the road the Prince of Wales Hotel in Southport was paying off its £13,000 overdraft in 1933 and 1934 and giving a 6% dividend to its shareholders as well. The Bristol College Green Hotel paid 12% for 1931/2 and put another 20% of undistributed profits to reserve.

Trust Houses, which was by far the largest hotel company in the countryside saw a sustained recovery after 1932. Net profits in 1937 were 36% up on 1929/30 and there was a 7% dividend. The growth in car ownership helped and also the substantial drop in interest rates - down from 4.5% between 1926 and 1931 to 2.9% in 1936. In addition, the salaried classes - the potential hotel users - were growing. They had risen by 10% since 1924, from 17.8% to 20% of the working population. When the government came up with a policy of cheap money, Trust Houses went out to buy hotels and by 1939 had 195 of them in total. If there was often neither hot nor cold water in the 45p - 55p a night bedrooms, they were still well supported.

There was certainly a case against investing in new facilities even if you could afford them. The *Daily Mail* gave the industry a much needed boost in December 1932: " There is the licensing trouble. If a person is anxious to build an hotel, he finds that every obstacle is put in his way. He cannot be certain in advance of obtaining a licence. He must wait till the building is erected, and even then a licence may be refused and all his expenditure will be in vain. Even for such necessary improvements as putting in extra bathrooms, evidence given before the Licensing Commission showed that in almost every case additional taxation is imposed. The hotel-keeper is confronted with the choice between equally painful alternatives. He may go smash because he has not fitted modern conveniences, and the public therefore refuses its custom; or he may be ruined because he has put in the conveniences and cannot pay the taxation and additional interest charges which they involve."

The question of whether you should actually promote your hotels more vigorously in bad economic conditions was a worry to many hoteliers. Admittedly, a report from Cornell University's hotel school in America had said that considerable research proved that you should. Against this, the somewhat less scientific idea that selling: "lowered the tone" was rife. That old bugbear, the hotelier's inferiority complex came back to haunt the delegates at the HRA's

241

Ritzy

conference in 1932. Sir Francis Towle took the HRA line, putting it down to their having to share a common licence with the pub owners. Mrs. V.W. Gresham, however, of the Torquay Hotel, Caterer and Apartments Association did not mince her words. She saw another threat to the status of her members and: "deprecated the use of road signs as tending to cheapen a place. "The delegates gravely agreed that: "they must be dignified to be effective." Dignity was, of course, even more necessary on the Sabbath Day. Both golf and playing sacred music in the open air were banned in Scotland on Sundays.

Many hotel companies also felt it undignified to actually talk about money to their customers in anything approaching public. An advertisement for Frederick Hotels in *Caterer* in August 1932 offered the readers an: "illustrated tariff on application to manager of the hotel." You might learn of the price of a Southsea Gas Oven - it was £37 - by reading their advertisement in the magazine, but the price of a bedroom in a Frederick Hotel - perhaps 70p - £1 - was still often stated, *even on the tariff*, to be: "on application." *Caterer* itself was less reticent and quick to change, if necessary. When one of its competitors decided to become a weekly, rather than a monthly magazine, the *Caterer* followed suit without hesitation and became a weekly from January 14th 1933; whatever else that did, it failed to improve the quality of the journalism at the time, with every scrap and scraping of news pressed into service to fill the weekly column inches.

The major companies realised that some form of promotion was essential, particularly in America. One report of the efforts made has survived. A Gordon's hotel manager, Brian Franks, sent it to his managing director when he got back from a trip to the United States in 1938. His efforts had been concentrated on the individual traveller, rather than on large company accounts. For example, Franks had a contact in the Chase Manhattan Bank and was entertained to lunch by her, as well as four of the Bank's directors. He reported that two of them had promised to stay at the Mayfair when they next visited London. He also went to a dinner of the Bon Vivant Club, where travel agents were members and he networked there: "They control at least 85% of the American business coming to London." The agents told him they were offered considerable hospitality when they came to the Grosvenor House or the Savoy and as: "they always come during the off season" Franks recommended Gordons did likewise in future. It would mean free accommodation and, possibly, free meals as well. There were also a lot of travel agents in the world, but if the rooms would have been empty otherwise, it was a relatively inexpensive marketing expenditure.

Franks wasn't happy with Gordon's representative in New York though he didn't feel it was her fault: "She is well known by the agencies and well liked. Her difficulty is the fact that she is a woman. It is obviously impossible for Miss Elliott to be particularly friendly with these men. She cannot go to their parties and meet them in bars, etc., where a good deal of their business is done." In the 1930s this was fair comment. The old habit of soliciting business from arrivals on the transatlantic liners continued. "Ward is endeavouring to obtain sailing lists from Cunard and the French Line before the arrival of the various ships, so that I can communicate with anybody I have met who is on board."

A number of other hotels had American representation but the most professional marketing weapon was undoubtedly the Savoy's press office. Able executives, like Ronald Tritton, Jean Lorimer and, later, Jean Nicol, were known to the press world-wide, and a regular flow of good stories kept the Savoy's name constantly in front of the international media. The Dorchester Press Office gave the Savoy a run for its money, though.

The growth in the use of motor cars and the continuing emission of smoke from chimneys led to an increase in both noise and pollution in the cities. The solutions were double glazing and air conditioning, but the latter seemed to involve wholesale reconstruction of the hotel. The Berkeley in London found an effective solution. They introduced double windows in 1936, using two sheets of glass 5/8ths of an inch thick, (1.5 cm) and three inches apart (7.2 cm). The air conditioning plant was built on the roof and the chimney flues in the bedrooms were used as ducts. Inlets for the process were put in behind fitted furniture and connected to the fireplaces, which no longer used coal and, therefore, didn't need the chimneys. There were 15 air changes an hour and peace reigned in the Berkeley bedrooms.

Across the Irish sea the Northern Ireland Hotel Association became Associates of the HRA. There were about 60 members of

Ritzy

the NIHA and they couldn't merge with the HRA because they couldn't afford the annual subscriptions. Even so, the guest of honour at their annual dinner on one occasion was Lord Craigavon, the Prime Minister of Northern Ireland. It illustrated the extremely parochial nature of the province and the paucity of the potential solutions for making the six counties economically viable. Separated from the new state of Eire, it was never likely to be able to stand alone. Looking round the Reception, if the noble Lord hoped for any major contribution to economic progress from the hoteliers, he was clutching at cheese straws.

Demands for better conditions for Northern Ireland hotel workers led to strikes in January 1936 as the NIHA tried to reach agreement with, this time, the National Union of Distributive and Allied Workers - another union banging its head on the brick wall of the hotel industry. The strike collapsed when the Union demanded the abolition of tipping! The members went straight back to work, presumably terrified that the union might win.

In 1931 the Royal Commission on Licensing included representatives of brewers and publicans but no hoteliers were invited to join the investigating committee. Nevertheless, possibly with the Trust House type of hotel in mind, it felt itself quite knowledgeable enough to say in its report that there was: "a generally recognized need to improve Britain's hotel stock. The majority of hotels in the country are out of date, the accommodation is unattractive, the catering is primitive and there is an obvious absence of trained hotel management."

Even if this were broadly true, it was no surprise that the Hotel and Restaurants Association went ballistic: "The Council feels aggrieved.....", "No evidence whatever ..upon which such a finding could be made...", "the statement is wholly contrary to fact...", "must have a prejudicial effect on the minds of our potential visitors" and so on. The blanket condemnation did owe something to the British disease of cultural self-flagellation. In fairness, 'out of date' is the other side of the heritage coin, the attractiveness of accommodation is in the eye of the beholder and catering can be judged primitive if you don't enjoy the food. Similar outbursts had been seen before and would be seen again. Some hotels deserved the criticism and some did not. Certainly, in the throes of a massive recession, the profits which pay for refurbishment were hard to come by. The government took no immediate action to help the industry improve the situation. Indeed, the opposite was true. The licensing hours when restaurant diners could drink in the evening were still restricted by DORA, the First World War Defence of the Realm Act.

The HRA had one victory in 1931. Margaret Bondfield, in the previous Labour government, had wanted to create a Trade Board for the catering industry to regulate hours and conditions. The HRA protested. When the Lord Chief Justice and his colleagues finally ruled on the subject, they held that 'Catering' was too broad a definition to enable uniform agreements to be reached. They decided that the August 1930 Terms of Hours Act was illegal. They said it was impossible to create: "a trade by definition." " 'Specified' does not mean anything the Minister chooses to call a trade." The hotel industry was too diffuse to be corralled into a trade; it employed everybody from cooks to carpenters and barmen to boilermen.

Even small changes would have helped a lot. Reeves-Smith was talking to Maurice Fowler, who became Editor of *Caterer* in 1934 and dominated its publication for the next 30 years. Reeves-Smith pointed out just one irritation. He said that if he wanted to get a step removed at the Savoy it would cost him £10. However, to get permission from the Licensing Justices to remove the step would cost a further £70 in legal fees. By contrast, in Italy in 1935, Mussolini had provided £166,000 for: "distressed hotels" and the Swiss government had given £666,000 to their hotel industry. To make matters worse, in Britain the cost of food, heating and lighting increased substantially during the 1930s - by 40% said the chairman of Grosvenor House. To make matters even worse, with a general over-supply of hotel bedrooms, the hotels couldn't maintain their tariffs.

If the Trust House performance looked quite good beside companies like the Savoy, the Cecil finally closed in 1930 and after that year Gordons never paid an ordinary dividend again. Dawnay, the chairman, had taken a 52% cut in pay since 1922 and the directors 46%, but their French hotels were a particular disaster in the 1930s and the Metropole Hotel in Cannes had to be closed and sold to the Bishop of Nice as a seminary. They were not alone in suffering poor business on the Riviera, where the effects of the recession were slow to arrive but still inexorable. In 1935 the Casino in Monte Carlo made

Ritzy

£13,000 profit where it had made £400,000 in 1934.

The major problem for Gordons had been their follow-up to the successful Mayfair Hotel - the Dorchester in Park Lane. They had bought the site, together with McAlpines, the builders, for £500,000. McAlpines started work a month before the Wall Street crash. The hotel opened in April 1931 in the depths of the Slump, Gordons had intended to pay for their share of the Dorchester by selling the Metropole, but property prices collapsed at the start of the Slump and by the time the Metropole was sold to the War Office in 1936, the price wasn't sufficient to pay off the accumulated debts. They managed to run the Dorchester from 1931-6 but they simply couldn't pay for their share of it. So McAlpines found themselves in the hotel business. Sir Francis Towle finally gave up the struggle and retired in September 1936. He told the shareholders that it was entirely his own idea, but a pension of £1,500 a year was some compensation for 16 years of very hard work. Inflation cut into it badly after the war, though. In 1937 Alfred Holland died. He had warned Gordon as long ago as 1897 that the company was heading in the wrong direction and resigned because of it. When he had left at the turn of the century the shares stood at £20. When he died they were £2. The manager in Monte Carlo showed prescience in pleading that they should keep the Dorchester whatever else they sold, but his argument did not receive sufficient support.

The Dorchester was really the only competition for the Savoy Group in London for many years. It was a major effort, completed with remarkable speed, when you consider that just one task was to remove 40,000 tons of earth from the site in order to build the garage, kitchens and Turkish bath. William Curtis Green, the architect, used 140,000 sq. feet (over 13,000 sq.m.) of polished marble concrete blocks, over 24,000 sq. ft. (2,230 sq. m.) of glass and 2,500 doors. The ballroom could seat around 500 for a dinner and became the most popular in London for VIP functions of that size. In 1934 the Grosvenor House made its swimming pool into a ballroom for 1,500 guests and the Great Room captured the really large London function market for the next 40 years.

What might have helped the luxury hotels was a greater degree of outsourcing. In 1939 the Savoy had its own power station, air conditioning plant, artesian well, bakery, ice plant (it could produce six tons a day), furnishing department, laundry and printing press. The company had: "silversmiths, seamstresses, carpenters, painters, plasterers, bricklayers, joiners, doctors, detectives and florists." There were about 1,000 staff, though of course, many of the specialists would be used throughout the group.

October 1934 saw the opening of the Kirk Sandall Hotel near Doncaster. It couldn't compare to the Dorchester in size but it did have one unique feature; it was made of glass. Built by the Pilkington Glass Company, the walls, floors, chimney pots, bar fittings, table tops and chairs were all glass. The outside of the hotel was: "shell-pink and turquoise-blue Vitrolite with a base of black." A particularly admired novelty was that: "Doncaster races is etched into the glass in the lounge." It was, of course, an admirable effort by Pilkingtons to prove that glass, as a material, could be used far more in buildings. The hotel was the company home of VIPs, particularly those visiting the Doncaster race meetings. It was a throwback to the Furness Abbey type of company hotel nearly 100 years earlier, but eventually Pilkingtons sold it. It is now The Glasshouse public house.

Overall, the fashion in decor was for simplicity after the convoluted extravagance of Victorian architecture. This emerged from the Bauhaus movement, an attempt in Germany early in the century to build decent housing for poorer people by cutting out the cost of the frills. Then it became fashionable and we get the graceful uncluttered lines of art deco. So, in hotels which wished to be considered modern, plain fitted wardrobes were in, but pictures on walls were out.

There is another reason why a Slump is not a bad thing for every company. If you can't afford cream, for example, it's good for custard manufacturers and custard sales did rise during the Slump. If you can't afford a new motor car, you may well have a degree of additional disposable income which can be spent on a new radio - or a few days holiday in a hotel. If you can't afford expensive hotels, you might settle for cheaper hotels which would benefit. Certainly, Lyons sailed through the Slump. The Strand Palace had been extended until it could now offer 1,200 rooms. In 1931, in the depths of the recession, Lyons formed a new company, Cumberland Hotels Ltd, to build a hotel in London at Marble Arch. The Cumberland opened in December 1933. It traded well at an inexpensive 11 shillings and 6 pence (57.5p) for a single room, with a private bathroom and English breakfast. In 1942 when my parents went to live there, the price had only risen to 13 shillings (65p). Strongly supported by their catering interests, Lyons continued to pay at least a 22.5% dividend. The Cumberland had a very simple, modern decor but its building costs were increased by legislation which made it illegal not to have the bedroom separated from the bathroom by a short corridor. Some years later this law was abolished but, by that time, hundreds of Cumberland Hotel bedrooms had useless lobbies.

King George V's death in January 1936 was a sad blow for the whole country. He was a very popular King and had served his country well. The *Caterer* reported the event in the form hoteliers would have expected: "King's death causes severe dislocation to the industry"! It reported in detail the loss of business which had resulted: "One provincial hotel, for instance, lost five functions, totalling 1,000 people, at the end of January, and for the first time in its history had to cancel its Saturday dinner-dance." Presumably, the end of civilization as they knew it.

Hotels remained the provinces of the well-to-do. The cost of living index had dropped 10% between 1924 and 1930 and a further 11% between 1930 and 1932. By 1938 it was just below 1930 and so, if you were in work, your money went further. The Come to Britain movement expanded slowly. In view of the Slump, the government reduced its annual contribution from £5,000 to £4,000. It restored it later in the 1930s and then in December 1938 tripled it to £15,000. War was declared nine months later. It was an epic example of too little and much too late.

No country in the Western world escaped the effects of the Slump. It was a struggle to survive and if you were junior staff and foreign as well, it was trebly difficult. Mario Gee, who eventually managed the restaurant at the Europa Hotel in Grosvenor Square in the 1960s, remembered those days very well: "If you were a waiter you had to learn French and you lived off your tips. Still, the Inland Revenue didn't pester you and you could take comfort from the fact that, if you wanted to be a manager, they were always promoted from the restaurant. You got one week-day off and every other Sunday, so it was a 5½ day week. You still couldn't get a work permit unless you were part of the exchange programme." The ruling was now that

The Slump years

for every Englishman who went abroad to work in the industry, one continental could come in his place: "Certainly, as a continental it was the hotel and restaurant business or nothing. You couldn't get a job as a road sweeper if you were continental; at a top class hotel like the Savoy, you might get £1 or £3 a week as a head waiter and the commis would get 10 shillings (50p) and a chef de rang 5 shillings. (25p). The other difference being that a chef de rang would get more from the tronc." (the pool of tips).

"Between Christmas and Easter was the low season. If you were out of work at Christmas, you wouldn't get another job till Easter. You always got a week off in the winter without pay. I can't remember anybody who had graduated from Westminster. Nobody there made their mark. Foreigners worked under foreigners in the best places. Tails would cost you seven guineas (£7.35p) and you could have a dress shirt made to measure for 10/6. (52 1/2 p.) Everybody wore black ties and no pocket handkerchief. I think my greatest achievement in my years in the industry was that my wife never had to go out to work."

If you fell on hard times, one solution was to turn to the Benevolent. Still battling on, it achieved another record year in 1938, raising a paltry £2,322. As the chairman pointed out with unjustifiable pride, the Benevolent had distributed £58,000 in grants and pensions since 1837. An average of £580 a year from the entire industry, for over 100 years, for the hotel and catering workers in distress throughout the country.

Admittedly, the days were gone when unemployment could mean starvation or the workhouse. There was a staff shortage in the industry by 1935 and the Denmark Street Exchange in London, which placed hotel workers, found 37,000 of them jobs in 1934. A good reference was still very important, though, and the power of the employers to hire and fire as they felt fit was a constant threat. Many of them were feared. Ron Jones started a distinguished hotel career as an apprentice in the Adelphi in Liverpool. When Arthur Towle visited the hotel the prepreparations went on for days. Jones says Towle would sack people on the spot who didn't look the part.

The same would be said of some post-war hotel leaders, who had been brought up in that milieu. When Towle sat in the lounge with his accompanying party, none of the staff would cross the carpet, but

249

kept to the edges of the room. Senior executives are often frightening to juniors without wishing to be; the aura creates the fear. But hotel staff were treated as second class citizens in the 1930s, if that well.

Women were also still having problems being recognized as equals. The HRA conference in Southport in 1938 enjoyed a paper given by Barbara Coutts on the: "Woman's point of view in hotelkeeping". Coutts was described in the advance publicity as: "Niece of Mr. D.G.S.Russell of the Lygon Arms, Broadway." She was well ahead of her time: "Public school boys have facilities for training in this country and abroad. There is no training school in hotel management for women. Public school girls who go into hotel work, start at the bottom and by picking up scraps of knowledge, gradually work their way up."

Auguste Escoffier died in 1935, universally admired and widely loved. He had started in a kitchen in Nice in 1859 at the age of 14 and devoted his life to his craft. The old scandal followed him to the grave, though. Eugene Herbodeau, one of his greatest disciples tried to cover it up when he wrote: "Escoffier, be it said to his credit, died a poor man." The implication was that, unlike some of his fellows, he had not taken bribes from suppliers, but he had. Herbodeau wrote later: "Escoffier impressed upon them, first and foremost, that the chief aim of a cook must be perfection, *however unremunerative it might prove;* (my italics) perfection for its own sake and the cook's own satisfaction." Unfortunately for the purist, very few businesses can be run that way.

The other side of this coin could be seen in the will of Mr. A. C. Gabb, head waiter for 49 years at the Grand Hotel in Eastbourne, who died in March 1934 and left over £20,000 in his will . In today's money, that made him close to a millionaire and he'd spent his working life as a head waiter and married the housekeeper. The importance of tips was far greater than the question of salary and, if the hours were long, the rewards - if you were in the right place at the right time - could be very considerable.

Reeves-Smith, as part of an HRA delegation to the Ministry of Labour in 1935, explained the normal working hours. During the year staff got 38 days off during the week plus 28 on Sundays. They usually got a fortnight's holiday a year and: "that meant that the whole staff was off duty for 10 weeks in the year." It also meant that, effectively, they worked a 6 day week. Arthur Towle told the Minister that: "90% of the employees were engaged for 65 hours a week, including Sundays" That would have included hours off duty during the working day for shift workers. The Trade Board enquiry in 1930 had shown that most hotel staff worked about a 50 hour week. Staff conditions had, however, worsened during the Slump as Gordons, for example, found themselves paying out 25% of the company's receipts on wages. In 1930, in a small gesture, the "Voluntaires" system of exchanging work permits for young people wanting to learn another language was extended to Germany.

The HRA continued to be run by the same coterie throughout the decade, though they agreed to work in concert with the Residential Hotel Association on matters of mutual interest. One fresh face was the successful candidate when a new general secretary was needed in 1933. The advertisement had made the necessary qualification very clear: " The successful candidate would have a public school education." Hugh Wontner could offer that and he had experience as general secretary of minor associations as well. It was good enough to get him the job and to start him off on a remarkable career in the industry.

On the face of it, the HRA was - and had always been - a democratic organisation. You had to be voted onto the Council, the Council voted for the Executive and one third of the members of both bodies retired each year in rotation for there to be new elections. In fact, though, every year the whole one third were reelected unanimously unless someone died or retired. The process was that someone stood up, said how much they owed to Reeves-Smith, or what a great job Francis Towle was doing with the International Hotel Association, or how grateful they should be for the time and effort put in by Salmon and, as a consequence, how about reelecting *the whole* one third. Members were not singly reelected but as part of the bloc. The Council could, constitutionally, be a massive 60 strong, so Reeves-Smith and the other leaders invited their friends to join it. The monthly reports of the association over the years hardly ever shows an element of dissension within the work of the committees. In fact, the note is of constant congratulation.

Congratulations for the efforts to get a Hotel & Restaurants Bill passed in the Commons. Introduced by Bracewell Smith MP in

Ritzy

April 1933, it died after the second reading. Another in 1934 also died after the second reading. And a third in 1936 when they couldn't even find an MP who had been successful in the Private Member's Bill ballot to put it forward; hopeless.

The key objective was always that elusive separate licence. It wasn't as if the industry had a poor case for it. The argument got bogged down, however, in a welter of accusation and counter-accusation. The industry saying a different licence from a pub would give hoteliers their justified higher status and the brewers saying it was class legislation. The government struggled with the fact that almost anyone who had a few rooms to sell could call themselves a hotel. A far more cogent argument for the industry was that an investor might think twice about putting money into a venture where the licensing justices could put him out of business overnight; this simply by withdrawing his licence which - even more infuriating to the industry - they couldn't do with a licence held by a theatre or a cinema. The absence of investment was damaging to local economies. They needed hotels to provide jobs and to encourage visitors to their parts of the country.

Take the Howard Park Hotel in Aylesbury, Bucks. In March 1933 a hotelier's son had bought a Rothschild mansion after the family had left and the first purchaser had been unsuccessful in trying to run a private school on the site. The young hotelier had worked in hotels in Britain and abroad and had taken a five year lease on the property. He had also spent £7,000 furnishing it. Now he wanted a licence and his application was opposed by the local Chief Constable. The reason advanced was that there were sufficient pubs in the area already. The police specified that the population was 1,494 and there were 12 licences. Therefore, they contended, no more were needed. Fortunately for the youngster the local justices turned down the police argument and granted the licence. If they had not, what would have happened to the expenditure on the lease and the cost of the furniture? If the government wanted stronger local economies and more jobs, this was hardly the way to go about it.

In 1931 the Royal Hotel at the Bridge of Allan in Scotland was refused a licence, in spite of the support of the Provost, the local church and Scottish Travel officials. The magistrates said there were enough licences already, though the total included 5 grocers.

The Slump years

The members of the HRA offered more congratulations when Reeves-Smith made representations to the government against the 40% rise in fuel oil prices due to increased taxation, but without getting an amelioration. Fighting on another battlefield, by 1936 the amounts paid out in corkage by the drink manufacturers to wine waiters and the butlers of grand homes had reached such proportions that the price of a bottle of brandy, champagne, liqueurs and wine was being increased to pay for it. The HRA had discussions with the Wine & Spirit Association. The HRA threatened not to have their members stock products where the manufacturer paid corkage. The WSA said that it was all the members of the HRA's fault for not paying their waiters enough. There was no progress but lots of thanks to the executive. It should have been work for the Prevention of Corruption Association, on which the HRA had a seat. The fact was, though, that in 30 years in Britain there had only been 869 convictions and that covered all industries and public sector employees. The fines had totalled £30,000 and 177 of the accused had gone to prison. £1,000 a year and six annual convictions. It was a good idea but conducted halfheartedly by successive governments.

Could the hotelier MPs have achieved more? Bracewell Smith, Salmon and Kimber, were just three back benchers. The power in the eating and drinking land were the Brewers; strong financial supporters of the Conservative governments, related to senior politicians, well represented in the House of Lords, members of the right clubs and major employers in many towns. The Brewers were important and the hoteliers were not. They had to settle for congratulations. As Prince Arthur of Connaught said at the Silver Jubilee dinner in 1935: "There is probably no more important industry in this country which, in the past, has been so grossly neglected" The guests murmured politely: "hear, hear". There was an element of whistling in the dark to keep up the spirits.

As usual, though, they were successful at stopping - or helping to stop - many proposals which would have adversely affected their members. They got the RAC to abandon the idea of charging hotels a fee for being graded in the motorist's guide and the Metropolitan Water Board to reduce their proposed charges. They were good at stopping things.

The best road forward was actually mapped out by Frank

Ritzy

Evans, a Brighton hotelier, when addressing the HRA's annual conference in 1933. He reported that there had been a lot of progress for the policies of Brighton hoteliers since he had won a seat on the town council.

The economic conditions and increased competition led to severe price cutting among the better London hotels during the decade. The last 10 years had seen the building of the Mayfair, Park Lane, Grosvenor House and Dorchester to compete with the Savoy group, the Langham, Carlton, Piccadilly and Ritz. It was agreed that there would be substantial fines if a hotel cut its prices below an agreed minimum of £1.75 for a twin bedded room with bath, and the HRA encouraged hotels out of London to adopt the same practice. It was price fixing on a large scale but it was perfectly legal if you could make it stick; it was, however, always suspected that someone was breaking the rules, but it was difficult to know who.

The big boost for the bottom end of the industry came with a bill to introduce paid holidays. In 1937 only 1,500,000 workers had a guaranteed holiday, paid by their employers. By 1939 this had increased to 11 million through government legislation. This created a vast new market. It benefited the boarding house owner rather than the hotelier but it was a very welcome help after so many difficult years. One entrepreneur who took advantage of the new situation was a South African fairground showman called Billy Butlin. He built his first Holiday Camp at Skegness, opened in 1936, and provided his customers with a standard of comfort and entertainment very substantially ahead of anything on offer at the price. Although Butlins isn't strictly part of the hotel industry, its expansion enabled it to buy such fine hotel buildings as the St. Georges in Cliftonville and the Grand in Scarborough. The new concept was widely copied and by 1939 there were 200 holiday camps of one kind or another. Arthur Towle opened the LMS Hotel's first holiday camp in Prestatyn in Wales that year. In the high season the holiday camps could look after 30,000 guests a week. Very useful for a multitude of purposes when the war broke out and many of them were commandeered.

Butlin built a great business and gave enormous enjoyment to millions of people. His mixture of professionalism, cheek and great public relations was well illustrated once when he was flying with his wife to the Caribbean for a holiday. Caught by the press on the airport, he was asked why he chose the luxury of such a far- away destination, rather than the more homely pleasures of a Butlins. Straight faced, he explained that he was only going to the luxury resort in the sun in order to discover new ideas that he could provide for his campers! He had tried so hard to improve their holidays that it was a feasible explanation.

The Coronation in 1937 provided a short term respite for the embattled London hotels. The Grosvenor House was on the route of the procession and did a brisk trade in seats, at a cost of 18 guineas each (£18.90 and in today's money about £1,000.) Even the Coronation though failed to bring tourism expenditure back to pre-Slump days. It totalled £48.5 million in 1937 as against £56 million in 1928. Tourist arrivals were 488,000 in 1937 but had been 692,000 in 1929. One welcome seed had been sown though in 1931. It was in the Local Government Publicity Act and it permitted the rates to include 1/2d (1/4p) for promotion. This would have a far reaching effect 15 years later.

The threat of war made 1938/9 bad for trade again. In times of great uncertainty, the price of houses collapsed - well, what would be your financial position if your house was bombed, as had happened in a big way in the recent Spanish Civil War? The tendency was to cut down on extraneous spending. The government was busy evading questions in the Commons on the need for a war risks insurance scheme. Hotel turnover, in such circumstances, is always among the first to be hit. There was also the continuing adverse effect of currency restrictions imposed by some European countries during the decade. A process which had started with Hitler trying to defend the Mark in 1936.

Preparations for war with Germany had started that long ago. An Air Raid Department had been set up at the Home Office and advised hotel association members, among others, of what to do in the event of an air raid.. By the Autumn of 1938 the Grosvenor House had gas-proof rooms, a shelter on the first floor, 75 fully trained air-raid wardens and 50 tons of sand to put into sandbags. Also in 1936 the Food (Defence Plans) Department of the Board of Trade was set up: "to develop plans for the supply, control and distribution of food in an emergency." Fifty million ration books were ready for distribution and there would be no hesitation, such as had marked

Ritzy

the move to rationing in the First World War, in using them. By 1938 schools were making plans for taking over country hotels to house their pupils, if evacuation became necessary

A decade which had started with dreadful economic conditions ended with a world war. The hoteliers who had survived the former, prayed they would also survive the latter. On September 3rd, 1939 Chamberlain declared war on Germany. The decade had gone from disaster to calamity and the forthcoming conflict was going to see a lot of both hotels and hoteliers failing to survive.

Arthur Towle stayed with the railway hotels and avoided his brother's fate.
Caterer.

Sir Francis Towle was a great hotelier overwhelmed by the Slump.
Caterer.

Lady Constance Honeywood was the token lady hotel chief in the 1920s, but she had to use her own money for the token.

Sir Bracewell Smith was a schoolmaster who went on to be Lord Mayor and Chairman of Arsenal.
Caterer.

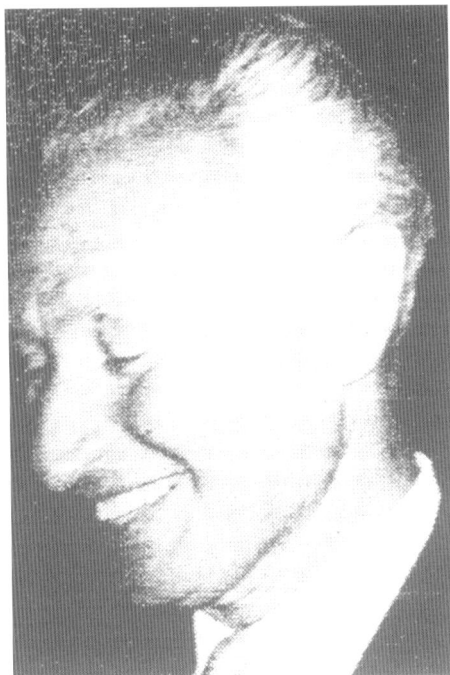

Fred Kobler created hotel sales promotion, total concentration on selling bedrooms and Grand Metropolitan – while looking out of his office window.

Sir Maxwell Joseph was a great property man, an indifferent hotelier, a wonderful entrepreneur and a fantastic gambler.

Lord Forte built the biggest British hotel company from scratch and against the odds.
Rocco Forte Hotels.

A.H. (Jack) Jones was a pioneer in very many ways, but should be mostly remembered for his contribution to hotel education.
Caterer.

Sir Hugh Wontner had one chance for greatness as Reeves-Smith's assistant – and took it with both hands.

Lord Crowther was a great journalist and economist who strayed into the hotel industry and the strain eventually killed him.
Caterer.

Professor John Fuller was the first to gain a Chair at a British University in Hotel Studies. It was he who felt that "the industry is scared stiff of brains."
Oxford Brookes University

Victor Ceserani is a devoted teacher of the craft of Hotelkeeping and Catering. Without him and his colleagues, the industry couldn't have managed its growth.
Caterer.

Martin Skan proved with Chewton Glen that the British can produce hotels every bit as fine as any in the world.

Sir Reo Stakis was a poor immigrant who built the finest hotel company in Scotland.
Caterer.

Cyril Stein was a great bookmaker and bet he could be a great international hotelier by buying Hilton International. He was right.
Hilton Group.

Jasminder Singh is a recent example of a refugee family enhancing the British economy. What would we have done without refugees?
Caterer.

L. SILLER	VIKTOR	SANTARELLI	LATRY	MANETTA	STALUGEUX	ZAVATTONI
General Manager	Chef de Reception	Manager, Savoy Restaurant	Maître des Cuisines, Savoy Restaurant	Manager, Savoy Grill	Maître des Cuisines, Savoy Grill	Banqueting Manager

Long before computers there were characters. These men were the team who attracted the visitors to the Savoy between the wars.

The Ross Hall class of 1962. These students and teachers were the essential ingredient for the expansion of the industry.
Caterer.

When George V and Queen Mary inspected the Mayfair Hotel they were greeted by General Dawnay.

A postcard for the opening of the May Fair Hotel

Judges at a cocktail competition in 1934.

The Oliver Messel suite at the Dorchester was not inspired by America. It did have theatrical overtones as Messel was a stage set designer.

This Stardust Mini Holiday brochure was produced by Grand Metropolitan Hotels and helped create the national habit for taking short breaks.

The London Hilton, one of the great successes of 1964.

This was a luxury motel bedroom in the 1960s. A lot of the ideas came from America.

Caterer.

Australian Oak wood carving in the Piccadilly Hotel restaurant, 1974.

Len Lickorish, CBE, the engine room of British tourism during its most important years of development.

Lord Forte (L) and Lord Crowther (R), agree the takeover. They came out fighting later.
Caterer.

Creative banqueting lives on in the skills of the Tower Thistle Hotel kitchens in London.
Incentive Travel & Corporate Meetings.

18
The Second World War 1939 - 1945

The war clouds had been gathering ever since Czechoslovakia had been sacrificed at Munich in 1938. Chamberlain may have called the agreement he reached with Hitler: "Peace in our time" but few believed him after the initial enthusiasm had dissipated. Hotels started to prepare for the coming conflict early. Staff were trained in fire fighting in anticipation of a blitzkrieg from the sky. Air raid shelters were constructed in the grounds or the most solid parts of hotels wherever possible.

Plans were made by the government to counteract Fifth Columnists. This was a phrase coined by the Spanish General Sierro during the Civil War recently ended. As his four army columns advanced on Madrid, he called his supporters behind his enemy's lines his Fifth Column. The fear of similar sabotage by Britain's fascists led the government, on the outbreak of war, to pass Regulation 18B. This enabled them to arrest and keep in custody without trial anybody they thought might help the enemy. Hoteliers of German origin were arrested in 1939 and Italians when Mussolini decided to join forces with Hitler in June 1940. As many continental staff also left the scene to join up, a lot of non-belligerent nationals found themselves promoted. The comparatively lowly Swiss night manager at the Piccadilly Hotel in London became the general manager overnight.

The government did not wish to be too hard on Italian hoteliers who had often been living in Britain for 20-40 years. If they had not become naturalised, they still did not appear much of a danger to the state. Nevertheless, exceptions couldn't be made and some Italians, like Hector Zavatoni, the Banqueting Manager at the Savoy, had been enthusiastic fascists. He would proudly wear his black shirt on Italian National Days. So they were rounded up and it was decided to send a large number of them to Canada to sit out the war in peace and comparative comfort. They sailed on the *Arandora Star* but the ship was torpedoed and sunk in the North Atlantic in July 1940. 470 Italians lost their lives, including Hector Zavatoni himself, Italo Zangiacomi, who had been the general manager at the Piccadilly and Cesare Maggi, the distinguished restaurant manager at the Ritz. Among those arrested but almost immediately released was

Ritzy

a young restaurateur called Charles Forte who would build one of the great hotel companies after the war.

The government had learned lessons from the First World War. Food rationing was introduced almost immediately in January 1940. It was later recognized that restaurants could augment the food ration, giving the owners the opportunity to exploit their position by raising their prices. So in June 1942 there came the Meals in Establishments Order which restricted the cost of a meal to 5 shillings (25p) and the number of courses was also limited. At the same time the hotel's supplies were restricted to a percentage of what they had bought prewar. The better hotels put up the margin of profits on sales of alcohol. The maximum menu price led to restaurant meals in Britain being underpriced, compared to the continent, for many years after the war, but alcohol being overpriced to make up for it. The Hotel Association managed to get small supplementary charges approved when entertainment was provided. There were, of course, shortages of every kind. The Savoy decided to augment their menus by rearing deer in the countryside and selling more venison. Chefs performed miracles of culinary invention, using the most unexpected ingredients, such as Snoek, which was a very obscure fish, dried egg and dried bananas. The German word ersatz was adopted into the English language to signify anything which was not, in reality, what it proclaimed itself to be.

There was a considerable illegal black market in food and drink and many prosecutions. Government control was strict; a typical instruction from the Minister of Food in 1942 was that hotels were not to serve turkey except on Christmas Day: "Pursuant to Article 8 of the Meals in Establishments Order 1942, as amended (S.R. & O. 1942, No. 909, as amended by 1942, Nos. 1494 and 1821)." In the early war years, however, the government was even more concerned to ensure that bombers had difficulty in finding their targets and the country maintained a total blackout out of doors after dark. For years the only lights were to be from burning buildings.

When the war started, not much happened for many months. It was a period nicknamed 'the Phony War'. The danger of air raids led to a massive evacuation of school children from vulnerable cities. Dulwich College Junior School was typical, moving into the Swallow Falls Hotel in Bettws y Coed in rural Wales. A large number of country hotels which were not requisitioned were still very badly affected by petrol rationing. Even a few gallons of petrol a month could only be obtained for essential purposes. If you weren't in a special occupation, like a doctor or a farmer, you just put your car into the garage until the war ended. At the seaside, as all the beaches were mined and piers separated from the land by destroying their middle section, the main attractions were no longer available. The seaside didn't return to normal until some years after the end of the war.

Anticipating air raids, additional large numbers of people fled or avoided the cities and the hotels suffered as a result: "Grosvenor House is at the moment almost literally hanging on by the skin of its teeth" wrote A.H. Jones, its Managing Director, and its bankers produced £50,000 in exchange for a charge on the hotel's assets. The ground rent payments were postponed, as were the debenture shareholders' dividends. The hotel had 70 guests and 1,000 staff on September 3rd, the day war broke out; 400 had to be dismissed immediately. By early 1940 advertising had been stopped, maintenance ended, the cabaret contract finished and the band reduced. There was practically no banqueting and only two floors out of seven were in use. By August 1940, however, two floors had been let as offices. If a company's offices were bombed, one option was to move into a hotel. London's work force was particularly badly affected and, even 10 years after the war, there was a shortage of offices. Management Selection, which became one of the country's largest headhunters, started life in one room in the Green Park Hotel. Grosvenor House lost money till 1941 and the Savoy lost money in 1940 for the first year in its history.

By 1943 profits could be made by London hotels again - if they had survived. One notable casualty was Cesar Ritz's Carlton Hotel in London which was totally destroyed in the Blitz. Another loss was the Langham which suffered hits and then was devastated by the blast from a large land mine which fell outside the hotel. The explosion fractured the hotel's water tank on the roof and the hotel was flooded out. It would be 50 years before it opened its doors as a hotel again.

Unlike the Great War, the government could foresee that the conflict was likely at least a year before. There was time to plan. In the first two weeks of the war some 200 hotels were requisitioned. They were used for many different purposes. The Ministry of Defence

Ritzy

took over the Metropole and the Victoria in Northumberland Avenue. Many civil service departments were evacuated to the resorts and spas. Even as late as 1943 the Great Room at the Grosvenor House was requisitioned by the Ministry of Works, for the Americans. The Willow Restaurant was the Officers Mess and an amazing total of 14,000 meals were served every day. The Americans took over the Washington Hotel in Mayfair as well. By the end of 1943 the Catering Wages Commission, investigating the industry, estimated that 1,832 hotels had been requisitioned - about 15% - 20% of the total hotels in the country.

After the fall of France in 1940 much of the population on the South and East coast of the country was itself evacuated. In a typical seaside town in those areas the Commission found a very substantial reduction in the available hotels. In 1938 there had been 16 licensed and 36 unlicensed hotels. By 1944 20 had been put out of action by war damage, 17 requisitioned and 3 were empty. Just 12 were still operating as hotels. After the war it was certainly going to take a long time to get back to normal.

It wasn't all gloom, though. There were soldiers on leave to accommodate and they came from many other allied armed forces as well. There were a considerable number mustering in Britain from 1939 onwards, hoping to take part in the liberation of continental Europe at some point in the future. Polish, French and other European forces fled from Europe. Elements of many Commonwealth armed forces were in Britain from the beginning and American forces started to arrive in 1942. Where they had mostly been posted outside Britain during the Great War, this time large numbers stayed in the country until the D Day landings in 1944.

Many of the black soldiers were refused accommodation. The sturdy independence of the St. Ermins Manager at the turn of the century in accepting black guests whatever his guests felt, had not become a principle. Learie (later Lord) Constantine, one of the greatest cricketers the West Indies ever produced, was turned away from a Walduck Hotel in Russell Square in London in August 1943 and a mass of outraged press publicity did not change the situation. It was still the case long after the war that the modest St. Ermins was the favourite hotel of the Foreign Office when they had to house a visiting African Head of State. The HRA had now become sufficiently liberal to deplore the refusal but still said that: "hoteliers had to consider their other customers"

As servicemen arrived on leave for a few days break, major city hotels became packed. Some hotels found themselves the appointed headquarters of irregular bodies; American news correspondents - neutrals until December 1941 - set up home in the Savoy and played an important part in spreading favourable propaganda on the: "Britain can take it" theme. From the point of view of the hotels every shortcoming in quality or service could be excused by trotting out the famous contemporary phrase: "Don't you know there's a war on." Petty larceny increased, however, with everything in short supply; shoes left outside bedrooms for cleaning overnight might disappear and management always feared for the security of their towels. Still, at least money did not have to be spent on redecoration - indeed, it couldn't be because everything was needed for the war effort.

The air raids started in earnest in 1940. The incendiary bombs of the period were quite small and civilians were recruited to deal with them if possible. My mother was given a bucket of sand and a stirrup pump to bring water to bear on any fire. She was then posted to the roof of the Cumberland Hotel in London, where we lived during the war, and told to keep a look out for anything that dropped and exploded! Where only 1,500 civilians had been killed in the 4 years of the First World War, more than 30,000 were killed in the Blitz. Not surprisingly, most prospective diners chose to shelter from the raids rather than eat out in hotels.

Life for the guests in the middle class Cumberland had not changed much since pre-war days. A single bedroom with a private bathroom was 13 shillings and 6 pence. (67p). The food was served in the Grill Room by waiters in immaculate full evening dress and there was an excellent curry trolley paraded round the room by a Sikh in a splendid turban and full national costume. Less ceremonial meals were available in La Fourchette and the enormous lounge was always packed at teatime. Air raids had not, however, been a pre-war feature of a stay in a hotel. When the air raid siren went, the guests could go into their bathrooms, separated from the bedrooms, and hope that the room curtains would absorb any blast from nearby bombs. If the raids were particularly heavy, everybody congregated in the basement where you could play chess in the Library until the All Clear siren sounded. The fact that the restaurant was also in the basement, well below ground, made it even more popular with the residents.

On one occasion bombs did blow out all the front windows of the Cumberland and my great grandfather was discovered walking around his bedroom on a sea of broken glass, murmuring: "I'm alive I am, I'm alive". He made a swift recovery from the shock but effective Housekeeping must have been difficult that day. Shortages came in many forms. With conscription and the exodus of many overseas staff, the number of male staff available to work in hotels diminished sharply but, unlike the Great War, single women were conscripted from the end of 1941 as well. It was the married women and the older generation who filled the gaps. A hotelier who had access to anything difficult to obtain could sell it at a handsome profit. In London there were three top quality ballrooms for large numbers where kosher food could be served under rabbinic supervision. To obtain a single popular date in the calendar, the Banqueting Manager at the Dorchester would ask for £250, (£7,000) in cash, in advance, as tips for his staff. How much they saw of this largesse was anybody's guess. In partial exchange, boxes of the hotel's excellent petits fours would be provided for the hostess when she left. Whether the company knew of this drain on their food profits is not known.

From 1941 when the Army Catering Corps was formed, many hoteliers were recruited into its ranks. The organisation was headed by a senior TH officer, Brigadier Richard Byford, but it was the brainchild of Isidore Salmon, as the major adviser to Leslie Hore-Belisha, the Secretary of State for War. (He of the Belisha Beacon in a previous government role.) It did sterling work in feeding the troops, and if an army marches on its stomach, British hoteliers made the long march that much more palatable.

Frank Bourne Newton, who had built the *Caterer*, died in 1940 at the ripe old age of 90. After he retired in 1923 he continued to write in the magazine: "From my Hove Armchair" and contributed as late as 1938 to the Diamond Jubilee supplement. Sir Isidore Salmon died in 1941, as did Sir George Reeves-Smith. The two had worked in tandem on the Hotel Association committees for 30 years. Sir Bracewell Smith filled the gap for a time but it was certainly the end of an era.

The creation of a coalition government, under Winston Churchill, introduced senior Labour Party politicians to the Cabinet.

One of the most important was Ernest Bevin, the Minister of Labour and National Service. A powerful figure in the Trade Union movement, Bevin's task was to keep up factory production with the minimum disruption from strikes. Bevin was happy to play his part in the war effort but he demanded a condition. He wanted a Catering Wages Act, to finally bring to fruition the efforts of Margaret Bondfield, one of his predecessors, who had not been able to get the equivalent measure through the Commons in her time. He wanted: "the entitlement of every worker to have his basic conditions, whether by collective agreement or by state regulations."

Bevin knew, of course, that organizing effective unions in the hotel industry was always going to be extremely difficult. The members were often peripatetic, moving from job to job and, therefore, difficult to keep together. If members were prepared to act as shop stewards and fight for their colleagues, they could be easily removed by management. The industry had any number of part-time workers because of the seasonal nature of the demand. If someone seemed obstreperous to management, their job could always be made redundant. Many staff also felt a reluctance to support the introduction of national agreements. The problem was the effect such an agreement might have on their income from tips. The Inland Revenue negotiated with each individual on their tax liability. As tips so often came in cash, they could be concealed from the taxman, and a compromise would have to be reached between the two parties, which usually favoured the tax payer. It was felt that a national agreement might upset this delicate balance. It was, naturally, not an argument which the union members actually wished to place on public record, but it mattered to them very much when their basic pay was low.

Churchill agreed to support Bevin and the bill was passed in 1943. The opposition mustered more votes than for any measure since the vote of No Confidence in the government after the evacuation of the British Expeditionary Force from Dunkirk in 1940.

Bevin was determined that all catering workers should be paid a reasonable basic wage. If that seems less than revolutionary, the fact was that most waiters really lived off their tips and always had done. Indeed, after the Act was passed, the change wasn't dramatic. Tips still exceeded wages by a fair amount. The bill was opposed by the Hotel Association with vigour. A Catering Trades

Joint Committee was set up, opposed to any form of regulation. They held that there was no evidence of low wages or dissatisfied workers. They said that Bevin's bill would be a threat to free enterprise and introduce: "fascist control of the industry." The *Caterer* supported a public enquiry and was infuriated when Bevin offered one *after* the bill was passed: "placing almost dictatorial powers into the hands of one individual is abhorrent to the British sense of liberty and justice." The industry bleated in vain. A Central Wages Commission set up five Wages Boards, including one for licensed hotels and one for unlicensed.

Another major influence on the postwar Hotel industry was to be the Beveridge Report in 1942. Sir William was asked to consider the problems of peacetime unemployment and recommended the setting up of more vocational courses to train young people after they left school. Among the suggested courses were some for the hotel industry and the government accepted the recommendations. Westminster College was still flying the flag at the time and it had been joined in 1940 by the brainchild of Arthur Towle (LMS Hotels) and his right hand man, Etienne Vacher. They had conceived of a hotel school in Scotland and the result was now Ross Hall in Glasgow. That was it; just the two institutions, but Beveridge was to transform the situation. New hotel and catering training courses started by being tacked onto Domestic Science curricula and many academic ladies, expert in the duties of housekeepers and parlour maids, suddenly found it necessary to study food percentages and balancing the tab. (Getting the accounts right at the end of each day.)

Beveridge did not attempt to recommend how many courses would be needed and might not have anticipated the enthusiasm with which domestic science teachers took to the idea of transforming themselves into more prestigious hotel experts.

In 1945 when the war finally ended, the condition of the British hotel stock was lamentable. There was little tourism and a large proportion of the jobs finished at the end of the summer season.

At this point, British hotels were also a favourite Music Hall joke. When the audiences stopped laughing at Mothers-in-Law, they started on Brown Windsor Soup and bad staff. "Waiter, there's a fly in my soup. Don't worry, sir, it won't drink much." From here the industry could only go up - and it did.

19
A pause for the thinker.
A.H. (Jay) Jones. 1906 - 1966

It is easier for us to reconstruct the past than it is for hoteliers to see into the future. When A.H. (Jay) Jones, General Manager of Grosvenor House in London was asked by *Caterer* in 1938 to write about his vision of the kind of hotel we might expect in the year 2000, it was a pretty tall order. Jones took it in his stride. He forecast Leisure Clubs, swimming pools with roofs that opened, 24 hour TV news channels and the possibilities of the atrium: "The controlling factor will be the demand for sunlight and natural air." In his article he also foresaw rooftop restaurants, valet parking, heliports, neon and adjustable lighting, individual temperature controls in bedrooms, video-conferencing and washing-up machines. He managed all this in 1938.

If there can be no doubt then that Jones was a visionary, there is also no question that he was one of the odd men out at the top of the industry in his time. He was born into a mining family in 1906 and, unlike some other leaders of the industry, he didn't try to disguise his modest forebears. As befitted his upbringing, he was a Socialist all his life and this did not make him popular in what passed for the industry's corridors of power in his later years. He left school at 15 to contribute to the family income and joined Yorkshire Amalgamated Products Ltd., in the Company Secretary's office. By the age of 21 he had been appointed Assistant Secretary. YAP built Grosvenor House, as they had built the May Fair Hotel for Gordons, and the company's founder, A.O. Edwards, took a keen interest in the work.

Grosvenor House was amassed in Park Lane in Mayfair on the site of the home of the Duke of Westminster. It was originally an enormous block of flats which Edwards meant to sell on, but when property values collapsed in the Slump, he had to run it himself as Chairman and Managing Director. It became part flats and part hotel. He decided to take Jones to London with him and left him to deal with the day-to-day business. The two Yorkshiremen got on very well in the somewhat alien London environment and in October 1931 Jones was made company secretary at the age of 24. The effects of the slump on the £2 million building can be easily seen from the decline in profits from £100,000 in 1930 to £5,000 by September 1932. Jones learned the hotel business from examining every conceivable way of saving costs.

From the beginning he had an enquiring mind and never took anything at face value. He started to look for better ways of running a hotel and he looked abroad to America. Where Bracewell Smith at the Park Lane and D'Oyly Carte earlier at the Savoy had looked for improvements to a hotel's structure and facilities, Jones, as a finance man, looked for better operational methods. The Grosvenor House was the first hotel to have an accounting machine and Jones bought the American textbooks on hotel accounting because he couldn't find any good British ones. He also took a keen interest in time and motion studies.

Edwards was keen on sales promotion. He went on sales trips overseas and produced direct mail, public relations and advertising campaigns. In 1934 he appointed sales representatives for the hotel in America - in New York and Hollywood. These activities were not unique, but when Grosvenor House hired banqueting salesmen, they were really pushing forward the frontiers. This early venture into professional selling was not always popular with the other staff. Talking to a banqueting old timer many years later, he told me: "We had sales people like you in Grosvenor House before the war. Banquet touts we used to call them." I didn't think he was trying to congratulate me on my choice of career! Jones competed in the Dinner-Dance market with the well-regarded Sidney Lipton and his Orchestra and even paid £50 a week for a man who would become one of the great variety stars in America, the ventriloquist Edgar Bergen, with his doll, Charlie McCarthy. Bergen was, in fact, a very poor ventriloquist - to maintain the illusion it was not a good idea to watch his lips - but he achieved his fame on radio, so it didn't really matter!

Perhaps Jones' most notable marketing innovation was the creation of one of the great London Special Events. A Special Event is a marketing ploy by which, when business is bad, you create an occasion which will transform it. Midsummer is not a good time for big dinner/dances - they're mostly held in the winter - so in 1935 Jones created the Grosvenor House Antique Fair and, nearly 70 years later, it still fills the hotel's Great Room for seven days. It was to be a further 30 years before the potential of Special Events began to be fully exploited.

In 1935 Edwards emigrated to South Africa, leaving the running of Grosvenor House to Jones as general manager, subject only to the board of directors. In 1939 Jones was promoted to managing director at 32, under an accountant chairman pressed for by the Stock Exchange. By contrast with Hugh Wontner's appointment as MD of the Savoy company in 1941 at the same age, Jones had better qualifications; he had been 11 years in hotels with Grosvenor House, compared to Wontner's three and in far more senior positions. If he had also been an actor, a public schoolboy and there hadn't been a war on, he would have made a good alternative candidate for the Savoy job when Reeves-Smith died. When the two men started to work together on the HRA a clash of principles and personalities was always likely.

Jones was a warm and friendly man and a fair employer, more democratic in his approach to the staff than was the prevailing custom. It was noted with amazement that he actually said: "Good Morning" to his commissionaire when he arrived at the hotel. As Jones recalled later, though: "The standard method of getting on and becoming successful in the trade was to accept being kicked around and then, when one was promoted, kick others around." The other side of the coin for the employee was that there were no industrial diseases like pneumoconiosis to clog a miner's lungs, more attractive surroundings in the public areas than in a factory, and often less heat and noise.

Jones could be tough if he had to be as he showed in 1939, when business collapsed. He also showed his leadership qualities in the wider industry. There was a price maintenance agreement at the time between the West End hotels to try to control price cutting. Some hotels wanted to break ranks because business was so bad but Jones persuaded them that a price war wouldn't benefit anybody. All but two hotels stayed in line.

Grosvenor House survived the war in good condition. It wasn't bombed and it made good profits after the Blitz. Jones, at the age of 34, volunteered for the Royal Artillery in 1940 but was soon released to help run the NAAFI, feeding the troops. He was put in charge of the operation in the South East of the country. He had a lot to do with the catering logistics for D Day, the invasion of France, and he was awarded the MBE at the end of the war. When he was demobilised in the middle of 1946 he went back to running Grosvenor House. A medical for a pension scheme established, however, that he had a faulty heart valve, probably from the effects of rheumatic fever as a boy or typhoid in 1938. He gave up cycling but not a heavy workload.

Within a few months he was caught up in one of the few hotel strikes the industry ever had. The end of the war found the unions in a militant mood, particularly with a Labour government sweeping the country in the election. There were old scores to settle and one of them was the refusal of hotels to recognize unions. The Savoy and others initially stood their ground when faced with lightning strikes by sections of their staff in October 1946. Jones at Grosvenor House, however, broke ranks; he met with the National Union of General & Municipal Workers and agreed to recognize the union if it recruited a substantial number of the hotel's workers. The union, in return, took Grosvenor House off the list of hotels to picket.

While Wontner was fighting the union tooth and nail, Jones persuaded the HRA to negotiate a London and then a national agreement with the union. The Council was initially in favour of: "standing together". Jones protested publicly: "Standing together about what?" The agreement stopped the strikes but it is quite likely that the GMWU's action would have been unsuccessful if the hotel companies had remained firm against recognition. Wontner didn't like unions - he floated the idea of Craft Guilds instead - but Jones had supported their cause, as his father had supported the General Strike 20 years before. Jones also recognized the ease with which staff could be victimised for standing up to management for better conditions. In an industry which regularly dismissed workers as demand fluctuated - there were usually a large number of redundancies at the end of the season in the late Autumn - it was very easy to get rid of shop stewards or even union members.

Jones, of course, had acted entirely within his rights but he had let down the right wing of the HRA - which was nearly all of it. Six years later they had a chance to get their own back. A government-appointed committee was addressing, among other things, the problem of split shifts. Many hotel departments need staff at lunchtime and dinner time, or morning and evening, but not in between. So the working day is split into two. The Wages Board felt that such staff should be paid more because there was little they could do between the periods of work except hang around. After argument about the need to satisfy the guests' needs by the shift system and the additional burden on small hotel proprietors of higher wages, the Board were prepared to recommend that small hotels be allowed to continue along the existing lines, but it wanted large hotels to pay the extra money. The HRA said this was unfair. If the small hotels could continue with the present system, then so should they all. Here indeed was an example of what small hoteliers had been complaining about for so long; the association working in the interest of the big companies at the expense of the minnows.

Although Jones would have benefited at Grosvenor House if the association's view had been adopted, he would have none of it. He denounced the policy at a meeting of the South West Hotel Division of the association: "They (the Wages Board) grant us what we want and we then refuse it." He objected publicly to the way that the Association had advised its members: "It is the most disgraceful document I have ever seen" he said. Basically, the Association Staff Relations Committee (the one that dealt with Wages Boards and Unions and on which Jones sat) had agreed to send the regional committees the pros and cons of the government enquiry report on split shifts. What the committees actually received from their Head Office were only the points *against* the report. Was this the fault of the permanent officials or the senior members of the Executive, like Wontner and others? Jones was outraged and named them all. He was furious that: "an association spokesman and a number of other colleagues actually had the nerve to admit that a referendum would produce a result unfavourable to their policy and, therefore, no referendum had been taken." As he was a member of the association's Executive Committee as well, he was very definitely speaking out of turn.

One week later, Don Russell, from the Lygon Arms in Broadway, Worcestershire, a member of the executive of the association, originally at the invitation of Reeves-Smith, stood up to propose the reelection of the Executive members for the following year. He invited the Council to reelect: "All....with the exception of Mr. A.H.Jones." The motion was carried by 15 votes to 11. Jones remarked later: "It was proposed without notice, without warning, without a request for an explanation, without a request to know my future attitude or anything else." After his non-election, he remained an assessor for the Catering Wages Commission but now as an independent. He severed all connections with the association and, instead, concentrated his energies on those areas of the industry's development where he was less likely to find himself in a small minority; tourism and hotel education. For the hotel industry it was an unmixed blessing.

As we now know, the Hotel Association had been originally set up to oppose that part of the Liberal Government manifesto in 1906 which dealt with reducing liquor licences. It was an Employers' federation and it was no friend to a Labour government. It had opposed the Catering Wages Act, and its attempts to get a hotel licence, separate from pubs, was labelled class legislation. It had struggled in vain to get the ear of successive governments.

Both the British Travel & Holidays Association and the Hotel & Catering Institute were, in marked contrast, the wish and pretty well the invention of the Labour governments between 1945 and 1951. The former to attract more tourists to help the balance of trade, particularly Americans with their precious dollars, and the latter to produce a better educated work force. As government initiatives they had an entirely different relationship with the corridors of power than had the HRA. The BTHA could look to government for technical help and finance, the HCI to the full cooperation of the Ministry of Education.

Jones served on the Hotel committee of the BTHA and helped to tackle the hoary old regulations which had always militated against attracting tourists. Initially, he worked hard on getting scarce supplies released for the hotel industry. In the high season there often weren't enough good *beds* for tourists! With many others, he wanted legislation to enable hotels, like manufacturers, to set off the cost of replacing plant and equipment against profits before tax. He wanted that extended to refurbishment costs as well. The Investment Allowances were finally agreed on plant and machinery in 1954 and extended to all items of equipment and furnishings soon after. In 1959 the government extended the hours when alcohol could be served with meals. In 1964 hotels finally saw the end of the Compensation Fund and it was also finally agreed that year that hotel residents could buy their guests drinks at any time. In 1965 August Bank Holiday was moved to the end of the month in order to extend the high season. Jones was in the thick of the agitation for all those measures.

His other great contribution to the industry was his work on the Hotel & Catering Institute. Jones was persona grata in government circles from the beginning; he had impeccable Socialist credentials and was one of the few very senior hoteliers to be passionate on the subject of hotel education. His MBE proved his commitment to the interests of his country. For the Minister of Education, Jones was 'one of us'.

He was elected the first Chairman of the most important HCI committee - the Associate Membership Examination Sub-Committee. The Committee set out to create the curriculum and structure for the industry's first management course. Jones was determined that it would be more than a craft course and the opposition to this concept was intense. As he told a Conference on Catering Education in 1962: "it was with the greatest difficulty that some of the subjects were accepted by the Committee and the Institute. .....hygiene, the principles of management, the economic aspects of the industry and accounting...."

As Chairman of the HCI, Jones looked back in 1960 on the arguments which had raged. On the balance between craft and management subjects: "whether it be all practical or all theoretical or what", what score would constitute a pass mark in the examination: "the task of finding examiners, invigilators, assessors..." He reflected in 1962: "The examination was inadequate, the examiners were difficult to find, assessors were almost impossible to find. Teachers...were not available....it needed a great deal of enthusiasm and belief...to get it established."

If you wanted enthusiasm and belief, Jones was the right name. He helped to set the exam papers and marked them. He pressed for more academic subjects to be included in the curriculum. Law, food chemistry and economics would take their place beside cooking and waiting. No detail was too small for him to attempt to improve. He was appointed Chairman of the Institute in 1959/60 and, in office, set out to launch the first National Diploma for the industry.

The Hotel & Catering Institute was run on a shoestring in its early years. In such circumstances an industry is either lucky to find people dedicated to the cause and prepared to make sacrifices for it, or they have to settle for second string staff because that is all they can afford. A third possibility is for young people, who might be prepared to take the low salaries, to be given senior jobs which they have to grow into at speed. The HCI had a devoted Secretary, Basil Edwards, but he was overwhelmed by the workload and resistant to change. Jones tried to get him to alter his ways, failed, and set out to fire him. This was agreed but at the Annual Meeting of the HCI Council in 1961, a critical resolution asked why Edwards had had no opportunity to rebut complaints or charges made in a report on his stewardship. The resolution was not carried but Jones had made the same complaints when he lost the HRA election.

Examination papers were now finalised on time, proper statistics were kept, correspondence was no longer six weeks in arrears. It was all boring administrative detail and Jones was prepared to deal with it. The numbers were impressive; among a host of other needs: "This means that examiners had been arranged for 152 separate waiting examination sessions, spread over 48 centres throughout the country."

Jones was ever frank. In 1961 he gave the HCI a valedictory address: "It would be normal to conclude these remarks by saying that I have enjoyed my two years in office, etc., etc., - but I cannot truthfully say this." He considered his term: "exceptionally difficult and very heart searching - but it has also been inspiring." The completed National Diploma was his legacy to the industry. It was a four year course and so structured that the craft content of the normal hotel course had to be cut in half to accommodate the new management subjects. The students spent parts of the first three years working in various hotel departments; kitchen, restaurant, reception, housekeeping and the accounts department. Hotels like the Grosvenor House and the Kensington Palace agreed to take them, initially with some reluctance. The concept was unproven but the students did well and the number of hotels willing to participate grew. Industrial release, as the process was called, became one of the distinguishing features of hotel courses and where Business Studies students often have difficulty in gaining experience in this way today, hotel students are well looked after.

Jones went out of his way to offer jobs at Grosvenor House to the new graduates coming out of the hotel schools. They were not universally popular candidates. I interviewed one of the Grosvenor House graduates for a job in my sales department in the middle 1960s. He had a hotel school degree and a second degree in Mediaeval Philosophy from Rome University, where the lectures had, of course, been in Italian, in which he was fluent. He wasn't Italian, though. He was Irish, from Londonderry in the North, and he was working as a clerk in the Accounts Department: "With all those qualifications" I asked him "why are you only an accounts clerk?" "I don't know" he said "When I told people my qualifications, nobody would offer me a job" ! Jones could give an example, but when he'd gone, the graduates could appear a threat to less intelligent management - and they *were* in the long run because they so often overtook them.

Jones welcomed graduates with open arms. Where the Dorchester next door would only give graduates a look round the hotel, Jones would offer them lunch. He took on six graduates every year. He knew exactly where the problem so often lay. As he wrote in *Caterer* in 1963: "The question of training people to think for themselves is too much neglected in our industry's training. If a young person has the capacity for...thinking impersonally, impartially, without prejudice, scientifically, philosophically...we would have much less need to worry in the future." "As he progresses, he must not start to live in the past, but his whole outlook should be for today and the future".

The idea of junior staff thinking, rather than carrying out orders given to them by their olders and betters, was almost revolutionary. The Towle dynasty did the thinking, as did the Salmons and Glucksteins for Lyons and the early entrepreneurs like Gordon, D'Oyly Carte and Reeves-Smith. Decisions were made in Board Rooms, not from ideas emerging from the shop floor. There had been a very few exceptions who still managed to make their mark, like Ritz and Escoffier, but only when they were well established. The idea that young people should think, rather than slavishly follow the company instructions, would have been seen as outlandish for years after Jones as well as before him.

If you read Jones' speeches today you're struck by the breadth of his thinking. He would talk about management theory, alluding to American academics and textbooks on the subject. As he told the teachers of management studies in 1951: "The fact that...the doctrines of Fayol, Taylor, Parker, Follett, Urwick and others are, for the most part, unheeded and unknown, does not blind me to the urgent need for making them known." He was quite right when he said in a 1955 speech: "There is a tendency for most of us (hotel men) to live in too narrow a field of thought". He was a disciple of the philosopher,

Ritzy

Marshall Skelland. He saw the hotel industry in the setting of the government's overall economic policy. He would quote Ministry of Labour demographics on education, where his contemporaries were looking myopically for more trainee chefs and waiters. Jones always banged the drum for better management courses. He was always in the vanguard, with the rest of the industry plodding along in his tracks, trying to keep up with his strings of fresh ideas. A situation which tends to be aggravating for those seeking a quiet life and frustrating for the proponents of change.

Unlike many of the major companies, Grosvenor House set out to expand. Jones bought hotels in Southampton and Hove and he started to build them in Sheffield, Liverpool and Worcester. In 1963, however, there came a take-over bid for Grosvenor House from Trust Houses which was successful. Jones was invited to join the board of Trust Houses and to continue running the hotel, but he had difficulty in adjusting to the new regime. For a man who had been independent for so long, the challenge of working as a member of a team proved unattractive. He was also not entirely on the same wave length as his new colleagues. He complained that he couldn't join in when his new Chairman, Sir Charles Taylor, wanted to talk about hunting. They hadn't hunted a lot in the mining village of Jones' youth. Taylor had been educated at Epsom College and Trinity College, Cambridge. He was the youngest Conservative MP when he was elected for Eastbourne in 1935 and was the man who told Gerald Kaufman, M.P. to go back where he came from - and he didn't mean Leeds! Jones was not: "one of us" again.

The moving force of Trust Houses was, of course, Geoffrey Crowther, who promised Jones that he could work out his contract, which had four years to run, without interference from the centre. One of the advantages of a chain of hotels, though, is the savings that can be made through central buying and central accounts. Crowther wouldn't see changes in these areas as interference. Jones, however, had been accustomed to having control over everything at Grosvenor House and resented losing the responsibility. Other minor items irritated him as well and eventually he resigned in 1965, feeling that Crowther had broken his promises. He left one of his graduates, Peter Mereweather from a new hotel school in Portsmouth, as hotel manager. Jones died within a year at the age of 59. There was still so much to do, he could still out-think his colleagues but, without a

274

power base or a strong heart, he couldn't influence the present. He had already influenced the future.

A.H. Jones helped to lay down the foundations of the modern British hotel industry. He was well ahead of his time and suffered the frustration of the man who can immediately see what is necessary but has to drag the great body of his fellows along at what he would consider a snail's pace. A considerable percentage of his achievements would only come to fruition after his death but he certainly deserves his place in the pantheon of *Caterer's* 1987 collection of *" Makers of 20th Century Catering."* Elizabeth Gadsby was the best Director the HCIMA ever had (1976 -1991) and although she never met Jones, she said: "I was quite surprised that anybody could be quite so revered by his friends."

20
The age of austerity: 1945 - 1955

No-one could say the post-war Labour Party lacked a programme, and if there was one thing that the Attlee government was determined to achieve more than any other, it was full employment. The sadness, bitterness and hopelessness of the dole queues during the Slump were branded on the Party's collective memory. They realised though that, to achieve this aim, an educated work force was an essential. So they set out to provide the educationists, the courses and the grants to enable youngsters to improve their qualifications more easily and make it simpler for them to get worthwhile jobs.

At the end of the war the hotel industry also needed far more professional staff straight away. The vast majority had left school at 14 with no qualifications and had learned by good - or bad - example. The German contribution had effectively ended in 1914 and the Italians were interned in 1940. Trained Continental replacements were impossible to obtain immediately after the war because of Labour's commitment to full employment for the British. That meant that immigration was initially discouraged, though there was one major exception which benefited the hotel industry. A Polish army had been formed in Britain during the war and had fought with distinction. When the war ended, most of them didn't want to return home to what was now a Communist country. The government allowed them to stay in Britain as an alternative, but many industries were barred to them by a powerful, protectionist and chauvinist TUC. An industry like hotels which was not unionised and needed workers was, therefore, a godsend to soldiers and government alike. A lot of Poles became hotel workers.

The varied effects of the war coloured a great deal of the country's life-style and attitudes for a considerable number of years after VJ Day finally ended hostilities. Take Maurice Menard, a Jersey man, who had been an assistant manager with the railway hotels before the war. Hotel managers are usually sophisticated in their own milieu but the war gave many of them the kind of experiences for which no amount of training could have prepared them. Menard was asked during the war to parachute into occupied France and run a hotel in which shot down allied airmen could stay, as they tried to get home along the route south into Spain. Betrayed to the Gestapo

The age of austerity

he spent 3 years in a concentration camp under sentence of death. By pure luck he wasn't executed and when he came back to Britain in 1945 it was, not surprisingly, totally impossible to upset him. Nothing could begin to measure up to the horrors he had been through. The inward looking hotel world of pre-war days was laughably small minded to such men. Who could fear Head Office after the Gestapo?

The more far-sighted leaders in the industry recognized that they would have to look to educating British youngsters in order to fill the gap. The solution of "Pay another 10 shillings (50p) and steal them from Lyons" - or the Savoy or the railway hotels, (the best three trainers) - was not going to be the long term solution. In December 1943 it had been agreed, with government encouragement, to form a Catering Trades Education Committee. This set about the organisation of training courses in technical colleges and established the City and Guilds course 150 for youngsters coming into the industry. By May 1946 the Ministry of Education was able to give detailed instructions to Local Authorities on the setting up of the courses. In 1946 Westminster finally started a hotel management course. By 1947 the CTEC had become the National Council for Hotel & Catering Education. In turn, this was dissolved and a new organisation was given responsibility for education, the Hotel and Catering Institute. It came into being in 1950 with 161 founder members and Sir Francis Towle as its first chairman. The HRA refused to take part as they felt that hotel schools, like the prestigious Lausanne in Switzerland, should be the aim. The Scottish Hotel School in Glasgow, Ross Hall, brainchild of Arthur Towle and his colleague, Etienne Vacher, opened with 79 students in 1948. It was a strongly management oriented course, as Towle would have wished, but unfortunately he died just a month before the first term started, at the age of 71. Sir Francis died in 1951.

By the end of 1949 4,000 students were taking full and part-time courses and much of the credit went to E.W.Collinson, who had been the chairman of the NCHCE, and G. Macauley Painter, who was a Ministry of Education Inspector. The growth in education was phenomenal. In 1946 the Ministry of Labour had encouraged local education authorities to set up programmes and, by the end of 1954, there were no less than 114 technical institutions offering hotel training courses to 8,000 students. This was more than the rest of Europe put together and partially reflected the enthusiasm of teachers

277

Ritzy

in Domestic Science departments for the extra status and rewards the new courses could offer. There were also many far-sighted heads of department who laid the foundations on which modern university departments were built; Mary King at Acton, which would become part of the Thames Valley University, Millicent Macdonald at Hendon (later Middlesex University), Dora Seton at Battersea (later Surrey University) and Nancy Blackburn at Huddersfield (now Huddersfield University).

There was no government planning to restrict the number of courses to any particular level and nobody considered whether the industry could absorb so many additional graduates. Without massive expansion, it probably couldn't but that growth did come about. The British muddled through again. They were helped a little in the years after the war by Swiss, Belgian and French students who were admitted in 1947, and by some of the 100,000 refugees from the European Displaced Persons Camps who were allowed to enter the country soon after. Work permits were also more easily available for immigrants from the Commonwealth and Empire. A lot of Cypriots came into the country and many of them were excellent waiters and progressed from there.

Why did so many British youngsters decide to come into the industry? After all, Westminster had always struggled to get students. The most rational explanation is that the training was now available locally and there was a grant from the government to pay for it. The hotel industry benefited enormously from both factors but what the government couldn't do was provide the trained teachers. Where were they to come from? Victor Ceserani was too good to be typical but he represented what the government hoped would emerge from within the business.

Ceserani had left school at 15 in 1934 to work as an apprentice chef at the Ritz. His family were from that rich source of restaurant professionals, Northern Italy, and this was fortunate for him because the senior chefs were only grudgingly prepared to teach apprentices and then only with the same national backgrounds. The tradition in Europe of the father paying a chef for training his son still did not apply in Britain, so the Ritz chefs remained reluctant to pass on their hard earned knowledge for nothing.

Cesarani's father and godfather had worked at the Ritz in the restaurant: " My father had the Royal station on the right hand side, by the windows, overlooking the park." It was no affectation to call it the Royal station either. Young Ceserani settled down to the strict discipline of a West End kitchen. It wasn't a typical choice for the boys at the Oratory School where he was educated: "When you said you were training to be a chef, you could see the disapproval flowing out of them." After war service in the Catering Corps he became Head Chef at Boodles Club, but a duodenal ulcer at the age of 30 made him question whether the constant pressure of the kitchen was what he wanted from life.

Although it meant a 25% cut in his salary, he decided to become a teacher. It could have been worse. Demobbed soldiers might face a 60% cut when they came back to Civvy Street and their former hotel jobs. After a year's teacher training Ceserani went to Acton Technical College as a lowly Grade A lecturer.

From there he never looked back. Few of his colleagues throughout the country had both his senior practical experience and his teacher training qualification. In the late 1950s a few of the Catering teachers formed the Catering Teachers Association and Cesarani was elected its first chairman. His quality as a chef had already been recognized. He was no: 48 on the roll of professionals invited to become members of the newly created Hotel & Catering Institute. The idea that both senior management and chefs could be in the same Association was a revelation after the: "class ridden and segmented" business he had always encountered.

The courses were developed by the City and Guilds Institute and Ceserani was not happy with the often esoteric aspects of catering he had to teach. When he was appointed the Head of the Department at what became Ealing Technical College: "I didn't allow the word 'management' to be used in the title of the school. I believed a potential manager should have experience in the kitchen, restaurant, housekeeping and reception departments. The students had to learn the basics if they were going to be good managers." Ceserani's classic text book, *Practical Cookery*, is now in its 10th edition and has sold over a million copies.

The balance - or lack of it - between academic studies and craft training was to continue to be a bone of contention through-out the future development of catering education. It tried to reconcile the competing demands of training in business management skills and the development of academic minds, with the ever increasing need in

Ritzy

the industry for more skilled craftsmen. It was yet another replay in academic circles of the HRA arguments between Francis Towle, from Cambridge, on the one hand and the Salmons and Glucksteins, who always started at the bottom in their company; many, admittedly, in later years, after also graduating from Cambridge.

Ceserani joined the catering committee of City and Guilds in 1954 and went to work to transform its curriculum. The committee had drawn its members originally primarily from the world of pubs and cafes. Most hoteliers had shown little inclination to devote time to education, no matter how much they bemoaned the lack of sufficient suitably trained staff. Ceserani proved again that if you want to change things, it's always easier from the inside than the outside. Over a period of years the less experienced City and Guild members departed and Ceserani encouraged more professionals to join him. In 1968 he went to Michigan State University, one of the finest hotel schools in the United States, to gain an MBA and to teach the students at the same time. It's a long way from a kitchen apprenticeship at 15 to an MBA at 49, but the hotel industry does have the advantage that, like Napoleon's foot soldiers, there's always a Field Marshal's baton in the knapsack.

The development of hotel courses had an interesting side effect. Over the years more and more hotel managers would start their hotel careers by going to hotel schools and they would learn to cook and wait, in addition to performing any of the menial tasks in a hotel. This meant that, unlike the management trainees taken from university by manufacturing companies, hotel management would fully understand hotel workers. They would be accepted as: "off the shop floor" and, if there was industrial unrest, they could take over the jobs of strikers. This created great difficulties for unions trying to organise hotel workers. The usual: "outsiders" and "oppressors" - the management - weren't filling their expected roles. Instead it was the senior union executives who came from outside the industry, who didn't know how to do the work and who were, therefore, less acceptable as leaders.

If the brainier young people were getting a better chance in life, the unions were still not satisfied with the conditions of their members in the industry. There was a short lived but acrimonious strike in 1946 which produced unwelcome headlines for the Savoy, but which petered out after some high pressure action by the union

280

leadership and shop stewards got out of hand. In December 1947 agreement was reached between the Unions and the HRA that a national council would be set up with six district councils to settle disputes. Union membership, however, continued to be very small, so the councils were seldom called upon.

The HCI would have liked its membership to be restricted, like other professions, to those who had passed exams. This obviously wasn't possible at the outset and the attraction of being able to put letters after your name, made membership very popular with established hoteliers. By 1954 the Association had over 7,000 members.

In 1950 John Fuller had become deputy secretary of the HCI. Late in 1953 he accepted a post as Head of the Hotel Management Department at the Battersea College of Technology. Thus started the academic career of a man who would become one of the first two professors appointed in catering education. Fuller had gone through the trainee mill at Lyons, worked on the continent and during the war had served in the RAF Catering branch, latterly with the rank of Squadron Leader. When he left in 1950, he joined the HCI. As another fine academic, Professor John O'Connor wrote: "He was a man of striking personality and appearance, fluent and wide-ranging in conversation." His most memorable remark, which he said more than once, pointed up the view of far too many members of the hotel industry in his time. He said: "This industry is scared stiff of brains!" Fuller was always seeking to expand his students' minds. Although I only started as a hotel salesman in 1954, he asked me to lecture on the subject at Battersea as early as 1956.

In 1948 the hotelier's exhibition, Hotelympia, returned for the first time since 1937. In 1950 it was notable for an educational conference which attracted 700 delegates; hoteliers, local authorities and academics all took a serious interest in in this burgeoning field. The membership of the HCI reached 4,421 in 1951 when a national apprenticeship scheme was started for cooks. Perhaps Goring and Reeves-Smith were wrong. Perhaps the British could cook. The HCI's first provincial branch began in Leeds in 1951 and in 1953 the first conference was held of teachers and examiners. It was a new dawn, very exciting, but there was a long road to travel. In 1954 there were only 200 catering apprentices in the country.

The Catering Wages Commission set up Catering Wages

Ritzy

Boards to agree the minimum workers should be paid. As we saw in the last chapter, it was imposed on the industry without consultation but the boards had both employers and unions represented on them: "In the opinion of Lord Shawcross, who headed the Catering Wages Commission, they (the employers) ignored - because they were politically naive - the fact that an industry which fights against the establishment of a union within its ranks, is likely to find itself opposed by a Labour government". Well, by Lord Shawcross' standards, the employers never did become politically sophisticated because the fight went on for the next 40 years. A.H. Jones said in 1951: "Management have for long been fighting a bitter rear guard action against the Trade Unions on the battlefield of the Wages Board. There has been no serious move for consultation." "Savage bargaining and grudging compromise" was the best both sides could achieve.

The Catering Wages Act certainly raised staff wages overall and between 1950 and 1965 they nearly doubled. Hotels started to add 10% for "service" to help pay for them. This was the beginning of innumerable disagreements between management, staff and guests. The management added the 10% for "service" and the guests asked whether they still needed to tip? The staff said: "yes" because they wanted the additional - potentially tax free - money. They said - and it was often true - that the service charge didn't get paid out to them. Obviously, as the total raised by the service charge was not the equivalent of the entire wages bill every week, it did get given to the staff, but if there was a surplus in any particular week, the management would be tempted to keep it back for quieter times. A substantial part of the wage bill was now, effectively, being paid by the clientele.

The management then hit on such duplicitous phrases as: "gratuities are at your discretion", suggesting that service charges and gratuities were two separate items. In fact, in certain areas, the catering wage minimum was a relatively unimportant part of the staff's income. That same waiter, Mario Gee, who we met in the 1930s, recalled that by 1950 he was getting £2 a week as a waiter in a good restaurant but could earn an extra £20 a week from tips. Wages could be the tip of the Glace Parfait. The average wage bill in a hotel in 1955 was still little more than 10% of the turnover.

Where the clientele continued to tip, the money was put

The age of austerity
into the departmental tronc (kitty) in areas like banqueting and the restaurant. The banqueting or restaurant managers then supervised the split between the different grades of employee in their departments. The more senior the member of staff, the greater their share. Without any accountancy training, the managers were then responsible for collecting the appropriate tax for the Inland Revenue. This was not always done with the accuracy the tax man felt was their due. "Pour encourager les autres" the tax man would occasionally prosecute a waiter or a banqueting manager and that individual would find himself in prison, first offence or not. One 63 year old banqueting manager got 15 months, only reduced on appeal to six months. Evading paying tax could be no joke and, like murder and treason, there was no Statute of Limitations to plead if the offence was years ago. It wasn't surprising that the Reunion des Gastronomes had voted unanimously at a meeting in 1943 for tipping to be abolished, but the RdG was recognized as a dining club and nobody paid any attention to the resolution. They returned to what they did best with the first post-war dinner in December 1953, the last one being in 1938.

The post-war hotel industry faced many problems. Once again, a world war had meant that the redecoration of hotels had, necessarily, been curtailed in the national interest. The hotels needed refurbishing but the materials were in short supply. Permits were needed to buy all sorts of items and, to make matters worse, their cost was increased by Purchase Tax. Where the raw materials of manufacturers were mostly free of tax, this did not apply to the hotel industry. Purchase Tax was an indirect tax and raised a great deal of money for the Treasury. It was aimed at the general public but the products hotels needed were taxed at the same level.

In 1945 all the hotels were shabby. Nothing had been spent on them for six years. Original white paint was a dark yellow, the upholstery was frayed, the tablecloths threadbare. Air pollution in the cities worsened the situation and dense fogs were a yearly meteorological feature. Most guests would have to pack their own soap to take with their hotel towel down the corridor to the public bathroom when they wanted a bath. There were still few private bathrooms. The wartime habit of not filling the bath with more than 6 inches (15cm) of water to save fuel made the experience even less attractive. In a large number of hotels for many years yet you would need shilling (5p) coins to get gas from the meter to light the

Ritzy

bedroom fire. At the good hotels the waiters might still be in full evening dress in the evenings, but food rationing was not to end totally until 1954. Journalist and man about town, George Augustus Sala, wrote about British hotels nearly 100 years before. He divided them into the expensive where: "wealth, pride, dignity, dullness and secrecy" were the distinguishing marks, and the family hotels which were: "respectable, clean and comfortable." After the Second World War he would have recognized similar conditions.

During the war rationing had been needed to distribute what was available fairly. To make the limited amounts go round. After the war rationing continued because the country hadn't got the money to import what was needed. Bread had never been rationed during the war but dollars for wheat were now in short supply; Lease Lend - the American wartime version of "Buy Now. Pay Later" - had finished with the coming of peace. In March 1946 restaurants weren't allowed to offer customers bread unless they were asked for it. That didn't save enough. So between January 1947 and June 1948 bread was rationed and customers had to choose between bread and pudding! Worse was to come for the hotels. In December 1947 the petrol allowance was withdrawn due to the continuing sterling crisis. That had a very adverse effect on hotels who catered for the motoring public. It was only in June 1948 that the allowance was partially restored. Hotel signs couldn't be illuminated at night until February 1950, the 5 shilling (25p) limit on the cost of a meal was only abolished in April of that year, petrol rationing in June 1950 and soap rationing in September. Most food finally came off the ration at the end of 1953 though meat rationing dragged on till June 1954. For 15 years hotels - like everybody else - were affected by rationing of one kind or another. To celebrate the final liberation, the Royal Victoria Hotel in Llanberis roasted an ox.

Fortunately for much of the industry, there was also great difficulty in getting foreign money unless you had to go abroad on business. Certainly, you couldn't get enough legally to go on holiday to the continent for long. While some people took advantage of criminal currency suppliers, the vast majority of the country continued to holiday in Britain. In 1951 only 1.5 million were taking any form of holiday abroad. This benefited the seaside hotels, of course, but initially the beaches remained mined. "Mystery Tours" by bus and the attractions of the pier and the seaside shows were, however, soon available again.

The total potential clientele for hotels would change as the standard of living improved in the country. It wasn't just that more and more people would be able to afford hotels but that, for million in the armed forces, their perspectives had been broadened by their wartime experiences. It was a very slow process. Most people before the war had never eaten in a good restaurant. A man called Frank Berni started serving steak in a pub called the Rummer in Bristol in the 1950s, it caught on and, over the next 20 years, Berni Inns would be the route by which millions of people learned how to eat out.

I remember a dinner in the mid-1950s for the foremen and their wives of the Scholl Manufacturing Company. The dinner had always been in the Scholl canteen but I persuaded Bill Scholl, who was the American chairman in Britain, to use a small London hotel instead. When the guests arrived, they stood awkwardly in the Reception room, silent and, as the science of body language has now taught us, in the Defensive Position. Only after enough gin and tonic had been poured down them, did they relax. Years later, Bill Scholl suggested they might like to try another hotel. The foremen objected strongly. They didn't want to go through that introductory experience again. The other two factors that massively increased the numbers prepared to use British hotels would be the experiences of holidays in Spanish hotels and of taking Short Break holidays, but they were still some way in the future.

The question of building new hotels didn't arise for a number of years because of the country's shortages. When town councils created their master plans for the redevelopment of their bombed town centres, however, they often demanded that the developers include a new hotel in the rebuilding. The property companies accepted this as a necessary part of their contribution to the town's amenities, in return for planning permission. Falkirk and Wakefield were just two towns which got new hotels on this basis. Out of town, as the roads were improved, a start was made on motels. The first was The Royal Oak Motel, just outside Folkestone in Kent. This was the brainchild of Graham Lyon, a Whitbread executive, inspired by the American example and it opened in June 1953. It had private bathrooms for all the bedrooms, your car was washed down while you slept, and your bedroom had such modern innovations as an iced water container, variable plugs for electric razors and the guest: "was awakened by an alarm clock which had already set going a mechanism which had made a pot of tea"; a Teasmade.

In November 1945 there were still 2,700 requisitioned hotels, though three quarters had been released by the following July. To encourage hotels to open as quickly as possible, bombed and requisitioned hotels were given an allocation of sheets, blankets and mattresses if they could reopen by that time.The Railway Hotels were still a power in the land. Arthur Towle had been succeeded at the LMS hotels by an accountant, Frank Hole. A keen hotelier, Hole set high standards and believed in the importance of hotel professionals: "Always have accountants on tap" he would say "but not on top." He was very conscious of the need for good financial controls, so that today he would be labelled a control freak. The core problem is a perennial one; the desire of hotel management to be independent of head office supervision and of head office to know what's going on at the Front. It's like the bit in the horse's mouth; if it isn't there, a lot of profits can bolt. In 1947 the Transport Act nationalised the railways and Hole got 57 hotels to run from 4 railway companies. These, after 1953 were known as British Transport Hotels and 18 of the smaller ones were sold in the next 10 years. The remaining hotels usually continued to outshine the competition up and down the country, with the exception of London. They still offered first class training to their staff and their ambiance was still feudal. Mess stewards would arrive at the offices of the senior executives, dressed in uniform and bearing coffee in china cups on trolleys.

To pay for what they needed, the hotels would have liked to borrow money from the banks but, as A.H. Jones said as late as 1951: "In prewar days it was at least possible to borrow money on the security of hotel property. Today, even that is extremely difficult." The fact was that many banks had their fingers burned during the Slump, with companies like Gordons, and the hotel sector was badly out of fashion. If a retail company went bankrupt, its property could be used by others, but what would happen with a hotel building? The Cecil had become part of Shell Mex House, just as Unilever had taken over the de Keyser in Edwardian times and replaced it with Unilever House in 1932, but the value of a defunct building was a small percentage of its worth as a major hotel unless the site was particularly valuable.

Shell and Unilever did very well with their purchases. Two

entrepreneurs in 1953 wondered whether there were other choice sites whose potential value was underestimated because they were used as hotels. Harold Samuel (later Lord Samuel) and Charlie Clore (later Sir Charles) were property men, though Clore had many other interests as well. They both agreed that the value of the Berkeley Hotel in Piccadilly was under-utilised as a hotel and the site could be sold for a fortune if the hotel was knocked down and offices built on it instead. They were right, but the Berkeley was part of the Savoy Group and the bid was fiercely resisted. Eventually both Samuel and Clore agreed to sell the shares they had bought, but the bid illustrated very forcibly that there continued to be two profits to be made out of hotels; the operating profit and the increase in the residual value of the building.

Fred Kobler, a Czech stranded in Britain by the war, wanted £600 to buy a share of a small hotel. The 16th bank he tried was the National Bank of Scotland who decided to lend him the money. That was why the bank eventually had the account of Grand Metropolitan, the 10th largest company in Britain in the 1980s, which Kobler helped to create. Kobler came to the hotel industry without preconceptions. He had started as an architect in Prague and then had spells in Lourenco Marques, Vienna and Paris, latterly trying to keep one step ahead of Nazi invasions. He was quite prepared to innovate. He looked at the balance sheet of a London hotel and immediately recognized that the profits were, primarily, coming from selling bedrooms; it wasn't rocket science. So he gave all his attention to filling his rooms.

He recognized that a lot of the business came from travel agents, so he cultivated them and paid them commission without question. This was a revolutionary approach for the time. With a shortage of suitable accommodation in peak periods, most hotel companies now wouldn't pay commission in the summer. Kobler became very popular with overseas agents, particularly in America which he often visited as he had family in New York. The Americans were beginning to come to Europe more, but a large number felt there was safety in numbers; they preferred to join groups. So Kobler took groups; they filled more beds. His competition, however, disliked groups because they felt they lowered the tone. They preferred individual guests.

Kobler liked to study the American hotel industry and during one visit he came across the practice of employing salesmen to sell hotel space. He decided that if the idea was good enough for the Americans, it was good enough for him. So he set out to find someone who could do the job in London. I was recommended to him by a mutual friend. He couldn't afford the £10 a week Cambridge history graduate salary I expected, I had no proper sales training or experience and I'd never worked in a hotel. By contrast with today's elaborate testing techniques to identify a candidate's suitability for a vacancy, I scored heavily when I told him about the Battle of the White Mountain at the start of the 30 Years War in his native country in 1620. He decided to take me on and, over some heated opposition from the rest of the management, his will prevailed, even though £10 a week was an assistant manager's salary.

Nobody knew - including Kobler - what a salesman was supposed to do and it was 6 months before I sold anything - a £75 a year hotel showcase the following spring! In the summer I went to America - a friend got me a free seat with the Pennsylvania State University Choir on a charter aircraft taking them home. In New York American hotel sales managers readily told me how they ran sales departments, I found a book on the subject, and that was the real beginning. Not quite a typical management training programme.

It is difficult to decide why more sales people were not employed earlier in the industry, apart from Grosvenor House in the 1930s and the occasional executive in Strand Hotels and Trust Houses. The business was there to go after but the occupation and concept of salesmen had a very low status. It wasn't really considered a respectable way to spend one's time and this attitude continued for many years. In the first book I wrote on the subject in 1963, the second chapter was entitled: "Is selling respectable?" It seemed an essential point to settle at the outset. The prospect of change for the hotel industry was unwelcome.

Grand Metropolitan was known as the Washington Group of Hotels at the time. It was a very laid-back company; Henry Edwards, who ran it on a day-to-day basis, was the lynch pin of the operation. Edwards would improve team spirit by getting the senior executives together to play table tennis. Kobler was very paternal and treated his coterie very much as family. The atmosphere was nothing like the normal formality in the industry.

The men leading the industry had changed with the death of

The age of austerity
Reeves-Smith, Salmon, the Towles and Bourne-Newton. The most prominent name was now Sir Bracewell Smith, who in 1946 became the first hotelier Lord Mayor of London since Sir Polydore de Keyser in 1887. Sir Bracewell didn't want to spare the time, though, and it was Hugh Wontner from the Savoy company who filled the vacuum. The Association acquired a new director in Eric Croft, whose engagement was announced in the HRA magazine in 1948: "Mr. Eric D. Croft to Miss C.M. Kelly." It wasn't a world where *Hello* magazine would have flourished. In 1948 the HRA finally merged with the RHA, the association for the small hotels, to become the British Hotels and Restaurants Association. The combined body still only had 2,000 members and an annual income of £14,000. As wages took up £7,000, the organisation still had very little spare cash.

At the end of the war the hotel industry had almost the total eating-out market because there were few good restaurants away from Soho. The standards of British food, however, were a favourite topic for music hall comedians. Brown Windsor Soup and jokes about poor service would always raise a laugh. To the Maitre d': "Charlie, did the waiter who took my order leave any dependents?" Standard patter. Seaside landladies were another favourite topic. Hotels were perceived as stuffy and formal and they were. Sometimes they were branded as worse though. In May 1951 the BBC broadcast a programme which stated quite outrageously that: "All hotels served filth to enrich the crooks who ran them." The BBC refused to apologise for this totally unbalanced definition and, when the BHRA complained, the newspapers joined in on the side of the BBC.

The government was desperate for dollars and the hotel industry attracted American visitors. The Olympic Games helped in 1948 and then, in 1951, there was the Festival of Britain; not quite as grand as the Great Exhibitions of 1851 and 1862, but impressive nevertheless. In July 1950 the government had promised to make a contribution to equipping and reequipping dollar earning hotels for one year. This was to help accommodate the large number of expected visitors and every effort was made to produce some wholly refurbished hotels. One that opened in time was Lady Honeywood's old Washington Hotel, now owned by Max Joseph, an estate agent turned property developer and hotelier. It had been commandeered during the war for the Americans. Apart from the fact that the so-called luxury hotel finished up with hardly any private bathrooms,

Ritzy
the newly installed third tap - the iced water one - never worked because it was too expensive to operate. Extravagant ice shows - a rink was put down in the main restaurant for the cabaret - didn't help by making a thumping loss. Bedroom business was fine in London during the Festival but afterwards it slackened off again for long periods of the year. This habit of overbuilding hotels for major events occurs again and again, but nobody ever seems to learn the lesson. It's often associated with the Olympic Games, and many an investor rues the day he believed that the largesse of the Olympics could be expected to last thereafter. Lady Honeywood died in 1956.

For a Britain crippled with debts, the promotion of tourists was worth supporting financially. The development of long range bombers during the war made it possible for civil aviation aircraft to be constructed which could fly the Atlantic. The Douglas DC4 was the work horse and could fly from New York to London in about 20 hours, only having to put down in Shannon in Western Ireland and Gander in Newfoundland to refuel. The great liners, like the Queen Mary and the Queen Elizabeth continued to dock in Southampton but their days were now numbered. The Travel Association had changed its name again in 1945. It was now the Travel Association of the United Kingdom of Great Britain and Northern Ireland. The more emollient United Kingdom had replaced the original Great Britain and the Industrial Development part of the title had been dropped. From a base of 203,000 visitors in 1946, the number of tourists steadily increased until the million mark was reached in 1955 for the first time. John Bridges was the head of the permanent staff of this early example of a private/public partnership. Bridges was an excellent PR man and realised the importance of that 1/2d (1/4p) Local Government rate first permitted in 1931.

The Association's funds depended a lot on membership contributions and Bridges went out to recruit as many local authority members as possible. Eventually he not only had 1,000 of them but a host of friends up and down the country. The board was elected by the members, so the quality was highly professional but, as time went by, the government abrogated the right to appoint eight members of the board and the chairman. Cronyism and the rewarding of faithful government supporters came to play a part in the appointments, delaying progress and making the professionals' jobs much harder.

After the war the spa towns were in serious trouble. Modern

290

medicine, like penicillin, made the water cure appear as primitive as it undoubtedly was. The buildings were dilapidated and the clientele who had survived the war were 6 years older, which was a very long time if you were still taking the cure. Dealing with an ageing clientele is a marketing nightmare.

The spa town which tackled the problem of its vanishing customers most successfully was Harrogate in Yorkshire. During the war every hotel had been requisitioned by one Ministry or another. Worse, the £100,000 the town had spent on improving the Baths and Well during the 1930s had made little difference to Harrogate's prosperity. A fresh start was needed and it was provided by Major Bill Baxter, the new entertainments and publicity manager. He recognized that the future had to lie in conferences and with a substantial promotion budget of £32,000 from a town with only 56,000 people, he was able to make a first class marketing effort, Harrogate became the home of Union and Association conferences from all over the country. When new Conference Centres became all the rage in the next 20 years, Harrogate's was to be one of the finest built. A lot of towns constructed such centres and, of course, their clienteles were from the same markets.

It would have appeared logical to create one database of the potential customers, available to all the towns, with the research bill paid by all of them. The American Convention Bureaux Association had been doing that for years. It was, however, an unpopular idea with the British resort towns, who wanted to keep their knowledge of their customers close to their chests and the data base had to be created by the English Tourist Board in the 1980s. Even then, there was no support from the towns and the initiative withered on the vine.

What certainly helped was the extensive implementation of holidays with pay, though in the long run, this was going to benefit the Spanish and Mediterranean Holiday industries more than the British. More could have been done. In 1953, the irrepressible A.H. Jones was speaking to the British Federation of Hotel and Boarding House Keepers. To lengthen the summer season he appealed for the August Bank Holiday to be switched from the beginning to the end of the month. That eventually happened years later. He also asked for factories to stagger their annual closing and for schools to have varied summer holiday periods in different parts of the country.

Ritzy

If Jones didn't get all he wanted, the old order was definitely in the process of change; a new cast of leaders, new markets and new ways of reaching them. At long last there was the possibility of real growth and a brighter future.

21
The start of major growth. 1955 - 1973

In developed countries the percentage of the work force employed in the manufacturing sector declined as the years went by. This was partly due to the increased mechanisation of the processes and partly due to a shift in the sources of output from the richer to the poorer nations. Typically, steel making became more mechanised and textile manufacturing started to go to cheaper work forces in Asia. Britain had two other problems in its traditional manufacturing sector; often dreadful industrial relations and poor management contributed to many companies producing unnecessarily expensive and shoddy articles and productivity was higher on the continent and in America. The result was that the country needed more jobs created in the service industries and the growth of hotels and tourism played its part in this. The change didn't come easily. The wages in hotels were poor by comparison with those on the factory floor, and the industry was still seen as involving servility and effeminacy (the idea that cooking was for sissies), with long and unsocial hours, and instability (because of its seasonal nature, a lot of people had to keep on changing jobs). It was also associated with foreigners and there were few pension schemes. The government didn't help when a senior minister dismissed hotels as "a candy floss industry". The hotel world was slow to change and the British were slow to adapt to a new economic world order.

So British industry suffered from the costs of over-manning while hotels looked around desperately for trained staff. The only solution for the hotels was a succession of influxes of overseas workers, allowed in by successive governments simply because there were insufficient British workers willing to take up the readily available, less skilled positions as chambermaids junior waiters and junior kitchen staff. From 1950 - 1978 the hotel industry benefited from successive waves of Italians and Spaniards, Caribbean and Filipino workers, until Britain's acceptance within the Common Market in 1973 created the much larger European labour force and far easier job mobility.

The task of filling the vacancies fell to hotel personnel managers but they were seldom professionally trained. It was just one of the jobs you took on while doing your training for the general manager's chair. An exception was Brian Worthington who decided to specialise in personnel work and, after gaining a National Diploma at Acton, went on to become Grand Metropolitan's personnel & training manager in 1965.

Worthington recruited largely in Spain, Portugal and Yugoslavia but ran out of applicants. So in 1968 he sent a direct mail letter to all the embassies in London, asking if they wanted jobs for their citizens in his hotel company. The Phillipine government found an agent and over the next 10 years more than 15,000 Filipinos came into the country to work in the hotel industry. The Ministry of Labour asked for minimum qualifications, which could often be forged or falsified back in Asia, but the migrants proved very good workers and solved a major problem. The Filipinos needed a guaranteed job in the U.K. and the Ministry would be told, in the appropriate wording, that: "No other suitable applicant is forthcoming from the indigenous labour force." Worthington also opened what he called a Job Shop at Grand Metropolitan's Head Office and the Ministry of Labour adopted that idea for their own Labour exchanges.

The Hotel personnel area also had to become a profession because of the Industrial Training Act in 1964. This envisaged Training Boards for many industries and in 1966 the Hotel & Catering Industry Training Board arrived with the power to collect a training levy, based on the wage bill of the hotel. The politicians had decided correctly, that the best way to make sure that firms trained staff, was to fine them if they didn't. If, however, companies could prove that they were spending the equivalent of the levy on in-house training, then they would be refunded the sums involved. So mostly small hotels paid the levy and the large companies started to spend more money on training than they ever had before.

In the normal way training often has to be seen as a luxury. If business is bad, the cost of training is one of the first budgets to be cut. Not this time. You either spent it yourself or you gave it to the HCITB to spend it for you. The clamour of indignation from an industry which had been complaining for years about the shortage of sufficient trained staff, was deafening.

The Savoy Company had shown their interest in the standards of training in the industry somewhat differently in 1961. The 1953 takeover bid had cost the Savoy Company a fortune to fight off. They would now try to protect the company against any other predators. A new class of B shares was created which had massive voting rights. Over 200,000 of them finished up in the hands of a charity formed in 1961 called the Savoy Educational Trust. The original Trust Deed, according to *Caterer*, specified that they shouldn't be sold "unless there are compelling reasons for taking such a course" and that all the Trustees should be directors of the Savoy. Bridget, Richard D'Oyly Carte's granddaughter had another large tranche. With other friends, known internally as The Concert Party, any future take-over bidder could find his way blocked by a small minority of the total shares. It was all perfectly legal and the dividends of the SET shares were to given away for charitable educational purposes. So they were, but in the mid-1980s the shares were worth well over £10 million and the distribution a paltry few tens of thousands.

Another result of the new emphasis on training was the growth of the hotel conference market. The need for suitable rooms for training courses for companies was augmented by more sales meetings and assemblies of every kind. Companies found that using their own office space for the purpose was uneconomic and hotels stepped into the breach. Countless palm courts, libraries, lounges, retiring-rooms, stables, garages and drawing-rooms were pressed into service. Conference facilities normally consisted of a baize covered table, rows of chairs, a blackboard, a lectern and a standing microphone. Anything else was very avant-garde. Air-conditioning, overhead projectors, tie- mikes and "the latest, state-of-the-art, audio-visual equipment" - the industry's appropriate piece of jargon - lay in the future.

Of course it was possible to be more professional; Birds Eye always hired the London Palladium, the greatest music hall in the world at the time, for the Chairman couldn't resist striding onto the same stage as had Bob Hope, Jack Benny and Danny Kaye; there were also smaller theatres available. The vast majority of companies, however, settled for the basic requirements.

The first brand new hotel to open in London since the war was the Westbury in 1955, owned by the Knott Corporation in America. The opening would not have received undiluted praise from later public relations companies. Naturally, the hotel was crowded with invited guests, anxious to see the new wonder. In each bedroom a member of staff had been strategically placed to safeguard the hotel's property; visitors wanting souvenirs on such occasions can

Ritzy

work out expensive! I had gone with a client who didn't want to see over the hotel by herself: "How much do you think this is?" she asked me of a handsome twin bedded room. "I suppose about £8" I replied. " Is it really?" said the watchful chambermaid nearby: "Isn't that disgraceful!" My client gave her a quizzical glance and said to me: "Nice, light rooms, aren't they?" The Chambermaid interrupted again: "Yes, but you're on the fifth floor. If you were on the third, you'd need the lights on all day"!

The railway companies had built their own hotels at their stations. Airlines were somewhat different. Sometimes, like the original railway companies, they built hotels in cities where their passengers had nowhere sufficiently luxurious to stay. Pan American created InterContinental Hotels to do just that under the leadership of an American industry genius called Juan Trippe. Air France produced Meridien Hotels and later Aer Lingus, the Irish airline, begat Copthorne Hotels. They were usually city centre properties, however. Almost all the British airport hotels were put up by hotel companies unconnected with airlines. There were only a few exceptions; for example, Aer Lingus built one of their Copthorne Hotels at Gatwick.

The first airport hotel in Britain was the Skyway which opened in 1960 at Heathrow. It was followed by Lyons' round Ariel Hotel which opened in 1961, took three years to build 180 rooms, cost a monster £900,000 and was difficult to make profitable with such heavy initial costs. One problem was that: "everyone was invited to comment and variation orders to the architect and interior designers were scattered like confetti." As the airport expanded, so more competitors came onto the scene. The name of the game was to get as close to the airport buildings as possible. From that viewpoint, many of the early hotels eventually found themselves drawn in the outside lanes in the race for business, as the newer hotels tried to hug the runways.

Until the 1960s, outside London, there was not a lot happening in the way of new construction. A lot of existing hotels were trying to modernise but there was a great deal to do. I well remember staying at one of the better hotels in Leeds in the 1950s. It was dark and gloomy, you still put 5p in a meter to get heat from the small gas fire, the food was dull, the furniture heavy and shabby, the bed linen rough and you traipsed down the corridor with your soap and towel for a bath. The staff were in black and the atmosphere was suitably funereal. That early Victorian critic, Albert Smith, would have felt quite at home.

There was a wide recognition that the quality of the nation's hotels had to be improved. The small hotelier, Fred Kobler, pleaded with his bank for money to spend on constructing more private bathrooms, a sine qua non for Americans looking for a decent place to stay. They also expected jugs of iced water on the restaurant tables. At a school reunion at the time, sitting next to one of the Bradford family who owned the University Arms Hotel in Cambridge, I pointed out that we provided this facility. His response was that if the Americans visited Britain, they should be satisfied to live the way we did! It wasn't an isolated example. Watneys, one of the great brewers, had just finished a new hotel called the Dover Stage to service travellers using the port. Not only were there no private bathrooms in any of the bedrooms, but the way the hotel was constructed made it impossible to add them easily in later years. It was, perhaps, fitting that Kobler's tiny company, Grand Metropolitan, bought Watneys in 1972.

A new hotelier was that Italian born caterer, Charles Forte, we've already met. Forte bought his first hotel, the Waldorf, in London in 1958. There were, of course, many naturalised executives with Italian origins in senior positions in the industry. In the 1960 census there were also 100,000 Italians in the country, but it was unusual for a major hotel company to be founded by an Italian born entrepreneur. What was more, the reputation Italians had for close families made many hotel executives uneasy about the influence Forte's relatives might possess. Michael Boella recalls joining Forte as a young man. His name sounded Italian and: "They were a bit wary of me at first. They wondered if I might be some distant cousin." Not that such concerns only applied to Italian families.

The amalgamation of hotel companies into larger groups continued throughout the 1960s. Spiers and Ponds went to Express Dairies in 1960, Queen Anne's Hotels - desperate to avoid the show business Danziger brothers' takeover bid - rushed into the arms of Trust Houses in 1965. Max Joseph's small group became Grand Metropolitan Hotels, a name which was far too large for the fledgling company and sounded like a branch of the Bakerloo line. Frederick Hotels, that creation of Blundell Maple with Fred Gordon as Chairman back in 1897, was sold to Fortes in 1967. The industry

Ritzy

remained dominated, however, by the reputation of the Savoy and the size of Lyons, Trust Houses and British Transport Hotels.

Lyons really took the bit between their teeth during this period. Between 1961 and 1975 they opened nine new hotels and bought 32. These ranged from the 830 bedroom Tower Hotel in London, which they opened in 1973 by Tower Bridge, to the 30 bedroom Glenborrodale Castle Hotel in Ardnamurchan in Scotland which they bought with 16 other Falcon Inns. A total of 5,500 additional bedrooms were added to the three large hotels in London. As an expert on Lyons has written, however, "Between 1970 and 1974, for reasons which are not especially clear, other than the wish to expand quickly, Lyons/Strand acquired the Kingsley-Windsor group and Park Court hotels." As far as Falcon Inns was concerned: "the rationale, other than expansion for its own sake, is difficult to understand." There must have been a degree of pride involved; Joseph and Forte were building empires and Lyons would not want to be left behind, particularly in view of their illustrious history in the industry.

Their power of innovation created one exceptional catering idea; the Carvery. The opportunity for the public to carve their own roasts, to slice off all their favourite pieces. It was first tried at the Regent Palace in 1960, after Christopher Salmon had found the concept in America, and it proved extremely popular. For the first time since the public had started to drift away to the new restaurant industry, the hotels found a formula to bring them back. The attraction was not only the food but also the fact that the public knew why they were going to the restaurant. It was a far cry from: "a wide range of national and international dishes" with which hotels hoped to attract the local clientele. That hardly ever worked but the hotels never gave up hope that it would. It was like the Pied Piper; all the hotel children followed the Savoy and the BTH hotels, because that was what *they* offered and that was where so many good hoteliers were trained.

The profitability of the Regent Palace Carvery, compared to the average hotel restaurant, was not usually allowed to cloud the hoteliers' loyalty to their hotel alma mater. Still, many hotels imitated Lyons' Carvery . The problem they found, though, was, that the public aren't as skilful at slicing meat as trained chefs. So there was more meat wasted and the *percentage* of profit on the turn-over dropped, even though the *total* profit went through the roof. Who cares, you might think? Well, food and beverage managers cared, they got greedy and they took away the knives from the guests and passed them back to the surgically slicing chefs. That took much of the pleasure out of the dining experience so Carvery profits fell away. Percentages improved though! It was a triumph for hotel accounting over common sense.

What Lyons were also very good at was the efficient operation of any business in which they took an interest. Their training was outstanding and their attention to detail legendary. Within hotels, time and motion studies were done on the work of chambermaids to increase productivity, television sets were put on pivoting pedestals and luggage racks cantilevered. Packaged and prepared foods were tested and absolutely nothing was too small to bother about.

Meanwhile, In Scotland the biggest hotel entrepreneur was a Greek immigrant called Reo Stakis. He built his own empire over the next 20 years, often using the same methods as Charles Forte, whom he resembled in style. Because his base was so far away from London, Stakis didn't get the publicity he deserved south of the border, but his Stakis Hotels were a beacon of hospitality in many a northern town and his knighthood, shortly before he died at the end of the century, was well deserved. As Charles Forte wrote in *Caterer* in 1987: "He has a good reputation for his honesty, shrewdness and ability. I have always found him genial, outgoing and generous."

Seaside hotels decay rather more slowly than those in towns. It's simply because there is less pollution to discolour the walls and eat into the fabrics. If their facilities were equally primitive, the better ones were still the social centres for the local community. For example, the Prince of Wales Hotel in Southport was packed out for dinner dances on Saturday nights. The manager - perhaps the only man ever to wear the sartorial mismatch of a rolled collar dinner jacket with a wing collared tie - ran a very good operation. The service was excellent - until he arrived at his personal table. Then the entire staff deserted their stations to gather round him in case there was anything he was missing! Only when satisfied that he had all he needed was normal service resumed. The waiters were jolly and knew most of their guests by name. The band was excellent, playing painted instruments which must have been originally manufactured some 40 years before. On the ground floor of the Prince was an enormous lounge in which the wealthy ladies of the town would gather throughout the day to take tea and gossip. The hotel buzzed, there were functions all the time and Henry Kimber's creation was still doing good business.

There were, of course, hotels like the Prince in many sea-side towns. One of the few to update its approach was the Imperial Hotel in Torquay. It was developed in a modern style and the manager, Michael Chapman, introduced Gastronomic Weekends which brought new customers to the hotel and gained excellent publicity for the business. I remember Michael Chapman, a very retiring man, doing his duty and walking round the restaurant greeting his regular visitors and enquiring after their health and enjoyment. The guests saw an urbane, immaculate figure, totally at his ease and in command of the situation. He kept his hands behind him, though, and they were wrung nervously throughout the discussion. He must have found the exercise excruciating but it was the classic approach, so he did it. The Imperial flourished under Chapman even if he was pernickety about who he allowed to book a room. It was part of a highly stylised regime which also included a voluminous set of rules; that you couldn't remove books from the library, you were asked not to take bedroom towels to the pool and you couldn't have a cup of tea in the restaurant after dinner. You could have coffee in the restaurant, but tea had to be in the restaurant annex. My wife, being pregnant at the time, was off coffee. A compromise was reached where the tea was served in a glass, so that it looked like a cocktail. You still couldn't get accommodation for much of the year.

Colour bars were still frequently applied in the industry. Back in 1953, Arthur Lewis, MP., had taken up the cudgels in the House of Commons after the Green Park Hotel in Mayfair had been accused of operating a colour bar. The owner freely admitted he: "actively enforced" such a policy and Lewis asked: "was it still the policy of the Minister of Food to withdraw or refuse a catering licence to hotels with a colour bar?" The Minister didn't know what he was talking about. He said he couldn't employ licensing regulations to stop such a practice and that there was no obligation under Common Law for caterers to serve anybody. He added, though, that he strongly disapproved of the practice. His disapproval had little effect; in the 1960s at the British Overseas Airways Corporation terminal at Victoria there was a typewritten list of every London hotel. By the side of each name was written in ink either the letter "C" or the letters

The start of major growth

"NC". 90% of them had "NC", which stood for "No Coloured." Grand Metropolitan was an exception which didn't prove a rule.

The new hotels would thrive and there were many more built in London in the 1960s; the Carlton Tower, the Britannia, the Cavendish, the Royal Garden and the Royal Lancaster were just some of the wave of hotels which would strengthen the industry in the capital.

The Carlton Tower, owned by the Hotel Corporation of America, opened in one of the most fashionable parts of London, Cadogan Place, in 1961. HCA couldn't use their company logo, though, because Fred Kobler had chosen it for his own company from the selection of letters 'filed' in his desk drawer some years before; it was certainly cheaper than hiring a design company! No permission had been asked and the logo, slightly modified, identified Grand Metropolitan Hotels as long as they existed. Eventually, the founder of HCA died and left the business to his children, Sonny and Esther Sonnabend. They changed the names of the hotels to Sonesta for at least an Archduke's ransom, in terms of reproducing the monogrammed material.

Gordons had been taken over by the Danziger brothers. They decided to upgrade the Mayfair Hotel in order that a subsequent sale of the company would bring in enough money to pay off the preference shareholders and leave enough for the ordinary shareholders too. The hotel was transformed. A truly fantastic Polynesian restaurant was built with tropical storms every hour, on the hour, and real crocodiles which had to be passed on to a zoo when they grew too large. New ballrooms and the glitziest lobby in town transformed the front. The hotel in the 1960s became the in-place in town; pop stars and the glitterati flocked to the now swinging decor. It had the desired effect on the value of the company.

The Danzigers' transatlantic approach left the industry singularly underwhelmed, as indeed did: "Swinging Britain" as a whole. Hotel commissionaires were still dressed as Russian archdukes and the management still went on duty in black jackets and striped trousers, looking like members of the Corps Diplomatique. The only concession to modernity was that waiters, traditionally in evening dress, began to discard their jackets and serve in bow ties, waistcoats and shirtsleeves. Instead of looking like penguins, they now appeared in the guise of out of work snooker players.

Ritzy

So, in 1965 Gordon Hotels finally came to an end. The rump - the improved Mayfair, the Metropole in Monte Carlo and the lease on the Grosvenor - was bought by Grand Metropolitan. The last Annual General Meeting, following assemblies of such aggravated shareholders that the press nicknamed them: "The Gordon Riots", was held in a small room in the Mayfair. Only a few of the Grand Metropolitan staff attended and the proceedings were over in 10 minutes. So died Gordon Hotels, but Fred Gordon wouldn't have been entirely unhappy with his successor. In the Minute Book of the Annual General Meetings - recorded verbatim in his time - he was saying in 1898 very much what Grand Metropolitan believed 70 years later. That the business was all about selling bedrooms. In an industry still dominated by Food and Beverage thinking, Grand Metropolitan at least agreed with him.

Fred Gordon had learned about Special Events in France; you can get good marketing ideas almost anywhere if you're prepared to learn. I was driving down to the South of France one summer and noticed that a hotel we stayed at was a member of the Environs de Paris Hotels and the Paris/Cote d'Azure Hotels. These cooperative marketing groups of independent hotels all helped each other and I thought it an excellent idea. So I mentioned it to a friend, Michael Blanchard, who ran the Whateley Hall Hotel in Banbury in Oxfordshire. He agreed and in 1966 formed Prestige Hotels, the first hotel co-operative in the country. Many others followed.

The key event of 1963 was the opening of the London Hilton. It was a skyscraper towering over Hyde Park Corner. The site had been provided by Charlie Clore, who we met trying to take over the Savoy in the last chapter. It was a great location and you could see the gardens of Buckingham Palace from the top of the building, which was said to irritate the Queen. The industry and the press waited with fervent hope and bated breath for the brash Americans to fall flat on their faces. They refused to oblige. The hotel opened perfectly. The General Manager, Louis del Como, a war veteran from Washington DC, led a very high-powered team and the hotel took London by storm. Mind you, the Americans took no chances. They had a franchised Polynesian restaurant called Trader Vics and the staff training for that operation went on for some weeks before the opening. Then the company flew in a second brigade from Los Angeles to back up the locals and then they took out half the tables

The start of major growth

the restaurant could accommodate! The first guests had never experienced such quality service. Where the Hilton made mistakes, few people noticed. The Malaysian Food and Beverage Manager, Euwe Hin Lim, found himself with the finest Rosenthal china for the restaurants, all of which was smashed in the first six weeks. Fine china doesn't get quite the same care in a hotel that you can lavish on it in your own home.

Hilton did bring some novelties to the British Hotel industry. Nobody was ever dismissed from the Hilton and neither did they decide to leave; they were either: 'involuntarily separated' or: 'voluntarily separated'. They also had some difficulty translating American expressions into British ones and it had to be pointed out that the hotel was not located in "Downtown Mayfair".

The London Hilton and the Carlton Tower had one thing in common; a successful restaurant. At the Hilton it was Trader Vics and at the Carlton Tower, the Rib Room. The Rib Room served slabs of meat, of huge American proportions, to a nation which had only come off meat rationing in 1954. It was a lovely room, decorated with brilliant cartoons by Felix Topolski. Almost every other hotel restaurant in the West End was steadily losing business to the restaurant industry and would continue to do so for years to come. The secret of Trader Vics and the Rib Room was that the clientele knew what they were coming for. Perhaps because both hotels were American, the British hoteliers did not learn the lesson. They stuck to their classic formula and steadily lost more and more money.

Charlie Clore had another site in Grosvenor Square but Hilton said they couldn't afford it as they could only build 150 bedrooms on it; the rules for building in Grosvenor Square are very strict unless the land is designated foreign territory, like the American Embassy. So Clore offered it to Max Joseph who negotiated a low price: "Well, Charlie, it's only 150 bedrooms" - and then built 300 in the space! Slightly smaller bedrooms, admittedly, than Hilton had in mind. That was the Europa which opened in 1964.

I had the responsibility for filling the Europa, among other hotels. Tourist arrivals to Britain had reached two million a year but the traditional problem remained. How could you fill thousands of hotel bedrooms over winter weekends?

The five-day week was coming in at this time and was initially considered a disaster for the hotel industry. Where there had

303

been businessmen staying on Friday night in order to go into work on Saturday morning, now that market disappeared. The industry braced itself for harder times. I didn't see it that way because the Americans were running Broadway theatre package weekends quite successfully; we learned a lot from the Americans. After all a five-day week also meant a two-day weekend so I negotiated with the railways to run package holidays, including the rail tickets and two nights in a hotel. Stardust Mini Holidays started in 1964 from Swansea, Cardiff and Newport to London. It was primarily promoted at the outset through dazzlingly bright red posters on railway stations. In the first year the company spent £1,000 and sold 325 packages. Ten years later Grand Metropolitan were spending over £1,000,000 and moving over 150,000 people from all over the country.

In addition to starting Short Break Holidays in 1964, the year also marked the beginning of a programme of Special Events, designed to fill the hotels when they would otherwise be empty. The first effort was the Guardian Bridge Tournament, which made the Europa Hotel's ballroom in Grosvenor Square the only one to be filled in London over Easter. It was called the Guardian Bridge tournament because we were turned down for sponsorship by the Times, the Sunday Times, the Observer and the Daily Telegraph! The tournament is still a feature of London's bridge life to this day and has attracted most of the great bridge players in the world. From such small beginnings came the spread of Special Events to cover activities for every kind of enthusiast; from bird watchers to quilt makers and from wine lovers to antique collectors. In addition, a whole range of purely educational Special Events have also brought guests to hotels who would not have been there otherwise. At the time we thought we were being totally original, but, of course, the Victorians with their own Short Break Holidays, had got there long before us.

The largest hotel company in the country was still Trust Houses, now chaired by Sir Geoffrey (later Lord) Crowther. Crowther was a great meritocrat. From Leeds Grammar he went on to Oundle, Cambridge (1928 President of the Union, like a lot of senior politicians) and Yale. His clubs were Brooks, Boodles and Yale. He had written 5 economics texts, including *Economics for Democrats* and *An Outline of Money*.

When I interviewed the jolly, cherubic establishment stalwart in 1963 he told me that it was very difficult to change Trust Houses until he became chairman and had the power to do so. He had been a director since the 1940s but his co-directors were not very commercially minded. Once in the seat, however, he certainly had vision. He recruited from the universities as well as the hotel schools. The idea that to get into hotels you had to have a vocation at an early age and then spend a long time training in the kitchens did not seem sensible to him "when other industries offer him more attractive conditions." He also wanted to attract women graduates, which was very advanced for the time.

Given their head, the executives pioneered. Some of their new hotels, for example, having their bedrooms and bathrooms constructed off-site and then dropped into place off a lorry.

A large number of the Trust Houses Hotels were managed by married couples who were good practical hoteliers but not great brains. At Head Office Crowther built a team of very clever executives. They included, for example, Diana Self, a graduate of the London School of Economics and a former head of the Economist's New York office. Self took on the responsibility for strategy and planning when most of the industry's entrepreneurs were flying by the seat of their pants. They were often very good at it, but Crowther brought to Trust Houses the disciplines of the wider economic world. Graduates came on two year management training schemes, as they would with a Unilever; they were paid the same starting salaries and they could expect senior positions at the end of it - unheard of before.

Crowther also wanted an industry research laboratory to solve technical problems - which still doesn't exist - and a standard bedroom for those companies who wanted to reduce building and refurbishing costs.

Crowther achieved neither objective and there was only slow progress towards producing products which were strictly for the hotel industry. For example, the public were offered attractive ovens with modern designs. New hotel ovens, however, were the traditional ugly Victorian ranges. The manufacturers spent their design budget on the general public and considered hotels a niche market. The concept of the international hotel market as far larger than many national domestic markets did not appeal to them. Much newly designed equipment eventually started to arrive from manufacturers overseas and British industry had lost another good export opportunity.

Ritzy

Incoming tourist arrivals were growing at a very satisfactory rate and the new Labour government in 1964 finally felt sufficiently confident of the country's balance of payments position to allow people to take whatever money they liked out of the country to spend on holidays. The balance of payments on tourism, however, actually showed a profit for the UK from about 1970-1985. For those 15 or so years overseas visitors would come in but the British had to get accustomed to going out; hence a profit. The BTA unwisely trumpeted this success. The problem was that the pendulum had to swing against them; there were more millions of Brits who would want to get away to the sun than there were tourists who wanted to come to the UK. Britain would continue to be remarkably successful in future years in attracting tourists but the balance of trade on tourism would eventually go into the red though when the Travel Industry got the package holiday market abroad properly organised and the nation's standard of living increased sufficiently. From 1986 this has been the case and it's unlikely to change.

John Bridges had served as Director General of the Tourist Association, since 1945. When he retired, his place was taken in 1963 by Len Lickorish and he held down the job as general manager for the next 23 years. The British Hotel industry owes an enormous debt to the work of the British Travel Association and its successor, the British Tourist Authority. Len Lickorish was in the finest tradition of TV's Sir Humphrey in: "Yes Minister". The idea of Lickorish ever being even slightly ruffled in public was ludicrous. He radiated calm and competence, smoking his pipe and offering you a handshake as soft and limp as an unfurled chamois leather. I watched him in action on many occasions, dealing with heated - and sometimes justified - complaints about the BTA with the air of a vicar, in line for beatification, explaining away the behaviour of a slightly mischievous choirboy. If you weren't involved, it was a Master Class in how to maintain total control without giving any impression that this was your steely objective.

When Lickorish took over, the revenue from overseas visitors was approximately £180 million a year. When he retired in 1986 it was £5,553 million. This achievement was particularly meritorious because the initial staff for the BTA often came from government ministries and the status of the organization hardly measured up to the Treasury or the Home Office. As a consequence those who chose to transfer were not often the pick of the Civil Service crop, but Lickorish built an excellent team from the material. In this his major help for many years came from his deputy, the Irishman, Frank Kelly, who many would have liked to see take over the reins at the appropriate time, but it was less likely in those days that an Irishman would lead Britain's tourist efforts than that a Swede would manage the English football team. Also when the moment arrived, the emphasis was all put on new blood and new thinking. What was wrong with the old thinking, which had stood the BTA in such good stead, was a less eye catching argument.

Only a handful of sales and marketing executives existed in the early 1960s. Even so they thought it worthwhile forming the Hotel Sales Managers Association in 1964. It was not likely to have much effect on the industry; only about a dozen practitioners wanted to join - and two of them were not strictly in the industry. The Association has grown to a very respectable size over the years but the membership are too junior in their own companies to throw their weight about in the national arena as an Association. The Hotel Industry Marketing Group continues to provide networking opportunities for its members, some interesting speakers at meetings, annual awards and social functions, but it is not a power in the hotel industry land.

Labour won the election in 1964 and Max Joseph had the largest political bet known at the time; £50,000 to win £37,500 on Labour's Harold Wilson. He reckoned he couldn't lose because his shares would go up if the Conservatives won. Wilson was devoted to the interests of his supporters and, as these were largely in the manufacturing industries, the government - short of money as usual - decided to tax the service industries. In 1966 they introduced Selective Employment Tax which was only levied on workers in the service industries. The tax was increased by 50% in 1968 and a further 28% in 1969. Happily for hotels, Edward Heath's government halved the rate in 1971 and abolished it, together with Purchase Tax, in 1973. The 1964 Licensing Act finally abolished the Compensation Authority - that old bugbear of the industry - for the days of refusing large numbers of licence renewals to satisfy the demands of Local Option were long gone. The existing funds could deal with the occasional case and the problem stopped being important.

Another body blow to the hotel industry was Chancellor Jim

Ritzy

Callaghan's decision in 1965 to disallow business entertaining for tax purposes, unless the guests were from overseas. The number of Expense Account lunches dropped catastrophically. The restaurant business at lunchtime in expensive hotels has never really recovered. Eventually, having waited for the good times to return for about 30 years, hotels started to encourage conference delegates to eat in the restaurant instead of in a private room.

Many British regions were looking hard at the possibilities of tourist attractions bolstering their economies, but they some-times had delusions of grandeur. In Scotland there was, for example, the creation of a ski village in the Highlands called Aviemore, which was opened in 1966. There *is* snow in the Highlands in some winters but you may still not be able to ski if the winds are too high! The development thus had serious problems from the beginning.

The Development of Tourism Act in 1969 was the government's attempt to improve Britain's tourism performance. It set up regional tourist boards, provided grants for worthy developments and laid the groundwork for hotel classification. Over the years the boards did good work, the grants produced a lot of new attractions but the attempts at classification never really improved on the work of the motoring organisations.

The Shangri La vision of creating the perfect hotel has a great appeal for all sorts of people. One such, Martin Skan, was from a sweet manufacturing company. Skan bought a very modest hotel with just a few bedrooms on the edge of the New Forest, called Chewton Glen. Slowly, over the next 30 years, Chewton Glen grew and Skan proved, against all perceived wisdom, that an amateur English hotelier could produce an individual small hotel of international quality and appeal. A hotel that would win accolades and prizes in international competition and make a very substantial profit each year into the bargain. A single hotel, unconnected with the great chains, has greater problems each year in reaching its clientele because of the development of ever more sophisticated - and expensive - methods of communications. By the 1970s an Austrian travel agent could make a booking at a chain hotel in Bath and the information would reach the hotel via a satellite in outer space and a central point in America. If Skan couldn't afford the technology, the customers consistently took the trouble to book Chewton Glen by phone anyway.

Skan was in the forefront of the development of fine country

The start of major growth

house hotels in Britain, most equally off the beaten track. There was Gerry Milsom at Le Talbooth, Dedham, Essex, Francis Coulson and Brian Sack at Sharrow Bay in the Lake District and later Bob Payton's Stapleford Park in: 'Sunny Leicestershire" as he called it..Chewton Glen won the most prizes.

Henry Edwards left Grand Metropolitan in 1964 after a row with Max Joseph. He soon decided to start his own company and Joseph backed him in buying three small temperance hotels. Joseph's rationale was that if Edwards' replacements didn't work out, he might need him back. Edwards built the small company up into Consort Hotels and then couldn't resist a considerable bid from Watneys for the business. So he started again and built Centre Hotels and this time Ladbrokes bought him out. So he started again and built Friendly Hotels.

Edwards has always been immensely hard working and likes to stick to his well tried methods. He built hotel companies by many routes. He might buy rubbish hotels and refurbish them. He might build new motels, take over the failures of other entrepreneurs or buy the surplus hotels others chains didn't want. He struck hard bargains but was absolutely scrupulous in all his business activities. His love of maroon, his Woodbine cigarette (until he saw the light), and his immense attention to detail and cost control were his trademarks. In awe and admiration, it was said that his idea of a perfect Sunday was to drive up to his hotel in Hull and count the paper clips.

To have been absolutely vital to Grand Metropolitan in its early years and then responsible for the creation of three successful hotel chains on his own, over a period of 50 years is a remarkable achievement - and one for which he could take the full credit - because in his own companies he was always the final arbiter. He inspired enormous loyalty from his staff but they looked to him for total leadership. His best qualities were that legendary ability to control costs and a thorough understanding of all the aspects of hotel-keeping. Like many another genius, Edwards has quirks. He is camera-shy and loathes personal publicity, but he deserves his place in the pantheon of those who built the British hotel industry. He finally resigned from Friendly when he was in his 70s but is still active outside the hotel field.

In 1969 the British Association of Hotel Accountants was created. BAHA's aim was to gather together the industry's financial experts and it was strongly supported by Jonathan Bodlender, of the accountancy firm of Horwath & Horwath. Bodlender was related to the founder of a major building society and was famous for his Savile Row suits and monogrammed Jermyn Street shirts. He was a good marketing man as well and Horwath & Horwath became famous for its production of the Uniform System of Accounts for the hotel industry. In constant touch with the members of BAHA, other financial consultancies initially found it hard to compete.

In 1971 the Hotel & Catering Institute merged with the Institutional Management Association to form the etymologically elephantine Hotel, Catering and Institutional Management Association. The acronym HCIMA, not surprisingly, appeared almost simultaneously. It was a professional association for the whole hotel and catering industry, with membership restricted very largely to those who had passed examinations or who had many years experience in the industry. The HCIMA was, initially, the guardian of the standards of hotel and catering education. The HCI had played the main role in helping to create the course curricula of colleges all over the country. HCIMA continued to help improve the content of the courses and were always represented on educational committees studying aspects of the subjects. This was their raison d'être. It was also fitting that those who had worked hard to gain knowledge should be able to mark the fact with the appropriate letters of membership grades after their names. The HCIMA developed chapters in the old Commonwealth countries and its membership roll swelled to over 20,000, but there is a case to be made that it has yet to achieve two legitimate ambitions; first, to be the father of an International HCIMA in which every country has its own Association - nobody else does have an HCIMA. There are no professional bodies, independent of the hotel owners or the unions, with members from every branch of the industry, from school meals and hospital catering to luxury hotels and Michelin starred restaurants. Second, to be the one-voice solution that successive governments have pleaded for the industry to provide. The major British hotel association remained the BHRA and that continued to be only an employers' federation.

The industry's support for the HCIMA had a downside. It enabled the hotel companies to continue ignoring the graduates from universities who had decided to take degrees in other disciplines. The industry remained largely incestuous and there have only been

The start of major growth

a minute number of graduates recruited for the hotel business from fine academic institutions like Oxbridge, the London School of Economics, Bristol, Leeds or Edinburgh University .

Two new universities in the 1960s had departments teaching hotel management; Surrey and Strathclyde. The department at Surrey came from the former Battersea College. Ross Hall was incorporated into Strathclyde University. Rik Medlik at Surrey and John Fuller at Strathclyde became the industry's first Professors.

The expansion of Grand Metropolitan took in Express Dairies in 1969 and Trumans in 1971. Express had 12 hotels and the financial press pointed out how well they would fit in with the others Grandmet operated. The fact was that Joseph wanted the milk company's cash flow and sold all the Express hotels except for the Viking in York. In 1971 the company bought Trumans, a middle sized brewer who also had a number of hotels. The brewers had not dominated the hotel industry as the size and resources of their companies would have enabled them to do. One reason was a determination to concentrate on their core business of producing beer, but another could well have been substantial share holdings in Gordons, purchased at the launch in 1890. Those shares had declined in value over many years to almost nothing and Gordons was the late Victorian blue chip hotel company. If that one wasn't profitable, was the hotel industry so attractive? For whatever individual reason, the Brewers were not major players in the hotel industry.

The contrast in viewpoints was illustrated by the way Trumans valued their assets. To Trumans a large pub in the country which sold little beer might be in the books at £1,500. To Joseph, the ex-estate agent, it was a large house and worth very substantially more.

In 1970 it was mutually resolved by the two companies that Trust Houses would make an agreed bid for Forte. The story of that marriage is told in Chapter 22. There were certainly attractions for both sides. Together it would be easier to raise finance and both companies had a lot of refurbishing still to do. Trust Houses were going to benefit from a strong team of professional catering experts and the combined hotel division would be very powerful. In addition, the assets of the two companies matched very well. The key question, however, was whether two firms with such dissimilar cultures could meld together.

1972 was generally a good year for the industry but 1973

311

Ritzy

would see the government Grant Scheme bringing new hotels onto the scene in profusion. The fat years were about to be replaced by some pretty lean ones.

22
A pause for the stars - Lord Forte, Sir Maxwell Joseph & Sir Hugh Wontner

Lord Forte - 1908 -

Charles Forte was a high profile leader of the industry for the best part of 25 years. He built a colossal company - Trust House Forte - and he built it from scratch. He wasn't born in the heart of England, like Fred Gordon, he wasn't hiding his past behind a screen of formality, like George Reeves-Smith. He wasn't academically minded, like A.H. Jones, and he wasn't shy, like Max Joseph. Forte was the migrant who made the grade both commercially and socially, a man who shrugged off a lot of discrimination and a number of setbacks. He is small in stature but larger than life. Ebullient and charming in public, a leader by nature. Of course, he had his detractors and no man is perfect, but there were too many ready-made insults to throw at him and he didn't usually deserve the calumnies which his enemies spread about him.

Lord Forte was born in Monforte, a small village south of Rome, in 1908. He comes from a tough family which he talks about in his autobiography. They had been minor lairds in the area and well-to-do by the standards of Monforte, until a late 19th century kidnapping and ransom demand for a member of the family left them deeply in debt. Forte's grandfather is famous in the family's folk lore for leading the villagers against the local terrorists and finally ending their threat. With a family back-ground like that, if Forte faced a battle throughout his long life, he didn't shirk it. He also became a fitness fanatic, capable of sustained exercise even at an advanced age. He was proud of his lineage. His father was certainly not portrayed as an Italian peasant trying to escape to the middle class; more a question of a local squire in reduced circumstances.

Forte's father came to Scotland a few years before the First World War and built up the Savoy Cafe in Alloa. He then sent for his family, Charles arriving with his mother in 1913. Forte went to good schools in Scotland and Italy and had 6 months training in accounting. He then started at 17 working for his cousin in a cafe in Weston super

Ritzy

Mare. Eventually he went into business for himself in 1934 at the age of 26. It wasn't easy to get extended credit from suppliers, or persuade friends to put up quite substantial sums of money. Forte had to coax and wheedle, sell the prospects convincingly, learn never to stand on his dignity. He was a proud man but he swallowed the medicine. From family and friends he raised the substantial capital of £4,000 and opened the Meadow Milk Bar in Regent Street in London. It flourished and Forte was on his way, even if milk bars did not have a high status in the economic life of the country.

Respect in Britain was not easy to acquire if you started life as an Italian small caterer. To make his future life more difficult, Forte was briefly interned during the War as an enemy alien under Section 18b. It was only for a few months though before he easily proved his loyalty to Britain.

So, an Italian milk bar operator who had been interned as a possible enemy alien. Not an auspicious start to a glittering career but Forte, at that time, came over as a young cheeky chappie, your friendly local caterer with an ever-ready smile and a sunny personality. In private, he was a budding entrepreneur, determined to make his way against the odds.

Contrary to some assertions, he did not surround himself with Italian top management. Throughout his business life there was a mixture of British and Italian senior management in his company. While, on the one hand you could point to expert hotel and catering executives like Leonard Rosso, Tito Chiandetti and Giuseppe Pecorelli, they were well outnumbered by businessmen like Eric Hartwell, accountant Dennis Hearn, ex-Chancellor of the Exchequer, Lord Thorneycroft (his Chairman for over 10 years), Lord (Alf) Robens, a former Labour minister and Sir Charles Hardie, who brokered his biggest deal. Though they were often in his debt for personal kindnesses, these were also his genuine friends and supporters. If he found room in his company for many of his original countrymen, he equally gave jobs to the native born. In later years even the Italian caterers came to be matched by British Forte trained executives like Garry Hawkes, Alan Hearn and Roy Tutty.

Forte was both paternal and charitable. A student had been offered a job with the company but there were cut-backs and the job offer was withdrawn. The student wrote to complain to Forte, who instructed his Personnel Department to honour the commitment. He encouraged young people and financed a Chair at Surrey University in the 1970s. You can't always be benevolent in business, though, and he and his business partner, Eric Hartwell, did not hesitate to make changes quickly if their managers failed to perform.

For some years after the war Forte concentrated on building up his restaurant business and the major problem was borrowing money for expansion. When his first great opportunity came in 1954, it was the chance to buy the world famous but run-down Café Royal. Bracewell Smith had sold it to investors but they couldn't make money out of it. Now they'd had enough. Forte soon settled the purchase price but this was the least of his problems. The agreed figure was £240,000 but the bank wouldn't lend Forte another penny. So he talked the vendor into taking £50,000, promising to pay the balance over 5 years. Then he couldn't raise the £50,000. So he asked the vendor to find him a friendly bank. The vendor was sufficiently charmed - or desperate - to ring the Bank of America, who also wouldn't lend the money to a complete stranger. So Forte talked the vendor into guaranteeing the £50,000 loan with the Bank of America! That was how he got the Cafe Royal.

It was an amazing piece of effrontery but he then paid off the whole purchase money in a couple of years. Forte always had immense charm, the total determination of so many migrants to succeed, and he had the wonderful capacity of serried ranks of Italian restaurateurs; effortlessly to mix first class cooking and administration behind the scenes with a perfect atmosphere for the clientele in the front of the house. It is partly reassurance that they know their food and wine as true experts, partly an ability to understand just what kind of approach is right for each client.

In the late 1960s and throughout the 1970s, the dominant, headline worthy, leadership of the industry was shared by Forte and Max Joseph, although Trust Houses had far more hotels than either of them. Grand Metropolitan consistently made larger profits than Forte. In 1970, for example, Forte's £5.5 million compared to Grand Metropolitan's £14.8 million. On one occasion, though, Forte beat Max Joseph at his own game. Joseph had recognized the potential of three luxury hotels in Paris, owned by an ex-dancehall hostess and wealthy widow, Madame Dupré Joseph did all he could to buy them but Dupré wouldn't even see him. Then Forte tried and when the lady refused a meeting with him on the grounds of ill health, he sent her a note of sympathy with masses of red roses. That ensured they got together and his charm secured the deal.

Forte finally created a hotel empire, but along the way he diversified in many other directions. At different times he bought Lillywhites, the department store, a publisher, three travel agencies a sweet manufacturer and a dozen seaside piers. He created the nightclub, The Talk of the Town, was very early into airport catering, in-flight catering and motorway catering, bought industrial catering companies and the Festival of Britain funfair in Battersea Park. If it looked capable of making a profit, it was worth a second glance. Some flourished, some grew enormously and a few were the wrong decisions in the short or long term. In the catering field it could be described as a planned evolution, using the company's catering skills more widely. Outside that world, it was opportunistic but none the worse for that.

In 1970 Forte set out on his most adventurous project, a marriage with Trust Houses. Both sides knew that it would be necessary for Trust Houses officially to take over Forte. The reason for this lay in the peculiar role of the Trust Houses Council. This body had half the voting shares in the company and, therefore, could obviously block any take over bid. Their task, however - created by their founders - was only to be responsible for the standards of Trust House Hotels. They had no power except to maintain those standards. Thus, when gaming became legal, the Council considered whether Trust Houses should diversify into that field. There was no unanimity of opinion among the members and so the idea was dropped. The running of the hotels, their purchase or disposal, were not areas in which the Council had any authority.

The chairman of Trust Houses was now Lord Crowther, the best Editor of the *Economist* since Walter Bagehot, a confidant of government ministers and a prominent member of the Establishment. Crowther was a powerful intellect, a fine journalist but not a brilliant administrator. He was more interested in the global concepts than the detail. What he had done some years earlier was call in McKinseys, the consultants, to run the rule over Trust Houses. Their recommendation was that a new Chief Executive should be appointed and the job went to Michael Pickard, an accountant with a good record. Pickard had set to work to bring modern business practices into the organisation. He found, for example, that the general managers in the hotels took no part in the planning of future budgets and corrected this. He improved the profits of the company very considerably by charging market prices and he brought on a number of able young executives. At the time of the take-over he was still under 40, compared to Forte's 63.

The take-over was primarily planned between Forte, Crowther and Pickard, with Sir Charles Hardie, a friend of both sides, acting as honest broker. The agreement was for equal numbers of Forte and Trust Houses directors in the new company. Crowther would be chairman for a year before handing over to Forte, who would initially be deputy chairman while Pickard would be chief executive. The top jobs were distributed between the senior executives from both companies and the deal was done.

It was to be the clash between the directors which led to a steadily deteriorating situation over the next 12 months. The two companies, in fact, fitted together very well. When the dust died down, THF was a highly viable organisation. It could almost be guaranteed, however, that there would be a major clash of personalities. Forte and Crowther were very different and the two companies had been run on very dissimilar lines. For years Crowther had had to try to coax his fellow Trust Houses directors into more modern thinking. The original ethos of Trust Houses was to restore derelict hotels rather than to make profits. Many of the Trust Houses board in the 1960s were liberal minded amateurs. That attitude had seeped into the company culture until Pickard started to revolutionise the thinking.

Crowther had hired university graduates for top management and developed a Head Office family who were encouraged to be innovative and to stand by their guns in argument. I wrote an article on Crowther in 1963 when he told me: "There is no doubt that the university graduate is superior to the man without that training." Forte didn't run his company that way. He might recruit from the hotel schools but most of his senior executives had had limited formal education. He ran a team of hands-on catering experts who knew their business backwards. Flair, experience and intuition had taken him thus far and he saw no reason to change his methods now. He made it quite plain, for instance, that he thought Diana Self's work on strategy and planning was a waste of time and money. To any outsider, the prospect of a deafening collision of cultures should have been relatively easily foreseen.

Ritzy

The clashes were not just at chairman and deputy chairman level. In his autobiography Forte says he couldn't understand why one of the Trust Houses directors, Brian Franks, said: "he hated him more than he hated Crowther". Well, Franks and Forte could hardly have been more different as well. We last met Old Etonian, Brian Franks, on a sales trip to America for Gordon Hotels in 1938. Over 30 years later he had become Colonel Brian Franks, one of the founders of the SAS and, at one time, Colonel of the regiment. He was posted to the SAS from the Commandos during the war and had performed nobly against the Axis. I met Franks for an article in 1962 when he had become the managing director of the Hyde Park Hotel and wrote: "If the industry is changing and moving on shifting foundations, he drops the anchor of his convictions very deep indeed." When his hotel company had been threatened with a take-over by the Danziger brothers in the 1960s, Franks had run to Crowther to be rescued. To Franks, Forte looked even more unacceptable than the Danzigers. He and Forte were just two directors who were very unlikely to be comfortable bedfellows.

It wasn't only personalities. Trust Houses was the biggest hotel company in the country and had been a famous name to the public for well over 50 years. They were part of the hotel industry Establishment. Forte was a Johnny-come-lately whose first hotel had only been bought in 1958. Lord Crowther undoubtedly felt superior to Forte, but if Forte had no university background, he was still a leader from a family of leaders and, now, for the first time since 1934 - 35 years - he was not in charge.

Forte would listen to the views of his co-directors but if he made up his mind, he would normally get his own way. The Café Royal exercise had not been prudent or for the faint-hearted, but it had been successful. With the new board it was different. For example, Forte believed that the company should buy the Carlton Tower in London. The Trust Houses directors thought the price too high. Forte was outvoted. In Forte's words: "my experience and knowledge of the hotel business was cavalierly thrust aside." Well, "cavalierly" is an emotive word and the Trust Houses directors didn't see it that way. They believed Forte was more interested in the large, famous hotels than in concepts like Trust Houses' Post Houses, which were superior motels. When Forte complained to his fellow Forte directors, he found warm support. The boardroom atmosphere started to curdle and different interpretations were made on even small matters, depending on which side you were on. For instance, Leonard Rosso had the responsibility for improving the hotels. He produced many useful recommendations. The question was whether these were good new thoughts or proof that Trust Houses executives couldn't run the company effectively. Or take the occasion when the amalgamated company moved to new offices, Forte felt his was far too small, which would have been a calculated slight. Whether it was or not, it further soured the atmosphere.

Crowther didn't help matters by exercising what can only be described as a juvenile sense of humour. He was accustomed to the free give and take of academic and journalistic relationships. He would make outrageous remarks and expect them to be made of him as well. He was small and tubby and knew it. He took the resulting badinage with good humour. Crowther had, in fact, set the tone at the outset of the companies coming together when he said in a *Times* interview "Forte has got to live with me." He might have meant the need to merge different styles. Well, Forte didn't see it as a one-way street.

The day arrived when Forte, Crowther and Pickard met to discuss their worsening relationships. During the course of the conversation Crowther declared that : "Italians were all cowards." It was stupid, untrue and insensitive but Crowther would have seen it as a bit of teasing. Forte took serious umbrage, as well he might. Hadn't his grandfather cleared out the bandits at considerable risk to his life. Crowther might have seen the remark as no more than jocular. Even so, the chairman of a major public company should have been restrained by a good public affairs director. As relationships went from bad to worse Crowther decided to renege on his agreement to resign with the excuse to Forte that: "the staff don't like you."

In an effort to improve the situation, Sir Charles Hardie was appointed a director in the hope that he would pour oil on troubled waters and hold the ring. Hardie was a great friend of Pickard. They had served together on another major board, but Hardie had also been on the Forte board in the 1950s and was a friend of Forte. Crowther thought Hardie was 'one of us' but, in fact, Hardie was determined to be unbiased.

It became a matter of the two sides having individual board meetings before the board meetings. Meetings were sometimes

Ritzy

called at short notice, which made it difficult for the Trust Houses director in Australia to arrive in time. The log jam was broken when Pickard was heavily - and as it subsequently emerged - unfairly criticised in a government report. The board voted by a slim margin, crucially affected by the absence of the Australian director, to dismiss him from his post. Pickard remained a director and Forte was not, at the time, elected to replace him, but the Trust Houses side decided that the only hope for future amity lay in a purchase of the combined company by an outsider. Crowther talked to Allied Breweries who did indeed try a take-over. Forte fought for his company's independence in the same spirit that his grandfather had attacked the bandits. He spent all his own money buying his company's shares to keep up the price and make the take-over more expensive for the predator. He got his friends to buy the shares too. Max Joseph bought some to support Forte, but told him that he would never have risked his own fortune to maintain control of his own company. Joseph, even more than Forte, was in business to make money; Forte wanted to defend his beloved company from the infidels. The take-over bid was fought off.

As Crowther's behaviour had become more and more antagonistic to the best interests of Trust Houses Forte, Hardie found himself with a casting vote on a proposal to dismiss Crowther and exercised it to approve the motion. Crowther was dead within a year. He might have made A.H. Jones so unhappy that Jones resigned, but this time it was another story. Crowther met A. H. Jones' widow at the opera and complained of Forte's treatment of him. Kit Jones told him: "Now you know what you did to Jay". Jones hadn't understood Crowther either.

When the Allied Breweries bid failed the Trust Houses directors all resigned as they had backed it. A number of the T.H executives were, however, given senior roles in the new company. Franks had left earlier. There had been an enormous row at a meeting with Forte and when Forte complained of his language and sentiments, the Colonel had had enough and walked out. Franks had been a powerful figure but it was Forte who had come out on top. Rightly or wrongly, this sent a message. A founder can count on support in the boardroom because he normally selects his board in the first place and they owe their advancement to him. An outside director brought in to run a company does not have that initial loyalty and in a major argument with a colleague, it is conceivable that a boardroom battle will result in victory for his opponent.

There was more to Forte, though, than simply sitting at the head of the table. If he was a tough businessman, he also had a public conscience. Early in his career he had decided to remove one-arm bandits from his motorway cafes and he banned Top Shelf magazines from the shops.. In later life he refused to have anything to do with casinos. He felt any addicts who resulted would be partly his fault. He strove mightily for the hotel industry as a whole. He played a major part in the early days of the London Tourist Board and used his senior position in the industry to propagate its arguments to politicians. THF won the Queen's Award for Industry on a number of occasions and played its part in the development of higher tourism flows. He helped the Benevolent substantially when it badly needed the money. He took his responsibilities as a leader in the industry very seriously.

Forte has one son, Rocco, who is the apple of his eye. Rocco was born in 1945, educated at Downside and, from the age of 15, earned pocket money in the school holidays working in various parts of the company. He went on to Pembroke College, Oxford, and became an accountant at Charles Hardie's firm. His varied social life and associations with lots of pretty girls made him good copy for the media. He went on to join the board of THF. Another sibling, Forte's daughter, Olga Polizzi, now a distinguished expert, was put in charge of interior decoration for the hotels after some time in the department, working under her aunt. If there was no competition for either post, neither had there been for Arthur Towle's daughter when she became his personal assistant at the LMS Hotels, or Towle himself when, with his brother, he took over the running of the chain from his father before the First World War. We've seen the result in Lyons of being born a Salmon or a Gluckstein. To outsiders it might appear to be nepotism but there is no shortage of similar examples of the same thing happening today in many other industries. What is more, the Forte shareholders had done very well out of trusting Forte's judgment and they didn't try to prevent Rocco's appointment.

Over the next 20 years THF expanded enormously, building up their Post House chain and becoming extremely important in industrial catering and many other catering fields. It was a huge success story with one exception. In 1981 Forte set out to buy the Savoy Hotel Company and the irresistible force met the immovable object: Sir Hugh Wontner. According to the Samuel/Clore camp,

Ritzy

Wontner had seen off their take-over attempt in 1953 by appealing, in part, to anti-semitic prejudice. Now the target was the Italian milk bar owner. Wontner suggested on many occasions that Forte should have stuck to his cafeterias' last. In his turn, Forte remarked on Wontner's: "great gift for supercilious indifference." The insults flew in the national press.

In the end the logic of a takeover bid by THF was not enough. Although Forte finished up with the majority of the shares, an anachronistic share structure meant that THF only had 42% of the votes. They never won control. It was one of Forte's very few failures. Having said that, the shares were bought for £50 million and were sold 15 years later for £400 million.

If he didn't succeed in winning the Savoy Group, he collected other Trophy Hotels in many parts of the world. Hotels like the King Edward in Toronto, the Plaza Athenée and Westbury in New York and the Ritz in Madrid. They were a wonderful collection and brought with them a great deal of kudos for the owner, but single luxury hotels in cities all over the world are very difficult to operate effectively from a strongly centralised base.

Few hoteliers are strongly linked to one political party or another. Guests come in all shapes, sizes and political opinions. Forte donated financially to Labour party leader, Hugh Gaitskell's Campaign for Democratic Socialism in the 1950s. Forte wrote: "I believe passionately in the Welfare State." What he was less keen on was unions. He believed in protecting the industry's managers by: "standing up to unfair demands by unions."

In the 1970 election he supported Ted Heath. In the 1980s he was even more supportive of Prime Minister, Margaret Thatcher. Not for Thatcher the automatic promotion of members of an ancient Establishment while Forte represented the benefit to Britain of a meritocracy. Forte has been a Conservative voter all his life and he is a self made man and a representative of the modern service industries. He became a Knight in 1970 and a Lord in 1982, a fair recognition of the part he had played in the industry's development as a major economic force.

Forte never lost his affection for the industry. He would chat happily to his most junior old-time employees and was never happier than meeting them at long service award dinners and talking over old times. Those who had built the business with him had an enormous affection for their boss, as was true in many other hotel and catering circles as well.

At his 80th birthday in the luxury of his Grosvenor House ballroom, Margaret Thatcher, herself, spoke very warmly of Forte's contribution to the hotel industry over the years. The tough, dynamic Italian migrant had reached the very top. Few members of the industry begrudged him his just rewards by that time. Shortly afterwards he retired and handed over the business to Rocco. In November 2001 he celebrated his 93rd birthday.

Sir Maxwell Joseph. 1910 - 1982.

Max Joseph was born in the East End of London in 1910. His father, Jack Joseph, was a Jewish ladies tailor, who turned to dealing in property in later life. Max's mother died when he was 10, his brother Theodore was killed in action during the 2nd World War and his stepbrother, Henry, a fine surgeon, died in Australia soon after the war. Life dealt Joseph a lot of hard blows but, as his cousin, Lord Mishcon, said: "As far as Max was concerned, if there was a problem, it had to be overcome." If his staff couldn't live up to that standard, they didn't last long with him. He could be a frightening figure.

From an early age he showed commercial flair. He would cut up pencils into sections and sell the pieces to his fellow pupils. His father was not an observant Jew but he felt that his sons should have a Jewish religious education. It didn't work. The style and method of tuition Joseph experienced put him off all forms of religion for life. A slim man, he was a determined fighter but shy in public. Nevertheless, it was said of him by his friends that he had a wonderful facility for: "backing into the limelight".

In 1925, at 15, he left school and joined Estate Agent, Ernest Owers, in Hampstead for £1.50 a week for a 10 hour day. In addition he got 2 shillings and 6 pence (12½p) for every "For Sale" board he got displayed. He said he concentrated on getting boards up more than selling houses. In the 1930s he borrowed the money from his father to start his own firm of estate agents, Connaught, Hooper, at Marble Arch in London. Even during the Slump he flourished and by the Coronation year he had the trappings of a Rolls Royce, a wonderful house in Hampstead and a beautiful wife. But in 1938 the bottom fell out of the property market because of the approaching war. What was a house worth if it might be bombed? Joseph had bought houses and they didn't sell for what he had paid for them.

In property matters Joseph was streetwise but this time he had been too optimistic. He was broke at the beginning of the war. He owed William Deacons Bank £40,000. (£1.5m) He joined the Royal Engineers, became a lance corporal, was stationed in the Home Counties and, in the latter part of the war, started to buy and sell small hotels. He could manage that in conjunction with his service duties. He began to learn something of how hotels were run and at the same time his finances improved. He wrote to Martin's Bank in 1945, whilst still in the army: "Although I found myself in the unfortunate position of owing nearly £100,000 (£3.5m) to the various banks during the war period, not for one moment did I doubt my ability to discharge in full my liabilities when conditions returned to anything like normal. Had I, at any time during this period, allowed myself to weaken, and pander to the stupidities of the Banks' demands for interest and repayments during the years 1941-1945, I should have found myself in Carey Street long ago."

His attitude never changed. In the 1970s, during the economic crisis after 1973, when Grand Metropolitan was hopelessly in debt to the banks, Joseph was asked by their representatives whether at least he might do something about the interest payments. He said: "no" and the banks knew it was useless to do more than wait for Joseph to sort things out, which he did when the economy recovered. If Grand Metropolitan had collapsed in 1973, it could have had a domino effect on large sectors of the economy.

Joseph was always a lover of the good life: casino gambling, the ladies, fine brandy, fine cigars and fine cars. He lived in the only farm house left in Kensington - with his own paddock in front of it. With such a life style, Joseph was strictly in business to build a fortune. When George Hill was made managing director of British Transport hotels in 1970, Joseph said to him: "Why do a job at which you can't make money?" Hill's salary was about £10,000 a year and there were no share options. It wouldn't have suited Joseph who was a steel-nerved gambler and, on occasions, put the largest stake that was allowed on a single number at the Monte Carlo casino. At times, it even came up.

A pause for the stars

Joseph's business deals were equally fearless and spectacular. He was exceptionally shrewd, particularly about the value of property. He had - and often must have needed - a good sense of humour. Dennis Hearn, a Director of Trust House Forte, was a fitness fanatic, like Lord Forte. He asked Joseph once what he did for exercise. Joseph told him he got all his exercise by following the hearses of his friends who were fitness fanatics! To an accounts clerk seeking advice on why suppliers kept asking for payment long after he had passed the invoices, Joseph explained gently "We....haven't... ..got.....any......money!"

After the war, one hotel that took his fancy was the Mandeville near London's Oxford Street. He decided to run it himself: "I became besotted with the hotel business." he said. Unfortunately, he was not very good at it. The Mandeville didn't make a profit until 1953/4. The lack of success with the Mandeville didn't stop him buying the Ford Hotel in Manchester Street or the Washington Hotel, which he refurbished. He ran it as a luxury hotel because he always wanted the best. Later in life he bought the Coq d'Or restaurant, one of the finest in Mayfair. He lost a fortune on that too; Joseph's mistake was to listen to the industry's Sirens who always recommended concentrating on the restaurant and bar. Fred Gordon had recognized that this was wrong, as we've seen, but that was 60 years before.

So, again, Joseph was in financial trouble. The solution was to sell 50% of his hotels to Fred Kobler in the early 1950s for £15,000 with Kobler taking on half the debts. Kobler was as cautious as Joseph was over-enthusiastic. The agreement was that Joseph should have nothing further to do with the running of the hotels. Kobler, together with a young refugee, Henry Edwards, set about operating the hotels with stringent economy. Kobler now had 40% of the equity and Edwards 10%.

Kobler had been on the run from Hitler since 1938. His brother-in-law had managed to get to America before the war but his sister and nephew had had to survive concentration camps. Kobler disliked Europe intensely and looked to America for inspiration. For example, if the Americans had hotel salesmen, he was going to have one. Recognizing the vital importance of filling bedrooms, Kobler gave instructions that the subject of food and drink was never to be mentioned in managers meetings. It wasn't Joseph's way but Kobler's deal allowed for no interference by Joseph in the running of

Ritzy

the hotels.

Kobler only promoted executives to general manager if they had worked as reception managers. This was unheard of in an industry dominated by the caterers and where the position of reception manager was normally occupied by a woman. This did not mean that Kobler only appointed women managers. He was a misogynist and appointed male reception managers. He recognized the importance of rooms having private bathrooms and built them as fast as he could. He concentrated on getting more business from America, using a good hotel representative, Henry Utell, for the purpose. He was a great innovator. Joseph concentrated on immense property deals, wheeling and dealing in the world he knew best. Slowly, very slowly, the hotels started to make money. Joseph buying new ones - the Green Park, Clifton-Ford, Flemings and the St. Ermins in London during the 1950s, with Kobler and Edwards running them. The St. Ermins deal was typical. Top Rate Income Tax was 83% but Capital Gains Tax was lower. It was more sensible for the owner to sell the property than to take the dividends. So Joseph was able to buy the St. Ermins for £500,000 and sell the freehold on to the Church Commissioners for £625,000 and an agreed 40 year lease. The hotel included an office block, the rentals from which paid the interest on the £625,000 easily. What Joseph did understand was the value of hotels: "Between 1950 and 1965 there wasn't a real estate man in the business who knew the value of hotels. I knew I had the feel. You can't devise a formula to value a hotel. You need a feel for the combination of property value and profit. I know hotels." That he did, but not how to make them profitable.

In 1957 Joseph decided to buy the Mount Royal Hotel at Marble Arch for £1 million. It was a hotel with 750 bedrooms, a former block of flats. The deal was agreed with Sir Bracewell Smith, who owned it. The only problem was that none of the banks he approached would lend him the money to pay for it! Disaster? Not at all. With only 24 hours to go before completion, he approached Sir Isaac Wolfson, the chairman of Great Universal Stores who was always prepared to help in an emergency if his company benefited substantially. Wolfson agreed to lend the money but Joseph had to pay a very high rate of interest.

The other hotels had been backed into the shell of a Public Company called Grand Hotel, Harrogate in 1956. The new name for the stock was Grand Hotels (Mayfair). Of this Joseph was chairman and he also ran the Mount Royal on his own account. Eventually, he proposed to Kobler and Edwards that the two companies be combined. This was agreed and now Joseph, who had the Mount Royal as well as a major holding in Grand Hotels (Mayfair), became stronger, with his friends, than Kobler and Edwards combined. The new company was called Grand Metropolitan Hotels and its shares became very popular. .

The first hotel Joseph ever built for himself was on the site Sir Charles Clore had sold him in 1962. There was an internal competition in the hotels to name the new baby. 2,000 entries were whittled down to a winner by the senior executives. Edwards told Joseph of the result and Joseph said "Oh, really. I've decided it's going to be called the Europa"! And so it was. Joseph was, in fact, taking a major interest in all aspects of the new building and Edwards disliked this unaccustomed interference: As an official biographer wrote: "Conflict followed and.....it was not likely that so masterful a personality as Maxwell Joseph would yield control of it (the construction) to Edwards. Nor did he. The course of the dispute is obscure but its outcome is clear. Edwards resigned from the Board, ostensibly for reasons of health, on January 1st 1964." Edwards was brilliant but still a young man. His view of Joseph's future was summed up when he told him that day: "without me, you'll never be anything." Kobler resigned too. He had had enough and retired to an estate in the country near to his beloved Glyndebourne. Working with Joseph had made him an ample fortune in just 10 years.

In 1964, Joseph left the running of the hotels to two accountants, Stanley Grinstead (later Sir Stanley), and Ernest Sharp. Sharp had been involved in Giltspur Investments, Joseph's company for his assorted industrial investments, and Grinstead at the Mount Royal and in Joseph's Union Properties. They were to prove an excellent team for the next 15 years.

The expansion of Grand Metropolitan was piecemeal. An early deal for some Scottish hotels, the purchase of the rump of Gordon Hotels, £3 million for two hotels in Paris and the famous Carlton Hotel in Cannes. When another site in Grosvenor Square became available, the company bought it and created the Britannia Hotel.

When you view the interior of the Britannia, it looks like an

Ritzy

18th century stately home which has been converted into a modern hotel. That was Joseph's instructions and, as the site was totally cleared before building started, the whole ground floor was make-believe Georgian; cunningly constructed out of plastic, with the air-conditioning ducts concealed below the pseudo-18th century rose mouldings in the ceiling. Joseph did not want what he called the Mid-Atlantic motel style of interior decoration.

There followed hotels in New York, Holland, Italy and Spain but there were also the takeovers of Express Dairies, Mecca, famous for its dance halls and Miss World competition, and Berni Inns. Why Berni Inns? Joseph had bought a small catering company called Levy & Franks. They had tried to compete with Berni and got the worst of it. So Joseph bought Berni to make sense of the purchase of Levy & Franks. As entrepreneurs Frank Berni and Max Joseph came from very different backgrounds, but there was never a cross word between them

These purchases had little to do with hotels but then, as the *Economist* pointed out: "The thing you have to understand about Grand Metropolitan's strategic plan is that they haven't got one." Grand Metropolitan were about making profits.

Joseph couldn't wait to get into casino gaming. The moment the announcement of its legality came, he pronounced the ballroom at the Mayfair Hotel shut. The builders moved in to transform it and the only problem was that there were 250 definite bookings for the room for future months. The sales manager, Robert Adley, had to find alternatives for the clients and try to avoid the company being sued for breach of contract. When this somewhat traumatic experience came to an end, Adley left and became an M.P.; presumably for a quieter life. Now Forte wouldn't have behaved like that because he disliked the social consequences of gambling. For Joseph, if the deal was right, that was all that mattered. When it was, he acted with his usual decisiveness; the take-over of the massive Express Dairies was substantially completed in a weekend

The profitability of Grand Metropolitan changed the City's attitude to the hotel market sector for the first time in 50 years. Joseph was helped in this vital area by the concurrent success of Forte and Berni. The City, which had had its fingers badly burned over the years, came to believe that hotel shares might be a good investment. They found in Joseph a source of good stories for the City pages. He

A pause for the stars

was usually referred to as Lance Corporal Joseph and the image of the little man defeating the giants was an attractive one.

As the share price of Grand Metropolitan increased, the opportunity to buy companies with the stock grew. Joseph's reputation in the City was of paramount importance to him. It had nearly been scuppered when he had some dealings with a pair of fraudulent Directors of the State Building Society in the early 1960s. He was totally innocent of any wrongdoing himself, but the problem of guilt by association emerged strongly. The Lord Mayor of London, no less, came to his rescue, praising his integrity.

Joseph's control of his company was absolute. During the slump of 1974 -1977 Grand Metropolitan's shares declined, with the rest of the market. They went from 240p to 18p. The company was terribly short of cash. At that moment Joseph decided to buy £500,000 worth of shares in the Savoy Hotel Company from Victor Matthews of Trafalgar House. The shares returned about 3% and the money would cost 15% to borrow. Some of the directors were livid and put the purchase on the agenda for the next board meeting. It was pointed out that the purchase had been completed without gaining their support. Joseph went a little red in the dead silence which accompanied this unusual outburst. The entire board of directors of the 10th largest company in the United Kingdom awaited the chairman's explanation: " Well" said Joseph "I think I know more about this subject than anybody else. Next business". And the Board went on to other items like lambs. Within 6 months Joseph sold the shares to Rothschilds for 60% more than he'd paid for them.

During that recession Joseph's personal finances were also problematical. He had once been thanked by the Board for buying a painting by Gainsborough of Ben Truman which had been on the wall in the Truman boardroom for years. He pointed out that such company capital should not be locked up in a painting. Everybody agreed. During the recession he sold it for more than twice the amount he'd paid for it to pay his tax bill. There was muttered criticism, a little adverse publicity, but he was entirely within his rights and was still sailing within the bounds of propriety. It also enabled him to keep afloat, as his personal fortune had been severely hit by the collapse in his company's shares.

The peak of his business career was the take-over of Watneys, which went into the Guinness Book of Records as the largest take-

Ritzy

over bid ever at the time. Watneys was one of the biggest brewers in the country and, traditionally, the brewers had been the ruling caste in catering. The resistance to being bought by a hotel company was fierce. When Grand Metropolitan bid for Watneys, there were no holds barred. At least one major institution enjoyed Joseph's hospitality at Ascot before finally deciding to accept the Grand Metropolitan offer and the lobbying was intense. It went down to the wire. When Grand Metropolitan announced victory, there were still voices suggesting that the counting was inaccurate. The margin was 52% - 48% in favour.

Like Fred Gordon before him, Joseph had many other interests as well. He developed another hotel organisation, Norfolk Capital, as well as property, investment and haulage companies. Yet he once told Peter Eyles, his managing director at Norfolk Capital and his son-in-law, that anybody who had to work longer than 4 hours a day at his job wasn't on top of it. Certainly Joseph was not noted for putting in long hours.

For all his toughness, Joseph was also a very charitable man. It was not just the donations he made to worthy causes. When the Mandeville restaurant manager, who had been with him in the early days, was dying , Joseph gave him today's equivalent of £50,000 out of his own pocket.

With the end of the slump, Joseph's personal fortune recovered. He discovered nothing had been done about his pension and a Board Meeting passed a resolution awarding him £166,000 for the contributions he would have to make in the next few years to provide him with a suitable figure. Ironically, it was an unnecessary expense. He died in 1982. Almost at the end he was knighted. The last time we lunched together, we talked in his Michelin starred restaurant about the cancer which he knew was incurable. He said that he had no fear of dying. Certainly, his career had been built on having no fear of anything.

Lord Mancroft was a great friend of Joseph and a wonderful after-dinner speaker. Joseph asked him to address an important group of Travel Agents because he was on holiday in the West Indies and said he had fallen sick. So Mancroft agreed to deputise and told the audience: "Max Joseph is very sorry he can't be with you today, but he has become ill in the West Indies. Well, you wouldn't expect Max to become ill in Walthamstow!"

Sir Hugh Wontner - 1908 - 1992

The advertisement for the post of secretary of the Hotel & Restaurants Association in 1933 was quite specific. The acceptable candidate would have to possess a public school education. The successful applicant was Hugh Wontner, who had been to Oundle. Wontner was born in 1908, into a family which had been prominent in the City of London since the time of the first Elizabeth and had provided several Masters of the Company of Feltmakers. Even so, his father was a well-known actor. It was not a profession which would have been likely to have been initially favoured by Wontner's maternal grandparents in those very class-conscious Edwardian days. Wontner grew up to be keen on acting like his father and performed with two well-known amateur theatrical companies, the Old Stagers and the Windsor Players. He had this in common with Sir George Reeves-Smith. The Savoy had also been built by a showman and the spirit of show business was present from an early stage.

Wontner left Oundle at 17 in March 1926 with only a pass in Drawing. He said he went to France for a while to the kitchens of the Hotel Meurice and then he served on the staff of the London Chamber of Commerce. Between the ages of 25 and 30 he was an efficient secretary of the HRA. It wasn't, however, an auspicious start to a glittering career; association officials were not considered high fliers and the hotel industry was not highly regarded in the upper echelons of society. Wontner did have one responsibility though which was out of the ordinary at that time. The HRA had agreed to help with planning the supply of hotel beds for visitors coming to the Coronation in 1937. Their secretary was the logical official to act as secretary of the committee formed for that purpose. Wontner did a good job.

George Reeves-Smith, still chairman of the management committee of the association, was impressed. He liked Wontner and, needing an assistant at the Savoy, he brought him over to the company in 1938. He was given the title of assistant managing director, though there could never be any doubt that Reeves-Smith would make all the important decisions. Reeves-Smith might be 80, but he was still putting in a full day's work. Wontner's title was useful, though. When Buckingham Palace wanted some help with their catering operation, it was the public schoolboy, assistant

Ritzy

managing director, Hugh Wontner, who was sent down the Strand to the Mall. There would have been far more expert Savoy executives available, but they were busy men and they might not have spoken as well. Wontner's successor as managing director at the Savoy, Giles Shepard, praises Wontner for speaking and writing English beautifully. Important attributes at Court and there appears to be no other logical explanation for sending a novice on such an important mission. Wontner received an MVO in 1950.

When Reeves-Smith died in 1941, the Savoy board split his position between Miles Thornewill and the 33 year old Wontner. Thornewill had been Reeves-Smith's right hand man and, like Rupert D'Oyly Carte, had been to Winchester. He had had legal training and he was appointed vice-chairman. Wontner was made managing director. There appears to have been no thought of appointing an outsider. Wontner was recognized as Reeves-Smith's protégé and he had obviously learned a lot in the three years he had been under the great man's tutelage. Even so, it was a risk. The Savoy was a major hotel company; three great London hotels - The Savoy, Claridge's and the Berkeley - staffed by some of the best profe ssionals in the country, as well as other prestigious catering operations. Wontner had never run any form of company. He was unproven even as a manager. Admittedly, he was available - he was not called up for war service - and he was from a similar background to the directors. It could easily be described as: "jobs for the boys".

What was in Rupert D'Oyly Carte's mind? According to Jean Nicol, the publicity manager at the Savoy in the 1940s Rupert didn't like either fuss or the limelight. He "enjoyed his tropical gardens in Devon whenever he had the time." He had left Reeves-Smith to run the hotels and, as far as the staff were concerned, Thornewill and Wontner would now carry out the same responsibilities. Wontner's strength lay in his belief in high standards. He once told me that a five star hotel must always have one member of staff for each guest; very expensive in the 1960s. Furthermore, no hotel could call itself five star unless every bath was 6 ft (1.8 metres) long.

The downside, of course, is that high standards are very costly. Predators in the years to come, anxious to take over the company, could always see the savings to be made. They pronounced the hotels badly run because of the costs. The costs, however, paid for the standards. D'Oyly Carte died in 1947 and Wontner was made chairman of the company at 39.

He also took over the reins at the HRA. When A.H. Jones spoke up for small hoteliers after the war against the big battalions running the HRA, on the subject of split shift payments for waiters, Wontner made sure that Jones was not reelected to the board of management. On the other hand, he did sterling work for the industry in dealing with the post-war government on the question of permits for the industry. Everything was in short supply and Wontner went to work to try to get the government to relax the quotas to benefit hotels.

Wontner was a terrible snob. A snob is defined as: "a person with an exaggerated respect for social position or wealth and who despises socially inferior connections." Chairman of the Savoy was an ideal job if you wanted to mix with people of social position and wealth. That he was a snob is attested by a wide range of people who knew him well.

For much of his career, Wontner was at daggers drawn with Charles Forte. They clashed when, in the 1950s, Wontner tried to get the hotel industry to only accept a credit card produced by the International Hotel Association, but to refuse to recognize others. Wontner had the foresight to realise just how much money would be lost to the industry by the payment of commission to card companies in the future. Forte was in favour of credit cards. At the executive meeting of the BHRA at the time, Wontner mocked Forte openly, telling his colleagues that Forte was not a hotelier but a milk bar operator. He repeated the same unpleasantry on many future occasions. When Wontner was under attack, he was inclined to appeal to the baser instincts of his supporters. Of course, when he took over the Savoy in 1941, Wontner, himself, had never run so much as a milk bar.

When Harold Samuel and Charles Clore tried to buy the Savoy Company in 1953, Wontner led a spirited resistance. The company couldn't reject the bid on its merits because accepting the offer would have been very much in the shareholders' interests. The defence concentrated on dismissing Samuel and Clore as speculators, which was a term of abuse at the time. In a debate in the House of Commons on March 25th 1954, Arthur Lewis, MP., for Labour, condemned: "the reprehensible conduct of Mr. Clore and his compatriots in connection with the Savoy Hotel",

Ritzy

while Lieutenant Colonel Bromley Davenport, for the Conservatives, asked on June 3rd: "Is it not in the national interest that our best hotels should be preserved as such, and would it not have been a tragedy if the group in question had been bought by speculators." Churchill referred to the takeover as a: "profit ramp by speculators" and the BHRA announced: "their profound concern at the attempt by outside interests to secure control of the Savoy Hotel Ltd.", expressing their: "full support for the directors, management and staff." In fact, Samuel and Clore had simply recognized the value of the Berkeley Hotel site in Piccadilly as a potential office building; an underutilised company asset. The Savoy said that the rebuilding of the Berkeley: "is in an advanced stage." In fact, it happened 20 years later, though in the 1960s Wontner saw the potential, selling the site and building a new Berkeley in Knightsbridge in 1972 with the proceeds .

It would be unfair to judge Wontner by the standards of the 21st century. He was a child of his time. Ron Jones, one-time general manager at Claridge's, has written that Wontner's most damning criticism was to say that someone was: "not a gentleman". Speculators could be classified thus, if this helped the cause. Wontner eventually bought Samuel's shares - Samuel had bought Clore's - and Samuel (Later Lord Samuel) made over £300,000 profit in 9 months. When it became obvious that the Berkeley would remain a hotel, the shares slipped back.

In 1973/4 Wontner was elected Lord Mayor of London. In the beginning of a catastrophic slump for the hotel industry, it was the unluckiest of timing. His company needed all his attention and he couldn't provide it. His various duties in the run-up to that point also explain a ludicrous error that cost the company dear. The government Grant Scheme gave £1,000 a room to new hotels, as long as work on the site was not started before a specific date. A minute amount of work was done on the new Berkeley site beforehand and the Savoy lost the grant.

Not being British could also be damning, as far as Wontner was concerned. He said of Lord Forte: "He is a very little man and he is Italian. So you have a recipe for folie de grandeur". And yet Wontner's company owed so much to its Italian staff. Few remarks could have been more wounding to them, particularly as Forte was naturally a folk hero to the Italian hoteliers throughout the country. Like many other utterances, it showed an immense arrogance and a monumental absence of tact. At the same time, he could be very witty; for example, when entertaining as Lord Mayor. He was in his element during state visits and a very good representative of the City.

The disease, for which arrogance was the medication, was the disdain in which careers in the hotel industry were held by society at the time. Until the latter years of the century, the industry was considered the last refuge of the man who had failed in his chosen profession. The unsuccessful law student, the man who had flunked his medical exams, the ex-soldier the army hadn't needed beyond the rank of Major. The seeds of hotelier self-doubt came from the world around them; they were, in fact, doing a hard job well. One the country needed; building an industry which would be great long after many of the traditional and reputable British manufacturing industries had collapsed.

Nevertheless, they were still looked down upon. When I said at Cambridge that I was going into the hotel industry, a friend who was going into Shell told me: "Well, you do realise you'll be living off your wits"!

This meant that, originally, Wontner knew he would have great difficulty being accepted into 'The Club', but his best chance was to adhere rigidly to what he perceived were the club rules. For those who didn't care for 'The Club' and who knew they had no chance of acceptance anyway, it simply didn't matter. It mattered to George Reeves-Smith and it mattered to his acolyte, Hugh Wontner. Wontner admired Reeves-Smith enormously. Reeves Smith deserved this for his careful tutoring of the young man and the effectiveness of the standards he set of top quality hotel-keeping. Wontner also must have recognized that if Reeves-Smith hadn't spotted him, he might have remained a lowly association secretary until it was too late to reach the dizzy heights he finally attained. He was immensely grateful to him.

This dislike of those who were not 'gentlemen' was part of what Wontner had been taught was necessary to keep up the reputation of fine hotels. To keep the riffraff out. What he had also experienced year after year in the cocooned position he held as the managing director of the Savoy, was constant flattery. It is often the way. When Sir Stanley Grinstead took over as chairman of Grand Metropolitan, I asked him how he was finding it. "Ever since I became chairman"

335

Ritzy

he said "I only hear the echo of my own voice." Wontner heard the echo of his own voice for 50 years and, as was often said by his colleagues, he did not like being argued with. The unending diet of people agreeing with him, admiring him, applauding him, hanging on his every word, was a drug which affected the soundness of his commercial judgments.

There was another side to him, though. He was very well liked and influential outside the industry - at the International Hotel Association, in the Corporation of the City of London, as a Catering Adviser to the Palace and as a very senior member of the BHRA. For many years after the Second World War, he was the most influential hotelier when it came to talking to the government. He was also extremely charming to his guests and supporters

Was the Savoy Company's profit record poor? It depended on your viewpoint. In his own defence Wontner once pointed out that the company had only failed to make a profit five times since its inception. That performance certainly compared well with, say, the Ritz which practically never made a profit in its first 70 years of operation. On the other hand, the profit performance in Forte's Grosvenor House was far superior to the Savoy.

The Savoy Group didn't grow to any extent in the 50 years he was effectively in charge. Wontner turned down the chance to buy the Ritz on more than one occasion. The original shareholders didn't demur.

Reeves-Smith had been a perfectionist and Wontner carried on the tradition. Where Reeves-Smith had invariably hired French chefs, the best Banqueting Managers were very often Italian. They were not Welsh! So when Bryan Evans was by far the best candidate for the job as a successor to Signor Contarini, one of the conditions of his appointment was that he must always be known as Evangelo Brioni. Which - and we're in the 1960s and 1970s - was what happened.

The Savoy Company particularly scored, in terms of the hotel industry, in the quality of its operational training. Over the years, thousands of hoteliers benefited from periods working for the company. They learned the way to maintain very high standards and they took the lessons with them onto their future careers. The Savoy remained the standard the industry wanted to emulate. Hotel restaurants up and down the country tried to copy the Savoy, though often with disastrous results where there was neither the local market nor the expertise to justify the attempt.

Wontner's last years saw him at battle stations against Charles Forte who tried very hard to take over the Savoy company. Forte's failure was due to the voting structure of the Savoy shares, giving one class far more votes than the other. The high voting shares were created to be held by one charitable foundation called the Savoy Educational Trust and a second, La Fondation pour la Formation Hôtelière, both effectively controlled by the company. Wontner had safeguarded the independence of the hotel company and, with it, his own position.

He ended his life in a penthouse in Claridge's and with an 800 acre estate in Scotland, a 150 acre estate in the Chilterns, a knighthood and a large fortune. Not bad for a public schoolboy with one pass in drawing.

23
The modern industry - 1973 -1987

For nearly 100 years the hotel industry had been complaining that the government neglected them. At last with the Development of Tourism Act's Grant Scheme, Harold Wilson's Labour party had given a substantial incentive to the creation of new hotels. The result was that substantial over-building in many towns and cities, coupled with an unexpected major oil crisis, caused widespread over-supply and many bankruptcies. Indeed, only a totally unforeseen series of unconnected events fortuitously prevented the situation becoming very much worse.

The problem was that the government grant of £1,000 a room for any hotel completed by March (later June) 1973 was in no way limited to a set number of new hotels. Consequently, where Anthony Crosland, the President of the Board of Trade, had total grants of about £6 million pounds in mind, the eventual bill was £68 million as scores of hoteliers, prospective hoteliers and entrepreneurs got onto the supposed gravy train. If many schemes hadn't been held up too long in the planning stage to qualify for a grant, the final figure would have been swollen still further. The number of new bedrooms built in London alone was 30,000. A price war of immense proportions was a strong possibility as, for much of the year, supply was going to rocket beyond demand. Certainly the tourists would find it much easier to get the quality of accommodation they wanted in peak periods, but an industry geared to maximum demand was always going to find it hard going in the off season.

The price war became a reality when, within a few months of the hotels opening, tourism flows collapsed in the wake of the 1973 Yom Kippur war; a forerunner of conditions after the New York Twin Towers atrocity nearly 30 years later. OPEC then quadrupled the price of oil, causing major inflation in the world economy, which reduced demand still further as companies drew in their belts. The other side of the coin, however, was that 10% - 20% annual inflation carried tariffs upwards very considerably, even if not enough for the hotels immediately. As a consequence, it was much easier to service the capital invested in the new hotels when the recession was over in 1976. Tragically, there had also been a major fire in a leisure centre in 1971 which claimed many lives. As the result of this, the government

The modern industry
had passed a swingeing Fire Precautions Act some years later, to make hotels improve their safety levels. As the cost implications were very high, a large number of small hotels had to close in the next few years, as they couldn't afford to pay for the new safeguards. By a most extraordinary coincidence, about the same number of beds that had been added through the Grant Scheme disappeared because of the Fire Precautions Act.

The Board of Trade hadn't contemplated the size of the demand for the Grant Scheme. The Foreign Office didn't expect the Yom Kippur War and the quadrupling of oil prices. The Home Office didn't anticipate the potential effect of the Fire Precautions Act and the Treasury didn't forecast a recession and high inflation. A complete shambles, from which emerged, at the end of the recession, a level of British hotel bed stock which had improved in quality by a very substantial margin. Alright, another classic case of the British muddling through, but it was still new hotels for old, as a British Tourist Authority Aladdin could now happily offer future tourists.

One of the hotels which was built to take advantage of the Grant Scheme was the Europa Hotel in Belfast, a hotel which gained the unfortunate record of being blown up more often than any other in the world. Whether it would ever have been profitable in those days is doubtful - a civil war attracts journalists but not visiting businessmen, who, if they do come for a fleeting visit, tend to have pressing appointments elsewhere in the immediate future. As, however, the government paid for both the war damage and the loss of profits, Grand Metropolitan shareholders, who owned it, didn't suffer.

The hotel was managed by Harper Brown, a cheerful Ulsterman who was a most professional hotelier. Before the Troubles, when he was managing a smaller hotel, he would improve the bar trade by ringing his friends, inviting them over, and paying for the first round of drinks. A party always developed. In marked contrast, as manager of the Europa, he carried a gun for some years and his heavy smoking eventually killed him. In spite of the continual stress, though, the clientele would only see him smiling and the press corps who covered the Troubles remember him with great affection. It would have pleased hoteliers if the growth of their industry had won equally universal support within the Labour government, which was returned to power in 1974. Instead, Ron Hayward, the general secretary of the party, went on record: "Napoleon said we were a nation of shopkeepers. If we are not careful we may turn into a nation of hoteliers and trinket makers for tourists." The Labour Party continued to be wedded, first and foremost, to heavy industry and the Conservatives still knew their bread was buttered on the farms in the countryside constituencies. Hotels remained such an economic pariah that, originally, they weren't even allowed to apply for the Queen's Award for Industry, a certificate for good export achievement.

After the experience of the Grant Scheme, the hotel industry might have been excused if they had given further involvement with the government a wide berth. This has always been difficult though. The problem always being that so many parts of a hotel's operation involve one government department or another. The Home Office deals with licensing and the Minister responsible for Transport controls signage on a lot of major roads. The Minister of Agriculture has responsibility for restaurants - the argument being that they're involved in food! - and the Department for Education and Employment has an involvement in hotel education. Over the years, the BTA had, normally been the responsibility of the Department of Trade & Industry. The co-ordination of the hotel and tourism efforts of all the government departments was always poor. The single exception would come in the 1980s, in Lord Young's time in Thatcher's government. Young would sponsor a new bill which created brown signs on roads for tourist attractions and he also set up a co-ordinating committee to deal with tourism matters. Unhappily, the latter didn't last long after he left office.

One major hotel company failed to survive the economic turmoil: Lyons. The pound plummeted against a number of other currencies and, particularly, against the Swiss franc. Lyons had borrowed heavily in that market to finance their expansion before 1973, because interest rates were much lower than in Britain. Then they couldn't pay the additional interest consequent on sterling's decline. In 1976 it became necessary to break the company up. THF moved in and bought most of the hotels relatively cheaply. Thus ended, very much with a whimper rather than a bang, the efforts of the Salmons and Glucksteins to build the first food empire.

It was only 35 years since Isidore Salmon had died, leaving the next generation in charge of one of the strongest companies in the country. It was a stark reminder that nothing is for ever. The last word on the subject should go to Lord Michael Montague, who was a Labour peer, a very successful businessman and chairman of the English Tourist Board for some years. Montague had lost his own hotel in Cyprus when the Turks invaded the island but, as he pointed out: "Hotels don't go bankrupt. Only hotel companies."

Rex Joseph was the last managing director of Lyons' Strand Hotel division and he had given the development of the chain his very best shot. He suffered from the fact that his was only a cadet branch of the Gluckstein family (his grandmother was Clara Gluckstein.) He wasn't a main board director. There had been 56 of those in all since the beginning in 1894; 16 had been Salmons and 11 Glucksteins. There had only been two Josephs. So the major decision on how to finance the expansion was not his, though anticipating the catastrophic results of events in 1973 was asking a lot of any financial wizard, even if he was a Salmon or a Gluckstein.

Another company which suffered badly was Mount Charlotte Hotels, a small provincial chain. In 1976 an ex-bartender from the George V in Paris, ex-banqueting manager of Grosvenor House and ex-manager of one of THF's smaller properties, joined the board. Robert Peel was all those things but he had also been educated at Eton and his brother, Charles, had a great eye for property values. In 1977 he was made managing director and Mount Charlotte was destined to become a major player for many years. They set up shop in unfashionable Leeds and they attacked their problems with ferocious energy. Peel was not famous for his ability to delegate and often seemed to run the company in the early days from the contents of his briefcase. He is a keen salesman, though, and it always helps when the client is approached by the managing director rather than a more junior employee.

There was a steady growth in the size and number of hotel chain operations. The leading companies in the 1970s were Grand Metropolitan and THF. Grandmet had bought the hotels of Trumans and Watneys when they took over those brewery companies. It was a sign of the times that a hotel company could buy a brewery when hotels had so often been unimportant trifles in brewery company operations. With THF absorbing Lyons and a large number of formerly independent hotels also becoming part of one chain or another, the group hotels started to dominate the supply in most cities. The days of the hegemony of the Savoy Group, Gordons,

Ritzy

BTH, Lyons and Trust Houses were over at last.

Indeed, only the Savoy Group survived when BTH was broken up by the government. Some of the railway hotels found new owners anxious to build on past glories. Some sank into mere shadows of their former opulence and importance. Smaller hotels started to combine together to get the benefits of better purchasing and marketing; Consort and the American import, Best Western, were but two examples,

The brewery companies were split on the importance of hotel operations to their future profits. Some were still uninterested; Whitbreads' board decided against setting up a Hotels Division in 1972. The famous old brewery company had inherited a number of hotels when they bought over 20 separate breweries between 1961 and 1971, but they left their regional operating companies to develop the ones in their area as they felt fit. They had some nice properties, like the St. Pierre Hotel near Chepstow, which also boasted a fine golf club. For the most part, though, the hotels were glorified pubs. Vaux, based in the North East, had 19 small hotels as far back as 1955 but it wasn't until 1972 that they set up a division called Swallow Hotels under Roy Tudor Hughes, who had been one of many Trust House executives to leave THF after the Forte side had won the day. He recommended Peter Catesby to succeed him. Catesby was a well-trained THF professional, who had actually started with A.H. Jones at Grosvenor House. It was he, as managing director, who made Swallow a hotel power in the North for many years. He also bought some hotels in the South but the main strength of the division was always centred around their traditional base. Bass ran Crest Hotels under the brilliant hotelier, Bryan Langton and Allied Breweries gave Chris Bond, a fine accountant, the responsibility for their Embassy Hotels.

In the 1980s a Warrington brewer, Greenall Whitley, bought De Vere Hotels and they, too, started to figure prominently. De Vere was created by Leopold Muller, a Czech refugee, very much in the same mould as Fred Kobler. Indeed Kobler said they came from the same village where Muller's father had been the local butcher. De Vere specialised in buying, among others, luxury seaside hotels, like Merton Cotes' Royal Bath in Bournemouth, the Grand in Eastbourne and the Grand in Brighton - the hotel which was blown up by the IRA in the mid-80's. De Vere often found themselves bidding for

The modern industry
companies in competition with Max Joseph. As Leslie Jackson, Muller's partner said, somewhat ruefully: "When we were outbid by Max, we always thought 'this time he's gone too far.' But he never had.". Greenall Whitley's hotels were the usual three star or less, superior pubs and, as Muller had said repeatedly that he wouldn't sell his company, the omens for the bid were not good at the outset. A cheque for over £40 million finally persuaded Muller that the time had come to retire. Grand Metropolitan, after buying Trumans and Watneys, put the hotels they didn't sell after the acquisitions into a new division called County Hotels, but this was never a very important part of their total hotel operations.

In 1979 Grand Metropolitan bought InterContinental from Pan American and a few years later another major American hotel company became British with the purchase of Holiday Inns by Bass. These developments illustrated just how far the British hotel industry had come from the days when Fred Gordon's operations in Dieppe, Cannes and Monte Carlo were just about the only hotels the British owned abroad. To have taken over Hilton International, InterContinental and Holiday Inns, besides the widespread international interests of THF, showed the new confidence of the City that British hoteliers were capable of competing with the best in the world.

Following the InterContinental purchase, Grand Metropolitan decided to liquidate their own hotel company. There were many reasons to dispose of a hotel company which had had such an influence on the industry over the past 25 years. The hotels didn't offer the same return on capital invested as the other parts of the greatly enlarged company Grand Metropolitan had become. The running of the organization had moved from an ailing Max Joseph to a board which looked on its hotel division as no different from any other. There was a massive capital appreciation to be gathered over the original cost of the hotels and the market for selling hotels was buoyant.

From a commercial point of view it made sound sense. The only thing against it was that the staff who had helped make the hotel division flourish were the major reason for Grand Metropolitan existing in the first place. Many of their interests were not served by being passed over to other owners, often when they were getting elderly and might need the benefit of the doubt about their

343

effectiveness; getting credit for their many years service with the company. That wouldn't be a factor the new company directors could take into account when they considered the best interests of the shareholders. The fate of the old timers troubled Joseph, but the good young Grandmet executives went on to equally, and often better, careers in the future.

The increased pace of buying and selling in the industry undermined company loyalty. Where Long Service Award dinners had marked the faithful service of so many employees over many years, this devotion to the company was often shown to be worthless. When companies were taken over, staff were duplicated, particularly in their Head Offices. So many were made redundant. Pension provisions for long service employees were a burden for their new owners. Most of the staff who found themselves under new management didn't stay long. Most hotel companies didn't have a pension scheme in the 1950s. When they tried to produce a decent one for their staff, the costs escalated alarmingly because of inflation in the 1970s. The companies couldn't afford to put in the additional sums needed to provide, say, 2/3rds of the retiring salary. Ron Jones, a distinguished general manager for Claridge's, worked 27 years for British Transport Hotels. He managed important hotels for them as well. When he resigned from BTH in 1969 to become general manager at the new Royal Garden Hotel in Kensington, he found that his pension when he was 65 was going to be worth £1,400 a year.

The staff's insurance - such as it was - was the ability to get another job somewhere else. You could carry on working into your 70s and 80s, so long as you were fit to do so. The high turnover of staff continued and now there would be clubs like the Old Metronians (Grandmet), who met, like Army Reunions, to salute the past. They still do. Similar gatherings remember Strand Hotels, BTH and - the latest - THF, after their 1990s takeover.

If calls for company loyalty were now likely to fall on deafer ears, the unions should have benefited. Yet they became less powerful during the time of the Thatcher government - in the hotel industry they had never been strong anyway. The fall-back position for the employers might have been to pay higher wages in real money terms to secure loyalty, but the abolition of the Catering Wages Act provisions by the Conservative government led to the industry sliding down the league table of national pay instead. Management had to struggle to respond to difficult economic conditions during much of the 80s and that involved keeping wage bills down. Loyalty was under attack all round. At least the serious arrival of the brewers was a development that improved the industry's products, as the brewers could afford the necessary investment.

The job of a hotel manager subtly changed over these years. The reality of the concept of Mine Host, the general manager, was that they no longer had the time to act in that role in a large hotel. The complexities of industrial relations legislation, health and safety regulations, forecasting and budgeting exercises for Head Office and the absorption of new computing skills were just some of the tasks which diverted their attention from their guests. In addition, due to the difficult trading conditions, the pressure to reduce staffing levels was intense. Management worked extremely hard, but the industry did have a singular advantage. The joy of working in hotels was that young people had a much better chance of climbing the executive tree very quickly. It was possible to get a management position in a hotel faster than in most other industries.

The development of hotel education went up a notch as more polytechnics introduced B.A. degrees in the subject. This led to students with higher 'A' level grades entering the industry, as the colleges offering degrees set the entry standards higher. Many members of the management in the hotel industry labelled the B.A. curricula too theoretical. The truth was that they wanted more cannon fodder to fill the vacancies in junior craft jobs and did not anticipate the increased intellectual competition of bright, young brains with any pleasure. In considerable parts of the industry not much had changed since the Towles and the Salmons had discussed the same topic.

The HCIMA could regard the rising standard of hotel education with much satisfaction. They had been very largely responsible for it and would continue to press for further improvements. The number of members rose to 20,000 and the influence of the HCIMA spread all over the Commonwealth through the development of a network of overseas chapters.

In 1977 the HCIMA appointed Elizabeth Gadsby as its director general. A diminutive lady from the world of agricultural associations, Gadsby was another in the Sir Humphrey mould. The two nominated positions of power in the HCIMA were the president, who chaired the council and the vice president, who chaired the executive. The vice president normally became president the following year. Serving both was predicated to be the director general. As many presidents were not worldly-wise in the industry's national affairs, Gadsby trod the delicate line between guidance and obstruction in the best interests of the Association.

The problem for the HCIMA was to get the leaders of the industry to devote their time to it. When they were simply invited to join the council, as originally with the HCI, it was easy enough. The HCIMA, however, had developed a democratic voting structure. There were two routes to the council; as a representative of a branch or as a national councillor. The former were voted for by the branch which had electoral turnouts akin to local council voting figures. To become a *national* councillor you needed about 20 times as many votes but, of course, you could then also be a defeated candidate. It transpired that not that many national figures were keen on risking rejection at the poll. By the end of the 1980s national figures had largely disappeared from the ranks of the officers. They chose to restrict themselves to serving the BHRCA which had never been madly keen on disputed elections, except in extremis, like the A.H. Jones affair.

The balance of students in hotel schools showed an increasing proportion of women entrants. They usually managed better results than the men, but the industry continued to be dominated by male executives at senior levels. The main exception was in the field of interior decor, where many a chairman's wife still persuaded her husband that she had bashfully kept the hidden skills of an Oliver Messel away from him, as had so often been the case with her predecessors in the past,. Max Joseph's partner, Eileen, was a reasonably typical example of the additional cost which so often resulted. She decided, for example, to put 8,000 sq. ft (800 sq.m) of pale beige carpet into the Europa hotel's ballroom in Grosvenor Square when it opened in 1964. Within 6 months it had to be shampooed every week and within 9 months it was thrown away. When the company built a new hotel, the Britannia, on the other side of the square a few years later, the lobby was dominated by another pale beige carpet. With exactly the same result.

Still, it was part of a long tradition; Arthur Towle, running the railway hotels before the war, had given the interior decor responsibility to his secretary, Miss Oxenford, who was also in charge of the company's housekeepers. The railway hotels had originally been decorated by some of the finest practitioners in the Victorian world, but Miss Oxenford's expertise was apparently sufficient to make the right judgments on any refurbishment to their work. As a director of another hotel company, I once asked a colleague who he felt should tell the chairman that his wife hadn't a clue about internal decoration. "We're right behind you, Derek" he told me. "We're some distance behind you, but we're right behind you!" Decorating a hotel is still not the same as decorating a private home. One of the very finest hotel interior decorators in the 1970s and 1980s was Bob Lush of Richmond Design but his skill in tackling the listed building authorities was as nought compared to his level of diplomacy in dealing with some of the family members of the hotels on which he worked.

The women graduates of hotel schools usually got a raw deal. It was true that a large number of them left the industry when they got married and had children. Even so, the number of women managers in the higher echelons of the industry didn't reflect their contribution or their ability. In the 1970s major chains like Hilton International had practically no women general managers. Major British companies had appointed female managers in a few minor properties and, of course, there were any number of husband and wife managerial teams, but that was it. There has been some improvement since that time but not a great deal. Men still dominate as general managers, head chefs, banqueting managers and financial directors. Women have been concentrated in sales and marketing, housekeeping and reception. General management still emerges primarily from the food and beverage departments.

Where women did make progress was in the ranks of sales and marketing departments. Grand Metropolitan, whose sales department was the benchmark for the industry, had stopped only employing men in the late 1960s after some gentle pressure, notably from Professor Rik Medlik of the University of Surrey. It was decided that recruitment on merit included the new women graduates. For other companies beginning to follow suit, the attraction of good looks seemed more important than intellectual ability in the sales area. The less clever girls were also considered more likely to be in awe of their superiors and easier for managers to control. This was felt necessary because

Ritzy

Grand Metropolitan's sales personnel had a fearsome reputation among a considerable proportion of the industry's managers for their determination to force the last ounce of marketing efficiency out of the hotels. Grand Metropolitan Hotels was by then a marketing-led organisation with a seat on the main board of the company for the director. The department was given an influence which was unique in its time and has never been replicated.

The main reason for this vote of confidence was the transformation of the weekends from dead periods for the Grandmet hotels in London to some of the busiest in the year. The Stardust Mini Holiday campaign had mushroomed and the company was handling 150,000 bookings a year, spending over £1 million on the operation. (About £10 million in today's money.)

These figures were so large for an industry still, for the most part, dipping its toes into the marketing ocean, that sales and marketing in Grand Metropolitan were effectively trusted to make their own decisions, subject only to the rubber stamping of the board. At a cocktail party Max Joseph made a suggestion to me about the Stardust marketing. I said it wouldn't be a wise move: "How many bookings have you got?" he asked. We were a few weeks into the season. "30,000" I said. He reflected: "Well, you'd better get on with it" he said. The national habit in Britain of going to hotels for the weekend is not matched to this day by a similar volume of business in other countries.

Special Events were also developing. In the midst of one of the most disastrous winters for business most hotels had experienced for many years, with London hotels discounting their rates by around 60%, Grandmet launched its most successful single Special Event to help solve the problem. It was a teach-in for hairdressing salon owners and it was run for 3 days at the Albert Hall by Vidal Sassoon. Sassoon was paid £25,000 (about £250,000 today) for an excellent three days work and the company's hotels booked in 2,000 hairdressers from all over the world. The package was for a minimum of 8 nights in January at the full standard rate for the hotels - plus 50%! Grand Metropolitan made a fortune but Sassoon's fee for a second event was considered too high. So it remained a one-off promotion, but it illustrated what could be done in the most difficult economic conditions.

While London was by far the greatest draw for overseas

visitors, there was a considerable growth in secondary tourism: "What do we do next when we've seen London?" Tourist Boards all over the country tried to make sure that the answer was to go to their area. Many entrepreneurs, recognising the potential of tourism, decided to go into the hotel business. Small Stately Home owners were targeted and the properties converted, usually with an additional bedroom wing adjacent to the old building. Hotels would emerge like Blackwell Grange, the old home of the Havelock (Indian Mutiny) Allen family in Darlington. Where once the town had been, primarily, a great railway centre, Home Secretary, William Whitelaw, even held a major conference on the future of Northern Ireland in the hotel.

The most popular tourist destinations were on the classic Round-Britain route, covering Stratford, York, Edinburgh, Harrogate and London. This still left plenty of business for Oxford and Cambridge, Bath and Brighton. Dublin had been very popular before the Troubles, promoted with terrific verve by Bord Failte, the Irish Tourist Board. The popularity of the whole of Ireland was, however, badly affected by the violence in the North. Tourists, who didn't know where Wales was and who asked about Scottish posters: "The Highlands and Islands of where?" were not going to find it easy to distinguish between the North and the Republic. It was also foolish of successive Irish governments to maintain Shannon in the West of the country as the main transatlantic airport. Where, after the war, flights to America from Heathrow had landed in Shannon, the invention of more powerful aircraft - particularly the Boeing 747 - really made Shannon redundant as a transatlantic passenger airport. But there were votes in the West of Ireland and Dublin lost its potential as a European hub airport, as fewer and fewer transatlantic air companies were prepared to land at Shannon before flying on to the capital. Eventually, they just overflew the whole country to London and left the passengers to take short haul aircraft back to Dublin. The British government, for its part, did Scottish tourism no favours by hanging onto Prestwick airport in Ayrshire when it was obvious that Glasgow airport was the sensible destination, once the runways were extended.

The Thatcher years (1979-90) saw a continuing increase in the number of incoming tourists. They also saw the end of the Welsh coal-mining industry and many of the principality's other heavy industrial plants. Tourism should have taken up much more of the resulting slack, but Welsh officialdom steadfastly refused to play the game. Successful tourism is usually about a pretend world; kilts and bagpipes, German oompah bands and beer festivals in lederhosen, Beefeaters, Cabbies, Bobbies and beret-toting Frenchmen. There was only one universal symbol for Wales; the lady in national costume with the tall, flat-topped, black hat. The Welsh politicians rejected it as old-fashioned and chose instead a red dragon, which was ideal - for the People's Republic of China! In fairness, it probably reflected the mood in the Principality. In a similar vein, talking to an Irish hotelier who wanted more British visitors, I suggested that his receptionists should, on hearing an English voice on the phone, say: "Ah, an' the top o' the morning to you." He was mortified. "We don't talk like that any more" he said emphatically. I tried to explain that visitors to Ireland did not come for the skyscrapers, the glaciers or the Great Barrier Reef, but it was an argument he couldn't accept. The most successful tourist countries - Holland is an excellent example - play at Tourism with great élan.

Hotels, naturally, had to adjust to greater numbers of visitors arriving from countries with very different cultures from those normally prevailing in England. The Japanese, for example, considered that trying to clean yourself in a bath where the water was getting steadily dirtier, was likely to defeat the object. They did their best with outlandish Western bath-room equipment. Before the installation of showers, they stood in the baths and threw water over themselves. This, until the hotels put drainage into the bathroom floor, had the effect of sending a lot of water through to the bedroom ceiling below! When the civil war in Lebanon ruined that country's tourist trade, a lot of Arabs turned to London for their holidays. Hotel waiters often had to get used to serving meals in suites on tablecloths spread on the floor in the Arab fashion. The days when the University Arms in Cambridge could expect the Americans to drink water at the English temperature, were disappearing fast.

Another innovation in hotels was Muzak, a device which enabled music to be played over hotel loudspeakers. An innocuous attraction unless in unskilled hands - like those of telephonists, who often controlled the equipment. Lacking instruction, they might well choose records of their favourite rock stars. With instructions, the staff could still be subjected to the interminable playing of *Jingle*

Bells throughout December. There is no recorded case of the tapes of the Massed Bands of the Brigade of Guards being played at breakfast, but it remains a distinct possibility.

Guests were also now able to enjoy Help Yourself Breakfast buffets. This was not an acknowledgement by the industry of a more informal life-style in the country. It was an attempt in the 1970s to save money by reducing the number of waitresses needed to serve the meal. Much as the guests welcomed the quicker service and the ability to pick and choose from a wide selection, the new idea was initially bitterly resisted by the hotel managements. This was because it would result in guests being let loose all over the restaurant, where the restaurant staff much preferred them to be safely moored at their tables!

Almost as interminable as the Iliad was the ongoing story of Forte trying to take over the Savoy Company. It rumbled on because the Savoy had those high voting B shares in their pocket. In 1984 the Savoy directors on the Savoy Educational Trust charity bought just 10 of the shares for £650, valuing their holding of 244,330 at nearly £16 million. If the Trust had distributed 1%, it would have come to £160,000. It managed more like 0.1%.

As the entrepreneurial founding fathers started to fade away, two newcomers appeared on the scene to carry the flag; the first was Jasminder Singh. A refugee from the persecution of Asians in Idi Amin's Uganda, Singh trained as an accountant and is a tall, quiet, relaxed, charming Sikh, who has given up the turban but retained all the courtesy of his forebears. He started in the 1970s with a small hotel in London , the Savoy Court, but expanded over the years to seven London properties, including a monster luxury hotel at Heathrow, called the Edwardian International. He now features on any list of the richest men in Britain.

The other major new player was Cyril Stein and Ladbrokes, his firm of bookmakers. Stein realised that his company had few permanent assets and that his profits were taxed without being partially hived off into buildings which would appreciate in value as the years went by. So he built three new hotels, taking advantage of the Grant Scheme. They were in Middlesbrough, Leeds and Bristol and were called Dragonaras. Some idea of Stein's personalised marketing approach can be gained from the opening advertisements for the hotels. At the time there was a popular full back playing for

Ritzy

Tottenham Hotspur called Cyril Knowles. When he did something spectacular on the pitch, the crowd would shout: "Nice one, Cyril" That was the headline for the Dragonara advertising campaign. The more retiring in the industry winced.

Stein would, however, go on to a great coup by buying Hilton International from the Americans. Next to buying IBM or Coca Cola - or Holiday Inns - there were few American icon companies to compare with Hilton. Stein had been outbid earlier, but the successful company got into financial trouble and sold the hotels to him. This automatically made him one of the international industry's great hoteliers. He is a spare, quiet man, very much in the Max Joseph mould. He had a similar ability to control his company but he was even better than Joseph at recruiting first class hotel executives. His original group included John Jarvis, who would go on to create a major British chain, Jarvis Hotels, David Michels, who would become CEO of Stakis and then CEO of Hilton Group itself in the 1990s and John Wilson who would become CEO of the now Singapore owned Millennium, Copthorne Hotels at almost the same time. David Michels had been originally recruited from Grand Metropolitan where he was the sales and marketing director from 1978 and so became the first marketing man to lead a major hotel company.

Singh and Stein, together with the THF heir apparent, Rocco Forte, were, at least temporarily, the last of the great British hotel entrepreneurs. As the size of the major companies increased and their founders died off, they were often replaced by the grey flannel suit men. There were plenty of very able executives, but they were more constrained by the institutional shareholders and their banks from the type of free wheeling that had epitomised Fred Gordon, Isidore Salmon, Max Joseph, Henry Edwards, Reo Stakis and Charles Forte. Still, if the newcomers weren't at the hotel poker table, playing with their own money, that didn't stop mergers and take-overs. If they seemed more conservative, it could well have been because they had far more to conserve than the entrepreneurial founders in *their* early days.

One way of getting the best out of general managers is to set them up in business for themselves and then share the surplus profits with them, after deducting an agreed annual profit for the company. This was the method devised by John Bairstowe, a former Estate

Agent, and it led to the creation of Queens Moat Houses. QMH bought, among other properties, the Grandmet County Hotel Division outside London in the early 1980s and built a very substantial chain on the back of this innovative idea. I had been managing director of the Grand Metropolitan company but never made the profits that Bairstowe managed. I asked one of my old managers one day how he did so well compared to my time in charge. "You work a lot harder when it's your money" he said. In principle it should have been perfect for both sides; when times were good, it was; when times were bad, the managers didn't make up the profits to the level agreed with the company. There was a nasty scandal and the banks had to fore-close.

Down at the seaside very little stirred. Unless the town attracted national and major company conferences, the outlook was grim for most of the best hotels. The seaside resorts, themselves, became more and more dormitory towns for the major industrial conurbations nearby. Southport for Manchester and Liverpool, Westcliff and Brighton for London, or Redcar and Saltburn for the North East. Where the areas were less attractive, the towns tended to become massive retirement homes, like Worthing, or temporary housing for the poor and immigrants, like Margate. The backbone of the business - the 7 and 14 night family holiday bookings during the summer - lost out to the alternative attractions of the Mediterranean and Spain. The guests who stuck to the old patterns began to funnel down into those with a horror of flying, the very conservative elderly and those who were too poor to afford a holiday overseas. As the standard of living rose, the last category also began to thin out.

The energy crisis led to hotels taking a very serious look at their consumption. For the first time, they were prepared to put pressure on the manufacturers. Dennis Hearn at THF insisted that the hot water used in washing up machines must be recyclable into the central heating systems or he wouldn't buy new machines. A solution to enable this to happen was soon found. It says much for the Victorians that the water for the hydraulic lifts was recyclable into the kitchen at the Westminster Palace Hotel more than 100 years before.

The 1970s saw union power at its peak and a determined effort was made by the Transport & General and the General & Municipal Workers to recruit membership in the hotel industry.

Ritzy

They had some success, with Centre Hotels, Henry Edwards' current company, agreeing to a closed shop and in many organisations there were proper negotiations with unions and shop stewards. The staff in hotels had more legal rights as well. The ability to go to an Industrial Tribunal had been established in 1964 to agree, among other things, disputed redundancy payments, but then there were less than 10,000 cases a year to cover all industries. The figure today is around 100,000. The cases swelled because unfair dismissal became illegal in 1971, sex discrimination and equal pay for women came into the orbit in 1975 and race discrimination was outlawed in 1976. Personnel managers had to learn new skills and the dictatorial practices of poor managements were severely curtailed.

Hotel booking agents had existed for many years to bring bedroomless customers into contact with appropriate hotels and their empty rooms. One such agency was Expotel, run by the brothers, Ranjit and Dev Anand. After a lot of hard work they also persuaded the hotels to pay them commission if they offered a company conference, rather than just someone who wanted a bedroom. This involved the hotels paying commission on the client's spending on food and drink, which had been excluded before. Once Expotel had made the breach, agencies started slowly to develop, concentrating exclusively on the conference market. They were single-minded in persuading customers to go to them direct, rather than to the hotels. As a consequence, over the next 20 years, hotels found that a proportion of their income on an ever increasing percentage of their important conference business, would be commissionable.

The agents would also be a barrier. They prevented the hotels from selling direct to the customers when the enquiry came from the agent; they could only quote the agent because they didn't know who the customer was. A small industry of these intermediaries grew up, now called Third Party Agents, providing no new business for the hotel industry, unlike Travel Agents who facilitated bookings from all over the world and had heavy promotional expenses. Just a flea on the back of the hotel elephant, seeking ever higher commissions, forcing prices down for their clients and, thereby, substantially reducing the value of the conference market to the hotel industry.

By 1987 British Hotels were a major service industry, recognized by government as an important provider of jobs, a respected power in the international hotel world and a vital support

The modern industry

for the British tourist industry. Britain was 5th in both world tourism international arrivals and the value of the money they spent. The league read France, United States, Spain, Italy and Britain. Our major overseas competitors in other markets - Germany, China and Japan - were further down the table. We possessed some of the finest hotels in the world - Gleneagles, Chewton Glen, the Connaught, Claridge's, the Ritz and the Savoy, Sharrow Bay, Turnberry and the Dorchester - to name a few. British hotel sales promotion, at its finest, was among the best in the world, the Americans being the only real competition. There were Michelin starred restaurants as well.

The industry had come a very long way over the 150 years, overcoming strings of difficulties, slowly adjusting to modern life and proud of its heritage. As the Mermaid at Rye in Sussex proudly proclaimed on its whitewashed wall outside the hotel "Rebuilt 1412."

24
Epilogue.

Well, that's the story. 150 years from tiny beginnings to a very large industry. There are a number of questions we can now consider.

Was the success inevitable?

Every country today has a hotel industry, so the British were going to have one too. The British Empire made London a great world capital, so when the tourism world created by fast air travel came about, London was almost bound to be a major European hub. Its close friendship and common language with the USA was also always going to be a major factor. Amsterdam as a hub, rather than Brussels, is a far greater achievement by the Dutch.

What is to the credit of the British - and that applies to the hotel industry as well - is the size of its success in tourism. Britain is a damp, off-shore island and yet it maintained its position, both in terms of arrivals and the revenue it got, as 5th in the World Tourism league until China got back Hong Kong. It's partly due to its position as the cultural centre of the English speaking world - Madrid has the same position with the Spanish and Paris with the French - but also it's because of long-term, first class marketing of the product. BTA, British Airways and British Hotel sales and marketing - at its best - were better during the 1960 - 1985 period than the vast majority of the rest of the world. The overseas tourists have been sold this country. By contrast, where so many British manufacturing industries have failed to survive, in many cases it has been because of their poor marketing.

Where did the British hotel industry go right?

Most of the major success factors for the British hotel industry weren't planned. It's comforting to write history as a carefully structured progression from point A to point B but the problem is that: "The best laid schemes o' mice an' men gang aft a-gley."

The Victorian British ruling classes considered it beneath their dignity to go into trade. Top management in British industry in the middle and late 20th century primarily came from the better universities. Practically nobody from those backgrounds wanted to come into the hotel industry. This left the field open to a lot of bright people who wouldn't have been given the chance to make the grade in more traditional fields.

The bright people came from a range of backgrounds. Fred Gordon, an unsuccessful solicitor, Isidore Salmon, from an immigrant family of cigar makers, Charles Forte, a small caterer from an Italian background, Max Joseph, a small estate agent. They were entrepreneurs and they built their companies without much help from the great and the good. Britain has always benefited from its immigrants. The country's tolerance to minorities has paid off again and again. Of course, in the hotel industry there were also a large number of British leaders whose families had been in the country for generations; Felix Spiers, Christopher Pond, the Towle family, Fred Gordon, John Blundell Maple, George Reeves-Smith, Bracewell Smith, Hugh Wontner, Geoffrey Crowther, Robert Peel, John Jarvis.

There were also a substantial number of leaders from immigrant families - first or second generation. There were a number of Jews at the top, particularly when the growth of the industry exploded after 1945. They knew - or believed, because that was just as relevant - they stood little chance of reaching that level with major organisations in other fields. So they built hotel companies; the Salmons and Glucksteins, Max Joseph, Fred Kobler, Henry Edwards, Leopold Muller, Leslie Jackson and Cyril Stein. There were other immigrants - Cesar Ritz, Charles Forte, Reo Stakis, Jasminder Singh. The field was open to them because the traditional ruling classes and captains of industry simply weren't interested. When you see what happened to so many of the industries which *were* run by the Establishment, it is a moot point whether you were better off without them.

Another major factor leading to the success of the industry was the inevitability of the ordinary management coming off the factory floor. Few hoteliers went into the board room without considerable or extensive experience of the world in which they would be working. Even today, the number of graduates from non-hotel school courses, who come into the industry, is quite small. The vast majority of the management knew their business. This crippled any attempt to unionise the work force. The major argument of the unions - that it was "us" against "them" - was cut off at the roots. Management could

Ritzy

cook, wait and make beds.

The other element that crippled the unions was that pay scales would always have to take into account the income the staff got from tips. Few tip-earning staff wanted that element of their pay to be controlled too thoroughly. The Inland Revenue has fought for its tax income from hotel workers for a very long time, but it has invariably had to compromise. If the Unions ever negotiated pay scales, with the level of tips on the table, a large number of tip-earning workers would not believe this would be to their benefit. In negotiations in the past, unions have been prepared to discuss actually abolishing tips!

Without unions there was practically no industrial unrest over the whole period. This meant, as a corollary, that hotels would become a low pay industry, compared to miners or car workers. The pension rights of most hotel workers were derisory. On the plus side, the industry didn't care about factors others than the ability to do the job. There were no restrictions because of nationality, accent, background or religion. Everybody was acceptable somewhere. It even applied to released prisoners. A washer-up's job might not be attractive but it was a way to start on the road back. It is true that women and black workers have taken years to reach the management levels to which they are entitled, but this, too, is markedly improving.

From the hotel industry's point of view, the absence of demarcation disputes, of strikes and wildcat strikes, made it possible to deliver the product on time and without interruption.

Eventually the industry also played its part in ending its contribution to British apartheid. There may still be restricted clubs of all kinds, quotas for this and "Full" notices for that, but there are no longer any problems in staying in 99% of British hotels. Even if Mr. Brown and Mrs. Smith want a double bedded room; unthinkable as late as 1970 when they would have needed to announce themselves as Mr. and Mrs. Smith. International tourism was a major contributor to breaking down the barriers.

Where the hotel industry almost totally failed over the whole period was in its efforts to influence successive governments. There were insufficient members of the Establishment to influence right-wing governments. There were no union leaders to influence left-wing governments. The government saw no votes in supporting hotels because the hoteliers never organised their political representation. There are, in fact, a large number of MPs representing constituencies whose economy depends on tourism and holiday making. At over 70, there are more than for any other industry. Yet MPs are not badgered in the way the farming constituency MPs have to answer to the farmers, or the miners' MPs had to answer to the NUM in the past. As Andrew Rawnsley writes about the effects of the Foot & Mouth outbreak in 2001: "The public responded all too well to avoid spreading the disease by staying out of the countryside. Massive collateral damage was inflicted on tourism, an industry worth twentyfold the value of the meat exports the slaughtering policy was designed to protect." But farmers protecting their meat export revenues had twentyfold the influence on government of the tourist industry.

I've still listed the failure to get government involved as something the hotel industry did right. This, even though they obviously tried to achieve the exact opposite. They lamented their inability to get government support. Yet, on the only occasion they really did achieve it - the Hotel Grant Scheme in the 1970s - the deluge of new bedrooms which were built as a consequence, practically bankrupted a whole range of hotels.

It was better for the industry, in most cases, that the government ignored them. Government involvement didn't save British Motor Cycles, British Ship Building or the British Mining industry. So, fortunately for the hotel industry, the government seldom noticed it existed. Where government really helped, it often did so without realising the implications. The creation of hotel school courses in the 1940s that did not specify a maximum number that could be run. Nobody had thought it through at the outset and that was the only thing that enabled the industry to have the modicum of skilled staff they needed to manage their own unexpected growth.

The Grant Scheme is another example. The British Tourist Authority was the adviser to the government on tourist matters. They wanted the industry to be capable of handling the maximum demand of the incoming tourist. As the Jumbo Jet was going to deliver several hundred passengers on each aircraft, that demand was set to increase dramatically. Gearing up an industry to maximum demand is, of course, a recipe for disaster when demand slackens off. If there are too many hotel beds, then there will be a price war. The bargain offers which result make the hotel element of the total tourism product a loss leader. That would have helped the number of arrivals as well and the BTA wouldn't have been unhappy.

Ritzy

As we've seen, for all the wrong reasons, the total British Hotel stock eventually finished up in much better condition than it had been before. Naturally, everybody took the credit for it.

What did the hotel industry do wrong?

It didn't modernise the product. The first hotel to have a private bathroom with each bedroom was the Carlton in London at the turn of the century. At that time hotels could have electric light, lifts, ballrooms and, indeed, almost everything we expect in hotels today. I don't think you can call trouser presses or TVs modernising the product.

What remained static were elements like uniforms, menus, wine lists, reception desks, commissionaires, morning dress and evening dress. The formality of hotels remained the classic way of doing things. The hotel industry continued to embrace its traditions as society, to a large extent, gave them up. The Victorian product was fashioned for the Victorian clientele. The 21st century product is, in many ways, equally appropriate for the Victorian clientele. The industry assumes that this is the way the public want it. They have no evidence for this. In fact, for example, the continuous drop in their share of the eating-out market over the last 50 years, would indicate exactly the opposite. Undoubtedly, the industry's biggest mistake has been to hand over that eating-out market to the restaurant industry. To lose a 50-year lead is to display a very high level of incompetence. The blind determination to continue with an increasingly outdated dining-room concept, without specialising in any culinary area, has proved steadily less acceptable over the period, but has had little effect on the thinking of the leading hotel companies.

Sooner or later, the industry will have to address the problem of trying to match their clientele's life-style, which has changed out of all recognition over the course of the last 150 years. At the moment many aspects of a hotel are almost a Disneyworld image of what life once was.

While the industry avoided the "us" and "them" conflict by promoting off the factory floor, it suffered in not attracting enough good brains from the major universities. The demand that a youngster should settle for a career in hotels before deciding on his university course - and settle for a minor university even if they were capable of getting into one of the major ones - simply shut the door on a mass of suitable candidates. The hotel industry could have made faster progress if it had recruited its fair share of the best brains in the country and developed management courses earlier.

Where will the battleground be in the future?

Because so few of the major companies were led by founding fathers after such as the Salmons and Glucksteins left the scene, Joseph died and Forte and Stein retired, the culture of many of them today reflects the training of their most senior executives. Most had a lineage in the Savoy Group, THF, Lyons, British Transport Hotels and Grand Metropolitan. The first 4 companies emphasised a formality in staff relations, a high degree of bureaucracy and a concentration on the minutiae in the creation of the product. Grand Metropolitan Hotels were very informal in their staff relations, far more sales and marketing conscious, avoided bureaucracy and were comparatively less concerned with the product than with the profitability of the operations.

In the past, all the chains put a lot of emphasis on company loyalty and their core of stalwarts who had served their organisation for very many years. This reciprocal loyalty of staff and management is much weaker today, partly because of leg law which makes dismissing an employee very difficult in lots of circumstances. The result in Italy, for example, has become quite ludicrous. Large numbers of top hotel waiters who are really permanent members of their hotel's restaurant staff, are reduced to one-day contracts. Hotel companies, like those in many other industries, don't realise what a decline in the level of staff loyalty actually costs them in lost profits.

As the British hotel industry marches into the 21st century, it has a great deal to be proud of and its major founders should be well-satisfied with the progress they made possible. However, a lot of British manufacturing industries, with apparently uncatchable leads, foundered in the 20th century. It could happen to the hotel industry as well. At least there is now no excuse for ignorance about how we reached the present position.

Bibliography

A.B.C. Hotel Guide, 1858, 1860, 1886.

Adam, W., *The Gem of the Peak - or Matlock Bath and its Vicinity,* Longman 1843.

Addison, W., *English Spas,* Batsford, 1951.

Baedeker, Karl, Publishers of Guide Books.

Becker, B.H., *Holiday Haunts,* Remington , 1884.

Bowden, Gregory Houston, *British Gastronomy,* Chatto & Windus, 1975.

Bowen, Elizabeth, *The Shelbourne,* Harraps, 1951.

Brinnis, John Malcolm, *The Sway of the Grand Saloon,* Macmillan, 1972.

Broemel, P.R., *Romance and Realities of Mayfair & Piccadilly,* Mills & Boon, 1927.

Bryant, Arthur, *English Saga,* Collins 1940.

Buxton Corporation, *Historic Buxton & its Spa Era.*

Carleton, Ethel, *William's Companion to Derbyshire,* Methuens, 1947

Carter, Henry, *The English Temperance Movement,* Epworth Press, 1933.

The Caterer, Hotel Keeper and Refreshment Contractor, 1878-1987.

Cecil, Robert, *Life in Edwardian England,* Batsford, 1969.

Clarke, G.E., *Historic Margate,* Margate Public Libraries, 1972.

Deane, Phyllis, *Industrial Revolution in England 1700-1714,* Fontana, 1969.

Dickens' Dictionary of London 1880.

Dow, George, *Great Central,* London Locomotive Publishing Co., 1969.

Ellis, Aytoun, *The Penny Universities,* Secker 1956.

Ensor, R.C.K., *England 1870-1914,* Oxford, 1936.

Exhibition Guide to London. 1851.

Fay, C.R., *From Adam Smith to the Present Day,* Longmans Green, 1928.

Feilding, D., *The Duchess of Jermyn Street,* Eyre & Spottiswoode, 1964.

Forte, Charles, *Forte,* Sidgwick & Jackson, 1986.

Gellati, Mario, *Mario of the Caprice,* Hutchinson, 1960.

Glicco, Jack, *Madness after Midnight,* Elek Books, 1952.

Hankinson's Guide to Bournemouth & District 1892.

Harrison, Brian, *Drink & The Victorians,* Faber & Faber 1971.

Hennessey, T. Hartley, *Healing by Water,* C.W.Daniel, Rochford, 1950.

Hern, A., *The Seaside Holiday,* Cresset Press, 1967.

Hill, C.E.W., *The Victorian Grand Hotels of London.* 1970. Unpublished.

Hill, George, *Figuring for fun,* Saints Press, 2000.

Illustrated London News, 1838-1914.

Incorporated Association of Hotel & Restaurants Monthly Reports 1910-1926. (Becomes the HRA and the BHRA - 1987.)

Jackson, Stanley, *The Savoy,* Frederick Muller, 1964.

Jones, Ron, *Grand Hotelier,* The Book Guild, 1997.

Kellett, John. R., *The Impact of Railways on Victorian Cities,* Routledge & Kegan Paul, 1969.

Laughton, Tom, *Pavilions by the Sea,* Chatto & Windus, 1977.

Lennard, R., *Englishmen at Rest and Play 1558-1714,* Oxford Clarendon Press, 1931.

Longmate,Norman, *The Water Drinkers,*Hamish Hamilton, 1968.

Macdermott, E.T., *History of the G.W.R.,* Great Western Railway Co., London, 1927.

Mackenzie, Compton, *The Savoy of London,* Harrap, 1953.

Magnus, Philip, *Gladstone,* John Murray, 1963.

Magnus, Philip, *Edward VII,* John Murray, 1964.

Malone, Roy, *Aston Lower Grounds*, Birmingham University, 1996.

Margetson, Stella, *Leisure & Pleasure in the 19th Century,* Cassell, 1969.

Matthew, Christopher, *A Different World,* Paddington Press, 1976.

Medlik, Professor S., *Profile of the Hotel & Catering Industry,* Heinemann, 1972.

Mee, Arthur, *Derbyshire, The Peak Country,* Hodder, 1949.

Moncrieff & Gardner, *The Peak Country,* Adam & Charles Black, 1908.

Montgomery-Massingberd, Hugh, & Watkin, David, *The London Ritz,* Aurum Press, 1980.

Lieut.-Col Newnham Davis. *Dinners & Diners,* Grant Richards, 1899.

Nicol, Jean *Meet me at the Savoy,* Museum Press, 1952.

Nottage, Jane, *The Gleneagles Hotel,* Harper Collins, 1999.

Owen, Colin C., *The Greatest Brewery in the world. A history of Bass, Ratcliff & Gretton,* Derbyshire Record Society, 1992.

Page & Kingsford, *The Master Chefs,* Edward Arnold, 1971.

Pattmore, J.A., *An Atlas of Harrogate.*

Peach, L. du Garde, *John Smedley of Matlock & his Hydro,* Bemrose Publicity, 1956.

Pevsner, Niklaus, *The Buildings of England,* Penguin, 1968.

The Piccadilly Hotel, Published by the Directors, Broadley, 1908.

Pimlott, J.A.R., *The Englishman's Holiday,* Faber & Faber, London. 1947.

Pope, W. Macqueen, *Twenty Shillings in the Pound,* Hutchinson, 1948.

Pope, Rex, *A consumer Service in Interwar Britain: The Hotel Trade, 1924-1938.* University of Central Lancashire, 2000.

Pudney, John, *The Thomas Cook Story,* Michael Joseph, 1953.

Rae, V. Fraser, *The Business of Travel,* Thomas Cook & Son, 1891.

Rawnsley, Andrew, *Servants of the people,*Penguin Books, 2001

Reader, W.J., *A History of Grand Metropolitan,* Unpublished 1986.

Redman, Nick, *The story of Whitbread and its hotels* Unpublished. 2002

Ritz, Marie, *Cesar Ritz,* Paris, 1948.

Roberts, John, *Europe 1880-1945,* Longmans 1967.

Royal Hotel Guide, 1856

Ruffs Hotel Guide, 1850.

Simmons, Jack, *St. Pancras Station,* Allen & Unwin, 1968.

Sims, George, *Living London,* Cassell, 1903.

Smedley, John, *Practical Hydropathy,* London 1877.

Smith, Albert, *The English Hotel Nuisance,* David Byce, 1855.

Sonpal, Chandra, *Balance of Payments and Travel Account,* British Travel Educational Trust, 1998.

Sparrow, Gerald, *The Great Swindlers,* John Long, 1959.

Tarbuck, Joan, *Southport as it Was,* Hendon Publishing Co., 1972.

Taylor, A.J.P., *English History 1914-1945,* Pelican, 1965.

The Times.

The Times Law Reports, Spokes vs The Grosvenor Hotel Company & Others, February 10th - 19th, 1898.

Vale, Edmund, *The Trust House Story,* Trust House, 1949.
Watts, Stephen, *The Ritz,* Bodley Head, 1963.
White, Arthur, *Palaces of the People,* Rapp & Whiting, 1968.

Index

Hotels mentioned in the text appear in the index under the entry for the nearest town. e.g. Bath, Empire Hotel. Entries in Italics are publications.